"A bold debut by a talented and energetic Generation X historian who dares think for himself. A fresh interpretation of rural life and the rise of the agriburb as a variation of sub/urban America in the 19th and early 20th century."

—Kevin Starr, University of Southern California

"The agriburb is a historic suburban landscape virtually overlooked until now. In *California Dreaming*, Paul Sandul recovers its rich history, situating this quintessential California landscape within the broad narrative of suburban history. This book extends our working concept of 'suburb' by adding a new, fascinating dimension."

—Becky M. Nicolaides, author of *My Blue Heaven: Life and Politics in the Working-Class Suburbs of Los Angeles, 1920–1960*

"If you want to know out of what stuff the California Dream was made, this book is for you. Looking closely at three agriburbs from northern and southern California—Ontario, Orangevale, and Fair Oaks—Sandul uncovers who had a hand in the creation of these communities, and how they profited by transforming their visions into realities on the ground. Sandul passionately argues that we all have a stake in how society remembers these landscapes, for those memories reflect power as well as shape our dreams for the future."

—Douglas C. Sackman, University of Puget Sound, and author of *Orange Empire: California and the Fruits of Eden*

"*California Dreaming* is an ambitious attempt to harness the three great forces in the development of the Golden State—land speculation, agriculture and suburbanization—to drive the story of three agro-urban colonies. It is a far-reaching disquisition on American habits of mind concerning agrarianism, suburbia and historical memory, as filtered through the myth-making machinery of local boosters."

—Richard Walker, University of California, Berkeley, and author of *The Conquest of Bread: 150 Years of California Agribusiness* and *The Atlas of California: Mapping the Challenges of a New Era*

"Sandul uses the lens of memory to help us better understand the origins and development of Ontario and other California 'agriburbs,' filling a gap in the history of the state's suburbanization. While many imagine suburban California filled just with bedrooms, Sandul thoughtfully brings agriculture back into the discussion."

—David C. Sloane, Professor, Price School of Public Policy,
University of Southern California

"Sandul unearths three fascinating case studies to examine the origins and legacies of California's 'agriburbs'—early twentieth-century suburban developments marketed with equal parts romantic agrarianism and genteel urbanism. *California Dreaming* makes provocative connections between booster visions for the future and the creation of local memory in later decades, writing the imagined picturesque rural aesthetic, nostalgia for small-scale horticulture, and exclusively white pioneer identity into the history. These insights contain valuable lessons for today's exurban entrepreneurs and public historians alike."

—Phoebe S. K. Young is Associate Professor of History at the University of Colorado at Boulder and author of *California Vieja: Culture and Memory in a Modern American Place*

"Sandul provides an insightful examination of the power of the historical narrative and the production of history. It compels us to reconceptualize how the California Dream influenced local communities that lay beyond the southern part of the state and consider boosters' tremendous influence to define landscapes and market lifestyles."

—Lydia R. Otero is an Associate Professor in the Department of Mexican American Studies at the University of Arizona and author of *La Calle: Spatial Conflicts and Urban Renewal in a Southwestern City*

CALIFORNIA DREAMING

BOOSTERISM, MEMORY, AND RURAL
SUBURBS IN THE GOLDEN STATE

VOLUME TWO

RURAL STUDIES SERIES

Sponsored by the Rural Sociological Society

VOLUME ONE:

Rural America in a Globalizing World: Problems and Prospects for the 2010s

Conner Bailey, Leif Jensen, and Elizabeth Ransom

CALIFORNIA DREAMING

BOOSTERISM, MEMORY, AND RURAL SUBURBS IN THE GOLDEN STATE

PAUL J. P. SANDUL

MORGANTOWN 2014

Copyright 2014 West Virginia University Press

All rights reserved

First edition published 2014 by West Virginia University Press

Printed in the United States of America

21 20 19 18 17 16 15 14   1 2 3 4 5 6 7 8 9

ISBN: 978-1-938228-86-5 (paper); 978-1-938228-87-2 (EPUB); 978-1-938228-88-9 (PDF)

Library of Congress Cataloging-in-Publication Data:

Sandul, Paul J. P.

 California dreaming : boosterism, memory, and rural suburbs in the Golden State / Paul J.P. Sandul.

    pages cm. -- (West Virginia University Press rural studies series ; volume 2)

  Includes bibliographical references and index.

  ISBN 978-1-938228-86-5 (pbk. : alk. paper) -- ISBN 1-938228-86-3 (pbk. : alk. paper) -- ISBN 978-1-938228-87-2 (epub) -- ISBN 1-938228-87-1 (epub) -- ISBN 978-1-938228-88-9 (pdf) -- ISBN 1-938228-88-X (pdf)

  1. Suburbs--California--History. 2. City promotion--California--History. 3. Suburban life--California--History. 4. Country life--California--History. 5. Wildland-urban interface--California--History. I. Title.

  HT352.U62C362 2014

  307.7409794--dc23

                                   2014025847

Cover design by Kelley Galbreath

Book design by Kelley Galbreath

Art Direction by Than Saffel

Cover images: Bees by iStockPhoto; Fruit from an original Hill Choice brand fruit crate label.

Dedicated to Tosha

TABLE OF CONTENTS

ACKNOWLEDGMENTS

I OWE A BIG THANKS TO MANY PEOPLE. None more so than my wife, Tosha. I dedicate this book to her (and our beautiful new baby boy, Max Prescott Sandul). I am also thankful to my family and friends. So thank you dad (Duane), mom (Diana), Glenn, Patricia, Aileen, Daryl, Jason, and the rest of my family, in-laws, and all my friends (and my pets too). Though not with us anymore, I must remember my darling first dog, Chewy, who died while I was away on a research trip. Also, another thank you needs to go to my dad, who, as a newspaper and public relations specialist, was my first and most trusted editor.

This book is a revision of my dissertation, "Harvesting Suburbs: Recalling the Suburban Side of California's Agricultural Colonization" (2009). Let me thank people involved with that: Lee M. A. Simpson at California State University, Sacramento (CSUS); Christopher J. Castaneda at CSUS; Randy Bergstrom at the University of California, Santa Barbara (UCSB); and Mary Hancock at UCSB. I have such respect and gratitude for each one of you, especially my mentor, Lee, without whom none of this would have been possible. Also at CSUS and UCSB are (or were) Aaron Cohen, George Craft, Jeffery Dym, Patrick Ettinger, Harold Marcuse, Shirley Moore, Charles Postel, Mona Siegel, and Karl Von Den Steinen. All of them had a positive influence on me. My graduate cohort at both places has meant a lot to me too. I have drawn much inspiration from them. So thank you; you all know who you are.

I must recognize that my work is built on the work of so many others. Some are historians and scholars today, while some are from days gone by. There has been nothing inconsequential about their work and their influence. While I could never list them all, as that is in many ways what a bibliography is for, in all sincerity, I want to recognize the unending influence of the late Carey McWilliams who, though I do not always agree with him, captured my imagination and fueled my desire to study California's suburbs and agricultural areas.

Thank you to John Archer at the University of Minnesota, David Vaught at Texas A&M, George Carlin, Rachel Carson, César Chávez, Charles Darwin, Richard Dawkins, Stephen Hawking, Paul David Hewson, Herman Hesse, Waylon Jennings, Helen Keller, Martin Luther King Jr., Bill Maher, Karl Marx, Willie Mays, Harvey Milk, NWA, Steven Pinker, Run TMC (not DMC), Peter Singer, Emmitt Smith, Jon

Stewart, George Takei, those involved with Dr. Who, freedom fighters across time and space, and to whomever really invented the Internet. You all have influenced my life. This book would never be as is without any of you.

Thanks to all the archivists and librarians at the many repositories I visited, as well as all the people who produced the primary and secondary sources I utilized once I got there. That is important stuff, no doubt, so I am thankful. Of particular help were the librarians in Ontario at the Robert E. Ellingwood Model Colony History Room, especially Kelly Zackmann. Patricia Johnson at the Center for Sacramento History also deserves much credit. In addition, thank you to the Historical Society of Southern California, which awarded me research money in 2008. I put that to good use in Ontario. Lastly, in Fair Oaks, I am thankful to the historical society and Carmelita's restaurant and Stockman's bar.

Thank you to all of my colleagues in the history department at Stephen F. Austin State University, especially those who were brave enough to have read something about this book and/or listened to me rant and rave, and to have offered me feedback to boot: Robert Allen, Mark Barringer, Perky Beisel, Philip Catton, Dana Cooper, Troy Davis, Andrew Lannen, M. Scott Sosebee, and Steve Taaffe. Newer history department colleagues, too, especially Karl Baughman, Aryendra Chakravartty, Brook Poston, and David Rex-Galindo, have also been a tremendous source of support and (in the positive sense) distraction. Still, life in the department, hence my life while writing this book, was only enjoyable because of all my colleagues around campus, as well as, and especially, the history department's administrative assistant Michelle Dorsett. In addition, I thank the many students who also had an influence on me, whether they know it or not. Thank you to my late colleague Archie P. McDonald. I am a better person and historian for having known you.

I am enormously thankful to the editors at the West Virginia University Press, particularly Carrie Mullen, and the Rural Sociological Society's Rural Studies Series, especially Mary Emery. Their insightful critiques and direction helped beyond words. To the reviewers, thank you so much. Your comments really did cause some fits and seizures but ultimately challenged me—and as a result, my work and I, or so I hope, are better for it.

Lastly, I am thankful to the Agricultural History Society for publishing an earlier draft of chapter three about Ontario in their journal. "The Agriburb: Recalling the Suburban Side of Ontario, California's Agricultural Colonization" appeared in *Agricultural History* 84, no. 2 (Spring 2010), on pages 195–223.

Anything wrong with this book is my fault and not the fault of somebody else.

BOURGEOIS HORTICULTURISTS IN AN AGRICULTURAL WONDERLAND

*I wish to have rural strength of religion for
my children, and I wish city facility and polish,
I find with regret that I cannot have both.*

RALPH WALDO EMERSON, 1844[1]

RECONCEPTUALIZING AGRICULTURAL COLONIES

George Chaffey Jr.'s biographer portrayed a mythic scene in 1928 wherein Chaffey came to California in 1882 to establish Ontario as an agricultural colony. He described Chaffey as a "solitary figure" standing atop the San Gabriel Mountains, taking in blue skies and purple sagebrush. Jackrabbits and coyote roamed, but because of infrequent rains causing wild flowers to come and go, the landscape only sustained sagebrush. "So this lovely slope lying at the foot of snow-capped Old Baldy," the biographer lamented, "is useless for cultivation unless water can be brought to it from the mountains." Nevertheless, Chaffey dreamed "a dream which shall come true." He envisioned a colony populated by "prosperous people setting a standard of comfort formerly deemed unattainable by ordinary people, extracting a generous living from a soil thought by generations . . . to be incapable of settlement." It would be a "rustic retreat without loneliness, a city without slums or saloons." He would build "a noble avenue" planted with a "quadruple of trees extending some seven miles." He pictured a "famous school" too. Chaffey only needed water to make his community. He did so by creating a pipe system bringing in water from Old Baldy.[2]

California's agricultural colonies, like Chaffey's Ontario, were farming communities established in the late nineteenth century and early twentieth century. They incorporated urban amenities like social clubs, good ("noble") roads, schools, and diverse services and businesses while also remaining within the socioeconomic orbit of nearby cities. They were also one part of growing metropolitan regions like Los Angeles and Sacramento. Ontario is one example of an agricultural colony, thirty miles from Los Angeles. Chaffey and his partners promoted Ontario as a rural-like community away from the city where a resident could fashion a middle-class lifestyle by tending crops on anywhere from one to ten acres of land.

Railroad service enabled residents to travel to Los Angeles within a reasonable amount of time to enjoy theaters and shopping. Nevertheless, the city did not always receive positive press. Cities like Los Angeles had reputations as bastions of crime, congestion, illness, and, not surprisingly for the day, immigrants, minorities, and activities often damned as sinful. Ontario featured its own local businesses, newspaper, shopping, banks, transportation, and communication systems to reduce dependency on frequent travel to Los Angeles for the touted finer things of urban culture. Upholding Ontario's difference from other rural areas as a measure of superiority, Chaffey christened Ontario "The Model Colony." He and his partners publicized their colony as a middle landscape, offering the best of both country and city. In Ontario, residents had a suburban lifestyle without want of city conveniences and amid what boosters called pristine natural surroundings.

Scholars do not often label agricultural colonies like Ontario in the 1880s through the early twentieth century *suburban* because of their agricultural orientation. Even so, they have distinct characteristics that mark them as suburban (e.g., homes, urban amenities, and connection to cities), though they are also rural through the embrace of agriculture and the theme of being a small-town community. The approach in this book is to argue for agricultural colonies as *agriburbs*—a mix of agrarian and suburban elements. Agriburbs were rural suburbs, planned, developed, and promoted as a means to profit from California's emerging agricultural marketplace extending nationally and, increasingly, globally at the turn of the twentieth century. Advertised as the perfect mix of rural and urban, they promised a better-quality lifestyle. They evoked the rural myths of agrarian virtue, a life on the farm in an exceptional environment.[3] Agriburbs were also ideally urban because of amenities like good roads, social clubs, cultural institutions, and businesses representing salient nineteenth-century symbols of modernity and progress. According to Chaffey's biographer, the model colony was "at once *Rus in Urbe* [country in the city] and *Urbs in Rure* [city in the country], where the best features of town and country life had been retained."[4]

Agriburbs, like Ontario lying thirty miles from Los Angeles, appeared separate from cities and adjoining subdivisions, similar to streetcar suburbs outside Boston at the time. Agriburbs remained close to cities via transportation routes and conceptually, however, to justify their existence and advertisement as suburbs, which typically, in more recent imaginations, mean places directly adjacent to an urban core. Clearly, roads, businesses, churches, and other so-called urban amenities existed in rural areas. Suburban boosters had nothing to gain in highlighting this and grossly slighted the quality and existence of such "amenities" in rural areas to distinguish their subdivisions. They had no problem exploiting the rural ideal, however, in concert with the suburban ideals of home ownership and, again, urban amenities. For example, another agriburb outside Sacramento—Orangevale—saw its boosters brag in the 1880s, "No part of California exceeds the localities [suburban homes] in picturesqueness of scenery and fertility of soil. They possess every attraction for those who prefer country to city life and already have the many solid advantages [including schools, churches, and infrastructure] so generally desired."[5]

Residents of agriburbs had agriculture. Specifically, they had horticulture, the intense cultivation of crops on small acres of land. Along with a rising suburban ideal, horticulture defines agriburbs as a product of their time. Without horticulture— which saw a booming science revolve around it, making smaller farms that much more productive, hence easily marked as modern—agriburbs very well might not have materialized given the vast amounts of land large, extensive farming endeavors required. The irony is this sowed the seeds of small farms' eventual decline by the 1920s as horticulture also sparked a role in increasing mechanization, intensive farming, and the accumulation of capital, including land. Land consolidation also saw the rise of agribusiness and more of a dependency on nonfamily labor, especially minority labor at odds with the ideal of suburban family farms.[6]

Agriburbs like Ontario and Orangevale were consequently neither rural supply lines of a city nor isolated colonies. They did not come into existence only because of urban sprawl or emigrant flight away from the dangers of urban life or solely because of some mass immigrant exodus of the wealthy class toward safety at the outer fringes of the metropolitan hinterland—an exurb.[7] Nor did they spring into existence fully formed. Agriburbs were an accomplishment: they came about because of both flight and exodus. Spurring on this migration was a cohort of local businesspeople like Chaffey who understood that what benefitted the urban or regional area, or the potential suburban resident or development, benefitted them. These local boosters purposefully harvested suburbs with an eye toward direct profit and metropolitan growth.

Boosters like Chaffey in Ontario and others in places like Orangevale epitomized the boosters who dominated California at the turn of the twentieth century. As many of California's boosters boasted of the state as unsurpassed for the location of an idyllic community, local boosters bragged how their community represented the best of the best. Local boosters such as Chaffey utilized narratives of place, class, race, lifestyle, and profit. Again fixing boosters to a particular area, they were also sophisticated businesspeople who understood that an image constructed to speak to the aspirations of its audience made good business sense. For people craving home, family, nature, health, culture, refinement, and rural virtue, boosters appropriated the fashionable images of the rural and suburban ideals throughout the nineteenth century. A single-family home in a natural California landscape with urban amenities made both a good place to live and a means of profit. Agriburbs, then, as one writer in the *Ontario Record* concluded in 1907, made it "possible for those in search of small home groves to obtain their desire and yet remain within the confines of a beautiful and progressive city."[8]

DEFENDING RECONCEPTUALIZATION

Looking at California's agricultural colonies as a type of suburb augments understanding the growth process in the Golden State at the turn of the twentieth century. It recasts the "California Dream" as synonymous with the suburban ideal. While California's scholars are correct to contend there is little evidence showing that California experienced a robust shift from extensive (large land holdings) to intensive farming (smaller farms) after the 1880s and became decidedly marked by little subdivisions and agricultural colonies for a time, the California landscape is large and complicated.[9] Regarding California's agriculture, the focus has largely been two-pronged: the nature of farming and/or farm labor. The point of the debates within the literature, particularly those surrounding the nature of farming, misses the role boosters like Chaffey deserve in the conversation. Their control over the conditions that shaped the form, development, and image of California's landscape was, and still is, consequential.[10] They had a profound role in how California developed and in constructing the proverbial California Dream.

Others looking at the California landscape have discussed agricultural colonies like Ontario before. California historian and journalist Carey McWilliams casts the longest shadow. In the 1940s, he homed in on Southern California's "citrus belt," including Ontario. He observed, "It [the citrus belt] is neither town nor country, neither rural nor urban. It is a world of its own." He called it an "agricultural wonderland" whereby an "orange grove is the perfect setting for a handsome suburban estate." He also created a neologism to describe them: *rurban*.[11] By the 1970s and 1980s, California historian Kevin Starr saw agricultural colonies as making a new life possible, "one possessing the benefits of country life and at the same time preserving values of diversity, leisure, and family living." For these "bourgeois horticulturists," California's rural life "showed a pattern approaching bourgeois suburbanism of later days."[12] Discussing Ontario, Starr said it "incorporated within itself an urban/

rural interplay deliberately orchestrated to preserve for middle-class horticulturists the feel and amenities of an urban community."[13] This sentiment also came through in Richard J. Orsi's 1973 dissertation-cum-*magnum opus* on California boosterism. Reviewing a 1870s booster tract about Los Angeles, he realized "the impression which emerged from the booklet bordered on the suburban."[14]

Many works exist about California's agricultural landscape, so many that slighting any one of them in this book is bound to happen. California's agricultural colonies have been called "the money-making cousin of the bungalow suburb" and places with an "eclectic mix of urban and rural characteristics" marked "by the predominance of luxuries and benefits not typically afforded to farming communities."[15] This list could go on, from "garden cities" to "irrigation districts" to "citrus towns."[16] The peoples of these areas have been called "bourgeois horticulturists," "a better class of people," "farmers," and more.[17] Furthermore, the ideal they were seeking has been labeled, among others, as agrarian, Californian, Jeffersonian, and, yes, even suburban.[18]

Situating the development of agricultural colonies at this time squarely within a suburban framework and then deconstructing it provides clarity to these disparate characterizations, none of which are completely wrong, but none of which are detailed. Such a framework reveals California's boosters appropriated a romanticized suburban ideal first popularized in the nineteenth century to sell the California Dream. The distinctive feature of California's agricultural colonies was that they were suburban. Recognizing some of California's development as suburban is not radical; rather, it enables a broader focus on the modernization and industrialization of society, agribusiness, and urbanization taking place and breaking up—or betraying—the agrarian idealism persistent at the time. In fact, as McWilliams alluded to and later historians such as Matt Garcia and urban critics like Reyner Banham have noted, urbanization in California occurred by way of suburbanization.[19] Agriburbs helped lead the way.

Accounting for the suburban nature of agricultural colonies is also reflective of current trends in suburban history. An understanding of California's agriburbs extends an appreciation for the diversity of suburban types. Recent historical literature concerning suburbs, labeled "new suburban history," concludes that earlier historians sketched out a vision of suburbia demographically, geographically, and functionally too narrow.[20] Much of the focus had been on the migration of the affluent from the city to suburbs, subsequently excluding migrators who were economically and socially marginal. This paints suburbs as predominantly white middle-class enclaves functioning as bedroom communities to cities whereby residents were dependent on job commuting, shopping, and leisure.[21] New suburban historians challenge these earlier depictions for their omissions: industry, retail outlets, local businesses, multifamily housing, blue-collar workers, minorities, and the poor. They have documented industrial suburbs, racial and ethnic suburbs, and more, moving beyond the white middle-class residential archetype.[22]

Though they were often mostly white and middle class, California's agriburbs also complicate traditional views of what constitutes a suburb. Of significance here is the commixture of work and residential space (i.e., a non-residential-only suburb based in agriculture), as well as a noncontiguous location near a central city. A common misconception of suburbs is that they resulted from a process of development spreading directly out of an urban core like rings on an onion and that they were primarily residential. New suburban historians have documented that industrial suburbs also mixed work and residential space along with a noncontiguous location near the city.[23] Moreover, the mixed use of rural-like suburbs with residents who commuted to work yet also had agriculture and livestock for food long ago received attention, notably from sociologist Harlan Douglass's *The Suburban Trend* in 1925.[24] California's agriburbs were not contiguous with or located near (within fifteen miles) large urban centers. They further show that suburbs have not always been *sub* and that the customary narrative of a suburb concerning its location near, and dependency on, a city is misleading because it does not encompass all of what suburbia represents or all the diverse suburban types (e.g., Ontario is more than 30 miles from Los Angeles). The focus here, however, is not on industrial suburbs, what one suburban anthology calls *manufacturing suburbs*, but on *harvesting* rural ones.[25]

Debate exists concerning some of the ways historians and others have chosen to define seemingly nontraditional suburbs. This debate applies to any discussion concerning industrial suburbs, like Dearborn, MI, or agriburbs, like Ontario, CA, because a common charge is that these places were not suburbs but something different, like "satellite cities" or "garden cities." Despite the inaugural study of satellite cities by economist Graham R. Taylor, who coined the phrase in 1915 and identified satellite cities as industrial suburbs, the term satellite cities, much like the term suburb itself, has evolved and is typically defined as small to medium-sized cities that retain, for the most part, autonomy despite being located near large metropolitan areas.[26] Satellite cities purportedly predate the local metropolis's suburban expansion, appear physically separated from the metropolis, and have their own bedroom communities and inner-city neighborhoods. However, as spotlighted in three case studies in the following chapters, California's agriburbs, while remaining physically separate from nearby metropolises, did not predate suburban expansion of a nearby metropolis. They *were* the expansion. They did not have their own nearby bedroom communities or inner-city neighborhoods (that is, before a robust agribusiness or industrial turn with World War I or a post–World War II expansion that saw many communities, like Ontario, explode throughout the Sunbelt). Finally, while they did have their own services, businesses, and work space, commuting to the nearby city did occur and figured in the boosters' advertising campaign. In fact, it would be a gaffe not to call attention to quality histories done about these nearby bedroom communities. These grew ever stouter following World War I and the resulting labor shortage, particularly concerning those areas populated by people of Mexican descent, as described by José Alamillo, Matt Garcia, Jerry Gonzalez, Gilbert Gonzalez, and Becky M. Nicolaides. In fact, these scholars have shown that these were rural, ethnoracial working-class suburbs in their own right, what Nicolaides calls "farm-fringe streetcar suburbs" and historian Carl Abbott calls "suburbscape[s]."[27]

Many who have focused on California's agricultural colonies certainly have come up with a variety of labels for them; irrigation colonies or districts or cities, and garden cities are key ones. For example, in *From the Family Farm to Agribusiness: The Irrigation Crusade in California and the West* (1984), historian Donald J. Pisani noted that historian Henry Nash Smith (1950) summed up westward movement succinctly when he concluded that rising urbanization and industrialization threatened the "agrarian ideal." Thus, the West had originally offered an opportunity to restore and strengthen an already seemingly tarnished dream.[28] This agrarian ideal, underscored by a small-farm ideal made possible through horticulture, meant the creation of a large middle class who would serve as the bedrock of Western society. While it did not turn out that way, Pisani identified the "promise" of irrigation in bringing about a small family-farm ideal centered on homes and horticulture. Specifically, critics of extensive, large-scale wheat hoped that irrigation in California would encourage the subdivision of large farms.[29] Pisani observed that the small family-farm ideal promised to strengthen the family and middle class. He therefore tracked the development of an "irrigation civilization" through "irrigation colonies" and "irrigation districts" in California that included "a wide range of civic institutions ranging from churches and schools to performing arts groups and literary guilds." He continued, "The small farms and dense settlement pattern required by irrigation would also dispel the isolation and dreariness of rural life experienced by farm families in the Midwest." Thus, *irrigation colonies*, such as Fresno and Riverside, but also colonies in Colorado and Utah, represented close-knit communities surrounded by farms that would sustain the establishment of civic institutions.[30]

These irrigation districts increasingly get associated with the garden city movement inaugurated by the utopian British planner Ebenezer Howard in 1898. As a result, such communities often receive the designation "garden cities" even if they began earlier.[31] Garden cities, much like irrigation districts identified by Pisani, not to mention historian Donald Worster, were, once again, planned, self-contained "satellite" communities located on the fringe of a nearby metropolis that commixed resident housing, industry, and, now, agriculture.[32] "The result," said Abbott, "was a semiurbanized landscape" that featured a community based in, and dependent upon, agriculture, yet complete with urban amenities such as libraries, schools, good roads, streetcar lines, parks, hotels, post offices, and media.[33] Looking at Runnymede (now East Palo Alto) in California developed by William E. Smythe in 1917, founder of the

Little Landers Movement—itself inspired by Howard's garden city model—historians Alan Michelson and Katherine Solomonson described it as a place of "small farms" and "garden homes." Citing the usual suspects of urban amenities, Michelson and Solomonson concluded such a garden city was a place where "the small farm merged with the bourgeois suburb."[34] Likewise, looking at Oakland after World War II, historian Robert O. Self identified how the Chamber of Commerce "married boosterism to regional planning," working toward the creation of an "industrial garden," thus mirroring garden cities, whereas industrial suburbs like those identified in Robert Lewis's *Manufacturing Suburbs*, were "tied to downtown Oakland and the port."[35]

In *A World of Its Own: Race, Labor, and Citrus in the Making of Greater Los Angeles, 1900–1970* (2001), historian Matt Garcia tracked social interactions, business and labor relations, and intercultural exchange in the citrus belt near Los Angeles. He opened with a discussion of the origins of places like Ontario, detailing Chaffey and his model colony, calling them *citrus suburbs*.[36] So Garcia, and others, like McWilliams, called these places suburbs too. One may wonder why a neologism like *agriburb* is necessary when *citrus suburbs* could suffice. The answer is simple: these suburbs, while undeniably citrus producers, had more. They grew many crops besides citrus, including almonds, grapes, figs, and more. While one could argue citrus is the major crop, and this does hold meaning for how these communities reflect on the past, citrus suburbs is a restrictive term nonetheless. Garcia adeptly utilized the term because of the famed "citrus belt" connotation in which citrus represented horticulture. As discussed later, horticulture and citrus, especially the orange, became symbolic of much more than a crop, but a broader vision for a better way of life. Namely, the idea is to summon the powers of the rural myth of agrarianism. The narrative undergirding the rural ideal holds farmers as the bedrock of the nation, even morally superior. Citrus suburb combines such a myth with the previously mentioned bourgeois suburb. Therefore, simply said, agriburb and citrus suburb mean much the same thing.

Agriburb is an accurate term simply because it encompasses more than citrus. It is a superior term because it imparts additional important information. Agriburb, as a combination of *agriculture* and *suburb*, summons the power of agrarianism and the cultural refinements of the bourgeois suburb. Citrus suburbs, while implying suburbs with citrus, does not explain what made these suburbs a specific suburban type, thus, further *functioning* as a suburb, nor does it provide context for the planning process and speculation that define its creation by placing agriculture at its core. Agriburb, however, grows out of the attempt to define suburban type, function, and the process of creation—retaining the same cultural meaning of citrus suburb but placing agriculture up front as definitive.

Whether called irrigation colonies or districts, garden cities, satellite cities, citrus suburbs, or a host of other names, places like Ontario are largely seen as, depending on one's urban or rural studies bias, either places akin to suburbs but in possession of agriculture or places that are agricultural but in possession of suburban qualities. Ultimately, all these names and descriptions are merely talking past each other to describe the same thing: rural suburbs, or agriburbs. At some point, a place that has all the familiar attributes of a suburb deserves designation as a suburb.

As captured so well in historians Becky M. Nicolaides's and Andrew Weise's *The Suburb Reader*, the wailings of journalists like William H. Whyte and Frederick Lewis Allen, writing in contempt of what they saw as Godzilla-like sprawl erasing the countryside both before and after World War II, have largely contributed to a limiting definition of suburbia.[37] Suburbia increasingly became what culturist John Archer has called "the places we love to hate." He traces a dominant view of suburbia bequeathed to us by early- to mid-twentieth century critics as a gross outcome and medium of mass society in an industrial-capitalist world.[38] Whatever the details be, new suburban historians have been at the forefront of countering such constriction.

While this book strives to expand upon the definition of suburbia, it should be noted that the California boosters at the turn of the twentieth century exercised a fairly rigid and constricted definition of suburbia themselves—the suburban ideal of nineteenth-century Romantic writers such as Emerson and landscape designers such as Frederick Law Olmsted. They did see suburbia as synonymous with the *bourgeois suburb* or utopias as discussed by those looking at irrigation districts or garden cities and so authoritatively described by historian Robert Fishman.[39] This Romantic suburban type, for many in the United States at the time, and today, represented the suburban archetype, casting suburbs as primarily residential areas of the well-to-do and connecting them to supposed healthful, natural surroundings. While still narrating a class- and race-based conception of suburbs, California's boosters pushed at the boundaries of that definition nonetheless to incorporate horticulture and the commixture of work and business with suburban residence—they did indeed mix the bourgeois suburb with the small farm. This happened, they claimed, because of the California Dream, as the environment and soil were so perfect as to allow for such a suburb. Agriburbs, however, were still indeed for the middle to upper classes. Even so, like industrial suburbs populated mostly by the working classes on the East Coast, residential and work space conjoined, as did, like suburbs of all types, leisure and shopping opportunities conjoined with residential space. A key element to discovering how such places could support the middle to upper classes came with the rise of what Californian historian David Vaught has called "the horticultural ideal" at the end of the nineteenth century, which again affixed agriburbs as products of their time.[40] Horticulture came to represent more than ornamental plants and gardens, becoming the basis for both a production community type, suitable for attaining and maintaining middle-class status, and a progressive community type in its own right (i.e., an irrigation district or garden city for Pisani or Abbott). In 1891, with such a redefinition of horticulture underway, the California booster Charles Howard Shinn explained California's agricultural colonies in perhaps the only way he could. "A California fruit-grower," he said, "is in some respects akin to the middle class of suburban dwellers near Boston and New York, with this very important difference, that he actually and constantly makes his living from the soil he owns."[41]

SPEAKING OF BOOSTERS

"Few people read the boosters anymore," bemoaned historian William Cronon in *Nature's Metropolis* (1991). Cronon did not so much defend the boosters and their "unabashed optimism about progress and civilization" as he attempted to redeem a study of their writings as a picture window into "what Americans believed—or wanted to believe."[42] Historian Carl Abbott has agreed. In *How Cities Won the West* (2008), Abbott highlighted the importance of the boosters in building up the West. "[M]y intent," he made clear, "is to emphasize the ubiquity of the city-building imagination and city-building impulse in shaping western North America. In the nineteenth century this imagination often took the form of bombastic boosterism because that *was* the rhetorical strategy available." Abbott reminds us that boosters were creatures and manifestations of a particular place and time; of politics and culture; of context. "By the later twentieth century," he wrote, "economic development professionals had taken over the job of urban population. Their publications now aimed at sophisticated corporations rather than naïve land speculators and benefited from training in economics, geography, and regional planning."[43]

Boosters and their writings, as Cronon and Abbott informed us, as did a few others, allow for a careful interrogation of what people believed or sought out as meaningful.[44] That booster literature offers this insight is self-evident, but worth briefly spelling out. Boosters sought to persuade an audience, akin to advertising in media or propaganda. They, presumably, read the market, made a determination about it, and then set about to influence it. The product of that process is not one that often opens dialogue or invites alternate interpretations; rather, it sets forth a collection of statements designed to impose meaning, impart specific information, and impel activity (i.e., move to California or, specifically, move to Ontario). Consequently, looking at how the boosters, as a "regime of truth," framed their discussion about the suburbs they had built and sold gives us a way of studying the meaning of these places to, at least, the boosters.[45] These boosters were both reacting to what they thought their audience (those "naïve" land speculators, not corporate fat cats) wanted and trying to convince them of what they needed. The agriburb is the result of this in California.

The boosterism involving agriburbs has had lasting consequences. It has directed the production of subsequent historical representations concerning agriburbs, thus influencing how people remember these communities and, in turn, affecting how these communities have built their local historical identities. For example, Fair Oaks, near Sacramento, developed in 1895 as another agricultural colony. The boosterism surrounding Fair Oaks worked to embellish the perceived uniqueness of the community, as well as its agricultural prowess, urban amenities, and local "pioneers," who were further cast as exceptional. By implication, such exceptional personalities made up the community, and contemporaries now bore the responsibility for carrying it on. Places such as Fair Oaks have cast anchor to such narratives to this day. The "History of Fair Oaks," for example, a short essay featured on the Fair Oaks Historical Society's website in the early twenty-first century, gets the point across.[46] Just over 2,000 words, the bulk of "History," like the histories of most agriburbs, tells the story of the community's "original design," early farming life, early businesses, and pioneer individuals. The climax is the freeze of 1932 that destroyed most of the crops and ended the period of Fair Oaks's days as an agricultural colony. That is where "History" ends.

The Fair Oaks history essay is distinctly limited in chronology and scope, but it mirrors the type of narrative representation first espoused by the boosters. The overwhelming purpose of "History" is to highlight the original design of Fair Oaks as an agricultural colony; no other design receives mention. Both "History" and other local representations concentrate on the time before the freeze. There is no discussion of the migratory labor of Japanese and others working packinghouses or, more strikingly, any event associated with the eighty-year history of Fair Oaks following the freeze. Fair Oaks's history lives in a bottle. It does not move beyond the themes crafted by the original boosters who, in effect, besides harvesting suburbs, cultivated memory—the remembrance of the past.

The attention to the early days of Fair Oaks and other agriburbs such as Ontario has helped divert attention from their suburban origins. Still, this attention to the early days reveals these communities' continual remembrance of the past. Their early periods appear in a myriad of local histories. In Ontario, for example, the colony period of Chaffey appears in student essays in the 1930s, the Ontario Diamond Jubilee Committee's history in the 1950s, the Ontario Bicentennial Commission's celebration in the 1970s, and local history books in the 1990s.[47]

While the presence of agriculture and pioneers seems to point to a rural past in agriburbs, the prevalent remembrance of so-called urban amenities throughout does not necessarily serve the purpose to show their suburban side. Urban amenities, like the "noble avenue" in Ontario, appear innovative in that they developed regardless of these communities' humble beginnings as agricultural colonies. At best, the urban amenities are part of a utopian garden-city ideal in which these communities constituted "a city without the city."[48] At worst, urban amenities seem exceptional. Neither scenario allows for a conception of agricultural colonies as suburbs, which is striking because such amenities, along with home ownership, reveal that agricultural colonies began as planned suburbs, especially when they are compared to most authoritative accounts of suburbs that also cite such amenities and home ownership as key markers of suburban places.[49]

Understanding the suburban side of California's agricultural colonization thus prominently exposes the accomplishments of boosterism specifically. Early promotional efforts concerning these suburbs reveal how a dominant cultural memory about each of these communities shaped—for the intent of boosting sales—and now largely contributes to diverting attention from their suburban origins. California's boosters constructed a narrative representation celebrating agriculture (in both the Jeffersonian sense and for production to market; i.e., Vaught's *horticultural ideal*), innovation (urban amenities in distinctly rural areas), and entrepreneurialism (middle-class lifestyle and material progress). These themes helped the boosters sell more lots while keenly promoting the growing metropolises surrounding them. For this reason, boosters were the original producers of narratives and representations ("memory") that have become the archival resources steadily used by others afterwards ("collected memory"). This causes researchers to focus on the dominant memory of a unique farming life, agriculture, innovation, and entrepreneurialism, and not on the suburban genesis of California's agricultural colonies.

Examining the influence of booster and subsequent historical representations also exposes much about the culture of suburbia. Critics and scholars like Herbert Gans, Edward Hall, Ada Louise Huxtable, and Jane Jacobs, who have never hidden their disgust with suburbs, argued that suburbs denied human needs for historical connectedness. Suburbs, they claimed, weakened individual and social identities by pulling people out of history.[50] Looking to agriburbs' local histories, memorials, performances, public history, and the words of suburbanites themselves turns these claims on their head and reveals both the lasting influence of the original booster narratives and the genuine use of the past by suburbanites. This suburban memory counters the more traditional imagery of suburbanites as uninterested in community and stories about the past, even if those stories get it wrong or are fabricated.

ADMITTING LIMITATIONS, CLARIFYING SCOPE, HIGHLIGHTING STRENGTHS

For historians it is tough to directly identify and justify the information not covered in their work. Rather than being a postmodern exercise in futility or a foolish attempt to cut off negative critiques at the path, however, the value of doing so is to highlight what is covered in this book more vigorously by taking special note of what is not covered. Specifically, this book is not a classical social or political history of suburbia broadly or of agriburbs. While demographics, issues of race, class, and gender all permeate throughout, the driving thrust is to analyze cultural representations and meanings—with an eye on how such things had personal and material effects on people and places. For example, a major thread that weaves throughout is an emphasis on boosterism and a local cohort of real-estate interests, or a "growth machine" (local elites seeking profit by stimulating growth; i.e., the boosters doing the boosterism).[51] The analysis narrows on how the boosters constructed representations of California and local places with the objective to profit from the sale of land and the enticement of migration and investment. Much space goes to deconstructing those representations and determining why such appealed to boosters who subsequently determined such would appeal to others. The focus is primarily on the former, not the latter, although explanations appear regarding why such representations would appeal to the boosters' imagined consumers. The focus, therefore, of part one and two of the book, is on how boosters packaged a unique suburban type at the turn of the twentieth century in California. To do so, part one ("California Dreaming") delimits both the suburban ideal (chapter one) and the California Dream (chapter two), with the California Dream chapter running a bit longer to explicitly compare them and show how they mirrored each other. Far from a focus on what some spatial theorists call imagined, designed, or first space (a story about place), the case studies concerning Ontario, Fair Oaks, and Orangevale that follow in chapters three, four, and five (part two, "Harvesting Suburbs") show how these places materialized or became what spatial theorists call material or second space. Admittedly, no significant ink goes to investigating suburbanites' everyday lives, behaviors, or, as spatial theorists say, their lived, practiced, or third space (i.e., people living in place).[52] Nonetheless, admitting this path, the achievement of this analysis is that it highlights the diverse and active role of suburban real-estate interests and boosters in the creation of suburban places.

The spotlight on boosterism continues into the final part of the book (part three, "Cultivating Memory"), in chapters six and seven, which focus on cultural memory. This focus extends beyond the turn of the twentieth century to the present. Although this shift might seem abrupt after several chapters defining the agriburb and putting a face on the boosters, the goal is to analyze further the lasting effects of the boosters' packaging of place. While this may come at the expense of providing a social history, the focus on memory accomplishes the goal of showing lasting booster influence beyond the turn of the twentieth century. This has an effect rarely found in accounts about suburbia: it explicitly shows the existence of suburban use of the past, which, like many good sociological studies, does point to suburban agents making sense of their lives. Admittedly, given the absence of minorities in the memories of these places, one can rightfully call the memory accounted for in the following pages as rather bad. Nevertheless, whether one calls suburban memory as revealed here good, bad, or even ugly, one cannot call it nonexistent. The suburban relationship to the past—at least for the purpose of constructing community identity if not individual—despite any moans, does exist. This focus on suburbanites' use of the past, furthermore, worked against trying to capture the histories of minorities in these communities. While critics may charge, and justifiably so, that such a focus only perpetuates the problem, even if doing so is to actually call it out, the benefit is a more intense spotlight on the silence of minorities so that the voices of those coming through loudest (i.e., the boosters and suburbanites) can be analyzed more thoroughly. It is, as the late theorist Michel Foucault might say, a "microphysics of power."[53]

Studying agriburbs, obviously, plays off rural studies. First, as Cronon and others made clear, the study of metropolitan landscapes means that we cannot separate the rural from the urban or even the suburban. Metropolises are more than their downtowns or patterns of sprawl. Agriburbs are also not just suburbs. Rather, if not clear already, they were part small farm. Rural rhetoric and imagery figured prominently in the growth process of California at the turn of the twentieth century, its suburbs, and, as discussed, its public remembrance of the past. Even in an era often lamented for the decline of rural America, rural America still plays a monumental (literally) role in the imagination of Americans and the narratives many find meaningful. Little good comes from studying metropolitan areas without taking into account rural accents and any Focauldian episteme (i.e., any apparatus of power that works to create and define knowledge).[54] Rural studies scholars can continue to point to the centrality of rural and agricultural themes in order to understand the histories of cities and suburbs, which too often—and mistakenly—exclude rural and agricultural themes.

This study of agriburbs, however, is not about unpacking the nature of farming or rural life in California. Rather, because other historians and commentators have so keenly unpacked the nature of farming and rural lifestyle already, the point is, first, that they have already done so and, second, more importantly, to ask what that means. Namely, scores of literature exist on the farming practices and lifestyles of California's agricultural colonies and farms. That literature comprises not only historical accounts but also booster narratives. Therefore, keeping in stride with a cultural analysis, the intent here is to examine the purpose and use of spotlighting farming practices and rural lifestyle by boosters and later scholars. The payoff is a better understanding of the tactics of boosters in packaging and selling rural suburban places (delimiting them as suburbs along the way) and the way scholars and others have decided to recount the histories of these communities, revealing, yet again, the lasting influence of boosterism and the existence of suburban memory.

Others have focused on the lasting consequences of boosterism, admittedly, as well as urban elites in general, and the effect on shaping memory and historical consciousness, in California and elsewhere. Important among these are works by Barbara Berglund, William Deverell, David Glassberg, Harvey J. Graff, Phoebe S. Kropp, Lydia R. Otero, and Cathy Stanton.[55] Common among these works is the use of the past as not just a means of exposing who does and does not do the remembering, or who does and does not dominate the production of historical narrative and, ergo, popular understandings of the past, but also on the use of the past as a device of social control. These authors reveal the assertion of dominance and social control of white, usually professional, elites over minority groups. These are hegemonic tales whereby historical narrative and other representations of the past, be they textual, evident within, architecture, commemorative, evident within pageantry, or more, are keen mediums in which whites have exerted control by making sure to, as Deverell makes clear, "whitewash" the past. That is, as Deverell says about Los Angeles, "Los Angeles is not so much a city that got what it wished for. It is a city that wished for what it worked diligently to invent."[56]

This line of inquiry continues in this book, but marrying the more intense study of the original boosters to the study of the legacies of boosterism. Recently, sociologist Laura R. Barraclough looked at the influence of boosterism in Southern California in *Making the San Fernando Valley* (2011). Her work and this book, her conclusions and ones drawn here, have a good deal in common. The same is true with Kropp's work, as well as those of others mentioned above. First, looking at the San Fernando Valley, Barraclough works to characterize what McWilliams called "gentleman-farming districts." Like other California historians discussed, she and McWilliams look at agriburbs. Yet, doing more than pour old wine into a new bottle, Barraclough explicitly connects gentleman-farming districts to suburbs, interchanging freely the two phrases.

Barraclough too is interested in what she calls "rural urbanism," the "production of rural landscapes by the urban state, capital, and other interests," which is another way of saying she analyzes the role of boosters operating as growth machines, as do Deverell and Kropp concerning Southern California. Barraclough unequivocally sees boosters' prominent role in the shaping of California's suburban areas. Her goal in doing so is to recognize "the relationships between American Imperialism, racial formation (especially the socio-spatial construction of whiteness), and the urban geographies of Los Angeles and cities of the West." She dissects how racial categorization and identity both shaped the California suburban landscape (and vice versa) and were further shaped by suburban actors and outsiders (i.e., third, or practiced, space). Other scholars do the same, though with less focus on suburbs.

Most of these works certainly do focus on race. Barraclough argues rurality is synonymous with whiteness. Further, she argues San Fernando Valley suburbanites appropriate, if not embellish, rurality through the inheritance and repackaging of a Western heritage myth and Spanish-mission past to legitimize claims to the landscape and contemporary social hierarchies entrenched in narratives of race and class.[57] Kropp and Otero, like McWilliams before them, also dissect the Spanish-mission past and, as Kropp states, they see "memory places" as "sites of cultural production and venues for struggles over public space, racial politics, and citizenship."[58] For Kropp and the others, myth became reality, thanks to boosterism, and shored up power for the white middle and upper classes, or, as Berglund states, boosters worked at "cultural ordering" to build "a social order more in keeping with nationally dominant hierarchies of gender, race, and class."⁵⁹ McWilliams's satirical treatment of the Spanish fantasy past is powerful, if not funny. Commenting on the role Helen Hunt Jackson played in shaping a romanticized memory of California's Spanish-mission past, by way of her novel *Ramona* (1884), McWilliams quipped, "Someday the Los Angeles Chamber of Commerce should erect a great bronze statue of Helen Hunt Jackson. . . . Beneath the statue should be inscribed no flowery dedication, but the simple inscription: 'H. H.—In Gratitude.'"⁶⁰

This book echoes much of these authors' focus on race and power, but key differences remain. Detailing the legacies of rural and urban land boosterism in not just Ontario, but also suburbs outside Sacramento, challenges the near-monopoly enjoyed by Southern California in studying the California Dream.⁶¹ In addition, as said, most histories concerning the early days of these places are more social, highlighting farmers, farming, labor, and city planning. This book rests on the original boosters. This is also a rare attempt to describe and then link Sacramento and its suburbs to larger phenomena extending statewide, regionally, nationally, and even globally. This is so striking because Sacramento is approximately the thirty-third largest metropolis in all of North America and, depending on favored definitions, about the twenty-third or twenty-fifth largest in the United States, with more than 2.1 million people.

Both suburban type and process are important in this book. This reflects historian Theodore Herschberg's call to account for both as well in the 1970s with the booming "new urban history" and anthropologist Setha M. Low's appeal in the 1990s to see "'urban' as a process rather than a type of [essentialist] category."⁶² Cities and suburbs, as well as rural places, are both a place and a process. So too are the metropolises and the regions that comprise them all. Therefore, in chapters three and four focusing on Ontario, Orangevale, and Fair Oaks, the goal is to delimit the exact characteristics of agriburb form. Doing so details exactly what made agriburbs actual suburbs in terms of their characteristics—and also their function. Regardless of whether form follows function (or vice versa), form and/or type and function reflect ideology, beliefs, and, with California in mind, dreams. Agriburbs were the product and the means of selling both the California Dream and metropolitan areas. They were and remain material landscapes and imagined landscapes that people live in. They were, ultimately, part of the process of metropolitanization, with boosters the key agents seeking to stimulate growth. Any interpretation of California's metropolitan regions—and suburbs, specifically—at this time must account for boosters and their role in form and process. Chapter five thus provides biographies of the boosters.

Finally, I want to reiterate that analyzing later boosterism—the period following the original boosters throughout the twentieth century to twenty-first century— shows the lasting effects of the original boosters and the way in which later residents (even suburbanites) appropriated new material and sometimes wove it into inherited narratives. Boosters first crafted these narratives, which have had lasting impressions in terms of how residents, suburban or otherwise, have come to ascribe meaning to their landscapes. They also use these narratives to understand landscapes—real or imagined—occupied by others and further distinguish themselves from such others. This dynamic is a means to understand a little about the culture of the residents themselves, especially suburbanites. Said differently, as Bruno Latour has pleaded concerning actor-network methodology, this line of analysis attempts to *"follow the actors themselves,'* that is try to catch up with their often wild innovations in order to learn from them what the collective existence has become in their hands."[63] Scholars like Barraclough, Kropp, and Otero are at their best with their analyses of the legacies of rural, Western, and Spanish heritage and their influence on local land use. The analyses of these themes in this book add to theirs, but the focus is more intensely on the themes of entrepreneurialism and Romantic agrarianism. They, and others, especially Berglund looking at rural exhibitions in San Francisco, look at these too, but such themes account for much more of this work. Rather than marking difference, however, all our studies together go a long way to reveal the dynamic ways in which boosterism and local meaning-making have gone to construct cultural memory.

Ultimately, the robust focus on the memory works (i.e., manifestations or articulations of cultural memory) of suburbanites and others marks this work as distinctive. The idea is to reveal that suburbanites actively engage the past to challenge older scholarship that says they do not. My intent, however, is not to create a straw man. Barraclough uncovers memory, but not as acutely. She focuses on land use and policy to reveal their influence on creating a racialized landscape and identity—as have others in regard to other localities. Case studies here narrow on manifestations of memory such as pageantry, memorialization, and historic preservation; scholars such as Martha Norkunas do the same, but with a more narrow focus on public history. Of course, unlike these scholars, suburbs are the special unit of analysis here. Most of these scholars seek to understand white privilege, while the objective here is to recognize the existence of suburban memory. Altogether, the culture and worldviews of suburbanites making their lives in California's agriburbs comes shining through. The legacies of rural and urban boosterism in California are undeniable as a result, and they are many.

Indulge a final word about the organizational structure and content of this book. While the three parts and their chapters received demarcation above, five smaller subsections also appear, receiving no chapter numbers. Namely, these subsections either provide some historical context or introduce relevant theory for the chapters that follow, or both. Placing such context or theory tightly in subsections happened because, first, they are indeed relevant, but, second, they mean to relay this information succinctly while not distracting the reader with potentially nuanced theoretical concepts or contextual minutiæ within the chapters themselves. Therefore, before chapter one, context about the Market Revolution and the rise of Romanticism appear to help ground the discussion on the rise of the suburban ideal. Before chapter two, a subsection about boosterism appears to position the review for understanding not just the California Dream, but also boosterism throughout the book. To begin part two, before chapter three, a review of historical suburban definitions and characterizations provides the framework for how dissecting agriburbs follows in chapters three and four. Before chapter five, a subsection on the growth machine theory portends the relevance of providing biographies of the boosters as such. Finally, launching part three, a subsection on memory provides a review of memory and makes clear the terms underscoring this work.

PART ONE

CALIFORNIA DREAMING

THE MARKET REVOLUTION AND ROMANTICISM

What hath God wrought?

NUMBERS 23:23

T he extraordinary changes taking place in the United States in the early nineteenth century have long impressed historians and contextualize the rise of the rural and suburban ideals at the heart of agriburb design. The reference to Numbers, "What hath God wrought," represents a key moment within this changing landscape. Admittedly, the King James translation can carry a negative connotation (particularly if wrought means twisted or destroyed, not created or produced), but in context the verse is one of accomplishment, foreshadowing the Hebrews' arrival out of Egypt, destined for the Promised Land. Most modern translations read something like, "What great things God has done!" Samuel F. B. Morse, contributing to the changes of the time, chose this verse as the first message to appear in his telegraph code in 1844. For him, and many others, it echoed the advancements of an exciting age.

Whether called the Antebellum Era (stressing war), the Age of Jackson (focusing on politics), the first Industrial Revolution (highlighting industry), or the Era of Reform and the Era of Good Feelings (examining sweeping democratic ferment and a soaring sentiment of patriotism), the United States experienced enormous changes in the early- to mid-nineteenth century. These changes, in one way or another, touched the lives of most Americans. What one historian called the "transportation revolution," others called a "market revolution" to explain profound political changes during the era that featured great innovation.[1] The economy began to transform from a largely subsistence economy of small farms and workshops whereby most local needs were satisfied through barter and exchange to a more capitalist commercial economy in which farmers and manufacturers produced foods and goods for cash incentives from an often distant marketplace. The United States experienced a powerful transformation from its early years to the Civil War. The population exploded, which included the arrival of larger numbers of immigrants. Cities arose while older ones grew. Manufacturing and industry began to rise. Transportation and communication technologies transformed the way people experienced their lives and imagined their futures. A middle class emerged that shaped and was shaped by the economic activities, political philosophies, and cultural values having a lasting influence on the spatial forms of the United States.

A review of changes caused by the market revolution helps to understand better the rise of the rural and suburban ideals. These changes had major implications in terms of industrial growth, immigration, slavery and ethnoracial conflict, political ideology and practice, social institutions and cultural patterns, and family life and household arrangements. The population totaled four million in 1790. By 1820, it reached ten million; by 1840, seventeen million; and by 1860, more than thirty-one million. Federal legislation slashed the price of land significantly: $2.00 an acre at a minimum of 640 acres in 1796; $0.125 an acre at a forty-acre minimum in 1854; and virtually free for 160 acres in 1862. Immigration, originally limited because of wars in Europe and domestic economic crises, exploded with about 600,000 immigrants, seventy percent German or Irish, arriving between 1831 and 1840. This compares with 144,000 arrivals between 1821 and 1830. As the population exploded and moved westward, thanks to King Cotton, nearly one million slaves relocated from the older slave states to the Deep South to harvest cotton production that skyrocketed from about 500,000 bales in 1820 to almost five million in 1860. The number of total slaves climbed from nearly 700,000 in 1790 to roughly 4.5 million in 1860. Those casting their lots in cities, particularly for employment in factories, contributed to the growth of urban areas as the number of cities with populations exceeding 5,000 rose from a dozen in 1820 to nearly 150 in 1850. Cities of more than 25,000 to 250,000 grew from three in 1800 to thirty-two in 1860.[2]

Rapid population growth, demographic change, and residential and occupational shifts were an outcome and medium of change in industry, communication, technology, transportation, and societal patterns. Transportation improved as more than 3,300 miles of canals in 1840 rose from about 100 miles in 1812. Steam ferries, omnibuses, and the railroad all significantly influenced migration patterns and commerce alike, as railroad lines boomed from more than 3,000 miles in 1840 to about 31,000 in 1860. Newspaper companies emerged as ninety newspapers with a circulation of about four million in 1790 escalated to more than 1,200 papers with a circulation of ninety million in 1835. Factories and mills, such as those in Lowell, Pawtucket, and Waltham, employed about three percent of the population—or 350,000 people—in 1820 and fourteen percent of the population—or two million—in 1860. When the era began, ax and plow served as the common tools of farmers in a predominantly barter and exchange economy. By the 1860s, however, within an expanding capitalist economy, farmers moved toward specialization and utilized horse-powered seed drills, cultivators, and reapers. By the eve of the Civil War, then, a vastly transformed, if not divided, United States arose. Many Americans struggled upon this changed landscape with issues raised by industrial capitalism, immigration, and urbanization and often interpreted such changes as a conflict and battle for the soul of the nation. New forms of consciousness, politics, and social life thus arose and shaped the tumults and innovations most often associated with the era.[3]

The ascendency of the philosophy of agrarianism, the rural ideal, came amid the backdrop of the market revolution.[4] Concisely, the ideal culminated, as one historian said, in the "belief that farming is the best way of life and the most important economic endeavor."[5] This view "celebrated farmers for their supposed centrality in a good society, their political virtue, and their moral superiority." Consequently, "farmers were society's heroes."[6] How this happened, of course, is complex. A line of regression could go back millennia to the ancient Roman poet Virgil. The immediate causes, however, come from Europe and the rise of Romanticism; hence some historians discuss *romantic agrarianism*.

Romanticism refers to the growing reaction to industrialization that first swept Western Europe beginning about the mid-eighteenth century. Noting that the term *reaction* might marginalize people with genuine beliefs in corresponding Romantic ideals apart from the industrial revolution taking place and, further, espouse beliefs with very long histories, we should realize that Romanticism has relatively modern roots. Industrialization reflected an industrial revolution with changes in production, manufacturing, improved waterpower, the advent of steam power and machine tools, infrastructure and transportation developments, urbanization, and so on. Incomes rose, populations grew, and the aspects of everyday life and all that such implies drastically changed.

Romanticism revealed a growing sense of loss amid this transforming landscape. Often coupled with conservative reactions to the French Revolution, industrialization helped create the fashioning of a mythological golden age championing a primitivistic philosophy that argued for the natural superiority of distant times, bygone eras, which industrialization, of course, threatened. This plea also came in the wake of the counter-Enlightenment, which argued the scientific method and its adherents had falsely rationalized nature, especially as more materialistic explanations appeared. Considered altogether, a nostalgic longing for a mythical utopia, lending to a useable past, arose that further expressed bewilderment with the seeming trivialization of the redemptive and, hence, spiritual, power of nature—of a pre-industrial society.

What had been lost had been regrettable. Romantics charged that industrialization ushered in an unwelcomed reordering of life and the creation of a social and economic order that seemed to brutalize those at the lower wrung of the ladder, working in the factories, mills, and mines and crammed together in deplorable housing. Industrialization contributed to increasing social unrest, political chaos, and fear. A rural golden age represented not just a classless society, but also a harmonious and stable one in which nature all (and best) by itself sustained life, all of which were good for individuals as much as their families, extending to society broadly. Industrialization, in contrast, upset it.

English poet William Wordsworth, French essayist François-René de Chateaubriand, and German painter Caspar David Friedrich are among a small sample of the European Romantics who fashioned a sacred view of nature and, accordingly, a desire to return to a pre-industrial world. In the United States, Thomas Jefferson, having spent considerable time in France as a diplomat, supported the view of nature as superior. He famously went on to extol farmers and farming, in contact with nature, as superlative and the foundation for the spread of a democratic society and the republic (i.e., Jeffersonian Democracy). Ralph Waldo Emerson, Henry David Thoreau, and Walt Whitman, among others, also represented an explicitly more spiritual reverence for nature in the United States by the mid-nineteenth century amid the market revolution.

The rural ideal, as covered in the following chapter, helped give birth to the suburban ideal, which, in its original articulation, historians often label *romantic suburbs*. Two other historical currents during industrialization and the growing market economy, however, are worth noting here. First, the transformations taking place both derived from and affected social hierarchies that experienced the creation of a new middle-class culture and consciousness.[7] Attempts to define the behaviors and values that ought to be considered "middle-class," along with the lifestyle appropriate to such class status, were what successfully marked the creation of a new middle class.

A new class and identity consciousness centered on values of democracy and freedom, and concepts of a "self-interested man" or "self-made man" became established as natural.[8] As economic life became more competitive because of the market revolution, a new "middle" America arose, and in overtly gendered and racialized notions, a new celebration of the successful young white male emerged whereby so-called entrepreneurs received praise for success.[9] Nevertheless, "the scheming speculations of the last ten years," wrote Reverend Henry Ward Beecher in 1846, "have produced an aversion among the young to the slow accumulations of ordinary industry, and fired them with a conviction that shrewdness, cunning, and bold ventures, are a more manly way to wealth."[10] Consequently, men had to prove themselves in the new competitive market economy. They had to demonstrate their ability to support their families—both as men and as members of a new middle class.

Ascension to middle classdom as a rule came through wealth. A lifestyle that correlated with, thus signaling to others, a higher income level and class status accompanied wealth as another signifier. Therefore, with newfound wealth, the new middle class sought to distinguish itself culturally, ideologically, materially, and spatially from everyone else (early examples of what scholars Thorstein Veblen and Pierre Bourdieu called "conspicuous consumption" and "distinction," respectively).[11] A redefinition of the American Dream and ideal lifestyle took place. A single-family home in the countryside, but still close to the city, emerged as an idyllic model and entitlement of middle-class Americans.[12] This ideal further transformed the United States, redefining the meaning of success. Suburbia and middle-class status represented a powerful redefinition of what it meant to be American in a time of great change.

Finally, as industrialization helped foster a lamentable loss of nature, as already hinted at, it also fostered a new historical consciousness wherein people were keenly aware of the changes taking place, some angered by them.[13] The same forces that gave birth to Romanticism and, subsequently, the suburban ideal, also led to the rise of a historical consciousness whereby lament for the loss of a romantic rural utopia manifested more robustly. Ultimately, whether an irony or an internal contradiction in the literature, or both, the argument is that this more vigorous historical consciousness (directly or otherwise) led to the proliferation of suburbs. Yet, as most suburban critics have made clear, we need to blame suburbs for a demise of historical consciousness. This contradiction is part of the analysis in the last chapters, yet it should remain in the reader's mind to appreciate better the significance of fashioning representations about suburban places.

CHAPTER ONE

THE SUBURBAN IDEAL

Sensible men gladly escape, earlier or later,
or partially or wholly, from the turmoil of cities.

ANDREW JACKSON DOWNING, 1850[1]

THE SUBURBAN IDEAL of the nineteenth century celebrated single-family homes away from cities but accompanied with urban amenities. Suburban image-makers painted an image of suburban residences as located within a sylvan environment. The hunt for the perfect location, the idealized physical and peaceful site for a suburb, began before the Civil War and continues today. California's boosters seized upon this growing suburban trend and proclaimed California as truly the Golden State, perfect for suburbs. Yet, as noted, this coupled with a growing celebration of the family farm. As a result, the romantic suburb married the small farm to create the agriburb.

Revealing the Romantic suburban ideal in all its parts reveals how California's boosters did seize upon such a model by the latter nineteenth century in the following chapters. Namely, this allows for a classic compare-and-contrast analysis. Ultimately, dissecting first the Romantic suburban ideal and second the California Dream shows how explicitly California's boosters crafted a suburban vision, mixed with horticulture, in hopes of harvesting suburbs.

THE SUBURBAN IDEAL

Llewellyn Park in Orange, New Jersey, receives recognition as the first planned suburb in the United States. It did not begin, however, after World War II, as most who picture suburbia as little boxes on a hillside might imagine. Rather, it began following the Mexican-American War in the 1850s as a fracturing nation edged closer to the Civil War. Llewellyn Park is the first of the so-called romantic suburbs. Picturesque cottages in a pastoral landscape were sought by middle-class Americans.[2] Romantic suburbs fit the application of Emerson's belief in the need to "unite rural and urban in order to promote spiritual and social advancement."[3] Romantic suburbs, like Llewellyn Park and, later, Riverside outside Chicago in the 1860s, were designed to harmonize with nature via Victorian houses amid curving roads, parks, preserves, and ponds. Planned as model-utopian communities in sylvan settings, they would providentially reform society.[4]

Few Americans could actually afford to live in elite romantic suburbs like Llewellyn Park. Even so, suburbs like this were both the manifestation and standard of a growing suburban ideal. They became the prototype for more romantic suburbs that followed, as well as to influence the less opulent suburbs that evolved afterward, from the streetcar suburbs of Boston in the late nineteenth century to mass-produced suburbs like Lakewood outside Los Angeles in the 1950s (which mandated tree ownership) and the luxurious Woodlands outside Houston in the 1980s. This suburban ideal also fed the rise of the California Dream whereby the Golden State incorporated suburban ideas to a more open Western landscape suitable for profitable farming.

Central to the emerging suburban ideal of the nineteenth century were several key points that Californian boosters later reassembled. First, the rural ideal championed by Romantics called for a check against urbanization and the retreat to more natural environments.[5] Second, the emergence of a more modern middle class also defined the era as suburbs became noted (hyperbolically—but still the point) for their prime potential to gather people of "certain tastes" together in a perfect environment that would lead to the blossoming of individuals and the nation. The perfect environment did not shun machines in the garden however. Suburbs called for a magical mix of city and country. Life amid trees did not mean life without businesses, social clubs, or good quality roads. Finally, an intensified rhetoric of home and family got voluminous attention as families, according to such rhetoric, grew more successfully in rural suburbs than elsewhere. These key points—the suburbanized rural ideal, the middle class in a middle landscape, and families and homes in a perfect environment— constituted the romantic suburb. Below is a tour.

THE SUBURBANIZED RURAL IDEAL

Landscape designer Andrew Jackson Downing said in 1850, "The republican home, built by no robbery of the prosperity of another class, maintained by no infringement of a brother's rights; the beautiful, rural, unostentatious, moderate home of the country gentleman, [is] large enough to minister to all the wants, necessities, and luxuries of a republican." He added, "and not too large or too luxurious to warp the life of manners of his children."[6] According to Downing, the countryside suburban home would make Americans better citizens or "virtuous citizens"—particularly vital given the perceived cacophony of problems brought about by industrialization.[7] This rural fantasy posited that suburbs would save America, foster republicanism and civic participation, stimulate neighborliness and community, and restore Americans' democratic spirit.

Suburban image-makers, repeating elements of romantic agrarianism, valorized a society of small-property owners who, while not exactly farmers, were close enough to nature and far enough from the city to mirror Thomas Jefferson's independent, rational, and democratic husbandmen who would help, in Jefferson's words, "preserve a republic in vigor."[8] Others agreed, such as architect and planner Frederick Law Olmsted, architect-author Samuel Sloan, and landscape designer Calvert Vaux. Olmsted thought suburbs would help further democratize and thereby equalize Americans, particularly by transforming them into a homogeneous middle class "of certain tastes." Sloan believed that home ownership, "allied to taste," filled the owner with a "love for it" and a "proportionate determination to uphold and defend it." "Such a man," he concluded, became "a good citizen, for he has a stake in society." Finally, Vaux maintained a suburban home "will, doubtless, help a good deal to clear away the obstructions that at present hamper the *social* progress of the spirit of republicanism."[9]

An increased middle-class antipathy, particularly toward the city, accompanied reported fears of increased immigration, industrialization, and urbanization by the early to mid-nineteenth century. Much of this evolved over concerns with congestion and traffic, crime and vice, and health and pollution. Suburbia became an imagined landscape for combating, even escaping, undesirable aspects of the city. "Flee the great cities!" cried Reverend Henry Morgan as late as 1880. He continued: "Oh young man, happy in your country home, come not to the great city!" For Morgan, liquor, prostitution, and crime were the "quicksands of city life."[10] In contrast, the suburban home emerged narratively as a safeguard of liberties and the authentic environment to promote better family relations, escape urban vices, and commune with nature in a healthful location or, as Catharine E. Beecher and Harriet Beecher Stowe imagined, "a healthful home" in a good climate with pure air and proper ventilation.[11] Authors from Beecher to Emerson, Jefferson, and Olmsted fabricated a set of representations and new—or at least retranslated—cultural values and perceptions of quality and taste that were decidedly anti-urban, pro-nature, and centered on race, class, home, and family. The suburb thus emerged as a middle landscape—an alternative to the city on the one hand and a mix of the best of city and country on the other.

Emerson, Jefferson, and writer/naturalist Henry David Thoreau were popular anti-urbanists who did little to disguise their disgust with the city, which contributed to the seemingly national desire to discover an alternative. Like Morgan, the anti-urbanists again bemoaned cities because of congestion, epidemics, pollution, and immigrants.[12] "I view large cities," said Jefferson, "as pestilential to the morals, the health, and the liberties of man." Emerson feared a brain drain as cities weakened the United States because they "drain the country of the flavor of youth, the best part of the population, and leave the countryside (in the absence of landed aristocracy) to be cultivated by an inferior, irresponsible class." Certainly we know that many urban leaders portrayed cities as vital centers that nurtured culture and innovation. Nevertheless, many others portrayed the city as the symbol of problems and wickedness: the city as menace. Cities could not suitably support the rapid population growth and lacked open, public spaces, which, as one nineteenth-century critic judged, meant "an evil of much more serious cost" because it would "keep without" that "ministering angel of health." "A man's health," Thoreau surmised, "requires as many acres of meadow to his prospect as his farm does loads of musk."[13] In this context, as Emerson noted, "nature is medicinal," and if Americans were sick because of industrialization, a maturing market economy, or large cities, then suburban homes in the countryside would provide the appropriate healing.[14]

THE MIDDLE CLASS IN A MIDDLE LANDSCAPE

Believing "our government will remain virtuous for many centuries as long as they are chiefly agricultural," Jefferson extolled a rural virtue contributing to a growing hostility toward the city and a romanticized fascination with nature. In this way, a suburb arose as an alternative residential middle landscape to set things right. In 1961, historian Lewis Mumford concluded romantic suburbs were places "to take advantage" of a "rural surcease." Suburban pleasures were "between rural and urban pleasures: eating, drinking, dancing, athletic sports, [and] love-making." Gervase Wheeler pointed to this ideal mix back in 1855 in his *Homes for the People, in Suburb and Country*. He concluded a suburban home "joined the social habits of the city" with "rural tastes." The suburban middle landscape then, while not rural, but not urban either, combined both. "To those who desire to dwell amid the beauties of nature and yet be within convenient distance of the city," wrote one contributor to *Suburban Homes on the West Jersey Railroad* in the late nineteenth century, suburbs had urban amenities whereby one could enjoy "excellent religious, education, and social advantages." Such advantages (as highlighted already in Ontario) included a library, opera house, public and private schools, and "numerous shops, stores, mills, lumber, and coal yards."[15]

Frederick Law Olmsted, in fact, as well as his partner Calvert Vaux, famously utilized the city and country mix as a principal foundation for suburban planning. Repeatedly recognized by historians as the key figures of suburbia's proliferation, they laid out sixteen suburbs, including Brookline, MA; Chestnut Hill, MA; and Riverside, IL. Olmsted and Vaux stated that suburbs were "not a sacrifice of urban conveniences, but their combination with the special charms and substantial advantages of rural conditions of life." The designers offered suburban communities with large lots and an environment that blended urban elements within "sylvan surroundings." This included curvilinear streets, parks, and shade trees. Previously mentioned, the showcase for this was in Riverside in the 1860s. This "best application of the arts of civilization" meant suburban residents would find "the advantages of society, of compact society, of the use of professional talent in teachers, and artists and physicians." Olmsted stated, "They want to be served in a regular, exact, punctual, and timely manner with superior comestibles, and whatever else it is desirable to have supplied to a family, freshly, frequently, or quickly on demand." Olmsted and Vaux said they designed Riverside "in such a manner as to combine the conveniences of the city . . . with all the beauties of landscape gardening and the essential advantages of the country." Ultimately, they believed their suburbs reflected a progress that "was never more rapid [than] at the present moment."[16]

HOMES AND FAMILIES IN A PERFECT ENVIRONMENT

The single-family home in a setting that combined the supposed better of two worlds certainly did emerge as a sought-after alternative to the growing storyline of dissatisfaction with industrialization. Suburban homes became a family's place of refuge. Preachers during this "era of reform," the so-called Second Great Awakening, cited the importance of the family as a safeguard against what they viewed as a morally failing society. The family home emerged as an emotional, rather than economic, unit.[17] Such books as Lydia Maria Child's The Mother's Book (1831), Reverend John Abbott's The Mother at Home (1833), Reverend Herman Humphrey's Domestic Education (1840), and Reverend William G. Eliot Jr.'s Lectures to Young Women (1854) depicted the middle-class family as the stabilizer of society. No government institution, political philosophy, or cultural practice could do what the family circle could do. "The foundation of our free institutions," Eliot said, "is in our love, as a people, for our homes. The strength of our country is found, not in the declaration that all men are free and equal, but in the quiet influence of the fireside, the bonds, which unite together the family circle. The cornerstone of our republic is the hearth-stone." Beecher and Stowe maintained that individual Americans and the nation would find salvation in the perfection of family life in suburban homes close to nature.[18]

The romanticization of the suburban single-family home represented a pattern of social and class segregation. The early days of suburbs saw the championing of the elements of class, culture, racial conformity, homogeneity, and uniformity, and not something as repulsive as they seemed to critics later. Notions of privacy and separateness gained saliency during a period when Americans grew concerned about their supposed security and quality of life. Therefore, the single-family home became the imagined place of refuge; and the locally controlled suburb, "united," as Beecher said, "by similarity of character and pursuits," emerged as a homogeneous fantasy to counter a heterogeneous urban landscape.[19]

While perhaps not as Machiavellian as some interpreters have characterized the middle-class movement to suburbia, suburbs as portrayed by Beecher and Olmsted nonetheless did reflect a middle-class longing for social segregation toward common interests and similarity, if indeed not away from ethnoracial and cultural differences. Regardless of motivation, homogeneity proved desirous as suburbs fostered a uniformity that minimized racial hostilities.[20] Suburban relocation also created a "spatiality of whiteness" or "possessive investment in whiteness" that minimized differences between ethnic whites and intensified the racializing—and radicalizing—of "others." Such racializing has had dire economic, political, and social consequences to this day.[21] So in suburbs, historically, the middle class sought and preserved social homogeneity, particularly in terms of class and race separation, whether as "clubbing together," finding "common interests," or, as Beecher and Stowe hoped, a "Christian family" in a "Christian neighborhood" that would be "the grand ministry of salvation" for the democratic citizen and the republic alike.[22]

FIGURE 1

"A Christian Home." This image comes from Harriet Beecher Stowe and Catherine E. Beecher's *The American Woman's Home: or, Principles of Domestic Science; Being a Guide to the Formation and Maintenance of Economical, Healthful, Beautiful, and Christian Homes*, published in 1869. Titled "A Christian Home," a single-family house (sanctified by the cross and signaling moral purity) is set within an ideal aesthetic of nature, complete with trees, waterway, and a garden. Notice that the likely father and daughter are tending to the garden as the likely mother and son stroll the clear walkway. All are dressed finely, signaling a higher-class status appropriate for owning such a "healthful," "Beautiful," and "Christian" home. Images like these, of families enjoying sylvan surroundings about their homes, emblematized the single-family home of the growing suburban ideal.

Depictions of the single-family home as a place of refuge also portrayed it as the proper place for women. An ideology of domesticity celebrated the home—where women presided and ruled—as the central institution of American life.[23] Removed from the city, women had to create a peaceful environment for their families. Because of industrialization that at the time largely excluded them from working, women's domestic roles were glorified. Earlier, advice givers such as Liza Farrar urged women to complete their domestic responsibilities because it was their duty. Domestic responsibilities came second to women's commitment to civic and family life by the nurturing of public-spirited males. By the 1830s, however, women such as Beecher and Sara Josepha Hale told women that domestic responsibilities constituted the means of social salvation. "And not only in domestic life is the moral effect of women's character and conduct thus influential," wrote Hale in 1840, "but the prosperity and greatness of the nation are equally dependent upon her."[24]

Catharine E. Beecher, one of thirteen children of the Reverend Lyman Beecher, is central to the consecration of domesticity.[25] Ironically, she never had her own home and family and rarely found herself on friendly terms with her siblings, yet she became the leading nineteenth-century theorist on the virtues of domesticity, value of home, and the importance of family. Believing in the doctrine of separate spheres and women's moral superiority, which she touted came to full fruition in the home, she put forth a "cult of true womanhood" as the basis for women to create a measure of their own power. Beecher subsequently linked architectural and landscape design with the domestic home ideal. She believed in the power of place and offered plans for an ideal middle-class home "in the country or in the suburban vicinities as give space or ground for healthful outdoor occupation in the family service."[26] She believed women were the "ministers of home" and could construct homes on "democratic" and "Christian principles," utilize technological innovations, and play a primary part in uplifting American life.[27] Focusing on family, home, nature, health, and security, Beecher helped shape the suburbanized rural ideal favored by middle-class families ever since.[28]

Historian Frederick Jackson Turner is famous for his vision of an exceptional American democratic spirit spreading across a "savage" frontier—the safety valve of the republic. Yet, in 1884, nine years before his famed "frontier thesis" roused the historical profession, he argued that the history of architecture provided evidence of a history of oppression. Nevertheless, in the United States, he lectured, "[T]he nineteenth century is striving to build humanity into a glorious temple to its God" through an architecture of freedom.[29] Turner and others, like Beecher, believed that the designs, layouts, and shapes of buildings could have a profound influence on the moral character of their inhabitants. The single-family home, synonymous at this point with the family inside, emerged in the minds of particularly those selling self-help manuals and pattern books as an island of stability in a modernizing society under strain.[30] Together with the invented appropriate familial relationships and domestic gender roles, said the suburban image-makers, the American family home would ensure America's inevitable march of progress. "He who improves the dwelling-houses of a people in relation to their comforts, habits, and morals," said one pair of

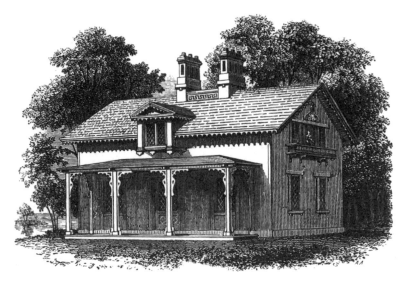

FIGURE 2

"A Suburban Cottage for a Small Family." This image comes from Andrew Jackson Downing's *Cottage Residences; or, A Series of Designs for Rural Cottages and Cottage Villas, and Their Gardens and Grounds, Adapted to North America*, originally published in 1842. Along with designers like Alexander Jackson Davis, who collaborated with Downing on this book, Downing produced premier design books among the many churned out in the nineteenth century. Downing and the others crafted a picture of an ideal home set among idyllic natural surroundings that would later become the bedrock of suburban imagery and design. In this image, notice not only the single-family home amid natural scenery, but also what appears to be a young woman in the window on the right, second floor. Perhaps she is the formulaic motif of the young wife waiting at home for her husband's return. According to Downing, in his caption to this image, which also features a floor plan, he makes note of the advantage for having the kitchen on the same floor as the living room so as "the mistress" can "have the management of the domestic affairs directly under her own personal care and supervision."

nineteenth-century architects "makes a . . . lasting reform at the very foundations of society."[31] The home became not only a place to live but also an emblem for family cohesiveness and identity, especially middle-class identity as it contributed to the definition of middle class at least as much as income level. As early as the 1830s, for example, some families were reportedly going bankrupt to appear middle class through lifestyle and home design (i.e., to keep up with the Joneses). "We have, again and again," wrote one observer, "seen families of limited means, forego the very necessaries of life, in order to keep up the appearance of being able to enjoy its luxuries, and this, because they were unwilling to seem inferior to those with whom they have been accustomed to associate in life."[32]

As Beecher is to domesticity, Andrew Jackson Downing is to the family home and to translating the rural ideal into the suburban ideal in the mid-nineteenth century. "We believe," said Downing, "about all things under heaven, in the power and virtue of the *individual home*." As author and editor of the *Horticulturist* (a journal title that, as will be seen, is more than a coincidence when discussing horticulture and suburbs), Downing espoused a faith in the power of "rural tastes" concerning homes, landscape architecture, and parks. Arguing that all "sensible men gladly escape, earlier or later, or partially or wholly, from the turmoil of cities," he added, "the love of country is inseparably connected with love of home." In the move to country houses a great transfiguration of the individual and family occurred by "not only augmenting his own enjoyment, but strengthening his patriotism, and making him a better citizen." Downing preferred people to live, as he haughtily saw it, more fashionable and tasteful lives. He suggested that in the city's hinterland the purchase of farmland and conversion of it into suburban property personified what Americans needed to do. He idealized love of rural life for middle-class suburban residents and sought to give advice, "practical methods," so as to "render domestic life more delightful." With a goal of bringing "men into daily contact with nature . . . in their country and cottage homes," he lectured, one "should look for the happiest social and moral development of our people" in such houses. "[I]t is the solitude and freedom of the family home in the country which constantly preserves the purity of the nation, and invigorates its intellectual powers."

Downing boldly offered "three excellent reasons" for "good houses." First, they were a "powerful means of civilization" whereby a "refinement of manners which distinguishes a civilized from a coarse and brutal people" is established and signaled the "progress of its civilization." Second, good homes had "a great social value," particularly best for the family and the "purity of the nation." Finally, Downing said, "[T]here is a moral influence in a country home—when, among an educated, truthful, and refined people, it is an echo of their character—which is more powerful than any mere oral teachings of virtue and morality." A good house in suburban communities "contributes largely to our stock of happiness, and to the elevation of the moral character."[33]

AMERICANS, THE SUBURBAN IDEAL, AND GOING TO CALIFORNIA

Suburbs assured hopes for the rejuvenation of America as suburban image-makers critiqued relentless capitalist expansion, immigration, industrialization, and urbanization. California boosters distinctly laid claim to the notion that California represented the supreme geographic location for the suburban ideal. Narratives of California as a land of homes, ideal for families, best for health, abundant in natural resources, and blessed with a pristine environment filled thousands of pages of advertisements that boosters spread across America. If one truly craved a single-family home in the countryside without sacrificing urban amenities, then one needed to head to California. The California Dream represented the peaceful romantic suburban landscape as envisioned by suburban image-makers.

BOOSTERISM

Western American history, especially from the late
19th century forward, is essentially the story of rapid urbanization
driven by investment in real estate, capital intensive agriculture
and industry, and social and cultural institutions. It is a story in
which capitalists transformed the West from a rural, agricultural
region into the nation's urban, industrial leader.

LEE M. A. SIMPSON, 2003[1]

Boosterism is advertising. It serves capital. This rests upon the fact that land in the United States, mostly, is a commodity and can be bought and sold. Boosterism is therefore about boosting the desirability of a product to entice a consumer to want it and, consequently, fatten the booster's wallet. This also reflects a real-estate speculation with imaginative vision. Stripping away, only for a moment, real estate's encompassment of appraisal, brokerage, management, marketing, and investment, real-estate speculation includes a piece of land, the air above it, and the ground below it—the physical, material, or built landscape.

With the rise of a robust market economy, advertising and the marketplace have evolved. Most histories of advertising narrow on the 1920s however. They typically begin with the propaganda of George Creel and the Committee on Public Information's massive advertising program for World War I, most famously the posters. Scholars further look at the 1920s as the rise of what one historian calls the "consumers' republic."[2] Advertising executives (aka "admen") and professional public marketing firms ushered in modern advertising.

Advertising has always been with us however, especially in cities with merchants and peddlers, or growing with a budding market economy through the first half of the nineteenth century. Yet, rather than advertising through admen, businesspeople such as boosters wrote and designed their own advertisements, commissioning printers and publishers to produce them and, more often than not, distribute them to newspapers, hotels, libraries, and reading rooms. In Southern California, boosters such as Robert M. Widney and the Los Angeles Chamber of Commerce underwrote publications and bore the cost of distribution throughout the nation, especially to the East Coast. Also take note that advertising before the 1920s occurred prior to the rise of radio, television, and film. The printed word reigned, largely from the 1820s forward as a market revolution got underway and as newspapers and other print publications increased in circulation. Lengthy written advertising campaigns reigned until about the 1890s, after which increasingly elaborate images, like the cover of this book, gradually filled the pages of magazines, journals, and the like because of better printing techniques, design developments, and ever-improving technologies.[3]

Between the Civil War and the 1920s, the period that correlates with the analysis of selling agriburbs, advertising both differed from and had similarities to advertising practices of the twentieth century. Indeed, as historian Pamela Walker Laird reminds us, a common theme in advertising across American history exists: progress. A major dividing line, however, is, again, the 1920s. The post-1920s era championed consumption as the driving force of progress. The era between the Civil War and the 1920s, in contrast, saw owners give greater attention to production and producers as the route to progress in their advertisements.[4]

Advertising campaigns, as historian Jackson Lears puts it, "urge people to buy goods, but they also signify a certain vision of the good life; they validate a way of being in the world. They focus private fantasy; they sanction or subvert existing structures of economic and political power. Their significance depends on their cultural setting."[5] In short, advertising seeks to urge (buy), focus (buy this), and sanction (buy this from me) or subvert (do not buy this from any of them). As such, advertising is often suggestive; it might seek to sell fantasy as much as to distribute information about any goods (admittedly, sometimes a pencil is just a pencil). Advertising is often seen as a representation of cultural values as it attempts to recast potential consumers' relationships with goods, services, environments, and even people—with the purpose of motivating purchase—and thus must be placed within a multi-voiced cultural context.

Advertising serves as a picture window into the consumers' minds, then the producers who, in turn, assess in some manner what they think will direct and urge consumers, or at least stabilize the market to their advantage as competitors and fickle tastes come and go. This is fundamentally a cultural analysis of what scholars call *representations* (i.e., the manifestation and transmission) of cultural values and beliefs articulated through products or ideologies such as advertising, journalism, religious and political speech, popular culture, and more. Related to *discourse*, the above logic also contends that the more any representation actually manifests—articulates—then the more likely the represented reflects a prevailing belief or value. Subsequently, a further assumption is that these representations appear frequently because they hold enormous potential to attract consumers; they are, as historian Jacob Burckhardt might say, "the recurrent, constant, and typical." This marks such advertisements as smart because they reflect, create, or somehow alter demand.[6]

The above analysis champions the symbolic use of goods and services beyond, but not at the discarding of, Marxian commodity fetishism that maintains consumers in capitalist societies come to perceive a commodity as possessing value in and of itself and not given value by the laborer(s) who made it. With insights from theorists such as Thorstein Veblen, the value of commodities extends to imaginary links, however realistic or not, however intense or not, spreading out from consumers' hopes and aspirations (granted, a pencil might just still be a pencil). People purchase goods and services as a way to project a sense of their own identity, however authentic or successful such consumption is at accomplishing this goal notwithstanding. People consume more than just a commodity. They consume ideas and beliefs, especially ones represented by any one commodity or even prevailing discourse absent a materiality per se, like political or religious beliefs.[7]

Given the cultural dimensions to advertising, and all the imagination it implies, advertisements hold the potential to tell us something about their creators—the boosters. In addition, advertisements tell us something about the time and subject matter for which the boosters designed them. First thing to make clear is that the terms *booster* and *boosterism* typically refer to the mid to late nineteenth century through the early twentieth century because, first, the boosters are not professional admen, and, second, their boosterism is verbose and dominated by lengthy written campaigns. These boosters also sell specific places. Boosters are real-estate speculators, whether developers themselves or otherwise interested investors who stand to benefit from an increase in population. Here is where the related term *growth machine* often comes into play.

While elaborated on in more detail later, the idea of the growth machine is that boosters and other interested parties come together to advertise and spark growth, be it in terms of population or capital. Members of growth machines share an intense interest in both the use, and, especially, the exchange of land. Most are real-estate speculators, but many auxiliary players include the media, politicians, utilities, chambers of commerce, and the like.

Boosters want to strike a chord. As said, boosters—what one scholar calls "regimes of representation"—want to make their product desirable; therefore, they fashion stories about their commodity, infusing it with salient cultural signs and symbols.[8] Such a view helps us look at boosters and boosterism as a product of their time. Establishing why they did what they did tells us much about the culture and values of turn-of-the-twentieth-century California, the American West, and even the nation. Delineating the content of the booster ad campaigns reveals the real power of the suburban and rural ideals at the turn of the twentieth century as they reflected dominant and desirable commodities. Boosters selling and packaging their land unmistakably reassembled these ideals in designing their rural suburbs and then selling them.

The boosters' advertising reflects the power of narrative and constructing stories about places. Looking at boosterism over time, public policy expert John Rennie Short identified two leading narratives: light and shadow. Light seems obvious enough for boosterism in relation to agriburbs: the appeal of the rural and suburban ideals. As light narratives, they imply a positive type of labor and availability of jobs, places good for home and family, low taxes, and an otherwise pro-business and morally upright environment. These are narratives of praise, and they are all present and accounted for in the narratives concerning agriburbs.[9]

Shadow represents the identification of the proverbial dark side that a consumer must avoid, whether by removal, containment, or the availability of alternatives. To avoid the dark side, of course, one can simply buy the boosters' product. By the turn of the twentieth century, amid booming urbanization, the shadow narrative emerged as that of the city as menace, filled with immigrants, crime, and sin. That is, one should flee to suburbs, especially Western suburbs, to avoid the troubles of cities, especially Eastern cities. Of course, you should not flee as far as rural farms. Accompanying the city-as-menace narrative was the negative image of extensive, large-scale farming that required vast amounts of land, mostly in the Middle West, notably plaguing farmers and their pocketbooks and famously igniting farmers' revolts via the Grangers, Farmers' Alliances, and the Populists (hence, horticulture and intensive farming were light narratives for boosters). Likewise, these places, according to boosters, had virtually no city conveniences like theaters or shopping districts. The shadow narrative looks to blame then. The concept is to identify scapegoats for why life in an industrializing age that saw wealth explode exponentially never truly trickled down to the masses and why they could not enjoy the so-called good life. Therefore, blame further represents a loss of control. Boosterism in the turn-of-the-twentieth-century California sought to deploy light and shadow as boosters created a product for sale that they thought would—for the lack of a better phrase—show them the money. This product is the agriburb in California. Boosters sold it.

CHAPTER TWO

THE CALIFORNIA DREAM

Going to California with an aching in my heart.

LED ZEPPELIN, 1971[1]

THE GOLDEN STATE HAD BEEN GROWING structurally, economically, and demographically in 1891 when Charles Howard Shinn declared that a California fruit grower was akin to a suburbanite out East, but with the important difference that a California suburbanite also farmed. Shinn moved from Texas with his family as a child in 1858 and witnessed the growth firsthand. A graduate of the University of California and John Hopkins in Maryland, Shinn, while working as a schoolteacher and newspaperman, authored numerous publications, most of which extolled farming, the environment, and so-called natural advantages of California.[2] Shinn, in fact, is just one example of many boosters who helped convert the image of California at the turn of the twentieth century into an idyllic land perfect for rural suburbs. The reputation of California as the ideal place for suburban farmers actually emerged between the well-documented breakup of large wheat and ranch land holdings in the 1870s through the rise of agribusiness by the 1920s. Far from inevitable, instantaneous, or complete, the growth of California during this period resulted from and contributed to the small family farm's emergence nonetheless.

The railroad also contributed to California's growth. Besides the transcontinental railroad, other rail lines such as the Atchison, Topeka, and Santa Fe ended California's seclusion from the rest of the nation. Moreover, transportation and shipping costs ran lower than ever with rate competition between warring railroads underway. Fruit growth, particularly oranges, boomed. Southern California impressively produced about 2,000 carloads of navel oranges in 1886 alone. Southern California's agricultural growth certainly has not escaped the attention of scholars. Yet growth took place in Northern California. For example, the capital city Sacramento, often slighted in most histories of California, shipped a measly thirty-three tons of fruit in 1870—but 3,161 tons in 1882; 20,000 tons in 1891; and

37,000 tons in 1898. California ranked eighth in the nation in terms of the value of orchard products in 1869—less than three percent of the national total. By 1899 California ranked first in fruit production with an output of $28 million, almost twenty-two percent of the national totals, enjoying near monopolies on oranges, as well as almonds, apricots, figs, lemons, walnuts, and, by the 1910s, grapes.[3]

Not surprisingly, California's population grew. Upon admission to the union in 1850, the thirty-first state ranked twenty-ninth in the nation with fewer than 100,000 people. But with the Gold Rush, agriculture, and urbanization, California grew to 380,000 in 1860; 865,000 in 1880; and about 2.38 million in 1910, ranking it twelfth largest nationally. This nearly tripling of the population between 1880 and 1910 took place primarily in cities—Los Angeles, Oakland, Sacramento, and San Francisco, for example, housed forty percent of the state's population alone—but, as will be seen, it had a decidedly (rural) suburban accent.[4]

The rise of the suburban family farm in California certainly emerged during this epoch of growth. Nevertheless, growth should not always be taken as a synonym for good or better. Modernizing California (and the United States), as a myriad of historians have shown, led to controls in the production and distribution of goods and services, extremes in wealth and poverty, racial hostility, declines in income, the rise of child labor, and unsafe and unsanitary work and living conditions. Still, in California, with the subdivision of large land holdings underway, the construction of homes did indeed occur, and suburban communities did form even if alongside incessant urbanization, industrialization, and the growing plight of those struggling to earn a buck. Agribusiness and the (re)consolidation of land also took place but unwittingly increased the reliance on and exploitation of minority labor. This served to undermine the family farm ideal as so well documented in recent historical accounts by José Alamillo, Matt Garcia, Jerry Gonzales, and Gilbert Gonzales.[5] With all this, however, California's boosters constructed the fabled California Dream as speculators and developers built entire communities based on horticulture and suburban lifestyle.

SUCH STUFF AS (CALIFORNIAN) DREAMS ARE MADE ON

In order to reshape the narrative and form of California's landscape as perfect for small farms and suburbs, supporters first had to turn on maligning land monopoly, which as a concept and in practice ran counter to any romantic hope of small farmers dotting the soil. Land monopoly famously ignited nineteenth-century political economist Henry George's scorn. He and others railed, "[L]and grabbers have had it pretty much their own way in California." They "molded" law, "dictated" legislation, and ran the land offices and courts.[6] In California, coupled with Spanish and Mexican land grants to ranchers—about nine million acres—and American land policies like the Homestead Act (1862), Timberland Culture

Act (1873), Desert Land Act (1877), and Timber and Stone Act (1878), capital-rich investors and speculators ruled land consolidation.[7] Champions of small family farms thus began their campaign for more access to land and ownership. They argued that with the growth of family farming "one million people could be put into these great valleys in ten years."[8] One later observer argued that "land owned in small tracts and occupied and worked by the owners" destined "all conflict between labor and capital [to be] adjusted; their differences reconciled and ended."[9] Eventually Mother Nature delivered a vital blow to ranchers and wheat growers as drought devastated them, precipitating the breakup of many large ranchos into smaller parcels. For this reason, Governor Robert Waterman exclaimed in 1888, "[A] great revolution is rapidly but quietly taking place." He continued, "[T]he larger land holdings are breaking up, and being sold . . . in small tracts to families that are seeking homes, where they can till the soil three hundred and sixty days in each year, and reap the result of their labor with less output than anywhere else in the civilized world." He concluded this would lead to "the building up of a happy and prosperous community."[10]

Reshaping the narrative of California did not mean starting from scratch. The boosters drew upon a deep well of iconic representations that had already held California as supreme. Certainly, the Gold Rush added credibility to this image for some. The Gold Rush, as Californian historian Kevin Starr pointed out, attracted Protestant preachers who saw in California God's plan for the advancement of "His" people. California, as demonstrated by the likes of such preachers as Joseph A. Benton, could potentially fulfill "His plan" for the spread of American Protestantism, its civilizing effects, and emerge, as they saw it, as a true paradise. Even before this, however, French, Russian, English, and even American visitors to Spanish- and, later, Mexican- controlled California touted its enormous opportunity to reap a rich harvest. Nevertheless, they were dismayed by the lack of agricultural expansion.[11] One early American visitor, after lamenting the inappropriate use of the land, observed in 1846 that California only awaited "being metamorphosed into a perfect orchard."[12]

California boosters from the 1870s through the early twentieth century carried forward a narrative of California as best in land and environment, making it that much more powerful. Rather than repeating and reusing the now-traditional narrative unaltered, these boosters, as representatives of local growth desires, packaged California in such a way as to further entice migration and capital. Boosters such as those covered in later chapters on Ontario, Orangevale, and Fair Oaks were developers of actual suburbs. Nonetheless, boosters in general focused on grand narratives. They applied their promotional acumen by seizing upon the growing popularity of the romantic suburb. Suburban imagery thus became a foundation for California boosters to articulate aggressively the California Dream and profit from it. The California Dream, therefore, evolved into the California Suburban Dream.

Negative representations stunted growth of California from statehood through the late nineteenth century, especially before the boom years following the 1880s when substantial growth is far more evident. This is a seeming paradox in the evolution of the California Suburban Dream, which also came about, as historian Richard J. Orsi has so authoritatively argued, as partly a defensive strategy—or counteroffensive—to prevailing negative images that existed alongside more positive ones about California in the latter nineteenth century.[13] Namely, while a dominant narrative emerges, do not mistake it as the sole narrative. To get to the punch line first, a major part of overcoming negative, or shadow, narratives about the Golden State included creating popular and positive, or light, narratives. California's boosters countered shadow narratives through their positive messages. The rhetoric, design, and cultural meanings of the rural and suburban ideals, as said, informed this counteroffensive precisely because they were relatively popular.

California's population exploded after the agricultural boom of the 1880s, sparked by expanding railroads and fruit developments, yet most of this was measured at the time as urban growth. Suburbs got lost in that era's census data. Places greater than 2,500 people qualified as urban, and areas with fewer classified as rural. Suburbs like Ontario did not surpass the 2,500 threshold until 1910; Orangevale, in 1960; and Fair Oaks, in 1970. The census thus embellished the rural and urban population numbers, especially as subdivisions picked up following the agricultural boom. Whatever the case, the overall lack of growth in the first decades after the Gold Rush worried California's boosters, especially as they competed with other Western states keeping pace with, or even beating, them.

Besides looking to criticize land monopoly, as well as the railroad, the Gold Rush became a victim to rightful criticisms too. A plethora of early news articles and Gold Rush "movies," shows featuring moving painted panoramas, proliferated on the East Coast. In connection, critics, not disguising their racism, bemoaned immigration, especially Chinese, to California with the Gold Rush and then the railroad. They likewise belittled shifts in the economy—demarcating it as unstable—caused from the changes of Gold Rush to wheat and cattle to, eventually, agriculture. The plight of labor, exacerbated by the Chinese and other immigrants, especially in San Francisco, also grabbed headlines. Repeatedly, sensational stories depicted California as violent and bizarre, populated by ruined miners, murderers, and the Chinese. Fire, earthquake, lynching, gambling, violence between whites and Native Americans, and even grizzly bears reflected a backward, distant country.[14]

While agriculture proved a favorite for many writers, some early rhetoric did condemn California's agricultural potential, typically citing the aridity and lack of irrigation. The climate also suffered ridicule. Hilton Helper, a noted critic of the South, in 1855, claimed every house had an infestation of vermin, adding, "Fleas, ants, and all sorts of creepy things are as ubiquitous as those that tormented Pharaoh and his people."[15] Others complained of dust, mosquitoes, malaria, small pox, and other ailments,

TABLE 1

Rural and Urban Population of California and the Four Major Cities of Los Angeles (LA), Oakland (OAK), Sacramento (SAC), and San Francisco (SF), 1850–1920

	LA	OAK	SAC	SF	SF (% of total)	National Rank	Urban Percent	Percent
1850	1.610	n/a	6,820	34,776	n/a	92,597 (29/31)	n/a	n/a
1860	4,385	1,543	13,785	56,802	76,515 (20.1%)	379,994 (26/33)	20.7	79.3
1870	5.728	10,500	16,283	149,473	181,984 (32.5%)	560,247 (24/37)	37.2	62.8
1880	11,183	34,555	21,420	233,959	301,117 (34.8%)	864,694 (24/38)	42.9	57.1
1890	50,935	46,682	26,386	298,997	424,460 (35.1%)	1,208,130 (22/42)	48.9	51.4
1900	102.479	66,960	29,282	342,782	541,503 (36.5%)	1,485,053 (22/45)	48.6	47.7
1910	319,198	150,174	44,696	416,912	930,980 (39.2%)	2,377,549 (12/46)	52.3	38.2
1920	576,673	216,261	65,908	506,676	1,365,518 (39.8%)	3,426,861 (8/48)	61.8	32.1

SOURCES: *See endnote no. 4 of this chapter. For urban and rural percentages, see Orsi, "Selling the Golden State," 14. Note: By 1920, San Diego overtook Sacramento.*

TABLE 2

California Growth Compared to Kansas, Nebraska, and Texas, 1850–1900

	California	Kansas	Nebraska	Texas
1850	92,597	n/a	n/a	212,592
1860	379,994	107,206	28,841	604,215
1870	560,247	364,399	122,993	818,579
1880	864,694	996,096	452,402	1,591,749
1890	1,208,130	1,427,096	1,058,910	2,235,527
1900	1,485,053	1,470,295	1,066,300	3,048,710

SOURCES: *Historical Census Browser, from the University of Virginia, Geospatial and Statistical Data Center, http://fisher.lib. virginia.edu/collections/stats/histcensus.*

making clear California should not be on anyone's list as a heath resort. In 1872, Mark Twain compared "dust-covered" California to "the lavish richness, the brilliant green, the infinite freshness, the spend thrift variety of form and species and foliage that make an Eastern landscape a vision of paradise itself." He wrote about "the eternal Summer of Sacramento," that "people suffer and sweat, and swear, morning, noon and night, and wear out their stanchest [sic] energies fanning themselves."[16]

Anti-California rhetoric had its logic, especially critiques emanating out of the East designed to stem the potential rising tide of California power and halt migration out of the region. Namely, if California could become a decent market for and of consumers, then great, but not to the point where it drained the East or, even worse, emerged stronger. These negative tales represented shadow narratives, conveying messages like do not go there, please stay, or come here instead. They continuously cited droughts, the lack of irrigation, poor markets, oppressive taxes, high land and supply costs, and especially land monopoly.[17]

Besides alleging California's economic backwardness, shadow narratives pinned down the social life and structures of California as equally backwards—a result and contributing factor to a poor economy. One writer for the *Salt Lake City Herald* summed it up in 1878, describing California as a "good place to send men to when they die to punish them for their sins."[18] Violence and vigilantism, especially in San Francisco and toward the Chinese, continued to garner much attention. According to the famed poet Joaquin Miller, "[T]he [California] country is full of tramps; everyone a heroic and war-like 'boy-cotter.'"[19]

California also lacked homes and families and, hence, family values, especially rural family values since agriculture had yet to boom. Following gross gender stereotypes and normative expectations one might expect of the age, much of this attention focused on California's women, living in a state with flexible marriage and divorce customs. Apparently California girls had too much liberty—lacking chaperons and openly dating— as "unfortunate women" abounded, along with divorcees, separations, and unsupervised children. California's women were also labeled lazy, pretentious, lavishly conspicuous consumers, reluctant to join charitable causes and, in seemingly every way, inferior to women living on the East Coast. Drunks roamed the streets too. California had the hardest drinking population, according to these sensational narratives. Even worse, California had too many prostitutes and opium dens, here throwing the Chinese under the proverbial bus again, but also blaming California's women as frequent abusers.[20]

THE CALIFORNIA DREAM

The previous chapter broke down the romantic suburban ideal to provide the basis for a compare-and-contrast examination. Dissecting the California Dream shows how California's boosters explicitly created a suburban vision, mixed with horticulture, in hopes of harvesting suburban migration and growth. With the state cast as economically unstable, with a bad climate and even worse social conditions, California's boosters had some heavy lifting to do. Once more, herein the power of the rural and suburban ideals and the celebration of single-family homes and small farms manifest. A more refined, but still rural-like class could help infuse California with a virtuous citizenry and usher in a more stable, productive economy. The means for reassembling the popular representations of the romantic suburb and the small farm rested in good salesmanship. While shadow narratives coexisted, suburbs, by the late nineteenth century, became largely light narratives synonymous with homes and families of stability, democracy, opportunity, middle classdom, and refinement.

California's boosters, following the previously mentioned breakup of large land holdings in the latter decades of the nineteenth century, claimed California as the most beneficial countryside. In fact, US presidents were reportedly not exempt from California's allure. Abraham Lincoln "had heard so much of the delightful climate and the abundant natural productions of California" that he "fixed his eyes on California as a place of permanent residence" once his second term ended. Apparently, Lincoln "thought that the [Californian] country offered better opportunities for his two boys."[21] California, like suburbs, signified progressive communities that promised a land of plenty and a democratizing agent for all. California, according to most promotional accounts, seemed the perfect stage for the materialization of the American Dream.[22] Through horticulture, what one California booster called "the fair goddess who is making the world young once more," California provided not just financial benefits, but also intellectual fulfillment, satisfying work, and cultural advancement.[23]

"Horticulture," wrote the editor of *California Fruit Grower*, "in the fullest sense of the term embraces . . . everything that makes our country bright, beautiful, ornamental, and enjoyable." He continued, "The great stride made in this State in redeeming it from a parched and unproductive waste and making it a land of plenty and great productiveness is due to horticulture."[24] California's horticultural dominance promised, according to booster literature, to bring a higher level of civilization to rural life and place. California boosters, such as the University of California professor of agriculture Edward J. Wickson, argued that a fruited garden in California, synonymous with horticulture, was the space of the most rapid and complete process of "Americanization." Agriculture in California, as with romantic agrarianism generally, destined the creation of secure homes of independent farm families. In this view, California would transform into something sweepingly democratic in principle while also offering high returns with light work in a pleasant environment. "It will appear natural," wrote one author just after statehood, "that California should be the most democratic country in the world."[25] California, the "most efficient advocate of that Young America of which she is the choicest and richest jewel," said another writer, represented the "happy results of Democratic progress, both on the individual and our republican system."[26] The California Dream constructed itself on and advertised itself as this suburban ideal. Therefore, the same key points that defined the suburban ideal—the suburbanized rural ideal, the middle class in a middle landscape, and families and homes in a perfect environment—organize the review of the California Dream that follows.

THE SUBURBANIZED RURAL IDEAL IN CALIFORNIA

Just as Beecher and Downing had extolled the moral dimensions of a proper home and lifestyle in the rural countryside, California's boosters applauded the moral dimensions of horticulture. California represented a realization of the agrarian ideal, Jefferson's proclamation that "those who labor in the earth are the chosen people of God."[27] Americans idolized Romantics' agrarian dream of a more enlightened and productive society. An agrarian existence, as the fairy tale goes, would foster democracy, particularly as farmers would create institutions to protect their own interests. Still, unequal land distribution and real estate speculation spoiled such an agrarian paradise, which Karl Marx, Henry George, and others famously said conflicted with a constantly growing capitalist system.[28] Nevertheless, according to booster publications, farming in California not only created and guaranteed egalitarian institutions but also restored and strengthened a faltering agrarian dream. California's farmers as a result became agents liberating and improving a land that many considered inappropriately used. California's farmers could then help stave off the debilitating effects of immigration, industrialization, modernization, and urbanization that supposedly rampaged nationally. "[I]n the hands of an enterprising people," wrote famed author Richard Henry Dana, "what a country [California] this might be."[29]

THE MIDDLE CLASS IN CALIFORNIA'S MIDDLE LANDSCAPE

The enterprising people of Dana's vision were none other than the emerging and growing white middle class. California's boosters, chroniclers, and resident supporters used words such as *businessmen, cultivation, culture, enterprise, -, industrious, intelligence, professional, refinement, talent,* and *well-to-do* to describe, as Wickson did, "the class of people which constitute the most desirable element in the up building of a great State."[30] The focus turned decidedly on the human ideal, on a conception of progress that mirrored the Lamarckian-inspired social Darwinism of Herbert Spencer and the rhetoric of Romantics. In the first book published in Los Angeles and the first narrative of Southern California's origins published in English, Major Horace Bell's *Reminiscences of a Ranger* in 1881 described a European conquest to show how order came to the frontier, how civilization subdued savagery. "Surely, we civilized the race of Mission Indians with a refinement known to no other people under the sun" and revealed to "primitive people . . . the mysteries of American citizenship."[31]

As boosters envisioned, California's population would grow in the mold of a small-farm family represented by a specific "class of people," a "cultured, refined people," who could become prosperous and even advance "beyond their class." These people would jumpstart California's growth, reclaim an untamed wasteland, and push America forward.[32] This variously labeled professional, talent-rich, enterprising, intelligent, cultured class was, as the prolific Southern California booster Charles Fletcher Lummis said, "the least heroic migration in history, but the most judicious; the least impulsive but the most reasonable." He added, "[I]nstead of by Shank's Mare, or prairie schooner, or reeking steerage, they came on palatial trains; instead of cabins they put up beautiful homes; instead of gophering for gold, they planted gold."[33] Lummis and others described a movement of middle-class families who arrived in comfort and invested in business and home, just as others had imagined suburbanites in suburbs would do.

California, said many boosters, promised a second Eden for the Anglo-Saxon home seeker. Joseph P. Widney, physician and prolific writer on treatise concerning health, epitomized this pseudo-scientific racial belief and said that God destined Anglo-Saxons to flourish in California and the Southwestern United States. California and the Southwest purportedly rejuvenated and reinforced both the health and spirit of the Anglo-Saxon race. A "racialist," Widney did not overtly argue that non-Anglo Saxons were inferior, but proposed them as being rather different (a racist view nonetheless). Repeating the gross racial science of his day, Widney argued that each race excelled within different particular climates: for example, Anglo-Saxons in the Southland and Africans in tropical environments. For Widney and other racial separatists, the California Dream stood for the rejuvenation of white Anglo-Saxon Protestant culture that helped construct a spatiality of whiteness and consolidate those with European ancestry, except of course Mexicans, into "whiteness." Consequently, those self-proclaimed refined and cultured people helped lay the foundation for the expansion of metropolitan regions in California and a more highly segregated landscape.[34] So as many scholars correctly look to the twentieth century to highlight an incessantly segregating society intertwined with suburbanization, the structural foundations were established far earlier in the nineteenth century and gave bigoted institutions and systems of belief sharper teeth, connection with the past, and a limited sense of culpability.[35]

California's narrated lifestyle, particularly its farming life, attracted professionals who, according to booster literature, would find in horticulture a form of agriculture suitable for profit and a comfortable middle-class way of life. California's promotional literature used unrelenting rhetoric to massage the egos of a largely middle-class audience in hopes of stimulating migration for the purchase of small landholdings and suburban houses. "From California the reversal of the westward course of empire—the return-flow of civilization will proceed," stated Wickson. California represented the land of sophisticated people and a land of "the most intelligent" people who required "both skill and industry," who were urbane and progressive.[36]

These "well disposed, industrious people" were the *avant couriers* of California's imagined manifest destiny to reclaim an untamed frontier.[37] Although many celebrated the theoretical agrarian nature of California's small-farm life, others cast California's farmers as modern businesspersons and manufacturers who embraced science and technology and practiced efficiency and control. "High-class farming," wrote one observer in 1905, appealed to the "bright and observing" who "utilize at all times the results of scientific investigation."[38] In the context of approaching agriculture as a commercial interest, as supported by the likes of Adam Smith (1776) and Populist Charles Macune (1887), California's boosters formulated a vision of improvement with business, education, science, and technology. These would combine to cast California as the best place for reaping the benefits of progress and development. Whether labeled bourgeois horticulturists, citrus scientists, modern businessmen, orchard capitalists, producers, or scientific farmers, California's small farmers, at least in white middle-class communities, favored brain over brawn, used knowledge and technology, improved and liberated the land, embraced marketing and advertising, and, subsequently, industrialized agriculture. In short, they were nothing less than forward-looking, irreducibly modern, and middle class.[39]

Citriculture, particularly the "glamour crop" orange, became the principle crop for the forward-looking, intelligent, refined, white middle-class farmer reflected in the light narratives between the 1870s and 1910s. The orange emerged as an iconographic symbol of civilized rural life, richness, class status, and prosperity.[40] Citriculture required only a little investment and promised high returns, the boosters held. "Orange culture must continue as has began," wrote William Spalding in 1885, "an industry suited to the most intelligent and refined people." "For [Californians], north and south . . . wherever horticulture . . . is crowned queen and welcomed friend, there are to be homes for the rich and poor," wrote another booster. Reports, or embellishments, of returns of $1,000 or more per acre within three to four years of planting commonly appeared. One observer suggested that a citrus orchard would return "not only competency, but an independent fortune."[41] Perhaps most impressive were testimonials from farmers (or so we are told) frequently used in booster publications throughout the period, such as Charles Nordhoff's *California for Health, Pleasure and Residence*. According to a farmer owning twenty acres of oranges, citriculture promised the good life:

Last year my trees paid the whole of my family expenses for the year; that was my first crop. This crop I shall make over five thousand dollars clear; after next year I am planning to take my family for six months to Europe, and I expect thereafter to have four or five months for travel every year, with sufficient means from my twenty acres to go where my wife and children may wish to go.[42]

Fruit became a leading representation of California. Southern California, for example, became the "orange empire," the symbol of richness—though, as José Alamillo has shown, lemons were prominent too.[43] Fruit culture, said one historian, "nurtured values of responsible land use, prudent capitalization, cooperation among growers," the creation of the "bourgeois horticulturists," and the vehicle for "rural civility." Another historian labeled fruit culture in California a "horticultural wonderland." Because of the illusions of easy wealth and living in a land of goodness and fruitful earth, citriculture "brought a new kind of agriculturalist—the intensive farmer, educated, middle class, capable of making a living on forty acres—and an aesthetic reshaping of the land."[44] Fruit farming represented a means and mode of existence that, as one farmer said, "[W]ould make us happy and rich in a short time."[45]

The narrative elements comprising California fruit farms mirrored the elements that suburban image-makers marked as the ideal: city and country mix; urban amenities in a community decidedly not urban; healthy climate and suitable physical environment; and a place for good homes, families, and the nurturing of children.[46] "The horticulturist," said one booster, "combines city life with country pleasure." "Here may be found beautiful rural homes, whose owners are within touch of social life, and enjoy the best features of the city and country." California's boosters and the suburban image-makers were for that reason describing the ideal place and lifestyle in identical terms. Such places represented civilized rural life because of their close proximity to nature, away from cities, but brimming with amenities. "The settler can have churches, schools, medical advice," wrote the author of *Letters from California,* "in short, all the advantages . . . a citizen possesses over a frontiersman."[47] California's farming communities had the institutions of a small city that emphasized outdoor and domestic pleasures, providing residents those outlets for supposed finer things that were the hallmark of their class status, aspirations, and anxieties.

CALIFORNIAN HOMES AND FAMILIES IN A PERFECT ENVIRONMENT

As noted, the home emerged as one of the key defining characteristics of California. The depiction of California as a land of homes strategically drew upon the veneration of homes glamorized by suburban image-makers. Continual reference to California's suitability for family homes, as seen, served as justification for pleas to subdivide large land holdings. The language of family and home plainly sought to attract migrants to the state by utilizing cultural representations distinctly appealing to the values and ways of life popular among the middle class. If people with money or those who could make payments wanted single-family homes, good boosters would then likely offer them such. The overwhelming majority of California's boosters did just that.

FIGURE 3

"Vision of the Golden Country." This "vision" comes from Benjamin C. Truman's *Homes and Happiness in the Golden State*, published in 1883. The scene is quite remarkable: snow-capped mountain in the background under a clear large sky; a river flowing through a canyon; and (one could imagine) beautiful fruit and butterflies within the trees and flowers at our feet. Images like this one splashed across thousands of pages of booster literature celebrating California's agricultural richness and beauty. It is, in many ways, an ideal scene meant precisely to evoke emotions such as awe and even longing. The Golden State, in other words, was truly golden and its richness awaited anyone willing to come.

"The overgoing [*sic*] sun shines upon no region, of equal extent," bragged booster Benjamin Truman in his *Semi-Tropical California*, "which offers so many and such varied inducements to men in search of homes and health." California's agricultural landscape offered not just a bountiful harvest, but also, as Truman again expressed in his aptly titled *Homes and Happiness in the Golden State of California*, "comfortable and happy homes." Talk of home, family, and California's agricultural possibilities echoed the suburban ideal of country homes. "Our public domain," said Charles Reed, president of the California State Agricultural Society, "our lands in general, should be divided up into small farms or parcels, each one of these the home and homestead of a family, dependent for a livelihood upon the cultivation of that homestead." Another observer for the California Agricultural Society commented that the subdivision of large land holdings in California into small-family farms would mean that "population will increase, wealth will appear every few miles, [and] a thousand pleasant homes will dot the state where now there are but scars."[48]

The promotion of family homes by boosters around California contributed to the suburban side of California's growth. Bernard Marks's *Small-Scale Farming in Central California* spoke of children, family, and home as much as agricultural prospects to stimulate migration to the Fresno area in the late nineteenth century:

> This pamphlet is addressed to those who will prize a home in which the flower-garden will furnish a bouquet everyday in the year without a single exception; in which the vegetable garden may be harvested and replaced in some part every month of the yearly twelve; in which a single acre may be so treated that it will support a cow in high condition the whole year through; in which a berry-patch a hundred feet square will furnish the family table with all its sugar, tea, coffee and condiments; in which the children may pick and pack for market enough waste raisins and figs to enable [them] to compete in child-wealth with the children of the rich; in which the solitary apple-barrel of the East is replaced by boxes of raisins, figs, pomegranates, almonds, and walnuts for the evening family circle.[49]

Likewise, others, such as Wickson, again pointed to orange culture. "The orange is an exponent of the possession of those natural characteristics of sky and air and soil, constituting the most desirable environment of human life—the highest desirability in the location of a home." In fact, several immigration societies were active in promoting California in terms of agriculture and home ownership. One leading organization, the California Immigrant Union, founded in 1869, wanted to attract "settlers." The Immigrant Union, after praising the state's agricultural and climate superiority, concluded, "Residents of those [other] States are easily induced to sell off their farms and seek new and more congenial homes in this State, and seldom regret the change."[50]

The Romantic praise of picturesque homes among pastoral landscapes thus barraged readers in California booster literature. Writing about Riverside, for example, *The Weekly Call* (San Francisco) captured three of the more salient elements in a larger theme of nature in California, explicitly echoing the sentiments of the suburban image-makers: weather and soil advantageous for agriculture, a more healthful climate, and an environment capable of cultivating a more advanced and refined way of life. Riverside, *The Weekly Call* reported, "is almost entirely settled by Eastern people [a synonymous phrase by this point for saying 'white people,' especially those descended from North and Western European stock], mostly of some means, many of whom have located there for health; some for the pleasure of its mild climate, and

FIGURE 4

"Residence and Grounds of O. W. Childs, Esq., Los Angeles." This image is from Walter Lindley and Joseph P. Widney's *California of the South: Its Physical Geography, Climate, Resources, Routes of Travel and Health-Resorts, Being a Complete Guide-Book to Southern California* (1888). Meant as a treatise on the so-called superior healthfulness of California via its climate, obviously noticeable in this picture is the similarities to Beecher's "Christian Home" and Downing's *Cottage Residences*. Notice the home is set among a pristine agrestic surrounding, but with well-maintained yards, shrubs, and a clear winding thoroughfare. Also, notice the sporadic placement of chairs, obviously meant for someone to sit outside, relax, and enjoy the scenery.

some for the purpose of raising semi-tropical fruits to which the entire surrounding country is devoted. It has an air of newness; the houses are all neat and clean, gardens well kept, and everything indicative of enterprise and thrift."[51]

As one Californian historian said, "[E]ver since the first wiggle of the first amoeba, climate has influenced the destiny of life."[52] Perhaps overly dramatic and deterministic, the sentiment captures the publicity of California's boosters who shaped what McWilliams labeled a "folklore of climatology."[53] Home ownership and urban amenities remain empty in allure without the appeal of the site itself. Historian Linda Nash has pointed out that *climate* and *health* were as much buzzwords for boosters competing for increased migration to California as they are for modern scholars who attempt to place "the stories of [agricultural] colonization and capitalist development alongside stories of health and disease."[54] Focusing on a straightforward economic pull did not suffice for boosters attempting to draw in migrants or historians analyzing the immigration. They also needed the attraction of the geographical image itself, of storied space, and its allegorical promise to reward culturally, economically, physically, and psychologically.

"Nature here runs a boom that is permanent . . . with a Harvest of grain, nuts, and fruits absolutely perennial," wrote one booster. The supposed superiority for growing virtually every type of fruit, grain, nut, or produce possible served as another central feature of California's rural environment. Another booster said, "Southern California seems to produce with proper care nearly every kind of tree, shrub, grass, herb, or tuber that is at all common or useful in the temperate zone, together with a large number of those tropics." Whether producing almonds, asparagus, grapes, lemons, or oranges, the land soaking up California sunshine proved, without exception, the best for the farmer anywhere. The natural advantages of California were so clear that not to take train, mule, or boat thousands of miles to break her rich soil, take a loan, put down an investment, build a house, and plow a field would be otherwise foolish. Repeatedly, boosters such as Truman, Wickson, and Widney, as well as hundreds of more local boosters, boasted of California's superiority, rich soil, horticultural innovation, and advantages for industry and manufacturing. Said Nordhoff, "[A]fter a thorough examination, I believe Southern California to be . . . the best region in the whole United States for farmers."[55]

California boosters cultivated a "California Eden" myth to harvest large levels of migration.[56] The glorification of nature repeated the viewpoints of Romantics that the countryside equated spiritual redemption tied to a model space. With that said, according to one environmental historian, "[E]ver since the nineteenth century, celebrating wilderness has been an activity mainly for the well-to-do city folks. Country people generally know far too much about working the land to regard unworked land as their ideal."[57] Nevertheless, California's rural landscape embodied images of the garden, frontier, and sacred nature as illusions that one could not only escape the troubles of the industrialized world but also spin a profit—the proverbial "win-win."

A promised unique relationship with nature characterized the heart of the California Dream. "The temperature is," concluded yet another booster, "perfection." He continued, "It is neither hot nor cold. A sybarite would not alter it." By the turn of the twentieth century, a Goldilocks formula had become *modus operandi* for most boosters throughout the state and characterized such disparate climates and environments as the shores of Malibu and the foothills of the Sierras. "This is paradise," wrote Warner. "It is very confusing to the mind of the new-comer to reconcile his necessity for winter clothing to what he sees and almost feels; in short, to get used to the climate."[58]

Of all the light narratives about nature's attraction, historian Kevin Starr has shown that nothing captured the imagination of the potential migrant in promotional literature better than the comparison of California to the Mediterranean. He points out that the Mediterranean analogy arose as an aesthetic metaphor for all that California offered—or hoped to offer. In the framework of a region supposedly best suited for the advancement of the Anglo-Saxon race, racists—or "racialists"—Walter Lindley and Joseph P. Widney maintained a "newer and nobler life" in California seemed tenable. They concluded that a (white) visitor could "discern the fair promise of a civilization which had its only analogue in that Graeco-Latin race-flowering which came to the shores of the Mediterranean centuries ago." "Whatever Greece, Italy, and Spain were in their noblest days," said Shinn, "that we hope to become, except that our facilities are greater, so our mingling of the beauties of a world may be greater."[59]

At once Greek, Italian, North African, Near Eastern, and Spanish, the Mediterranean metaphor had behind it the force of a region steeped in history and the force of a region celebrated for its ideal climate and topography. California regularly received self-comparisons to Italy from the 1870s forward. Italy had beauty, Greece had art, and both were celebrated forbearers of republicanism and democracy. North Africa and the Near East symbolized a vast desert set to bloom and the supposed home place of Christ. Spain and Mexico had long histories in California that were simply too obvious to ignore, and the celebration of a Spanish and Mexican past established a connection and a narrative sense of place that gave new migrants a sense of continuity. "California has the climate of the lands which have given the world its noblest religion, its soundest philosophy, its highest art, its greatest poets and painters and sculptors and musicians," said Lummis. He continued, "There does not seem to be anything bad for the intellect or the heart in the sort of climate that has mothered Jesus of Nazareth, and Homer and Socrates, and Praxiteles, Plato, Virgil, Michelangelo, Titian, Correggio, Velasquez, Saavedra, and all the interminable list—even to Napoleon."[60]

Whether focused on such places as Los Angeles or San Diego, scores of booster publications publicized specific places and California in general (including Northern California) as a healthier place, particularly for the "invalid."[61] Whatever California's Mediterranean climate could do for fruit or mind, it could also do for body. According to boosters, California's therapeutic qualities could cure anything from tuberculosis to a wide variety of other pulmonary diseases. The imaginary curative powers of California's climate transformed health into a natural resource and along with other such Western places as Tucson, California's countryside represented "geographies of hope."[62] After the arrival of the railroads in the 1870s, a "health rush" ensued as many came to seek out the benefits of an imagined restorative climate. "The air, when inhaled," wrote Truman, "gives to the individual a stimulus and vital force which only an atmosphere pure can ever communicate."[63]

TOWARD A COMMON DEFINITION OF AGRICULTURAL COLONY, HORTICULTURE, AND SUBURB IN CALIFORNIA

The picture of the small-farm ideal in California abounded because of the notion that profitability from horticulture could earn the Californian small farmer more money than the farmer with more land in a different place. Less land required, of course, also meant less money needed to purchase the land and more available for the purchase of equipment, possibly labor, and a home (though, in reality, falling crop prices negated much of this promise). Boosters routinely employed the vocation of horticulture to communicate the validity of their faith (or growth fantasies) in

California's agricultural potential and promise for a better country life. They also used the term *colony*, as in agricultural colony or irrigation colony, with irrigation serving as the means to facilitate a more intensive and profitable type of agriculture. The term *colony* received loose treatment in California, no doubt, but usually referred to the subdivision of an area into small parcels of land. In such colonies, however, boosters and others pointed out that these new farm areas, through horticulture, retained a level of amenities. The ways in which boosters and subsequent historians have characterized and detailed specific elements of California's agricultural colonies and horticulture beg comparison to how suburban image-makers depicted the ideal lifestyle. Terms like *colony, horticulture,* and *suburb* markedly described similar things in like ways, which suggests such terms were nearly synonymous. Perhaps historian Glenn Dumke proved keenly insightful to call the "boom of the eighties" a "suburban phenomenon," but he limited it to only the so-called boom of the 1880s and to Southern California. More accurately, it is better to define more of California and its growth from the 1870s through World War I, particularly in connection to agriculture, as representative of a suburban phenomenon.

In 1848, Andrew Jackson Downing reiterated Jefferson's Romantic characterization of the American farmer when he wrote, "The cultivators of the soil constitute the great industrial class of this country." In numerous articles written for his journal the *Horticulturist* in the 1840s through the early 1850s (he tragically died young in 1852), Downing depicted "horticultural pursuits" as what made "one's country worth living and dying for." Downing, along with a parade of suburban image-makers, fervently believed (or said they did) that "horticultural pursuits [possessed] a political and moral influence vastly more significant and important than mere gratification of the senses. . . . Horticulture and its kindred arts tend strongly to fix the habits, and elevate the character, of our whole rural population." Downing glorified "retirement to country life" as a "universal pleasure." In "a good country residence" a house was "no longer a comfortable shelter merely, but an expression of the intelligent life of man, in a state of society where the soul, the intellect, and the heart, are all awake, and all educated." In the single-family home, amid the city-country middle landscape, "we believe," said Downing, "in the improvement of human nature necessarily resulting to all *classes*, from the possession of lovely gardens and fruitful orchards." Through horticulture, Downing and others imagined "the advantage, morally and socially, of orderly, neat, tasteful villages; in producing better citizens, in causing the laws to be respected, in making homes dearer and more sacred, in domestic life and the enjoyment of property to be more truly and rightly estimated." In short, Downing's horticultural paragon defined the suburban ideal, like the belief of the model family, home, and community life by Beecher, Olmsted, Vaux, and others. The place for this was the nearby countryside, of which, as the boosters said repeatedly, California had plenty.

"The best advice," Downing said for the best location of a country home, "is . . . to choose a site . . . where nature offers the greatest number of good features." California seemed such a site. California's environment, metaphorically for some but literally for others, was paradise and most emphatically, as Downing desired, a site where nature offered the greatest number of good features.[64]

The way in which Downing and suburban image-makers used the term "horti-culture" fell more in line with the historical definition: "the cultivation of a garden; the art of science of cultivating gardens, including the growing of flowers, fruits, and vegetables."[65] A horticulturist therefore practiced the "art" of horticulture, one who practiced gardening "scientifically." In comparison, California's boosters often used the term horticulture to describe intensive agriculture, specialty crops, and farming on small amounts of land. Horticulture, as a descriptive term, represented an economic endeavor pursued for the sake of increasing profits. Economics alone did not define horticulture at this time though. California's boosters and farmers used the term to depict both a particular type of agriculture and a way of life that mirrored the language of suburbia. "Horticulture," said one nineteenth-century observer and shared earlier but worth repeating, "is the broad term applied to fruit growing in California, but it covers far more than this one branch of this wide-spread industry. Horticulture in the fullest sense of the term embraces every portion of the fruit grower's, gardener's and landscape worker's art; in fact, it covers everything that makes our country bright, beautiful, ornamental and enjoyable."[66]

Horticulture unquestionably dominated California boosterism as a way to profit and lifestyle. It was special because of its purported social advantages. Historians have long recognized that the benefits of horticulture, as lauded by boosters, extended beyond the financial.[67] David Vaught, for example, correctly asks us not think of California's (white) farmers "as agrarians nor as industrialists, but as horticulturists" who "fervently believed they were cultivating not only specialty crops, but California itself."[68] An 1892 *Yolo Weekly Mail* article demonstrated this point for Vaught: "There is something in horticulture which quickens the notions and enlarges the ideas, and therefore within its ranks is found a class of people who enrich a community with new blood, new brains, and fresh energy."[69]

California's boosters consistently bragged that horticulture required great skill and knowledge, attracted stable and intelligent people, and fostered community pride, all while appealing to a middle class. California's horticulture fostered "neighborliness, strong local social, cultural, and political institutions, and economic progress, all in an environment that was esthetically pleasing as well."[70] California emerged as the "highest and most perfect stage" for the manifestation of "the American Dream itself," a dream that numerous historians have shown intimately conjoined with the suburban ideal.[71] California boosters held that horticulture would be the medium implemented by, as Wickson said, the "class of people which constitute the most desirable in the upbuilding of a great State."[72] The ethical dimension of horticulture, therefore, promised a subdivision of land that would stimulate the rise of small farms, displace migratory labor, and introduce into the state's rural society a conviction that farming must be a way of life rather than simply a speculative investment.[73] Perhaps there is no mistaking California's suburban heritage when Frederick K. Cox (a later figure in the case study of Fair Oaks), in a presidential address to the State Agricultural Society in 1891, declared that the "pursuit of horticulture may be the happy means of dotting the land with small holdings." These "small holdings," he continued, "will be the seat of happy homes, whence shall proceed a generous brood of men and women reared amid the most congenial environments, perfect types of American manhood and womanhood, and fitted for every duty and performance of life."[74]

California's horticultural fantasy of an ideal farming life happened most visibly, then, in the development and promotion of agricultural colonies throughout the state. Colonies are, in fact, what link California with the suburban rhetoric of the nineteenth century most clearly. Still, *colony* offers a difficult term to deal with. Historically, a colony is a specific community type and political entity. In classical Greek and Roman use, a colony meant a farm, an estate in the country or a rural settlement. The term, in more recent times, also describes a territory occupied by like-minded individuals, whether culturally, economically, politically, racially, or spiritually (perhaps, indeed, a perfect way to still describe suburbs for many people). Although both usages represent well how *colony* applied to California's agricultural settlements at the turn at the twentieth century, in more modern application, the term represents a territory under the immediate political control of a geographically distant state. Here, images of British or other European empires manifest. It perhaps seems far-fetched to compare colonial Fresno to Colonial Williamsburg or Riverside to Hong Kong, although perhaps not unwarranted. Many historians, such as Carl Abbott, have discussed the West's characteristics as a colonial territory under the control of, and for the exploitation of a geographically distant state in Washington or, at least, business interests in nearby or even distant cities.[75] Abbott and others have pointed out that California's agricultural colonies, like colonies generally, were dependent on outside capital, largely stimulated, of course, by "relentless publicity." Also, again like colonies elsewhere, California's agricultural colonies grew dependent on low-wage workers, typically minorities, as much as investors. As highlighted, this trend sowed the seeds of small family farms' decline and precipitated the logic of capital accumulation and the rise of agribusiness.[76]

The term *colony* as employed by boosters and historians certainly implies key colonial themes such as empire, exploitation, racism, and capitalist expansion. In fact, take historians previously spotlighted, such as Alamillo, Garcia, Gilbert Gonzalez, and Jerry Gonzalez, who have already discussed the suburbanization process within and concerning the Mexican-American communities of Southern California. They prominently do so by using terms such as *colony* and utilizing frameworks such as colonization and empire. Specifically, they discuss semi-rural *colonias* (colonies) composed of working-class, first- and second- generation Mexican Americans. First, however, a caveat: I do not mean to circumvent or trivialize the inequalities of these segregated *colonias*, at least compared to white so-called agricultural colonies or at the expense of the vibrant activity in such communities that these scholars make clear. Still, the story is that some *colonias* evolved into *barrios* through a process of what historian Albert Camarillo calls *barrioization*. *Barrios*, in contrast to *colonias*, were Mexican-American suburbs (or pockets therein), largely thanks, as Jerry Gonzalez has shown, to the agency of the residents themselves fighting urban renewal and removal projects and housing segregation. In any case, *barrioization* in this context is a distinctly Mexican-American process of suburbanization according to Camarillo. To be clear, the point here is not to challenge this argument. Rather, the point is—much like how Nicolaides and Abbott refer to working-class, ethnoracial neighborhoods as "farm-fringe streetcar suburbs" and "suburbscape[s]"—that *colonias* like Pico, Jimtown, Rivera, and others in Southern California *were* suburbs. Admittedly, this is nitpicking. *Colonias* were working-class, ethnoracial minority suburbs. *Barrios* were more middle class, and a little more residential. So *barrioization* is just as much about the making of (or moving to) middle-class, residential-based suburbs (i.e., what suburbs narrowly are in the minds of many Americans—and scholars—to this day) as much as it is about the complex processes of racial and spatial identity construction, class anxiety, and integration. They imply and inform each other, and the scholar cannot always so easily do without them.[77]

Not surprisingly, terms like *empire*, *exploitation*, and *expansion* convey negative connotations. While perhaps such terms are not always negative, however, boosters at the turn of the twentieth century certainly did use the term *colony* to brand agricultural communities in an economic sense. Historians have discussed colonies in terms similar to French legal sociologist René Maunier's theory of colonization in which colonization is a capitalist achievement tied to race, politics, economy, and imperialism.[78] For example, Dumke argued that chambers of commerce and boards of trade "were extremely interested in colony migration which promised to enhance the value of surrounding properties."[79] Another historian characterized the colony system in California as an orchestrated way to profit.[80] The depiction of colonies in California as a real-estate speculator's castle in the sky has remained consistent from booster William Bishop in 1882 to historian Dumke and others more recently.[81] Not coincidentally, the portrayal of suburbia as a system of capitalist expansion and real-estate speculation dominated by an economically powerful and politically influential elite runs easily in sync with a comparison of suburb and colony.

The desires of a white middle class—or aspiring middle class—defined both the suburban and agricultural colonial experience, at least in literary representations. Just as suburban scholars have worked to show that suburbs, while intertwined with real-estate capitalism and market forces, are more than mere speculative ventures and involve a variety of socio-cultural factors and imagined lifestyles, so too have those describing the middle-class colony system in California. One of California's pioneer historians at the turn of the twentieth century defined such colonies in California as the joining of people "from the East who were imbued with the same purpose."[82] The joining of people with the same purpose in colonies, or "with other believers" who "settle among friends," was the same depiction given by geographers, as well as by Starr who referenced a "homogeneous" group who lived in social and economic cooperation.[83]

The way of life described by boosters and subsequent historians is an obvious connection between colony and suburb, and vice-versa. Suburbs promised community life and urban amenities in a beautiful rural landscape. So too did California's small farms. California historians have long commented on the vast array of "amenities" offered in California's "colonies."[84] Once more, colonies were subdivisions, usually in five-, ten-, and twenty-acre allotments, sustained by a matrix of institutions and infrastructure established by developers, such as banks, bridges, canals, ditches, merchants' stores, and newspapers. Suburban image-makers depicted a community that afforded ample leisure time to enjoy finer things amidst a plethora of urban amenities without the crime and vice of cities; similarly, colony organizers and leaders paraded forth "amenities" such as churches, clubs, parks, stores, theaters, and a thriving commercial district. Such amenities, in both middle-class suburbs and colonies, represented the perfect blend, then, of a city without a city and a country life without isolation. A California agricultural colony was the ideal suburb in an ideal environment.

That the term *colony* is reflective of an increasing celebration of the thirteen colonies and the American Revolution, particularly as the centennial approached in 1876 and remained a vibrant symbol years thereafter, is indicative of another possible (even redemptive or counter) connotation associated with the term and its usage at the turn of the twentieth century in California—and elsewhere. Actually, before continuing down this train of thought, it should be clear that California's boosters did not perceive the term *colony* (or *suburb* for that matter) as branding these places in the negative (shadow) sense held by modern scholars and critics. Words can have multiple meanings, to be sure, and in an imperialist age (and all the meanings of race, class, and subordination that phrase implies as well), colony and empire were not necessarily dirty words, but rather the opposite. A rising commercial and professional class employed patriotism to bolster their trade interests as a viable business approach as early as the 1820s. This tactic reinforced the attempt of the rising middle and professional classes to place their pursuit of gain and advancement in the context of patriotic activity. To romanticize and celebrate colonies, particularly as they embodied the original thirteen colonies of the Revolutionary era, in one way or another, played off a powerful emotional symbolism. As the eminent historian Percy Miller long ago reminded us, even the Puritan "errand" into the wilderness, the supposedly great motivation behind the growth of many English colonies in the so-called New World, reflected a nobler errand and represented a longing for a better way of life.[85]

The agricultural colonies of Ontario in Southern California and Orangevale and Fair Oaks in Northern California provide comprehensive examples for detailing California's suburban phenomenon, links between colony, horticulture, and suburb, and the existence of the agriburb as a unique rural suburban type. Boosters reiterated the suburban and Californian rhetoric of home, family, nature, and urban amenities to persuade readers that Ontario, Orangevale, and Fair Oaks were the best places to live. In addition, Ontarians, Orangevaleans, and Fair Oakians were farmers who, boosters said, hoped to earn a dollar amid California's booming horticulture, achieve or maintain middle-class status, and better themselves and the nation. The following chapters (chapters three, four, and five) explore how and why boosters packaged the California agricultural colonies of Ontario, Orangevale, and Fair Oaks as agriburbs.

PART TWO

HARVESTING SUBURBS

SUBURBAN DEFINITIONS, ARCHETYPES, AND LIMITATIONS

We created a landscape of scary places,
and we became a nation of scary people.

JAMES HOWARD KUNSTLER[1]

P ART ONE DESCRIBED THE RISE OF the suburban ideal, providing historical definitions and representations, dissecting some of their problems and limitations, and then providing an archetype model of suburbs. This provides context and a framework for what follows—defining the agriburb in the case study sites. Historically, a suburb has been defined as a place that exists outside a town or city—either *sub*-urban or *sub*-town. The town or city must be nearby to constitute a suburb. For example, around 1342, Benedictine monk Ranulf Higden discussed the "subarbes of Rome." This understanding of suburbs remains common. Perusals through dictionaries reveal more examples, as the definition of a suburb remained salient for more than 350 years. "Suburbian," according to Thomas Blount in his 1656 *Glossographia*, is "belonging to the Suburbs or out streets, and parishes of a Town or City." Noah Webster's *An American Dictionary* in 1828 defined a suburb as "a building without the walls of a city, but near them; or more generally, the parts that lie without the walls, but in the vicinity of a city," which essentially remained the definition for *Webster's* through the 1980s.[2]

According to definitions advanced by the U.S. Census Bureau, suburbs refer to unincorporated and incorporated communities of moderate density typically located outside a central city or cities. Suburbs rest within a metropolitan area and are under an urban center's sociocultural and political-economic orbit. As of 2000, just more than fifty percent of the United States' population resided in suburbs, though suburbs became the majority during the 1970s with more than forty percent, besting rural and urban areas. Most Americans now shop and work in suburbs and spend an increasing amount of their commute, leisure, and travel time moving from one suburb to the next. The Census Bureau in 2000 listed 390 suburbs, what the agency calls Metropolitan Statistical Areas (MSA), up from 284 in 1990, 152 in 1940, ninety in 1910, twenty-nine in 1880, and nine in 1850. An MSA is a suburb outside a central city or twin cities of more than 50,000 people. From 1850 to 1940, scholars have shown that the census can account for MSAs as "metropolitan districts" that comprised an "outer fringe" that included places that neighbored the city and an urbanized fringe, as well as incorporated townships with greater than 150 persons per square mile but less than 1,000 per square mile.[3]

The problem with census and historical definitions is that suburbs have not always been *sub*. Understanding them as such creates a bias in our minds when discussing them and risks becoming a barrier for many as they try to conceive of the agriburb. Different economic, political, and social forces fostered the creation of suburbs outside Rome, England, and the United States, not to mention ancient Babylon and the suburbs of the Levites mentioned in the Hebrew Bible.[4] In fact, urban historians have pointed to a unique urbanization process in the United States, one that categorically did not include walls, possessed ambiguous and evolving boundary lines, and grew to a shape molded by the pursuit for profit.[5] Likewise, new suburban historians, while citing similarity to England, point to a unique suburbanization process in the United States.[6]

One should avoid getting caught up in the definition of the term *suburb* as if suburbs, in reality, have been constantly one thing. Suburban function, type, and suburbanization as a process are contingent on historical phenomena and context. They evolve—meaning continuity is a reality, yes, but adaptation is too and, well, the appearance of new species, if you will pardon the metaphor. New suburban historians, as discussed in the introduction, have tried to make this clear. Namely, they narrow their lens to focus on suburbs within a particular epoch and geographical region—North America. Still, they expand the definition of a suburb to include working-class and middle-class residential communities, as well as industrial communities, not directly tied to an urban core nor defined as residential-only.[7] The historical definition of a suburb regarding its geographical location near a city is therefore misleading. As argued, it does not encompass all of what suburbia represents or all the suburban types that have come into existence. Volumes like *Manufacturing Suburbs* document industrial suburbs that were not distinctly tied to an urban core and, further, featured mixed residential and industrial use, while historians like Andrew Wiese and Becky Nicolaides have documented working-class and minority nonwhite suburbs.[8]

Another difficulty with an emphasis on physical location and place is that it risks reducing the importance of imagery and imagination, of storied space. Suburbia is as much a cultural symbol and intellectual creation, even lived space, as a geographical, material place. Suburbia's critics, such as Lewis Mumford, Peter Blake, and James Howard Kunstler, to name a few, have made this abundantly clear.[9] A connection between the values people have and the kinds of communities they create, and vice versa, seem palpable too. American urban sociologist Robert Park, for example, believed changes in physical and spatial structure directly affected social practice, concluding, "The physical or ecological organization of the community, in the long run, responds to and reflects the occupational and the cultural." Moreover, culture is a "structured and structuring structure."[10] Suburbs therefore encompass more than geographical location or material form. Changing conceptions of the family, home, privacy, separateness, nature, and domesticity, accounted for in the previous chapters, all shaped and were shaped by the territorial organizations and transformations occurring in the United States during the nineteenth century.

It would be a gaffe not to note how popular culture works as a prevailing force in shaping the conception of what suburbs are for many Americans. Perhaps none is more salient than the 1950s and 1960s notion of the nuclear family of dad, mom, two kids, a dog, with a large grass lawn in the front yard of an attractive house with a garage. Depicted in this light, Beaver and Wally Cleaver; or Princess, Bud, and Kitten Anderson; or David and Ricky Nelson ate dinner, always followed by dessert, with mom and dad at the family table with Ward, Ozzie, or Jim reading the newspaper in the study afterwards as June, Harriet, or Margaret cleaned the dishes. The same went for Fred, Wilma, and Pebbles Flintstone in the Stone Age and George, Jane, Judy, and Elroy Jetson in the Space Age. All of these are well-known television characters from the period. Collectively they presented a picturesque light narrative of the American family in suburbs that represented proper family values and relationships, appropriate (sexist) gender behaviors, and a tireless, and especially patriotic, devotion to strong moral character. It was irrefutably white and indisputably middle class and residential.[11]

The problem with this quaint image of suburbs is life there has not always been so quaint. Given the dominant discourse of the day, never is there mention that Beaver might have unexplored sexual feelings toward his friend Whitey, that Princess may have had a self-induced abortion, that Ricky could never face the terrible truth that marijuana led to heroin addiction, or that Fred and George beat their wives behind closed doors. Clearly silly, the point is that the gap between Hollywood and reality about popular cultural depictions of suburbs is real. Many from the same era expressed conflicting views and produced counter, shadow narratives. Journalist Frederick Lewis Allen complained in 1954 that growth came "too fast," and destroyed all that made suburbs attractive.[12] William Whyte famously perceived a dangerous trend toward conformity at the expense of individualism for the "Organization Man" in the "New Suburbia" in 1956. Betty Friedan gloomily described the "problem that has no name" in *The Feminine Mystique* (1963) to alert people to the psychological consequences facing suburbia's homemakers.

Movies like *Mr. Blandings Builds his Dream House* in the late 1940s and Norman Lear's television program *Mary Hartman, Mary Hartman* in the 1970s satirized life in the suburbs as well. Also in the 1970s, as the United States became a suburban majority for the first time, fictional psychopathic serial killer Michael Myers, born and raised in suburbia, returned from the mental hospital to kill his sister, the babysitter, in John Carpenter's 1978 release of *Halloween*. The 1980s did not let up. *Nightmare on Elm Street*, for example, also localizes horror in the suburbs. Recently, among innumerable other examples, *Disturbia* (2007) took Alfred Hitchcock's 1954 urban, apartment complex horror-thriller in *Rear Window* and relocated to the suburbs. In the 1990s, to rewind, the Bundys typified the dysfunctional family in *Married with Children*. More movies followed, from *The Truman Show* to *American Beauty* and *Pleasantville*.[13] On one hand, suburbs stand for home, family, and community and, on the other hand, they signify conformity, uniformity, consumerism, racism, structural (and physical) violence, and elitism.

The problem with the Hollywood image of suburbia and even the critiques of that image is that suburbs are not just white, middle-class residential communities as seen in popular representations from *Mr. Blandings Builds His Dream House* to *Leave It to Beaver* to even Ice Cube's *Next Friday* (2000). The point is to free ourselves intellectually from these archetypes by recognizing their power to restrict how we come to understand what suburbs are and what they mean. This thus allows for conceptualizing the agriburb, not to mention industrial suburbs, working-class suburbs, or minority suburbs.

New suburban historians have turned out quality work to broaden our understanding of suburbs, at least in academia (however narrow the subgroup within that population is notwithstanding). With that said, most suburban histories since the mid-1980s still fall back in some way on the suburban account of Kenneth T. Jackson's *Crabgrass Frontier: The Suburbanization of the United States* (1985) in which he contended the United States possessed a unique suburbanization process. "This uniqueness," he concluded, "involves population density, home ownership, residential status, and journey-to-work."[14] Much like historical and census definitions, the first distinguishing element of suburbs identified by Jackson is low residential density and the absence of discernible divisions between city and country. The second distinguishing feature of a suburb is a strong desire for home ownership. The third feature is the limitation of suburbs as residential, which Jackson further argued correlates to a socioeconomic distinction between the center and the periphery—in other words, middle-class status and income are elements that further define suburbs. The final distinguishing characteristic of the suburban experience is the length of the average job commute, whether measured in miles (twenty plus) or in minutes (ten plus).

New suburban historians complicate and challenge—though sometimes complement—Jackson's description of suburbs. Nonetheless, Jackson's definition of a suburb provides a well-defined model to which the agriburb model can compare. Case studies of suburbanization provide further challenges to—or at least differentiate from—Jackson's generalizations and help describe the elements of the agriburb as it happened in these places. To be clear, besides noting intellectual gratitude and fondness for Jackson's work, the intent here is not to create the proverbial straw man. The intent is to use a well-defined and popular model that corresponds to other popular and historical definitions. This makes describing an agriburb straightforward. Therefore, in the next two chapters covering Ontario, Orangevale, and Fair Oaks, Jackson's model

CHAPTER THREE

THE MODEL COLONY OF ONTARIO AS THE MODEL AGRIBURB

*The plan for the colony is of
the most advanced and liberal kind.*

ONTARIO, LOCATED IN SAN BERNARDINO COUNTY, 1883[1]

"I F HE WERE AROUND TODAY, the founder of Ontario and Upland would carry an iPod and a BlackBerry," said one contemporary local reporter, "after improving both."[2] Such cleverness seemed to merit a statue commemorating the founder of Ontario and Upland (once part of Ontario) in 2005, George Chaffey.[3] The Chaffey statue is a thirteen-foot bronze depiction of Chaffey standing firm on an outcropping of rocks (San Gabriel Mountains) looking out on the San Gabriel Valley as he holds a compass in one hand and a surveyor's scope in the other. The statue is a representation of Chaffey's own recollection of a fateful day in 1881. "From the plateau of the foot of the mountain," he said, "I obtained a bird's-eye view of the whole area I proposed to acquire, and while I was standing there looking at it, I saw what Ontario was to and did become."[4]

Chaffey's vision for "what Ontario was to and did become" represents an agriburb that integrated romantic agrarianism with urbanism. As California's boosters celebrated the state's landscape and environment in general, Ontario's boosters bragged how their community represented the best of the best. A review of the promotional literature shows Ontario's boosters speculated in real estate. They took a scattered approach to appeal to as many potential migrants and investors as possible. For example, for a farmer in Iowa, Ontario promised urban sophistication and a profitable business venture that displayed farmers' astuteness. For a Chicago businessperson, Ontario promised life among flowers without sacrifice of familiar city convenience. Yet, in tune, Ontario also promised the absence of publicized city vices or problems such as alcohol and pollution. For all, male or female, city or rural dweller, working class or already middle class (but all still white), Ontario symbolized a middle-class way of life advertised as exceptionally American.

THE ESTABLISHMENT OF ONTARIO

The establishment of Ontario could have been the inspiration for any number of Hollywood films or other tall tales about the creation of communities in the so-called Wild West. Men armed with rifles, guards on post, fence wire ("devil's rope"), and concerns over water rights were all present and accounted for in the spring of 1882. Representatives of the firm Chaffey Brothers clashed with representatives of the Pomona Land and Water Company over the purchase of a land option first offered to Joseph Garcia by a group of San Francisco investors called the Cucamonga Company. No doubt this symbolized real-estate capitalism at its seemingly most wild. The land in question actually changed hands several times, as the Cucamonga Company had bought the land eleven years earlier from Isaias W. Hellman of Los Angeles, who had been the last of several owners of an original Mexican land grant in 1839. Luckily, in 1882, cooler heads prevailed before guards representing the competing real-estate interests soaked the soil with their blood. In short, the Chaffey Brothers won the battle through negotiation, secured Garcia's option, and on September 18, 1882, paid the San Francisco investors $60,000 for 6,216 acres located between San Antonio Creek and Cucamonga Creek along the San Gabriel Mountains. The Chaffey Brothers purchased an additional 250 acres at $20,030.80 and another 114 acres at the mouth of the San Antonio Canyon for $11,000.[5] At this point, as Chaffey allegedly recalled in 1925, "The plan for laying out Ontario was thought of under some old peach trees." He continued, "That is where I went to plan this scheme. I laid out there all day long and after a time I had it pretty well in mind. I got my surveyor and the thing was under way."[6]

The Chaffey Brothers Company included George Chaffey and his brother William Chaffey, both of whom hailed from Kingston, Canada, located in the Ontario province. In 1877, William's brother-in-law Dr. Joseph Jarvis, M.D. visited Riverside, California, and purchased a tract of land. Returning to Kingston in 1877 or 1878, Jarvis extolled what he conceived of as the virtues of Riverside and urged his brother-in-law to relocate. William's parents, George Chaffey Sr. and Ann Chaffey, joined him and his siblings Charles and Emma and moved to the "Canadian Tract" in Riverside's Arlington District later that year. Although dates vary, story has it that the elder George, along with William and Charles, scouted land near Pomona in 1880 and/or 1881 in a profit-driven fantasy of reproducing the success of Riverside, not to mention Pasadena. Whether already in Riverside or back home in Kingston, the Chaffey family informed the eldest of the boys, George Chaffey Jr., of their find. As the story has it, William, a so-called horticulturist and soil expert, scouted the possibilities for an "agricultural wonderland."

TABLE 3

Distribution of Chaffey Promotional Material for Ontario

Places in which the Chaffey Brothers sent promotional literature to advertisers or interested real estate agents			Places in which the Chaffey Brothers sent promotional literature to advertisers or interested real estate agents
UNITED STATES		**CANADA**	
Anaheim, CA	West Durham, ME	Barrie, Ontario (2 times)	Arizona Star, Tucson, AZ
Los Angeles, CA (4 times)	Homer, MI	Berlin (now Kitchener), Ontario	Fruit Grower, Riverside, CA
			Agent, San Francisco, CA*
Riverside, CA	Minneapolis, MN	Collins Bay, Ontario	Bancroft Lithograph Company, San Francisco, CA
San Francisco, CA (5 times)	Sedalia, MO	Elora, Ontario	Central Pacific Railroad San Francisco, CA
Denver, CO (3 times)	Hartford, MO	Goderich, Ontario	Rural Californian, San Francisco, CA
Aspen, CO	St. Charles, MO	Kingston, Ontario	Merchant Publishing Co., San Francisco, CA
Collinsville, CT	Sidney, NE	Lambton Mills, Ontario	Hawk Eye, IA
Washington, D.C	Omaha, NE	London, Ontario	Poweshiek Company, IA
Storm Lake, IA	Rye, NH	Nova Scotia	2 Agents, Chicago, IL*
			Ontario Steel Co., MN
Traer Tama, IA	Silver City, NM	Toronto, Ontario (12 times)	Globe, Toronto
			Ontario, Canada
Chicago, IL (7 times)	Brookfield, NY		
La Grange, IL	Niagara Falls, NY		
Kansas City, KS	New York, NY		
Topeka, KS	Coshocton, OH		
Newton, MA	Paddy's Run, OH		
Holyoke, MA	Harrisburg, PA		*Offered 5 percent commission to agents on land sales*

Data tallied from correspondence found in the Chaffey Letters. Chaffey Letters, Binder 1, Book 1: January 23, 1882, to March 10, 1885, letters 1-265 and Book 2: March 15, 1883, to November 14, 1883, letters 1-175; and Binder 2, Book II: November 14, 1883, to September 4, 1885, letters 176-486, compiled by Ron Baker and transcribed by M. Tikfesi, Robert E. Ellingwood Model Colony History Room, Ontario City Library, Ontario, CA. Remember, in addition to these places, booster organizations like the Los Angeles Chamber of Commerce also sent out materials from Ontario and other communities to libraries, hotels, tourist agencies, newspapers, magazines, and, in a quasi-exchange program, to other chambers of commerce throughout the nation.

Often the case in arid Southern California, water presented a problem. But this was not a worry, as the younger George was a marine engineer and shipbuilder. The family, according to the sources, regarded him as the best one to assume the task of bringing water to a so-called barren land to make it bloom.[7] Besides, here lay a fantastic business opportunity. Chaffey, who reportedly became "excited by the strange enthusiasm of his father and brother for a land so different from their beloved Canada," joined the family in cultivating their dreams of speculative real-estate ventures.[8]

The Chaffey Brothers' first speculative venture was Etiwanda (near Ontario), reportedly named after an Antiguan chief and Chaffey family friend in Canada. On Thanksgiving Day in 1881, the Chaffey brothers met with Garcia and offered him $30,000 for 560 acres of land, water rights, and even his house—since then known as the Garcia-Chaffey house. After signing the deed in January 1882, the Chaffey brothers purchased an additional eighty acres in February at a grand total of one dollar. The brothers then subdivided the land and began to advertise. What has impressed residents, historians, and others since the first years of Etiwanda's establishment were the numerous amenities. The Chaffey brothers organized the Etiwanda Water Company, a mutual (i.e., a private corporation organized for the purposes of delivering water to its stockholders and members at cost) and pipe system of irrigation designed by Chaffey, which became the standard for water system management in Southern California (discussed in detail later). The first long-distance telephone call in Southern California took place between San Bernardino and Etiwanda in 1882, and the Chaffey-Garcia house lighted the Southern California night sky for the first time with electric lights on December 4, 1882. Etiwanda, a "community of firsts," seemed on the cutting edge of technology and implementation of community planning without sacrifice of romanticized rural virtue.

The Chaffey brothers infused Etiwanda, and later Ontario, with the nineteenth-century symbols of progress. Historians have long understood that technologies like communication, electricity, irrigation, and transportation were essential to constructing America as a modern nation. Not all Americans, however, particularly rural Americans, directly experienced or used such technologies. Nevertheless, technologies were—and are—as commonly and powerfully imagined as experienced or used. New national networks of railroads, interurban and intraurban transit, telephone lines, electricity, and even regional irrigation projects were critical as tools and light narratives. While they facilitated a more integrated regional and national economy, "they taught," said one historian, "Americans how to imagine themselves within that economy, and gave them vivid metaphors with which to do so."[9]

Although Etiwanda could make a great case study to describe the details of an agriburb, so too could numerous communities from Pasadena to Riverside to Redlands. Ontario, though, perhaps more than the others, stands out for two reasons. First, Ontario is the community that numerous historians single out as an archetype of Southern California's distinctive development at the end of the nineteenth century.

Ontario is, for this reason, a well-known case study, and familiar to those who study California. This first reason bleeds into the second. Ontario serves as a good case study for delineating the details of an agriburb because it has such a long, rich, and extensive body of historical literature on which to draw. So, while foregoing providing a new case study, the intention here is to reinterpret a well-known and well-documented area in hopes that doing so will make the analysis that much more powerful, though new case study sites come in the next chapter. With all that said, the Ontario boosters, not to mention hundreds of subsequent historical narratives, recall the establishment of Ontario as "the most perfect plan ever adopted by a colony in this State."[10] While not exactly validating that claim, this case study adds depth to it.

When Chaffey sat, seemingly Zen-like, under peach trees in 1882 after purchasing land, he set out to establish a "model colony" based on three principles. In 1884, his business partner Robert M. Widney listed the three principles that constituted Chaffey's vision. "First—distribute the water for irrigating purposes over the whole tract and to each farm lot in concrete and iron pipes, requiring some forty miles of piping. Second—improve the main thoroughfare so that it will be a thing of beauty and usefulness forever. Third—furnish a college for the education of the people of the colony."[11] Concerning the first, the Chaffey brothers created the San Antonio Water Company on October 25, 1882, to which they sold the water rights they had previously acquired in land deals, and laid down forty miles of conduits. After tunneling in San Antonio Canyon, Chaffey discovered a vibrant underground stream and constructed the first underground water tunnel in Southern California.[12] About the second: Chaffey envisioned Euclid Avenue as an eight-mile, 200-foot-wide, double drive lined with trees to serve as the thoroughfare where the streetcar system connected to the Southern Pacific depot in downtown. About the third: on March 17, 1883, ground broke for the laying of the foundation for the Chaffey College of Agriculture, which, for a time, served as a branch of the Los Angeles-based University of Southern California (USC).[13]

Ontario's boosters worked quickly to build institutions and infrastructure designed to appeal to potential migrants and investors. With infrastructure and institutions, boosters could promise that life in Ontario would reflect an urbane existence without the problems of a city and upon a soil perfect for the cultivation of profitable produce in a comfortable and healthy climate. Perhaps this sounds familiar. What might seem like repetition here is actually part of a comparative approach. Such repetition is central to the bigger idea: Ontario's boosters, like their counterparts throughout California, employed the language of suburbia and, themselves, were contributors to articulating and disseminating the so-called California Dream. These boosters were thus about the business of boosting. At any rate, Ontario's boosters continually cited the potential for land values to rise exponentially, particularly regarding fruit and related markets. The boosters also understood the appeal of urban amenities to draw in migrants and investors and, in turn, influence the likelihood that land values would indeed rise. In addition, the arrangement for and capital investment in urban amenities could be (and were) used as essential enticements in the boosters' publicity campaign.

Ontario's boosters touted a variety of benefits in the new "agricultural colony." Opening the pages to their 1883 and 1884 booster publications shows an extensive advertising approach, as they likely wanted to appeal to every possible interest. They paraded advice and information cited or otherwise presented as authoritative, even factual, especially through such simple things as impressive tables, charts, and signed testimonials from doctors and other purported experts. The boosters filled the pamphlets with information concerning planting and pruning, irrigation and cultivation, diseases and insect pests, picking and curing, sorting and packing, and the raisin and citrus industries. The information potentially appealed to an experienced farmer or someone otherwise knowledgeable in agriculture. The material

FIGURE 5

"Ontario, Bancroft Lithograph." In attempts to publicize the "Model Colony," the Chaffey brothers and their partners commissioned this lithograph in 1883. The train and road reflect the intentions of the advertisers to portray Ontario as advanced and technologically savvy. Yet, the open area to the mountains, the rail car full of lumber, and the elegant hotel also communicate a sense of naturalness, refinement, and growth. The train of course meant a lot to the budding colony, particularly for farmers, but also for the Chaffeys to sponsor excursions. Still, before a railroad station made it a bit easier to sponsor train excursions, essentially a nineteenth century version of an "open house," the Chaffeys would meet, according to one early excursionist, "prospective purchasers" at the train station at Cucamonga with a carriage and then take them to either Etiwanda or Ontario. This early excursionist, reporting on his trip of December 27, 1882, reported of having lunch with the Chaffeys and then given a tour of colonial lands via carriage. Here the Chaffeys, in this one case William, made the sales pitch, explaining the plans for a pipeline, the subdivision of tracts, and the planning of streets. The sales pitched worked too. The next morning, according to the excursionist, he and his wife returned to claim a "stake" and "it was here that the first domicile, in the shape of a tent, was erected in the city of Ontario," as the excursionist oversaw the construction of his home (*Ontario Daily Record*, January 12, 1911, transcribed in Conley, *Dreamers and Dwellers*, 28–29). Lithograph courtesy of the Robert E. Ellingwood Model Colony History Room, Ontario City Library.

demonstrated the boosters' understanding—or at least dedication to secure people who understood—the complexities and details of farming and production for market. The reader therefore saw that the necessary and correct steps were taken (or promised) to develop a successful agricultural region. Then again, the detailed information in the pamphlets concerning agriculture potentially appealed to city dwellers or people otherwise unfamiliar with agriculture to assure them that the boosters knew what they were doing. The pamphlets' material served as corroborating evidence of the reliability of Ontario's agricultural prowess.

The advertisement of urban amenities served the same sort of purpose as the information concerning agriculture. Touting urban amenities, as well as modern technologies increasingly associated with urban life in the positive sense, likely appealed to city dwellers. The promotional material aimed to guarantee that the benefits of the city would be present. Still, as shade trees, parks, and the agrarian rhetoric underscore, boosters pushed Ontario as a city without the supposed problems of a city in the negative, shadow sense. The adoration of urban amenities also likely appealed to farmers or people otherwise not often associated with urban living. The booster pamphlets promised urban culture and amenities without leaving the rural countryside behind; new residents could escape the vilified seamier sides of city life.

The list of urban services promoted in Ontario's booster literature included transportation, communication, electricity, water supply, educational institutions, religious institutions, social clubs, a post office, stores, a hotel, public library, and more. The railroad, though, towered over all. The railroad, a cultural symbol of modern-industrial society at the time, provided access to market for aspiring prosperous farmers while also providing a convenient connection to emerging urban centers and nearby communities such as Los Angeles, Riverside, Santa Monica, and Orange. The railroad created an extensive regional network that also reached out nationally. Certainly, among other lines, thriving agriculture and regional networks grew with a second Southern Pacific line running to San Diego (1882), the Santa Fe Railroad (1885), a link with Santa Fe at Cajon Pass (1885), the Chino Valley Railroad (1887), and the Los Angeles and Salt Lake Railroad (1903).[14]

Euclid Avenue undeniably served as a showpiece in promotional literature. "A grand avenue," wrote the boosters, "200 feet wide, named Euclid Avenue, will lead from the railroad to the mountains, and be illuminated at distances of a mile by an electric light." The boosters further promised that on Euclid "will be built a double track cable railway" propelled by "water power" and lined with "shade trees" such as eucalyptus and palm. If any doubt remained about the role of Euclid, good roads, or railroad links, the boosters spoke plainly. They stated, "[L]et him [a new buyer] remember that when he has so purchased the cheap lands it will cost him vast sums to add to it these things which alone elevate and build up the human race into higher

FIGURE 6

Euclid Avenue. This image, depicting Euclid in the late nineteenth century, comes from J. A. Alexander's biography of George Chaffey in 1928. Notice in addition to the road itself, lined with trees, the text under the picture prompts the reader to follow the much-praised road to the mountains in the background and then to appreciate the amenities, i.e., hotel and school—the duality of rural and urban in one setting.

culture, enjoyment, and civilization."[15] Therefore, no one moving to or investing in Ontario needed to worry, as the boosters thus provideth.

Besides trees, railways, and Euclid Avenue, Ontario offered educational institutions, from high schools to normal schools to an agricultural college, the "aim of which shall be to bring to the inmates of these homes the improving influences of mental and moral culture." Religious denominations were "well represented here," said the boosters, "and either have or are securing suitable places to worship." To highlight their investment in "public and quasi public improvements" the boosters again cited such things as railroad lines, a telegraph line, cross streets, electric lights, stores and shops, and a newspaper. They said that because "homeseekers coming to this country . . . desired a tract of fruit land surrounded by all the comforts and many of the luxuries of life, they determined to find here a settlement that should out-rank all other localities in natural and artificial attractions." According to the boosters, "A constant intellectualization has been going on around the farm" and Ontario would attract "men of good business judgment."[16] These amenities and Chaffey's "most perfect plan" show the suburban quality of Ontario, particularly when compared to the suburban analyses by Kenneth T. Jackson and others. Therefore, now using Jackson's definition, let us undress the story of Ontario recounted here to reveal its suburban character.

Ontario: A Model Agriburb

LOW RESIDENTIAL DENSITY AND LACK
OF DIVISION BETWEEN CITY AND SUBURB

The first distinguishing element of suburbs identified by Jackson is low residential density and the absence of distinguishable divisions between town and country. Concerning low residential density, Ontario at the turn of the twentieth century meets Jackson's criterion well. Ontario's population reached 683 by 1890 and remained under 23,000 until the 1950s, all within an area of approximately 6,582 acres, or 10.3 square miles.[17] Nonetheless, many rural-seeming areas, particularly nearby Colton and Redlands, show similar low-density numbers of less than or at about 1,000 per square mile—at least until 1920 concerning Colton, and 1950 for Redlands.[18]

As discussed in the introduction, the lack of a sharp distinction between town and country (or city and suburb) is where Ontario seemingly does not compare to a typical suburb. But let us dissect this more locally. Ontario's noncontiguous location to the three nearest county seats—Los Angeles, Riverside, and San Bernardino—is important. First, it again potentially explains why scholars fail to recognize Ontario as a unique rural suburb because a common misconception of suburbs is that they resulted from a process of development spreading out of an urban core.[19] The

TABLE 4

Ontario's Population & Density, 1890–1950*

Year	Population	Density/People per acre	Density/People per square mile
1890	683	0.10	66.31
1900	722	0.11	70.10
1910	4,274	0.65	414.95
1920	7,280	1.11	706.80
1930	13,583	2.06	1,318.74
1940	14,197	2.16	1,378.35
1950	22,872	3.47	2,220.58

*Ontario's land size registered as 6,582 acres, or 10.3 square miles (640 acres=1 sq mi) from 1890 to 1950

SOURCE: California, Department of Finance, "Population Totals by Township and Place for California Counties: 1860 to 1950," compiled by Dr. Campbell Gibson, 2005, available online at the California Department of Finance webpage: www.dof.ca.gov.

emphasis here is on geographic location, on the distance between suburb and city. Second, Ontario's noncontiguous location to an urban center such as Los Angeles— or at least growing urban areas—reflects one of the appeals drawing what Ontario's boosters called *colonizers*. The emphasis once more is on location, the geographically measurable and visually physical separation and distance between suburb and city.

Ontario, as mentioned, may not seem a suburb because it lay approximately thirty-eight miles from Los Angeles and just over twenty miles from Riverside and San Bernardino, with divisions marked by "unsettled" areas between. Recall, however, not all suburbs are contiguous with or located near (within 10–15 miles) a large urban center in the United States. Many suburbs, particularly working-class and industrial suburbs, emerged among waves of industrialization and building construction from the mid-nineteenth century to the mid-twentieth century. In fact, earlier railroad suburbs did not connect directly to cities either in the 1830s and 1840s but by transportation routes, which suburbanites often took the lead in funding.[20]

As previously mentioned, the problem regarding an emphasis on physical location (second, or material, space) is it often ignores the importance of imagery and imagination (first, or storied, space). The significance of Ontario's noncontiguous location to major urban centers rested upon its appeal. While a principal appeal came by way of connection to cities such as Los Angeles, Riverside, and San Bernardino, via the railroad, Ontario also needed to stay separated by a rural landscape. It thus functioned as more than a residential community. Ontario invoked a rural ideal.[21] It appealed to middle-class dreams of success in horticulture coinciding with, and contributing to, the general agricultural boom in Southern California in the 1880s. A booster brochure produced in 1883 by Luther M. Holt's Riverside Press and Horticulturist Steam Print, *Ontario, Located in San Bernardino County, California on the Southern Pacific Railroad*, captures the middle-class appeal and spirit of horticulture typical of the period, particularly fruit production:

> The result of careful, judicious cultivation of agriculture or horticultural products is profitable. Some products yield a profit of $50 per acre. The small profit is from grain crops. The large profit is from fruit crops. In fruits, one man can properly cultivate and market 20 acres of land, leaving sufficient time to properly care for poultry and animals needed to use up ordinary fallings about the place. . . . This country is of such character that each twenty-acre tract of our lands fit for cultivation, by proper cultivation, and a capital of say $2,000 to $3,000, invested in improvements, will support and educate a family; not in extravagance, but with the comforts and necessaries of life.[22]

Ontario did exist within the socioeconomic orbit of Los Angeles and surrounding neighborhoods via transportation routes and capital flow, and it could facilitate the development of other areas. Though such a sentiment went unspoken, Ontario's boosters proved that actions, as the saying goes, speak louder than words, sponsoring excursions from Colton, Los Angeles, Riverside, and San Bernardino in March 1883 to entice nearby residents to invest or resettle.[23] Regarding fruit production, Ontario's boosters touted the railroads' benefit to production for market to demonstrate that life in Ontario paid monetarily as well as culturally. The 1883 booster pamphlet, *Ontario, Located in San Bernardino County, California on the Southern Pacific Railroad*, as well as another pamphlet published by Holt's press, written in 1884 by Widney, highlightsthe importance of the railroad for Ontario:

> New markets will soon be opened up for Southern California. The new Southern railroad route, now completed, and the prospect of two or three other independent lines being finished to Southern California within the next two years will furnish, it is hoped, cheap transportation to the heart of the Mississippi Valley. These routes will enable us to find a market where millions of people will want our fruit.[24]

The adoration of agriculture in primary sources and subsequent histories concerning Ontario is typical, particularly for California. As we saw, images of California agriculture and its profitability apply to numerous Californian communities from northern vineyards to the orange groves of Southern California. Boosters throughout California promoted the state's horticultural promise. The glorification of agriculture, particularly citriculture, not only dominated larger accounts and historical narratives concerning California, but also local accounts of Ontario. Many California historians emphasize the importance of California agriculture and fervently cite Ontario's growth within a few short years to underscore the larger trend of land boom. So, having discussed the adoration of agriculture at the state or regional level, the idea here is to revisit this theme—as well as other themes—by localizing it (i.e., minimize the scale of analysis).

Within two years of Ontario's founding in 1882, the acreage of fruit registered at 7,678. Most acres were devoted to citrus, particularly oranges and lemons. In 1883 alone, Ontario shipped 207 train carloads of oranges and lemons and 104 carloads of deciduous fruits and raisins to market. The stunning growth and agricultural production in Ontario that increased following the boom of the eighties receives great attention, though it did stumble during the lean depression years of the 1890s. Perhaps most striking is the lasting power of agricultural production in Ontario and nearby areas as a major source of employment through 1960 despite the rise of nonagricultural industry throughout the region, particularly the electrical appliance company Hotpoint. Yet, one observer remarked in 1907, "It would be an impossibility for a person to remain more than a few minutes within the limits of Ontario without realizing that here oranges are grown."[25]

HOMES AND FAMILIES IN A PERFECT (YET MODERN) ENVIRONMENT

The second distinguishing feature of an American suburb is a strong desire for home ownership. Recall that renowned suburban image-maker Andrew Jackson Downing once said, "We believe, about all things under heaven, in the power and virtue of the *individual home.*" Downing strongly advocated the so-called purifying power of rural tastes about homes, landscape architecture, and parks.[26] The advertisement of home ownership in Ontario reflected the intent of boosters to sell Ontario as a suburb. "The cost of building neat, plain houses," asserted the boosters in the 1883 promotional, "is about $200 per room of 9x12 feet, and about $250 per room of 12x14." The boosters continued:

> Having secured both land and water, they [the Chaffey brothers] immediately set about laying the plans for a settlement that should attract the very best class of people that come to Southern California to secure homes and engage in that most pleasant and remunerative business—the growing of fruits indigenous to Southern California.[27]

Speaking of home seekers, the boosters added that the colony would appeal to those "who desire to enjoy a sort of suburban life, engage in fruit culture and make homes for themselves and families." The notion of "happy homes" championed in the 1883 pamphlet resounded further in the 1884 pamphlet, which aptly carried the subtitle *Information for Those Seeking Homes in Southern California.* One part read, "Two hundred and thirty-eight thousand four hundred and ninety-nine 77-100 dollars have been spent by the [Chaffey] company up to July, 1884, in preparing Ontario for pleasant and profitable homes."[28]

Home ownership in the framework of drawing potential migrants and investors did not stand complete. Rather, hinted above, other elements augmented the lure of home ownership: economic investment and profitability, climate, and the rural ideal. Ontario boosters said that they planned and invested $238,499 on improvements, adding, "The plan of the colony is of the most advanced and liberal kind," which included joint stock ownership in a mutual water company and water rights. They even proclaimed in a phrase—destined to become one of the most repeated in Ontario's historical literature—that the boosters set up "the most perfect plan ever adopted by a colony in this State." This "most perfect plan," again, included three parts: irrigation and a water system, good roads, and education through an agricultural college.[29]

The boosters wanted to depict Ontario as innovative—exceeding supposed norms of other rural-seeming communities that included agriculture. In both 1883 and 1884, Ontario's boosters accredited the colony with a dizzying array of infrastructure and idealized attributes. Such attributes included the leisurely cultivation of just about every item capable of growing under the sun, such as apples, lemons, limes, grapes (raisins), oranges, peaches, pears, prunes, and wheat. Likewise, the advertised low price of acreage in Ontario, compared to surrounding areas, figured prominently in the publicity campaign. Land sold for $150 per acre for town lots (business district), $200 per acre for horticultural lots, and $250 per acre for villa lots just outside the business district of town. In comparison, lots in Riverside reportedly (described by Ontario's boosters) sold for as high as $500 an acre, Redlands' "unimproved land" at $200, and Crafton at $200 because of "the unfinished condition of the water system." The underlying points centered on first, how Ontario land, which the boosters declared improved because of irrigation and other amenities, came cheap; and second, how the land values of some places, particularly in Riverside, skyrocketed in value in as few as three years (they claimed Riverside land once sold as low as $75). They went so far as to add a section to the 1884 pamphlet boasting that land near Bordeaux, France, "has sold as high a figure as $16,000 per acre."[30] The motive here rested on the notion that Ontario's horticultural promise and business investments (that included the boosters' own

FIGURE 7

The Mule Car, ca. 1890. In 1887, Ontario's "gravity mule car" made its first run up Euclid Avenue. The uphill trip toward the San Gabriel Mountains reportedly took 90 minutes, while the downhill ride only took 30 minutes because the mules, as seen here on the left, rode along as passengers in a pullout trailer. The mule car ran until 1895 when finally replaced by an electric streetcar. Courtesy of the Robert E. Ellingwood Model Colony History Room, Ontario City Library.

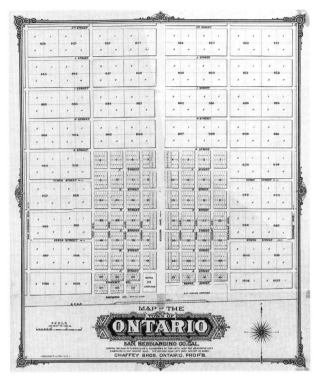

FIGURE 8

Map of Ontario, California, 1883. This map shows the "town" laid out in the popular grid system, first used in North America in Philadelphia in 1682. The grid system became nearly universal and synonymous in the planning of Western cities during the nineteenth century and early twentieth century because it allowed the rapid subdivision and auction of a large parcel of land. Courtesy of the Robert E. Ellingwood Model Colony History Room, Ontario City Library.

contribution of more than $200,000) could easily foster an agricultural production and profitability superior to Bordeaux.

The boosters paraded forth a host of institutions that meant to signal Ontario's sophistication and its supporting infrastructure for the hyped-up benefit of all of Ontario's citizens. "They [the boosters] simply propose," the 1883 pamphlet read, "to invest a large proportion of the profits of the sale of the tract in permanent improvements for the benefit of the settlers."[31] In fact, historians—local or not—name Ontario, behind Etiwanda, as one of the first communities in the West to have electric lighting.[32] Ontario seemed to have everything a would-be-colonizer could ever fantasize about in cultivating work and home on the fringes of Los Angeles.

The promotion and design of Ontario to include urban amenities are what delineate the suburban side of Ontario's origins. Certainly home and nature correspond to the ideal image of suburbia as imagined by the likes of Beecher, Downing, and Olmsted, but so too did, according to Olmsted, "the easy gratification of certain tastes" and "numerous luxuries." Added Olmsted, as if he had Euclid Avenue in Ontario in mind, "The main artificial requirements of a suburb then, are good roads and walks, pleasant to the eye within themselves, and having at intervals pleasant openings and outlooks, with suggestions of refined domestic life, secluded, but not far removed from the life of the community."[33] Olmsted was rather specific in his letter to the Riverside Development Company that an ideal suburb possessed a supreme climate, purity of air as "aidful [sic] to refined and healthy domestic life," drives, walks, and recreations, a public park, and water supply.[34] This is exactly what the boosters of Ontario promised and sold as they incorporated the design and promotional imagery of romantic suburbs, even while expanding it to include horticulture. On the one hand, Ontario's boosters did utilize a gridiron system of street design in the business district as a way to maximize house lots and provide an illusion of orderliness and prosperity. On the other hand, Ontario's boosters prized their tree-lined boulevard and pastoral feel. Likewise, the railroad station and other amenities such as social clubs, leisure spaces, telephone service, electricity, and trolley service became a source of pride, the symbols of Ontario's urbanity without it being urban.

But wait, the boosters had more! The creations of a mutual water company and the Chaffey College of Agriculture emerged as the boosters' *pièce de résistance* designed to sway any remaining skeptics of the "most perfect plan" and win possible cynics over concerning the social-mindedness of the founders' "liberal" intentions of the most "advanced" kind. California in the 1880s, particularly the arid south, dealt with a need for irrigation.[35] Water did not flow abundantly in arid Southern California. The founders of the model colony realized that and understood the legitimate concern of potential migrants. To douse such fears, the boosters devoted apt space in their two pamphlets of 1883 and 1884 highlighting the high rainfall or high water levels in Ontario (or nearby storage ditches) and Southern California.[36] Lack of access to water, attributable to earlier appropriation of water rights, also gave rise to negative critiques of California and threatened the boosters' hopes for the profitable settlement of Ontario. To overcome this obstacle, they designed a mutual water company to grant stock and water rights to all landowners in Ontario.

The mutual water company plan established a corporation (the San Antonio Water Company) in which each owner of Ontario property held stock. The fact that the boosters set up a corporation is in and of itself revealing. Historians have highlighted the significance of larger corporate capitalism's rise over smaller competitive capitalism in the late nineteenth century.[37] By the 1880s, incorporation emerged as a modern way of doing business and not a special state-conferred privilege. Accompanying this new business norm, corporate capitalism tended to shift power away from shareholders to directors and managers.[38] The boosters established a legal institution offering them limited liability, full power, and a chance to maximize profits. These were smart executives aware of the law and keen to develop institutions to secure larger profits beyond the simple grab and sell of land—a point that further attests to the thesis that Ontario began as a planned agriburb, not an abstract "colony" system dependent on initial real-estate sales to a consortium of farmer-purchasers. The boosters' biographies, covered in chapter five, work to substantiate this claim further.

The Chaffey College of Agriculture, another so-called innovative institution offered to the "settlers" of Ontario, reflects another creative method of indirect profit-seeking by the boosters. The Chaffey Company established a trust in which it turned over more than 300 acres of property, plus an additional twenty acres personally donated by Chaffey for the campus. The trustees, headed by Widney, were in actuality the charter members, first directors, and regents of the University of Southern California who, for a time, made the Chaffey College a branch of USC.[39] Again, the formation of a trust, run by directors of another corporation—USC incorporated as a private religious university in August 1880—illustrates the business shrewdness of Ontario's boosters. They established their trust in November 1882 on the heels of the first great trust that same year—Rockefeller's Standard Oil—and celebrated the laying of the cornerstone in March 1883 with a speech by the noted California booster and educator Edward J. Wickson.[40] Again, their economic and legal cleverness underscores how the boosters wanted to establish a strong suburban community to secure larger and sustained profits. USC benefited as an embryonic college that received free land and an opportunity to expand while also hoping to increase enrollment. The proceeds from the sale of lands formed an endowment for the construction and operation of the college.[41] The boosters also benefited. As with the water company, the boosters found a way to establish a supposedly needed and valued institution that appealed to migrants seeking refinement. The creation of the Chaffey College of Agriculture grew out of speculative imagination and provided a middle-class cultural establishment that could entice migrants to move to Ontario.

We cannot shortchange the appeal to climate and health in Ontario. The boosters accounted for this too. As we saw, literature concerning climate and health in California and histories of its promotion is vast. In Ontario, the promotion of health and climate ran in sync with a Californian booster literature whereby boisterous claims about the Golden State celebrated its self-proclaimed superior natural environment.[42] Climate and health, recall, augment home ownership and other amenities. They become more powerful in their appeal because the site of their location emerges as the fulfillment of the "geography of the ideal."[43] Such an appeal to the pristine landscape of Ontario mirrored the type of natural environment suburban image-makers called for, as they argued for "a healthful home" in a good climate.[44] This view of climate and health also mirrored the conception of nature popularized by Romantics. Recall that Emerson noted, "[N]ature is medicinal." So, now at the localized scale, if Americans were somehow sick from maladies caused by increasing industrialization, modernization, and urbanization, then suburban homes among Ontario's beautiful orchards would provide, literally, just what the doctor ordered according to Dr. Joseph P. Widney's praise of Ontario and the Southland.[45]

Remember that a principal element to the celebration of California's environment was the Mediterranean analogy.[46] As California, particularly the Southland, regularly received comparisons to Italy from the 1870s forward, Ontario's boosters followed suit. Boosters and others in Ontario, such as writers in *The Ontario Record* (1905), labeled Ontario as "The Italy of America."[47] Ontario's Mediterranean climate could aid the superior growth of a farmer's fruit or the advancement of his heart, mind, and body. "The climate is perfect," wrote the Chaffey brothers to an inquirer in 1882, "and one which will be sought after by invalids and those desiring to make pleasant and happy homes."[48]

One of the premier figures in the promotion of California's healthfulness was the brother of Chaffey's partner Judge Robert M. Widney, fellow USC director, and a trustee for the Chaffey College of Agriculture: Dr. Joseph P. Widney—medical doctor, clergyman, public health author, and one of the key boosters spotlighted in chapter five.[49] Dr. Widney's influence on Judge Widney's promotional pamphlet *Ontario* in 1884, as well as the 1883 pamphlet, is clear. The pamphlets utilized the "climatic studies" of Dr. Widney and informed potential settlers that Ontario possessed "the finest climate in Southern California for persons affected with pulmonary diseases."[50] In a section titled "Health Resort" in the 1884 pamphlet, Ontario receives credit for having cured a man's "indigestion, sleeplessness, neuralgia, and rheumatism." "Children who would languish and die for lack of vital strength in other lands," Judge Widney wrote, "will here grow to health and strength." He added, "Adults whose systems are annually deteriorating, will here prolong in health and comfort the days of their sojourn." Ontario, in health and beauty, truly seemed a model colony, or, as Judge Widney wrote, "The second Garden of Eden."[51]

THE MIDDLE CLASS YET AGAIN IN A MIDDLE LANDSCAPE

The final enticement for drawing migration to Ontario, which accompanied home ownership and the rural ideal, coalesces with the third and most important distinctive characteristic of American housing patterns, according to Jackson. He argues socioeconomic distinctions between the center and the periphery mark suburbs as unique. New suburban historians have complicated this view. In fact, much of the labor force in Ontario consisted of Mexican Americans and Asian Americans (at the fringes actually, in Upland—a "farm-fringe streetcar suburb" or "suburbscape"). Ontario, however, resembles Jackson's conception of a predominantly middle-class white community.[52] Jackson's conception of a suburb as a bedroom community, however, as well as his thesis that the final distinguishing characteristic of the American suburban experience is the length of the average journey to work, inadequately explains the early development of Ontario. Ontario undoubtedly remained a predominantly middle-class white community before the post–World War II boom.[53] Nevertheless, suburbs were also semiautonomous enclaves that combined work and home as much as they were developed as bedroom communities, which thus undermines the commuter element and narrowly conceived function of suburbs highlighted by Jackson.

In line with Jackson's notion that suburbs were white, middle-class communities, California's boosters, particularly Ontario's boosters, specifically targeted a middle-class audience by publicizing the rural ideal.[54] The literature on the rural ideal, like the literature on irrigation, agriculture, or climate, includes a vast number of texts. Specifically, it is important to remember that the image of rural simplicity in an increasingly modern, industrial, and urban society potentially appealed to both middle-class urban Americans and rural Americans fearing the modern industrialized city, increasingly filled with foreign-born immigrants, as it would corrupt individuals and wipe out any modicum of social control and undermine a "search for order."[55]

We can again localize this phenomenon with Ontario. The Chaffey brothers, according to the 1883 booster pamphlet, purchased land east of Los Angeles and offered it "for sale in such quantities as will suit the pocket of the humblest of farmers."[56] Despite the deep-seated popularity of the rural ideal upon the breast of most Americans in the late nineteenth century, the plight of farm life also received publicity. The difficulty facing American farmers became a popular topic of public and political distress in the form of farmers' alliances and Populist revolts in the last quarter of the nineteenth century. Farmers in the late nineteenth century faced the cruel coupling of dropping prices on one side and high costs on the other side.[57] If American farmers throughout the country felt so downtrodden and abused by the economic and political systems, why would Ontario's boosters tout a farmer-lifestyle as the ideal type of middle-class community, let alone assume such a plan the best? While certainly explainable in the context of the strong appeal of agrarianism (actually, that is the explanation because the agrarian myth grew even stronger as a result; i.e., more light narratives came out from the dark ones), the boosters' word choices might seem perplexing if we accept the argument that they were intelligent executives with genuine dreams. The explanation offered here centers on gender and class. Such is also another way of demonstrating how these boosters creatively and zealously reassembled powerful cultural representations and, for this reason, better sold their suburb.

While I highlighted gendered language and evolving social norms concerning women by discussing Beecher earlier, middle-class male aspirations are also important and proved significant to the appeal of horticulture and the farming life in the advertisement of Ontario. As the United States shifted to a largely modern, industrialized urban nation, increasing numbers of men lost their economic independence. The number of salaried, nonpropertied workers reportedly grew eight times between 1870 and 1910.[58] Historians have previously pointed out that concerns about "over-civilization" and "feminization" threatened Victorian ideals of masculinity, virtue, and vitality, as well as concerns over the loss of social control, epitomized by the large cesspools of "immoral" immigrants and "degenerates" inhabiting the city.[59] Farming therefore offered a rhetorical antidote to overcivilization and industrial capitalism as a man could till the soil and reap the profits of his own labor—independent of any authority, manager, or boss—while, at the same time, purportedly avoid the problems plaguing farmers throughout the rest of the country.

A model of "masculine domesticity" emerged in the 1870s, according to historian Margaret Marsh. A suburban man voluntarily took on more domestic chores (such as lawn mowing), spent more time with his children, made his wife a regular companion instead of his "male cronies," and took a more general interest in the affairs of the home.[60] Ontario offered a man all of this. The suburban man in the agriburb could potentially bypass the glass ceiling imposed by bureaucrats in the commercial sector and subsequently claim a sense of moral authority and superiority over the home because the suburban home in the agriburb reflected a commercial venture itself. As a consequence, the man, as the allegorical top bureaucrat of the agriburb home, challenged the moral authority of his wife in the home that suburban and domestic advocates originally claimed intrinsic to the female gender and what made women of the middle class both truly American women and middle class. In contrast, as

FIGURE 9

The Oakley family in their orchard with the Chaffey College of Agriculture in the background, ca. 1888. Like other middle-class families in Ontario and surrounding communities, the Oakleys exemplified both an image of gentility and hard work in the pursuit of profit among California's beautiful orchards and vineyards. Notice their fine dress, particularly the woman in front, as well as the child in the background holding a doll. Courtesy of the Robert E. Ellingwood Model Colony History Room, Ontario City Library.

developed in the next chapter, the importance of shopping and social clubs became a principal element in boosters' advertisements (likely) aimed at women.

In the 1883 promotional pamphlet, the boosters lamented, "How shall the young man be led to appreciate these charms of country life, without quenching his ambition, curbing his youthful energy, and repressing his longing for a life of enthusiastic action?" The boosters proactively addressed concerns that farming failed to provide a forum for transforming young boys into strong intelligent men with the necessary "commercial skill" needed to survive in an industrial world. When a young man began "to think the thoughts of manhood," the boosters wondered whether "agriculture [might] seem most distasteful to him." Presupposing many might view farming as archaic in nature, lacking the "skills" necessary and championed by an industrial society, the boosters praised California agriculture and proclaimed, "Agriculture will be the science of the future." Horticulture provided young men with an opportunity to develop wisdom as they honed the "financial skill required in carrying a[n] [agricultural] venture from the point of beginning until it yields a dollar in return." California agriculture, according to the boosters, required commercial awareness, financial skill, intelligence, science, and promoted robust health. With a successful farm in California came "intellectual and moral advancement." "It is to make them better farmers," the pamphlet concluded, "and [echoing Downing] better citizens."[61] Ontario's boosters, again, mirrored sub-urban image-makers in their portrayal of democratic citizenship as more compatible with rural rather than urban environments. Ontario's boosters created an image of the archetypal middle-class male, who likely made the final decision on whether to move to Ontario or not, celebrating a male farmer's intellectual prowess, physical strength and health, democratic citizenship, and love of family.

The promotion of Ontario as a middle-class haven follows some other distinct lines of thought wrapped within class and upward mobility: producerism and civility. "Vast numbers of men came here with no capital," declared the boosters, "who, to-day, are worth from $4,000 to $50,000." They continued, "But they were men who were not afraid to work hard, and late—who lived within their income, and saved annually—for such there is still room."[62] The boosters proclaimed that migrants did not have to come from wealth, but be hard workers capable of using their heads as much as their hands. The land in Ontario, they wrote to one potential migrant, was "lying dormant waiting the necessary capital and brains to carry them to perfection."[63] The boosters made both public and private announcements aimed at potential migrants, likely filled with middle-class anxiety or aspirations, whereby they warded off so-called scruff that could give Ontario a bad reputation and lower not only the boosters' investment value, but also reduce the potential migrant and investor's investment value and sense of middle-class identity. Ontario presented "many opportunities for good investment," wrote the Chaffey brothers to a Kansas City inquirer and "the life is 'pioneer.'"[64] Through hard work, a comfortable income and life awaited. Likewise, in a quote shared earlier, the boosters pronounced in the 1883 pamphlet, "Having secured both land and water, they immediately set about the plans for a settlement that should attract the very *best class of people* that come to Southern California to secure homes."[65] As historians note, middle-class America underwent transformation and, more to the point, looked to the past nostalgically to interpret what a "better class of people" might be—and to identify themselves as belonging to it, as the bulwarks of moral social order.[66] In Ontario, the better class of people found a rural ideal set in the past glorification of agriculture and an advertised dry community free of alcohol, slums, prostitutes, crime, and many non-whites. Ontario thus had the infrastructure of a city without the supposed degeneracy. In comparison, Americans also looked forward, as science, technology, and business cunning symbolized modernity and middle-class sophistication. Ontario's boosters appealed to an aspiring middle-class audience as they remarked, "Men of good business judgment and foresight see these facts and unhesitantingly [sic] purchase here for homes. We venture the statement that in the State of California there is not a collection of men who will average in wealth, business ability, judgment, and foresight as high as purchasers of land at Ontario."[67]

ONTARIO REVISITED

Ontario was an agriburb. Ontario, as a planned rural suburb, constituted a speculative imagining and real estate venture designed to yield a profit. The way of life in Ontario, as represented by the boosters, reflected the way of life and urban amenities so extolled by suburban image-makers. Suburbs promised community life and urban amenities in a beautiful rural landscape. So too did Ontario. As reviewed, California historians have commented on the vast array of amenities offered in California's "colonies."[68] Such colonies, recall, were subdivisions, such as Ontario, and supported by institutions and infrastructure typically established by developers in longer settled communities. Good boosters like those in Ontario understood that to attract people they needed to provide a variety of amenities. As suburban image-makers depicted a community with plenty of leisure time to enjoy finer things with a level of urban amenities, so too did Ontario's boosters. They highlighted amenities that were, according to them, good for "mental and moral culture." Such amenities, in both suburbs and colonies, represented the perfect blend of a city without a city and a country life without isolation.[69]

Now the focus turns north, as Northern Californian boosters also used the language of suburbia to draw potential growth as they sought to earn a profit as well. The communities of Orangevale and Fair Oaks outside Sacramento were two such ventures where their boosters emphatically envisioned a suburban type that mirrored the agriburb model like Ontario. A review of these communities widens the geography of an analysis of the suburban side of California's agricultural colonization to show a larger phenomenon. Such a review also provides another case study that further details and verifies the verity of the agriburb.

CHAPTER FOUR

THE AGRIBURBS OF SACRAMENTO

*There is one especially great advantage to
Sacramenteans in the opening up and development
of these suburban tracts, and that is the facilities
afforded business men for enjoying the comforts and
privileges of country homes, without interference
with their business interests.*

SACRAMENTO UNION, MAY 8, 1888[1]

PACKAGING THE PLACE OF SACRAMENTO

The promotion of Sacramento began long before Orangevale and Fair Oaks ever
emerged in the minds of Sacramento's boosters. These communities were part of a
far broader publicity campaign by Sacramento's growth coalition to profit from the
promotion of Sacramento and its surrounding countryside. Expectedly, the Gold
Rush and mining figured prominently in publicity from 1850 forward. Still, the
packaging of Sacramento as a place of agricultural profitability began early on as
well, particularly in the lavishly illustrated *History of Sacramento County, California
with Illustrations Descriptive of Its Scenery, Residences, Public Buildings, Fine Blocks,
and Manufactories* by Thompson & West publishers in 1880.[2] The Thompson &
West publication represented just one of dozens of booster pamphlets that emerged
between the 1870s and 1910s, all designed to romanticize the Sacramento region.
In particular, the narrative laid out in the Thompson & West publication proved
salient in the decades to come. It showed a long-term packaging of Sacramento as an
agricultural metropolis that boasted the best agricultural landscape with urban amenities. Sacramento's boosters, therefore, employed the agriburb model of suburbia

in Orangevale and Fair Oaks as a way to profit from the direct investment in such communities and from their inclusion in a broader metropolitan publicity campaign.

Some of the brash booster publications produced between 1880 and World War I concerning Sacramento include Thompson & West's *History of Sacramento County* (1880), *Sacramento: The Commercial Metropolis of Northern and Central California* (1888), *Sacramento County and its Resources* (1894), the Sacramento Chamber of Commerce and Board of Supervisor's *Resources of Sacramento County* (1899), *Souvenir of the Capital of California* (1901), "Northern California: The Story of the Sacramento Valley" in *Harper's Weekly* (1903), the Sacramento Chamber of Commerce's *Sacramento and its Tributary Country* (1904), the Sacramento Chamber's *Greater Sacramento: Her Achievements, Resources and Possibilities* (1912), and *Sacramento Valley and Foothill Counties of California* (1915).[3] These publications had many recurrent, constant, and typical themes, particularly after 1887 (formation of Orangevale), and then again in 1895 (formation of Fair Oaks), especially regarding the use of Orangevale and Fair Oaks as examples of Sacramento's agricultural bounty and superb community types, business intelligence, and general sophistication. In the boosters' words, these writings gave "a simple, unadorned statement of facts such as will give those unfamiliar with the region a clear and comprehensive idea of the city and county, its representative homes, its business establishments, its farm and orchard sections, its products, commerce, trade and trade relations, its social and refining features and its importance in the economy and growth of California."[4]

One of the numerous, conspicuous themes that germinated from the broad publicity campaign included Sacramento's quality in comparison to not just anywhere U.S.A. but Southern California in particular. The packaging of Sacramento as not only a model place, but rather as the best place, mirrors the representation and promotion of place as a commodity by boosters throughout the nation in general. The juxtaposition of Sacramento with Los Angeles had logic. Los Angeles and Southern California already benefited from a large, well-conducted publicity campaign richly captured in histories by the authors Carey McWilliams, Mike Davis, Greg Hise, and many more.[5] While not wanting to slight Southern California's broader boosterism and the scholars who have deftly chronicled such, the point here is finally to acknowledge that, from the late 1880s at least, Sacramento's boosters set out to reap from the Southern California harvest in publicity and embarked on a serious booster campaign in their own right. It is worth reviewing.

Comparing Sacramento to Los Angeles, the boosters wrote that the "Valley of Sacramento is a garden and Sacramento is the 'urbs in horto' [city in a garden] of it. It is our first glimpse of the celestial flowering kingdom of the Christian world." While many in the Southland made similar statements, boosters in Sacramento claimed that the soil and weather in the Sacramento Valley were better than in Southern California. As the promotion of Southern California had cast that region as the perfect place for the growth of just about any produce, Sacramenteans claimed Sacramento that much better. Not even northern Italy and the Riviera could compare because Sacramento had an average temperature of 61.0 degrees and 238 clear days to Italy's average temperature of 60.0 degrees and 220 clear days. Sacramento's boosters boasted *ad infinitum* that produce in the region came to maturity about six weeks earlier than in Southern California, thereby giving Sacramento a commercial advantage by reaching the market before Southern California produce had a chance to either enter or saturate the market, adversely affecting value.[6]

The packaging of the Sacramento metropolitan area as a commodity placed emphasis on the region's so-called natural advantages, which, in turn, fostered more advantages in agriculture, commerce, socio-cultural life, and community and family life. In addition to the climate and soil, they lauded the region's mountains, rivers, trees, and even aroma. "The prevailing breezes come laden with ozone from the sea, or bearing balsamic piney odors from the forests of the Sierra Nevada." Neither tornadoes nor cyclones threatened the area. Any concerns about flood or fire met with pledges of newly built levees, strong buildings, and municipal services. Entire booster pamphlets, such as the 1880 Thompson & West publication, actually publicized the problems of flooding and fire disasters just to highlight Sacramento's progress or to counter, as Orsi argued about boosterism generally, existing shadow representations. "Perfect safety," they claimed, "has been secured." Mortality rates, they not surprisingly claimed, remained lower, particularly in comparison to Southern California. Sacramento enjoyed low humidity, sporadic droughts, and the temperature never burned too hot, never chilled too cold. Sacramento boosters thus exclaimed, "There is no spot on earth where fruit culture can be carried on more profitably, where greater variety can be produced, or where crops are surer than in that portion of the great Sacramento valley occupied by the county of Sacramento."[7]

In this "richest portion" of California, boosters explained, "hardly a foot of its land is not susceptible of successful cultivation, and the major part of it will favorably rank with the best land in the Union." The key to unlocking the array of benefits within this land, recall, meant hard work and intelligence as the boosters extolled the virtues of producerism and "scientific modes of cultivation." The boosters boasted in 1888, "They [Sacramento's lands] but await the application of enterprising labor to render them principalities to their possessors." Like boosters throughout California placating potential migrants, boosters in Sacramento praised the intelligence, modernity, and masculinity of Sacramento's potential future small farmers, particularly within the context of horticulture.[8]

In fact, horticulture, as prosecuted in California, is an art that demands a rare combination of qualities for perfect success—more, perhaps, than any other profession or calling. When you see a man obtaining, every year, phenomenal returns, you may feel assured that, in addition to being favored by natural conditions, he has intelligence, judgment, practical experience, energy, executive ability, and business sagacity. Any man of these qualities can be assured of phenomenal returns from fruit culture in this county. Fruit-growing is the business of all others which offers a premium to brains and work. A community of fruit growers is a community of able men—often cultured men—as different from a community of purely grain-growing farmers as can be. And the wealth created and the permanent prosperity insured in a fruit-growing community, the small homes horticulture creates, and the dense population it supports, all make a marked contrast with the results seen in a community devoted to general farming.[9]

Highlighting Sacramento's natural advantages distinguished a light narrative of Sacramento as an "agricultural empire" where one could benefit from "perfection in horticultural development." The natural resources, such as Sacramento's American and Sacramento rivers, augmented Sacramento's proficiency. "Think of it! A navigable river winding through millions of fertile acres more than 300 miles, and not only does this magnificent stream afford irrigation and shipping transportation, but as a source of food supply, it is unsurpassed." Sacramento boosters cast the area as a premier fruit-growing center as they presented various reports and statistics of profits made, shipments, and total tons of fruit produced. The boosters also paraded forth Sacramento's railroad heritage and vast railroad system to proclaim Sacramento as the transportation hub of the Pacific slope, which, of course, reportedly benefited the local grower, not to mention industry. In their words, Sacramento emerged as a "natural distributing point" and had "a practical monopoly on transcontinental fresh fruit transportation."[10]

As a land described as capable of growing fruit of every kind, not to mention nuts, wheat, alfalfa, and hops, the boosters proclaimed that the Sacramento area had established a profitable business sector through a perceptive "business intelligence." Those same rivers, climatic conditions, prosperous lands, and transportation systems that made agriculture successful also provided commercial advantages. Boosters claimed Sacramento enjoyed the benefits of a bustling site of business as they touted the Chamber of Commerce, banks, retail trades of every kind, factories and mills, industries, and the Southern Pacific Railroad Company. Given such advantages, they claimed, "[P]anics and speculative excitement never disturb the people of the city."[11] Sacramento, "the commercial metropolis," benefited from a vast system of railroads, roads and bridges, and, as the boosters liked to claim, a growing population and a large base of nationwide consumers who were accessible via transportation networks.

According to the boosters, Sacramento's agricultural and commercial strengths sustained social and cultural life, which further contributed to the region's agricultural and commercial growth. Sacramento's boosters highlighted Sacramento's pastoral feel, including a wealth of trees, flowers, and parks. Nevertheless, in Sacramento, claimed the boosters, a "displacement of the old for the modern" had taken place. The boosters bragged about Sacramento's urban amenities, cultural life, and infrastructure to demonstrate the area's modernity. They, as perhaps expected by now, highlighted churches;

schools; asylums and hospitals; fire and police departments; hotels; libraries; an art gallery; post offices; water supply; sewer system; transportation; lighting and heating; and numerous clubs and organizations, such as literary guilds, Free Masons, and Odd Fellows. "The social advantages of churches, educational and fraternal organizations are numerous," one booster pamphlet claimed, affirming the point by adding, "[The] solid foundation of real Christianity is the basis of our real civilization." Sacramento's plethora of churches "kept back the scruff" and the population supposedly "comprised the cream of the society of America and Europe"—meaning white people.[12]

Sacramento also had homes and, more importantly, the hyped republican, civic-minded families living inside. Advertised as a "city of homes," it emerged as, even better, "A city of homes and flowers, the residence portion being embraced in choice foliage, and the streets well shaded." Packaging life in Sacramento as "very near [in] approach to the ideal," the boosters described the area as having both "graceful and classical architecture," but it also had a soul, such as the church. "As a rule, present the home life and surroundings of a people to the intelligent stranger, and you give him the master key to their civilization and character, social state and conditions of thrift." Life in the Sacramento area lent itself to beautiful homes in a modern, yet bucolic, landscape that featured urban amenities, refinement, good business, so-called traditional values (or, as the boosters said, "rural conservatism"), and an agricultural industry that could support men of intelligence, but even men of "average intelligence."[13]

Within the context of the broader publicity campaign concerning the entire Sacramento metropolis, Orangevale and Fair Oaks were subsequently presented as proof, as examples of bloated claims. "Besides the bottom and the plain lands, there is still another class of productive land in Sacramento County. This is the rolling land at the beginning of the foothills of the Sierra Nevada. The rolling land lies north of the American River and is no doubt the most picturesque part of all of Sacramento County. It includes the prosperous colonies of Orangevale and Fair Oaks, noted for their production of citrus and semi-tropical fruit. Practically all the oranges grown in Sacramento County come from the pretty groves on the gentle slopes of Orangevale and Fair Oaks." Orangevale and Fair Oaks were more than just speculative real-estate ventures for a few. They were also talking points for boosters throughout the region. "The Orange Vale Colony is a striking illustration of self-supporting small homes," while Fair Oaks was an example of water supply, and both held citrus production and the profitability of small farms. When embellishing the splendor of the Sacramento Valley and its fertility, the boosters would invoke a "panoramic view" of Fair Oaks. When need for proof of the region's citrus and fruit dexterity came along, a picture of a prize-winning orange tree in Orangevale appeared. Orangevale and Fair Oaks were therefore good for both individual place entrepreneurs speculating in real estate and a Sacramento metropolitan growth coalition hoping to reap profit from their promotion. They were Sacramento's "subs in horto."[14]

ORANGEVALE AND FAIR OAKS IN THE HEART OF CALIFORNIA

As with Ontario in the previous chapter, to best compare and contrast Orangevale and Fair Oaks to Jackson's model of suburbs, reviewing briefly the formation of these communities provides essential context. The creation of Orangevale as a settled community resulted from a series of land deals that date back to California's Mexican period in 1844. According to the Sacramento firm of Buckley and Taylor in 1895, the Mexican governor of California, Manuel Micheltorena, first granted the land that included Orangevale to Joel Dedmond on Christmas Eve in 1844. The land grant, known as the Rancho de San Juan, included nearly 20,000 acres. The first land sale occurred in August 1845 to John Sinclair. Sinclair then sold the land to Hiram Grimes in February 1849 for a mere $5,000. While Grimes officially received a US Land Patent on July 9, 1860, he (and soon others) sold off small parcels throughout the 1850s. In 1861, Serranus Clinton Hastings, California's first chief justice and third attorney general, purchased most of the San Juan grant for $36,000. Hastings eventually sold parts of the land, including portions to prominent business partners Frederick K. Cox and Crawford W. Clarke. Cox and Clarke eventually sold what they owned to a land company that formed Orangevale. Most importantly, however, Hastings sold land to an Irish farmer, John T. Cardwell, in the 1880s. The Sacramento boosters—who included prominent businesspersons Harris Weinstock and Valentine S. McClatchy, co-owner and editor of the *Sacramento Bee*—purchased land from Cardwell and other landholders, and eventually they sold their combined acres to their booster organization, the Orange Vale Colonization Company (OVCC), in 1887 and 1888.[15]

Five of the company's trustees appeared before a notary public on September 2, 1887, to place their signatures on articles of incorporation. McClatchy, George M. Mott, Thomas B. Hall, Phillip C. Drescher, and Weinstock each signed the document to create the colonization company. They also announced some lofty goals, which included the construction of bridges, ditches, and buildings, as well as loaning money to cultivate farmlands. The trustees envisioned the creation of a farming community, yet they had an even grander goal of forming an intricate system of suburbs on the fringes of Sacramento's rural landscape, which would include bridges, buildings, and real-estate projects. "As a practical demonstration of the fact an extensive acreage is no longer necessary to support an average family, and land well selected, a comfortable home and living can be made upon a ten or twenty acre piece of land," said some of Sacramento's boosters earlier in 1884. They later added, "[A] score of the best businessmen in Sacramento, in 1888, formed and incorporated the Orange Vale Colonization Company."[16] Explicitly, the OVCC represented the community as not only a paradise inhabited by small farmers, but also as a thriving suburb of Sacramento where middle-class urbanites could escape the city's buzz. The *Sacramento Union* reported this sentiment in an 1888 article. "There is one especially great advantage to Sacramenteans in the opening up and development of these suburban tracts, and that is the facilities afforded business men for enjoying the comforts and privileges of country homes, without interference with their business interests."[17] The article boasted of plans for schools, churches, transportation routes, and homes. The trustees of the OVCC did not create a mere agricultural colony full of farmers. More daringly, they used an agricultural model of suburbanization not yet seen in Sacramento.

The OVCC featured thirty-six businesspersons from Sacramento, including McClatchy, Weinstock, Mott, Drescher, and Hall, all of whom served as the original directors. Robert Devlin, a prominent lawyer with a successful practice, served as a secretary. He helped draft Sacramento's third city charter as well; served as a member and president of the Board of State Prison Directors; and, in 1905, began a seven-year stint as the US district attorney for the northern district of California. George Katzenstein, listed as a director, also promoted the creation of the Orange Vale Water Company by 1896. He had a prominent business career. Most notably, beginning in 1868, Katzenstein served as manager of the Earl Fruit Company, the most extensive shipper of deciduous fruits in the state. The company and its heads divided the Orangevale land into ten-acre tracts and imported fruit trees from Florida.[18] The articles of incorporation for the OVCC list their purpose:

> To purchase and sell real property; to purchase, construct, maintain, and sell bridges, irrigating canals and ditches; to purchase, appropriate, maintain, and sell water rights and privileges; to purchase, erect, and sell buildings, fences, farms, and other land improvements; to cultivate and farm lands, and to lease, colonize, or sell the same; to borrow money, and to loan money upon ample security; and to do and to perform all and every act and thing necessary to the transaction of a general real estate and colonization business.[19]

These men advertised small lots to potential migrants throughout the United States, particularly in Northeastern and Midwestern states, such as Minnesota. They even included a morally upright anti-saloon clause. Yet when the national Depression hit, precipitated by the Panic of 1893, it largely eliminated migration to Orangevale, so the company dissolved in 1896.

Sacramento's boosters and other promoters, including the two newspapers, the *Sacramento Bee* and the *Sacramento Union*, endorsed the city's suburban areas, including Orangevale. Articles appeared intermittently in the two newspapers in the late 1890s and the early 1900s publicizing the growth of suburban areas. Both newspapers produced large, spirited booster pamphlets that, while designed to promote all of the Sacramento metro area, made sure to focus on the city's burgeoning suburban areas as well. The *Sacramento Bee* published *Sacramento County and Its Resources* in 1894, and the *Sacramento Union* published *Souvenir of the Capital of*

California in 1901. The *Bee,* with McClatchy as an editor, crammed its pages with sensational stories and pictures of Orangevale. Likewise, the *Union* bragged about the community's agricultural productivity and even highlighted local William Calder's Orangevale residence, called "The Palms," as an example of the beautiful suburban homes on Sacramento's fringe.

Orangevale, though its name suggests otherwise, produced all types of fruits. Several local histories show that Orangevale emerged as the center of Tokay grape production, a distinction it held until the development of Lodi's vineyards in the first decade of the twentieth century. Boosters did not limit their praise of the area's soil to its citrus-producing ability. They also named almonds, apricots, berries, figs, melons, peaches, pears, pecans, plums, prunes, and walnuts. Still, orange cultivation in the early years expanded significantly.

The OVCC organized in 1887 to rival Southern California's booming citrus industry. Although farmers planted many types of deciduous fruit trees during the 1880s and 1890s, it was, again, with hopes of competing with Southern California as the citrus center of the world that inspired many valley farmers along the eastern foothills to plant oranges. Farmers planted more than 250,000 orange trees and 50,000 lemon trees north of Sacramento between 1888 and 1891. Orangevale itself shipped twenty carloads of oranges and 200 carloads of deciduous fruits in 1899. Orangevale had 500 acres of oranges planted by 1894 and helped Sacramento County put forth the best display of budded oranges at the California State Mid-Winter Fair. Orange acreage blossomed to 2,000 by 1915 and reached its peak by 1925. By the late 1920s, however, the community's orange production dropped, mainly because consumers preferred orange juice to whole oranges and because a national law affected the sale of oranges not yet considered ripe. Farmers were further devastated when, in the winter of 1932, a frost swept the Sacramento Valley and killed most crops. This effectively ended Orangevale's period of agricultural productivity.

The early farming boom in Orangevale had a lasting effect, namely the development of community and social services.[20] Owing to the growth of community services, transportation, and infrastructure, Orangevale survived the lean Depression years between the freeze and World War II. Despite nature's blow, Orangevale's population exploded in the 1950s and 1960s, thanks to the rise of military bases, a shopping mall, and a nearby defense corporation that offered steady employment. The construction and widening of bridges over the American River, the development of highways (such as Interstate 80), and improvements to Orangevale's main street, Greenback Lane, helped sustain growth as well. So while Sacramento's dreams of suburbanization did not produce a sizeable population in Orangevale at the turn of the twentieth century, the boosters did get the necessary infrastructure that enabled Orangevale to become a more stereotypical bedroom community of Sacramento during the population boom that followed World War II.

The promotion of Fair Oaks as an imagined farmer's paradise began much like Orangevale.[21] For all practical purposes, the Fair Oaks colony first began on August 29, 1873, when the real-estate firm of Cox and Clarke acquired the large tract of land that became Fair Oaks for $20,500 and began to parcel land out for further purchase.[22] Subsequently, General Charles Howard, who publicly spoke of his concern that American farmers might "revert to the European peasant type," and James Wilson, an advocate of silver and currency reform in the age of Populist revolt, of the Howard & Wilson Publishing Company of Chicago, secured rights to sell land in the tract in 1895.[23] The company contracted with Cox and Clarke to market the land, although it does not appear that they received title.[24] Whatever the case, the Howard & Wilson Company had the land surveyed, mapped, and began to promote Fair Oaks.[25]

Like Orangevale, Howard & Wilson advertised Fair Oaks as an innovative agricultural colony and promised electricity and the construction of a bridge, suburban railway, and water system "for the homeseekers favor." "It is a section," the publishers wrote, "of sunny skies, sun-kissed fruit and pretty flowers, where bountiful nature has strewed her gifts with lavish hands." They also highlighted the successes of the neighboring colony of Orangevale and their own previously established colonies in Louisiana, North Carolina, and Florida.[26] Howard & Wilson featured Fair Oaks in its quarterly, *Farm, Field and Fireside*, as a place with no frosts, perpetually blooming flowers, temperatures rarely above ninety degrees or below thirty degrees, and, of course, no booze. About 300 people resided in Fair Oaks by 1897 and bought land in five, ten, and twenty-acre tracts at an average of thirty dollars per acre—ten dollars of which went to a fund for the building of a railway. By 1898, however, again in the midst of a national Depression, few came to Fair Oaks or Orangevale and investment began to diminish. Howard & Wilson withdrew from the colony and took with it unfulfilled promises of infrastructure.[27]

Because of the failure of the Howard & Wilson Company, and the dissolution of the OVCC, McClatchy formed the Fair Oaks Development Company (FODC) in 1900 to both keep the budding suburb from failure and to protect his investments in Orangevale and generate profits from the sale of land. With the sale of most of the land in Orangevale, the OVCC had dissolved in 1896 after the sale of Fair Oaks's tracts went to Howard & Wilson and because of Howard & Wilson's promise to supply a bridge, railway, and water system to the area. With the withdrawal of Howard & Wilson, however, came the need to develop a new group for promoting Fair Oaks and overseeing the construction of a bridge and other services.

McClatchy's concern for the need to protect his own investment and that of his fellow Orangevale investors had been mounting since at least 1899, just a year before the formation of the FODC. McClatchy had openly become frustrated with the delay of fruit shipments out of Orangevale. For example, in several letters to his groundskeeper in Orangevale, F. E. Linnell, McClatchy urged for no delays in the deployment of fruit from Orangevale. "We [Thomas B. Hall and McClatchy] also desire to impress upon you

FIGURE 10

"We Colonize the Earth," 1897. This booster piece appeared about Fair Oaks in the Howard & Wilson Company's 1897 *The Heart of California*. Notice what seems to be an angel or Miss Liberty guiding a team of trains like a horse master, echoing the theme of Manifest Destiny to go Westward. Courtesy of Center for Sacramento History, Paul Sandul Collection, No. 2006/030/277.

FIGURE 11

"Among the Scattered Oaks. Landscape View on the American River, in the Heart of California," 1897. This picturesque scene, and many like it, appeared in Howard & Wilson's 1897 booster brochure, *The Heart of California*, to flaunt Fair Oaks's rural landscape. Courtesy Center for Sacramento History, Paul Sandul Collection, no. 2006/030/606.

our wish that shipments be hurried forward as much as possible, not stopping for any reason so long as there is fruit to be shipped." On one occasion, McClatchy expressed concern over the delay of about 1,000 boxes of oranges, what he called "sufficiently colored for shipment," not shipping out in a timely manner. "Please understand that it is our wish that everything be pushed; so far as concerns the crop which is owned by or under the direction of the [OVCC's former proprietors] committee in any way, it is to be shipped at once." McClatchy, though, offered the defense that timely shipment benefited the entire Orangevale community. "Permit me to say also that the more Orangevale is built up the more work there will be for those who are there." He continued, "I say this in the interest of all parties [Orangevale citizens, fruit growers, and investors]. I have no present selfish motive in the matter since I have not offered my own tract for sale."[28]

In winter 1900, McClatchy assembled information concerning the shipment of fruit out of Orangevale to various markets as he developed plans to form the FODC. In letters to Linnell and Hall, as well as six identical letters to various Sacramento executives, McClatchy inquired if they knew how much fruit from Orangevale they had shipped to aid in his attempts to develop a railroad project to create a line from Fair Oaks to Sacramento.[29] At the same time, McClatchy attempted to foster a relationship with local merchants in hopes that a railway from Fair Oaks to Sacramento could advance such business—he even sent some fifty to seventy-five boxes of navel oranges for sale to a local grocer.[30] McClatchy and other landowners in Orangevale then sent a letter, signed by Hall, to other principal owners concerning "the matter of bids for the disposal of the Orangevale orange crop." Hall announced, "The best interests of the growers, both now and in the future, would be conserved by sending the fruit for sale to Messrs. Sgobel & Day, of New York, whose reputation for ability and integrity is at least equal to that of my firm in the fruit business."[31] McClatchy, as well as Hall, had clearly grown concerned about Orangevale. With Howard & Wilson now gone from Fair Oaks, McClatchy took the initiative in developing Orangevale's neighbor. Such an undertaking not only represented a good real estate venture, but also a means to securing vital infrastructure and services in Fair Oaks that would benefit Orangevale as well, particularly concerning fruit deployments, such as a bridge over the American River and rail service direct to Sacramento.

McClatchy drafted a contract for the FODC to acquire the rights to sell the Fair Oaks lands owned by Cox and Clarke in the same month he sent out letters inquiring about the shipment of fruit from Orangevale (April 1900). McClatchy outlined the terms for how the promotional company would acquire the rights to sell the land, how it would be sold, how the profits would both be split between the parties and go to paying for land improvements, and the conditions required on behalf of FODC to fulfill the terms of the contract. The construction of a railroad line and a water system that would benefit potential residents emerged as the primary conditions marked out for the FODC.[32] McClatchy devised a scheme for which he and his partners in

FIGURE 12

Fair Oaks, Sacramento County: In the Heart of the Fruit-Growing Section of California. Promotional pamphlets such as this 1900 booster publication were designed to attract so-called settlers and investors to the "promised land" of Fair Oaks. Notice here the boast of a supreme natural setting as well as advantages. Courtesy of Fair Oaks Promotional, Paul Sandul Collection, 2006/030/004, Center for Sacramento History, Sacramento, CA. Note that the Paul Sandul Collection, named after me obviously, is the result of my donating Fair Oaks history materials to the Center for Sacramento History. Specifically, as I worked on a book, *Fair Oaks*, for Arcadia publishers, I gathered many images from private individuals and local organizations. I donated all the materials I collected to the Center, as well as the Fair Oaks Historical Society. The Center's policy is simply to name the collection of materials they receive from a donation after the donor, which, though I collected it all from others, was me. Hence, this is why my name is attached to the collection.

the FODC—McClatchy, L. T. Hatfield, Charles Dickinson, Stephen Kieffer, and Walter Raymond—bought the rights, for one dollar, to have the "exclusive option to purchase the real property" in Fair Oaks for a period of five years at thirty dollars per acre. McClatchy also secured for the suburban boosters the rights to control water, the parceling of lots into at least five acres each, "except in town sites, which may be of any quantity," a right of way to the lands, including "a sufficient right of way for a railroad."[33] Like in Ontario, Sacramento's boosters were keen and perceptive businesspersons, experts in the law, and talented as they created organizations and companies that mirrored the innovative business practices of the day as they strove to maximize profits while limiting their liability.

With an agreement in place between Cox and Clarke and the FODC, the group officially incorporated on September 8, 1900, and set out to promote its investment under
the influence of its trustees. Joining treasurer McClatchy and secretary Hatfield, who
are discussed in more detail in the next chapter, were the Reverend Charles Dickinson,
Kieffer, and Raymond.[34] Dickinson, a preacher from Massachusetts (coincidentally
from Olmstead and Vaux's Brookline), served as president of the company and likely
provided the company with a good face, a sense of moral authority, and wholesome-
ness. Kieffer, an engineer for the city of Sacramento and a Fair Oaks resident, served
as the company's engineer and manager. He likely provided the company, as well as
Fair Oaks proper, a sense of modern technology and science. Raymond served as the
vice-president and brought, once again, an outside influence with much-needed capital
and resources. He co-founded the successful Boston advertising agency of Raymond
& Whitcomb in 1879 and ran a prestigious hotel in Pasadena. Thus, while serving
as president of Raymond & Whitcomb in 1900, he brought along his advertising
expertise and resources to promote Fair Oaks more effectively. He also provided the
FODC a valuable sense of entrepreneurialism.[35]

McClatchy immediately set out to draft a promotional booklet for Fair Oaks,
which not only helped the boosters' plans come to fruition, but also helped convince
the Sacramento Chamber of Commerce finance the construction of a bridge at Fair
Oaks.[36] The FODC's booklet—*Fair Oaks, Sacramento County: In the Heart of the
Fruit-growing Section of California*—promoted Fair Oaks as a paradise and a growing
suburb. It provided promotion for the entire Sacramento metropolitan region that
clearly pleased the Chamber. The booklet opened:

> This modest booklet, then, shall open for you the gate to the Promised Land.
> It shall tell you how you may become possessed of the home so attractive in
> your dreams, but far more charming in the reality. For the home it offers
> you, under the cloudless skies of Fair Oaks, the suburban residence district
> of Sacramento, in the heart of California, while sheltered by magnificent
> oaks and looking, as far as the eye can reach, over picturesque swells of
> orchards of orange, olive, and all kinds of deciduous fruits, and vineyards
> of Flame Tokay, yet offers all the conveniences of a developed and settled
> community, in fine residences, water piped under pressure to the door,
> educational facilities, postal delivery, suburban communication with a
> large city, etc.[37]

The FODC rigorously pitched Fair Oaks as an innovative agricultural colony. The
company highlighted the fruit market and claimed that the Sacramento region shipped
"seven-eighths of all the Californian deciduous fruits seen in Eastern markets." They
proclaimed, "Fair Oaks is also in the early fruit belt, much smaller in exact, which grows

and ships fruit earlier than all other sections of California." Land in the "Promised Land" also came cheap for those of "moderate means" and easily climbed in value. Furthermore, the booster tract claimed "Sacramento City is a great jobbing centre, supplying the northern portion of the State and Nevada with goods of all descriptions," and, in a likely appeal to women, who could certainly influence migration decisions, the department stores were "equal to anything in San Francisco."[38]

To provide further proof of the FODC's good faith and reliability, they invited, on the part of the Sacramento Chamber of Commerce, a searching investigation into its plans, methods, and responsibility, "because of the injury to Sacramento's standing that mismanagement of such an enterprise would entail." The Chamber, in a letter dated October 29, 1900, stated that the FODC had, on five points (land quality, integrity of the title, water rights, integrity of directors and managers, and plans for further development), "good" and "perfect" standing. Concerning the integrity of the directors and managers of the FODC, the Chamber stated, "The Directors and active managers of the company are men of excellent standing, of responsibility, and of well-known executive ability, and are well calculated to inspire confidence in the enterprise."[39]

Despite the promotional efforts of the FODC, the business venture still failed in the mind of McClatchy, and the suburban real-estate organization folded. McClatchy cited several reasons for the failure: they did not possess enough capital; they did not have many purchasers; the Southern Pacific Railroad delayed in building a road; and, most importantly, they failed to finalize a water deal. Without such a deal, the FODC could not fulfill its contract with Cox and Clarke because they were unable to secure a water system, which the deal required them to do. The deal between Cox and Clarke and the FODC also depended on the suburban real-estate organization selling 1,000 acres within the first year and securing the building of a main water pipe within two years. Although the FODC dissolved, they were nonetheless successful in bringing about the construction of a bridge and railway to Fair Oaks that not only serviced the local community in Fair Oaks, but also provided for improved transportation of fruit in Orangevale and the further development of both agriburbs. The freeze of 1932, however, altered the course of both communities' history. Again, the freeze hit during the Great Depression and effectively wiped out Fair Oaks and the other surrounding areas that were major producers of fruit. Fair Oaks continued to grow, however, but did not experience a so-called population boom until after World War II.[40]

LOW RESIDENTIAL DENSITY AND
LACK OF DIVISION BETWEEN CITY AND SUBURB

Again, utilizing the model of suburbs advanced by Jackson, recall that the first marker of suburbs concerns low residential density as well as the lack of separation (or development) between city and suburb. Concerning low residential density, population numbers in Orangevale and Fair Oaks at the turn of the twentieth century remained low. Fair Oaks, in fact, had only approximately 300 residents by 1897. Orangevale and Fair Oaks, listed together for a time under the Mississippi Township by the US Census that included neighboring Citrus Heights, recorded 630 residents in 1900; 1,225 in 1910; 1,651 in 1920; and remained well under 10,000 until the 1960s, all within an area of more than 9,000 acres.[41]

The lack of distinction between Fair Oaks/Orangevale and Sacramento, as mentioned before when discussing Ontario, has likely led to historians and other researchers failing to recognize agriburbs as rural suburbs. This is particularly so because, as argued, a common misconception of suburbs is that they resulted from a process of development spreading out of an urban core. Orangevale and Fair Oaks, then, like Ontario, challenge—and ultimately dismantle—such conceptions of suburbs and their contiguous location vis-à-vis central cities.[42]

Orangevale and Fair Oaks' noncontiguous location also reflected good advertising. Just like Ontario and its nearby city centers, Fair Oaks and Orangevale needed to connect to Sacramento City but remain separated by a rural physical landscape. Remember, that is what gave the communities their appeal. Their noncontiguous location represented a middle landscape.[43] Orangevale and Fair Oaks retained a level of urban amenities usually only found in long-settled communities. Orangevale and Fair Oaks, like Ontario, also appealed to the success of horticulture.[44] An article that appeared in the May 31, 1900, issue of the *Union* captured this:

> Mr. Taliaferro, who owns only an acre of land, has some of the novelties [the many different types of fruit that can grow in Fair Oaks], and is realizing large sales and good prices. Mr. Taliaferro is an expert gardener, and from his one acre, he has sold, for the first month, over $100 worth of fruit.[45]

In contrast to the appeal of the rural ideal of Orangevale and Fair Oaks, these communities remained relatively close in proximity to Sacramento, approximately twenty miles away. The developers promoted the construction of bridges, roads, and railways that connected those living in Orangevale and Fair Oaks to the "jobbing centre" of Sacramento. A May 8, 1888, article about Orangevale in the *Union* highlights the importance of this infrastructure: "If the Townsite is attractive, hardly less so is Orangevale Avenue, as the approach to this model colony is called, which skirts the banks of the American River as far as the Lincoln cut, and is romantic enough for anything. It is a well-graded road, with the picturesqueness of an avenue or park-walk. In its construction it has been found necessary to erect no less than three bridges, which are open to traffic already."[46] Orangevale and Fair Oaks thus became the outer poles of Sacramento City and could facilitate the suburbanization of the areas that lay between (categorically defying any conception of them as edge or satellite cities). Recall, in November 1900 the FODC produced their brash booster booklet, *Fair Oaks, Sacramento County*. The FODC promoted Fair Oaks as a rural paradise on the one hand and as a suburb close to the city of Sacramento on the other:

> Sacramento City is a great jobbing centre, supplying the northern portion of the State and Nevada with goods of all descriptions. It has four large department stores equal to anything in San Francisco, and shopping can be done there as economically and as satisfactorily as in the larger city. The schools of Sacramento, including the Crocker Art School, afford all their advantages to the residents of Fair Oaks.[47]

Another statement about a railway connecting Fair Oaks to Sacramento perhaps best reflects the boosters' rural suburban dreams. Under a title heading, "Suburban

FIGURE 13

Fair Oaks Railroad Station, ca. early 1900s. In the summer of 1901, Southern Pacific built a railway spur and station in Fair Oaks to help facilitate commuter traffic and crop shipments. In addition to such traffic, the railroad, in both Ontario and the Sacramento region, helped the boosters hold "excursions" whereby they would lead a group of prospective buyers to tour the area. In fact, in Orangevale, before the completion of the Fair Oaks Station, the boosters resorted to leading an excursion by carriage in the summer of 1890. Gracing the front page of the *Sacramento Daily Record-Union* on June 16, 1890, the story of eighteen "citizens of Sacramento" unfolds as they made their way to the new colony in the morning, not returning until 8 pm. They first stopped at the "Villa," a stick-style structure overlooking the American River, where "they were entertained by several officials of the colonization company." They were then "afforded an opportunity to ride leisurely over the entire colony tract," whereby the boosters made sure both they, and now the *Union* readers (à la good advertising), made note of the streets, avenues, water pipes, and "ornamental trees" in their subdivisions. Courtesy of Center for Sacramento History, Paul Sandul Collection, no. 2006/030/334.

Railroad," the FODC promoted Fair Oaks as a rural suburb that included the promise of agricultural productivity and profit:

> Railroad communication will be made between Fair Oaks and Sacramento City. The railroad, while intended mainly for quick suburban passenger traffic, will be also so built as to permit of the loading at the orchards of the regulation fruit cars, so that they can be drawn direct to Sacramento, and there attached to the eastbound fruit trains without the loss of time or the expense incurred in double handling.[48]

HOMES AND FAMILIES IN A PERFECT AND MODERN ENVIRONMENT

Home ownership emerged as one of the major draws in attracting migrants to Orangevale, Fair Oaks, and the Sacramento region in general. The advertising of home ownership clearly reflects the intention of the boosters to characterize Orangevale and Fair Oaks as suburban types because it most categorically fits the suburban ideal. According to the *Bee's* 1894 publication, *Sacramento County and its Resources,* the "primary object" of the OVCC's efforts "was to prepare the way and provide homes for the better class of colonists, who were invited to build their homes among our people, and thereby add to the material prosperity of the locality." The idea of property ownership and building one's own house appeared repeatedly as a selling point throughout the Orangevale and Fair Oaks boosterism. Frequently referring to houses in the language popularized by suburban architects and designers, such as *cottage homes, country homes, happy homes,* and *self-supporting small homes,* Sacramento's boosters extended the light narrative of successful property ownership to home building. Concerning Orangevale, the *Bee* stated, "Everything in and around the colony has this end view: the upbuilding and the prosperity of the small homes." Another promotional effort about Orangevale expressed this same view as the boosters declared, "Every large American city has a suburb—a place for country homes. . . . We must have a place for country homes [in the Sacramento area], and no more beautiful spot can be found than in Orangevale."[49] The FODC also boasted of home ownership opportunities in the newly established suburb. On the opening page of the company's publication in 1900, a "modest booklet," they announced that it "shall tell you how you may become possessed of the home so attractive in your dreams, but far more charming in the reality." They continued by further describing the suburban dream of Fair Oaks:

> For the home it offers you, under the cloudless skies of Fair Oaks, the suburban residence district of Sacramento, in the heart of California, while sheltered by magnificent oaks and looking, as far as the eye can reach, over picturesque swells of orchards of orange, olive, and all kinds of deciduous

fruits, and vineyards of Flame Tokay, yet offers all the conveniences of a developed and settled community, in fine residences, water piped under pressure to the door, educational facilities, postal delivery, suburban communication with a large city, etc. It shall tell you how money put into such a home may yet be made to pay as a business investment, and in a few years maintain the wife and babies as well.[50]

Home ownership in Orangevale and Fair Oaks as a selling point coupled with the benefits of these sites as actual places. Sacramento's boosters packaged home ownership in relation to the place of Orangevale and Fair Oaks while they advertised and had developed amenities and infrastructure that purportedly enhanced the quality of these places in comparison to other places, such as Southern California. The boosters in Sacramento, like in Ontario, persistently highlighted the power of place, its rurality, and agricultural prowess, "in terms of horticulture," they said. They painted a picture of small-home cottages and self-supporting farms dotting an aesthetically pleasing rural landscape that included a soil perfect for farming and playing and an environment atop the soil perfect for sustaining such farming and play. They, too, promoted Orangevale and Fair Oaks as the manifestation and fulfillment of some geography of the ideal. Remember that, according to the boosters, the natural environment of these agriburbs allowed for the superior growing of most produce. These fruits were not only superior in their quality and a commercial advantage for a farmer producing for market, but they

FIGURE 14

Broadley Home, Fair Oaks, ca. early 1900s. The Broadley home was built in 1898 on Sunset Avenue in Fair Oaks. This home, like the Oakley's home in Ontario, was the ideal of the middle-class single-family house among orchards and trees. Courtesy of Center for Sacramento History, Paul Sandul Collection, no. 2006/030/665.

also came to maturity quicker than in Southern California, yet another type of advantage for the commercial well-being of a farmer. In an article describing an excursion in the summer of 1890, the *Union* extolled Orangevale's fertile soil. "All the gentlemen in the party versed in horticulture declared that they had never seen more rapid and healthier growth than the majority of trees and all the vines in the colony tracts shown, though none of them have been in the ground three years, and many but one year." They added, "[N]o Southern California colony of equal age ever made so good a showing." In the 1900 publication of *Fair Oaks*, the boosters also praised superior climate, topography, and soil. They contended that Fair Oaks had just as good a climate as, if not superior to, Southern California and Italy. They added, "[U]npleasant extremes of heat and cold" do not threaten either crop or comfort. Purity of air, healthy rainfall, and nearby rivers and ground water also allowed for the success of farming with or without irrigation.[51]

"You are interested in California, of course. Who is not?" asked the boosters in the *Fair Oaks* booklet. They continued, "You have probably entertained the wish, if not actually the hope, of some day acquiring in that land of sunshine and flowers, far from snow, blizzard, and sunstroke, a home." In Fair Oaks, the boosters promised that one could live "in God's own country." Orangevale and Fair Oaks's charm lay in its natural environs—which would have surely been the envy of the Romantics—providing its residents the opportunity for a home among orchards and vineyards. Orangevale and

FIGURE 15

The Woman's Thursday Club of Fair Oaks, 1912. The Woman's Club of Fair Oaks organized in 1902 for the purpose of "social intercourse and intellectual betterment of its members." The Woman's Club, still active, has participated in innumerable activities in Fair Oaks, from donation drives to tree planting and entertainment programs. Note the dress of the women and the fashion emblematic of the middle class of the era. Courtesy of Center for Sacramento History, Paul Sandul Collection, no. 2006/030/255.

Fair Oaks, along the American River, had a "picturesque bluff" and their "thrift and comfort were apparent everywhere, and the scene was one well calculated to enlist the admiration of everyone capable of enjoying the beauties of nature." In fact, said the boosters, Orangevale and Fair Oaks were unrivaled in California when it came to scenery and soil productiveness, not to mention urban amenities in an otherwise country landscape with a healthful climate. "It was spring when we arrived in Fair Oaks," recalled Robert Broadley on his family moving to Fair Oaks in 1897. "The wild flowers were in bloom, and I thought we had surely arrived in Paradise." Perhaps it was paradise, because people reportedly lived longer in Fair Oaks than anywhere else, which the boosters pointed out through a profile of Victorianno, a 136-year-old Native American from the region.[52]

Sacramento's boosters bestowed Orangevale and Fair Oaks with all the symbols of rurality (i.e., light narrative) without necessarily assigning them all the symbols of an isolated rural hinterland (i.e., shadow narrative). They infused Orangevale and Fair Oaks with all the symbols of urbanity without the city as well. Orangevale and Fair Oaks were therefore the perfect mix of city and country so romanticized by the suburban image-makers. Rambles, parks on the beautiful bluffs overlooking the river, and shade trees of eucalyptus and palm lined the communities' streets and "picturesque" avenues. One could hunt quail and jackrabbit as easily as one could catch a ride on the train and go shopping in the department stores that purportedly rivaled anything found in San Francisco, and "shopping [could] be done there as economically and as satisfactorily as in the larger city." You could even visit the Metropolitan Theater via train to Sacramento to take in a show. Rambles and parks laid adjacent to towns with laid-out plots and roads, including curvy roads like Winding Way, which had steel pipes pumping water underneath for the benefit of irrigation and the family home. "The force of the water," reported the *Union* of Orangevale in 1890, is "sufficient to throw an openbutt stream from a hydrant from six to ten feet perpendicularly into the air, and with an inch nozzle to reach the second-story of any building." Among orchards and vineyards, schools, churches, clubs, transportation routes, good roads, electricity, merchant stores, and a water system offered the "luxuries" and "conveniences" so extolled by Olmsted that made a rural existence not only tolerable but supposedly superior to anything found in the heart of the American city. On top of that, according to the boosters, "These evidences of social life will rapidly multiply." While Orangevale and Fair Oaks had good roads comparable to anything found in the city, theirs had shade trees and traversed a beautiful countryside. "Along the pleasant avenues, sixty feet wide," said the boosters concerning Orangevale in 1894, "were hedges of Monterey cypress, with here and there a dark-leaved eucalyptus, or a bright-green fan palm extending its broad hands over the soil as though in the act of blessing it." While Orangevale and Fair Oaks had parks in which to take in all Mother Nature had to offer, they had a town center with dry goods stores, a post office, hotel, banks,

FIGURE 16

Fair Oaks Bridge, 1902. The original bridge over the American River at Fair Oaks, though washed out by a flood, but ultimately replaced, both served the boosters' advertisement of Fair Oaks and the farmers they were supposed to serve with commuter transportation to Sacramento and crop shipment. Courtesy of Center for Sacramento History, Paul Sandul Collection, no. 2006/030/301.

and a railroad depot, complete with connecting bridges that could whisk them away at a minute's notice with "no trouble reaching the city at about any hour of the day." While Orangevale and Fair Oaks had the best class of people, a class of entrepreneurs comparable to the supposed best of the city, their residents would not succumb to the evils of the bottle, because both enforced temperance. Residents could go to church, join the Woman's Club, learn in school, but they could never go to the saloon or barroom, and they would never have to fear the crime and vice plaguing American cities.[53]

THE MIDDLE CLASS IN A MIDDLE LANDSCAPE AGAIN

According to Jackson, the final distinguishing aspects of suburbs are middle-class status and commuter transportation. Class status and aspirations certainly did provide a major enticement for drawing migration to Orangevale and Fair Oaks. While much of the work force in Orangevale and Fair Oaks did consist of Asian Americans and other minorities, these agriburb communities remained predominantly white and middle class residentially. Yet these white middle-class suburbanites were not simply commuters working in Sacramento City or elsewhere and only sleeping at home. Orangevale and Fair Oaks were not merely bedroom communities. While boosters undoubtedly designed Orangevale and Fair Oaks to appeal to a white middle class or those aspiring to such status, residents had to sustain their middle-class lifestyle by tilling the soil as scientific farmers.

The railroad facilitated Orangevale's and Fair Oaks's viability as agricultural colonies. Reminisces of old-time residents recorded by the local newspaper in the 1950s, the *San Juan Record*, mention some of the particulars of rail travel in the early history of Orangevale and Fair Oaks. On one hand, these recollections reinforce the notion of the possibility for commuter travel; that is, these suburbs did indeed function, in part, as bedroom communities. Emma E. Bramhall, for example, recalled, "When we first came here to Fair Oaks [in 1902] there was one train a day to Sacramento, which left early in the morning and returned in the afternoon, leaving Sacramento at 3 o'clock." She also noted, "There were two ways to drive into Sacramento": down the unpaved road of Folsom Boulevard or over the San Juan Grant itself before Fair Oaks Boulevard opened in 1918 and connected to J Street. Civil Engineer and prominent Fair Oaks resident Stephen Kieffer wrote in 1902 about the details and importance of the construction of a bridge over the American River at Fair Oaks that linked to a railway. He concluded, "At last Fair Oaks, with a magnificent bridge spanning the river and a convenient train service connecting with the capital city of the State, was leaving behind the 'good old days' of the pioneering period and was beginning to look to the future as the great suburban district of the capital city—a place of fine homes."[54]

Despite the presence of the railroad for commuter travel, the railroad's importance clearly lay with the service it provided farmers hoping to reach market and turn a profit. Agriculture in Orangevale and Fair Oaks were the means to achieve improved socioeconomic status. The railroad allowed farmers to ship more efficiently, cost effectively, and to all points and markets, reportedly, around the nation. Progressive

FIGURE 17

Landis Packinghouse, ca. 1890s. A rare glimpse into an Orangevale packinghouse in the late nineteenth century. Often it took the entire family to prepare fruit (and, more often, hired labor). Here the Landis family is packing boxes for the Earl Fruit Company. Notice the workers include men, women, and children and, whether for photographic reasons or not, symbolizes the small-family farm ideal in agriburbs and California's agricultural colonies. Center for Sacramento History.

extraordinaire Harris Weinstock even worked to make sure they would get both a better deal once in market and better protection en route (discussed more in the next chapter). Therefore, while providing "communication" between "Fair Oaks and Sacramento City" for "quick suburban passenger traffic," the railroad also permitted "the loading at the orchards of the regulation fruit cars, so that they can be drawn direct to Sacramento, and there attached to the eastbound fruit trains without the loss of time or the expense incurred in double handling."[55]

Sacramento's boosters specifically targeted a middle-class audience by publicizing the then all-too-familiar agricultural wonderland ideal that encompassed horticulture, science, and technology at that time. First, the price of land in Orangevale and Fair Oaks, while not dirt cheap, was advertised as low and, more importantly, a solid business investment; in the case of Fair Oaks, for $125 to $200 per acre for "acreage lots" of five to ten acres, or for "town lots" of one-half to one acre at as low as $250, it "offer[ed] the lowest high-grade lands in California." In the case of Orangevale, the boosters stated, "Not the least important feature of the enterprise is that a person with only a few hundred dollars as a beginning can, by laying aside each month a small portion of his salary or earnings, soon become the owner of a tract in Orange Vale." Even better,

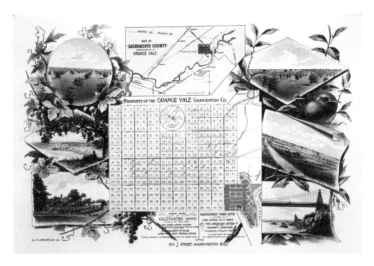

FIGURE 18

Map of "Orange Vale," ca. 1892. This map and its images show how the land was originally conceived and how Orangevale was advertised as a thriving community with streets along a grid pattern (urbanity), meticulously planned parcels, profuse orchards (rurality), and a bridge across the American River to access market. The map and images represent the commixture of traditional agrarianism and the embrace of modern technology and design. Furthermore, the naming of the streets in Orangevale arouses both the spirit of its rural and modern narrative. As the *Sacramento Union* reported in September 1887, Orangevale's roads "are appropriately designated by names signifying the different varieties of fruit for which the colony expects to become famous." The north-south roads, which residents still traverse today, have nut trees for names, and the east-west roads have shade trees for names, with expectations for Main and Central Avenues, which were named after water lines. Courtesy Center for Sacramento History, no. 2002/092/001.

they could "thereafter secure freedom from all other occupation, if desired, except the supervision of this property."[56]

Second, the improvement of the land is what brought wealth by way of cultivating orange groves, almond trees, and lush grapes. "As an example of the fecundity of the soil of Orange Vale Colony," said the boosters, "it may be stated that H. Carmichael sold his first crop of almonds on five acres from four-year-old tress for $625." To accomplish this image of robust fertility and growth, the boosters fervently advertised how much they invested in the community, providing all of the valued social services necessary for a middle-class lifestyle along with easy, quick access to market, which in turn would produce the income necessary to maintain a middle-class lifestyle. They reportedly hired horticulture experts to oversee and offer sage advice. They convinced Sacramento County to pay for the construction of bridges and even managed to finagle the Southern Pacific Railroad Company to pay for the construction of a road. They also had other roads built, and they sent sample fruits to various markets to supposedly whet the appetite for, and enhance the reputation of, fruit grown in the "Heart of California."[57]

ORANGEVALE AND FAIR OAKS AS AGRIBURBS

In every respect, Orangevale and Fair Oaks were to become, in suburban historian Robert Fishman's phrase, *bourgeois utopias* of the middle class. The novelty of the Sacramento boosters' scheme, of course—as found in Ontario, Fresno, Runnymede, and other places described by California historians as in tune with the "horticultural ideal"— was that suburban middle-class lifestyle came by way of agriculture. According to the boosters, the key to unlocking the harvest of a highly rewarding crop and thereby middle-class lifestyle required more than just an ability to use plow and hoe. It required, as one could guess by now, "brains" and "intelligence." Knowing when, where, and what to plant were essential as the boosters bombarded their literature with information on fruit types, picking and canning information, railroad services and their benefit, and the superiority of the soil and climate. The mere fact that one showed the intellectual foresight and strength to locate to Orangevale and Fair Oaks in the first place was ostensibly a sign of their intelligence because it, according to the boosters, revealed a man, and sometimes woman, of business savvy and acumen. Sacramento's boosters therefore massaged, yet again, the egos of an aspiring middle-class audience. By working hard, the agriburbanites of Orangevale and Fair Oaks were producers, a producer class, and not a debtor class (which was how the boosters described most other farmers in the nation). "The man with modest means can, with brains and energy," said the boosters in the 1900 *Fair Oaks* publication, "make and maintain at Fair Oaks an attractive home as readily as a millionaire." By utilizing their intelligence by specializing in the growth of cash crops made possible and more profitable through advancements in horticulture and scientific agriculture, agriburbanites reflected the essence of a "most desirable class of residents" and hence hyped as refined, cultured, and devoted to family, home, God, education, and democracy.[58] They clearly loved nature but welcomed modern luxuries and conveniences that stood as hallmarks of modernity and middle-class status. In fact, the boosters painted the influx of a "most desirable class of residents" as good for the entire region and positioned it as justification for the use of county resources in the upbuilding and promotion of Orangevale and Fair Oaks. Theirs was a metropolitan vision of growth good for everyone:

> Sacramento is indeed favored by her surroundings, and cannot help but becoming a great center of business and population. It behooves her people of means to foster and encourage all such enterprises as that of the Orangevale Association, and similar ones now being carried out nearer to the city. Every dollar expended in developing enterprises of this character acts as a magnet in attracting hither home-seekers from the East and less-favored sections of the coast, and will in the near future through the increased business and wealth of this community.[59]

The Sacramento boosters, as well as the boosters in Ontario, obviously worked to make their vision for growth a reality. Without them, agriburbs, yet alone the California Dream as we know it, would not exist. Therefore, while most attention until now has specified the constituent parts of what made these agricultural colonies, in fact, suburban types, the boosters themselves are yet even more evidence. Namely, as boosters-cum-real-estate speculators, these boosters came together as a local cohort to stimulate growth and make a buck. They did this as they also championed various reform causes to which the agriburb seemed to belong. To understand better, then, how the agriburb came about, the boosters themselves need a face, contextualizing them and their lives so that their real-estate activities and desires to create an agriburb manifest more clearly, and hopefully, undeniably.

WELCOME TO THE GROWTH MACHINE

The tendency among historians to focus on commercial incentives behind boosterism may be due not only to the actual importance of economic interests in local affairs but also to the fact that noncommercial motives tend to become buried or even indistinguishable when combined with commercial ones.

ELVIN HATCH, 1979[1]

I N 1976, SOCIOLOGIST HARVEY MOLOTCH penned a landmark essay, birthing the field of urban sociology, "The City as a Growth Machine: Toward a Political Economy of Place."[2] His thesis is simple: coalitions of land-based elites (i.e., growth machines), tied to the economic possibilities of place, drive local politics in their quest to expand the local economy and accumulate wealth. The economic and political essence of cities is growth. The boosters of Ontario, Orangevale, and Fair Oaks, as the terms *boosterism* and *boosters* already imply, represented such growth-machine coalitions. Also called *place entrepreneurs* or *rentiers*, these boosters unmistakably organized cooperatively to improve their prospects.

Growth-machine members typically rally together as organizations, or further work through other organizations, to benefit collectively (e.g., organized as a private business they often receive government subsidies and/or tax breaks—aka welfare), utilizing benefits.[3] Growth-machine members, like boosters, typically are local landowners, real-estate speculators, or astute businesspeople in a position to profit from the specific land use in an area. Some rather wealthy, politically connected, and powerful people take an interest in land use and exchange and seek to drive policies in the seemingly unending capitalist quest to make money. Regardless of precise political affiliation, moral philosophy, or specific business type (i.e., growth might attract competitors for any particular business attached to the growth machine apparatus), most place entrepreneurs agree growth is good. They even portray their effort as a public good because it supposedly increases economic activity that, á la trickledown hopes, benefits all.

Agriburb boosters formed growth-machine coalitions to bolster their development goals in budding metropolitan regions. Together, these boosters organized land, water, and railway companies, participated in local, regional, and state politics, created local municipal organizations such as the chamber of commerce, and participated in numerous reform and social clubs. These connections included not only links to the local government but also to governors of California and leaders of various corporations and institutions. While investing their own capital, they formed alliances and worked through government and corporations in an effort to spread and redistribute costs.

Scholars mix in their acceptance of a growth machine to describe the development of urban and metropolitan landscapes, including their suburbs and rural hinterlands. Many scholars concede that growth truly is the economic essence of most localities, and coalitions of land-based elites drive it. Yet most do not like what they see. They contend that in promoting the economic possibilities of place, while the economy can expand, it does so sometimes unevenly and comes at a terrible cost. Ultimately, new homeowners arise as a result, and they become part of the elite as well. Further, their interests narrow on property values. Community thus means homogeneity of race, class, and, especially, home values, and, even worse, the most important social movement in suburbs and metropolises is that of affluent homeowners engaged in the protection of home values and neighborhood exclusivity.[4] Pro-growth policies created a modern suburban middle class fervently opposed to growth, creating an antigrowth essence of place in many of America's more affluent, white, middle-class suburbs. Growth coalitions have also received blame for the alteration and even destruction of the physical environment, often coinciding with the expansion of an economy that has organized vast spaces and connected them to a larger regional, even global, one.[5] The growth machine capitalists have further displaced minorities in the more recent postindustrial era by supporting preservation and revitalization efforts in the areas most minorities live, thereby dislocating them.[6]

Other scholars, who still agree growth characterizes urban and suburban areas, do not portray growth coalitions as so one-dimensional and, therefore, complicate a solely profit-driven analysis. Some see light, or at least a few sunbeams. For example, while historian Sam Bass Warner Jr. certainly lamented the exploitation of the less powerful and the manipulation of land-law use, he also bemoaned a heritage of viewing the land as a basis for liberty rather than as a community resource. Therefore, while one could argue ideology and economics go together, and they do, ideology (like sociologist Max Weber argued about the spirit of capitalism generally) can receive as much blame for the consequences of unrestricted city growth.[7] Historians such as Arthur Schlesinger Sr., Eric Monkkonen, and geographer Robert Lewis have also looked beyond economics to contend that cities, suburbs, and their leaders often, and innovatively, created new infrastructure to deal with either an increasing population concentration or phenomena beyond their control, or a negotiation of both.[8]

The growth machine can be triumphant when placed under the correct microscope. Schlesinger argued the city helped to create a more dynamic culture and collective human experience. Historian Lee M. A. Simpson concluded women were important participants in California's growth machine and, instead of harming the population, made possible policies that enhanced the quality of life for the general population, as women worked to beautify their cities, promote images of cosmopolitanism, and stimulate tourism.[9] Finally, the dean of California boosterism, Richard Orsi, long ago pointed us to a better way of understanding boosters without succumbing to a narrow economic-only point of view or slipping into hagiography. First, in his 1973 dissertation, "Selling the Golden State," then in several articles and, more recently, *Sunset Limited* (2005), Orsi has shown how boosters and huge corporations like Southern Pacific made substantial efforts not only to profit for profit's sake but to also promote agriculture, land ownership, water resources, sustainability, and conservation.[10]

Other scholars argue that growth is not the only thing at work in the development of cities and suburbs. These scholars have focused on entrepreneurs' seemingly sincere desires to raise society itself. Historians who emphasize interests on dynamics other than growth have attempted to characterize the by-now infamous capitalist elite in terms of reform and social control (i.e., Gramscian hegemony). While reform and control are terms with negative connotations, historians discuss an urban landscape where those in power have not necessarily pursued growth in hopes to raise their fortunes, but rather in hopes of spiritual and social growth. Middle-to-upper-class elites work through both private and public institutions to impact reform and foster social control. Therefore, while Schlesinger saw this as a triumph of innovation, historian Robert Wiebe saw this as the "sinking of the classes."[11]

The work of those who subscribe to the growth-machine theory reveals an undercurrent of anger and a dismissal of the notion that good intentions might have been involved and could be worthy of more consideration. Indeed, as depicted in such studies, it seems that the elites of the growth machine rarely seem to seek change, reform, or development because of humanitarian motives. In the classic Marxist sense, they seek development and social control to maintain and increase their own power. Unlike the Marxist ruling classes, however, which conflate their class interests with the general welfare, the growth-machine elite is Foucauldian because development is consciously, albeit often anonymously, about self-interest. While some scholars do name names, like Jeremy Bentham for Michel Foucault or Cardinal Roger Mahony for geographer Mike Davis, it soon becomes evident they are merely symbolic. What is truly lurking behind all the symbolism, the shifts in power, and determining forces, is the old culprit of capitalism, which is all the more vicious because it refuses to go away.[12]

So what were the motivations of California's boosters, as growth-machine members? Simpson argues, "[B]oosters likely believed their own rhetoric."[13] Again, Orsi, not to mention Kevin Starr, argue the same. Warner also reminded us, "Today suburbs are increasingly assigned all the evils of American society." He continued, "[B]ut in the late nineteenth century they created a wide spread sense of achievement."[14] All these observations reflect two opposing views of suburbs that open the door for considering an alternate vision of boosterism and the growth machine. Specifically, the well-chronicled consequences of America's move to suburbia and metropolitan growth has given way to the possible discounting of the more well-meaning intentions of those who toiled to make it possible and those who actually moved there. Orsi, Simpson, and Starr are right. The prevailing focus on the assumed evils of suburbia and metropolitanization eclipses the motives and explanations offered by boosters for their choices and business transactions. Recall sociologist Elvin Hatch's lament at the start of this piece. He said the same. Historians often focus too narrowly on economic interests and fail to identify noneconomic motives.

When we do learn about the boosters and read their writings, for example, we read about a host of issues and concerns that center on, among other things, the rural ideal, home, family, class, and urban crisis, which, admittedly, do raise fears of race and class bias and a longing for exclusivity. Regardless, something more, something else is present in the residential choices of most Americans besides fear and prejudice, if those two are factors at all.[15] The motivations of the boosters, such as those of Ontario, Orangevale, and Fair Oaks, are multifaceted and complex too.

A review of some of the boosters' biographies reveals not only shared profit-driven speculation but also involvement in reform agendas, rhetoric articulated in the language of raising society, and, seemingly, a genuine desire to create a better community for the benefit of most residents. Economic motives are not always indistinguishable from, nor antithetical to, social agendas (and one is not always more pure than the other). A gross desire for profit needs not to be so gross or exclusive from humanitarian or noneconomic motives. The growth machine needs not always be so evil, so villainous; it might just simply be. Ultimately, the boosters envisioned agriburbs as middle landscapes. The boosters themselves seemed to genuinely believe in the rural and suburban ideals and the narrated power of horticulture to improve society and foster better lives—or at least white people's lives—thus, suggesting their boosterism was more than merely a strategic rhetorical device put to the service of their capital interests. Agriburbs thus manifested in the desire for profit and for developing a better society, even if the boosters' utopian visions seem either passé or repulsive to us today.

Short biographies of the boosters also help address a few other critiques of the growth machine.[16] First, the growth-machine analysis is often cast, as odd as it may sound, as too empirical. Some charge it as more about data collection and fitting the proper pieces into a puzzle than a theory. Whatever the case, as biographies of agriburb boosters reveal, their correlation to a growth machine does pay dividends and exposes a cohort of land-based businesspersons and others coming together to profit and reform society.

Some say the growth machine is too local, missing the top-down doings of influential actors and structures at state, national, or international scales. In contrast, some see the growth machine as too broad. The complaint is that the growth focus narrows too intensely on the top-down doings of elites. Doing so ignores marginalized members of society and lacks a focus on quotidian practice and lifestyle, the so-called poetics of everyday behavior, and the appropriation of space by others. As agriburb boosters again make clear, however, they most certainly account for larger trends at the state, national, and even international scales, most evidently in their use of the rural and suburban ideals, not to mention the California Dream. Likewise, as argued in the final chapters about memory, boosterism has had an effect on the lives of everyday suburbanites as evidenced in their use of the past plainly spoken in the language first created by the boosters—*machine language*, if you will.

Lastly, some charge that the growth machine is no longer applicable in a postindustrial era, especially with the rise of a New Left, "spaceship earth" consciousness, liberal environmentalism, or even restrictive right-wing antigrowth movements. To boot, many also charge that the growth machine is not applicable outside the United States, even in Western Europe as growth polices there have been historically far more centralized. These critiques have merit. Yet they remind us that the boosters under analysis in the following pages are, again, a product of time and space.

CHAPTER FIVE

THE BOOSTERS

*Welcome my son, welcome to the machine. What did you
dream? It's alright we told you what to dream.*

PINK FLOYD, "WELCOME TO THE MACHINE," 1975[1]

SACRAMENTO'S PLACE ENTREPRENEURS

"The world is moved by action," proclaimed Sacramento booster Harris Weinstock in
a lecture before students of the College of Commerce in San Francisco in 1905. He
continued, "[A]nd only he who has the power of action can hope to make progress—can
hope to leave a 'foot-print on the sands of time.'" Weinstock added, "Thrift, fidelity,
industry, brains and conscience are receiving higher rewards today than ever before,
and are destined to receive still higher rewards in the days to come." He advocated
the philosophical and sociological view of a racialized social Darwinism and asked,
"What think you is the chief cause . . . leading to the superiority of the Anglo-Saxon."
He answered, "It is none other than his power of initiative, and the power to do things.
The power of self-reliance and self-helpfulness." He proclaimed, "You may throw an
Anglo-Saxon where you will and, as a rule, he will fall on his feet." He proudly declared,
"Whatever progress the Anglo-Saxon has made beyond that of other races is largely
due to his spirit of independence, self-help, and self-reliance; to his power of initiative,
and his readiness to assume responsibilities."[2]

Weinstock's speech exemplifies the mindset of the consortium of boosters who
joined him in founding Orangevale and Fair Oaks, as well as the boosters in Ontario.
Weinstock and his associates, and George Chaffey and his, were not just boosters but
also growth-machine members who treated land as a speculative venture, a space on
which they left their collective footprint. As they implemented the "power of initiative,"
these boosters commodified place and packaged it for consumption, which, according to
spatial theorists like David Harvey, structures "the construction of built environments."[3]

Ontario, with the Ontario boosters, and Orangevale and Fair Oaks, with their
boosters, grew out of growth interests. These communities were vehicles through which
the boosters sought to meet their interest-driven needs. The boosters in both Ontario

and Sacramento actively speculated in real estate and relied on their ability to change successfully the relationship of one place—an agriburb—to other places. They packaged an agriburb as a desirable commodity—to tell you what to dream, if you will, to stimulate consumer desire. As place entrepreneurs who desired to boost profits, these boosters organized collectively. In their respective locales, together these entrepreneurs organized land, water, and railway companies, they ran political and bureaucratic offices, and formed local institutions. The boosters, therefore, attracted the construction and development of urban amenities and the infrastructure that, in their own words, benefited the entire region despite the fact that investments and capital flowed to and primarily benefited only their respective suburban interests. These are growth-machine cohorts who, like many others, saw the entire metropolis (Sacramento) or region (Southern California), not just isolated places, as the stage in which they operated—and needed to operate.

The profit motive certainly motivated the boosters in their development of agriburb communities. In fact, their development of Ontario, Orangevale, and Fair Oaks was essential cogs in a wider wheel of publicity for both the Sacramento metropolis and the Southern California regions, the principle areas surrounding Los Angeles. At the turn of the twentieth century, these boosters strived to benefit from a broader endorsement of California, as exemplified by the writings of boosters covered in chapter two. Their goal was to compete with other regions to attract migrants and investors to their communities. These boosters recognized a far-reaching business opportunity when they saw one. Built on the backs of boosters championing California in general, agriburb boosters worked diligently to take advantage and construct an image of their places as model places to live that equaled, if not surpassed, anywhere else in California.

While the Ontario boosters, like Ontario itself, receive a lot of coverage in the historical literature already, short biographies of the boosters there and in Sacramento still reveal sophisticated businesspersons engaging in a myriad of business-related activities, political institutions, and economic ventures throughout their lifetimes. We can place the agriburb business ventures, the formation of corporations and trusts, within the lifetime of the boosters' activities as they continually involved themselves in speculation and creative endeavors designed to produce profit. Following the lead of anthropologists and those who advocate "life history," the emphasis here is on the notion that people experience events throughout their lifetime and, therefore, any given event or action requires scholars to appraise such events or actions in the context of an individual's entire lifetime.[4] While one might see this line of inquiry as going off the rails from spelling out how agriburbs were a unique suburban type, the point is complementary.

By pulling away the layers, we come to reveal that the boosters' motivations for promoting their respective agriburbs centered on making a buck. Ultimately, a key defining feature of an agriburb, like most planned suburban developments, is that it had a growth-machine cohort working to sell it.

The goal of life history studies, particularly as expressed by ethnographers, sociologists, and historians, such as John Dollard, is to understand better an individual's particular action, and hence the scholar "will peer down the long avenue of the individual life to see how the present day event matured."[5] Life history aims to historicize the events or actions of an individual's life. This includes analyzing the life activities of any given individuals and appraising their actions within the context of the culture in which they live, the family they were born into, and the friends they keep, and the social context in which they act. Additionally, it is important to take note of what, if any, social structures influenced the activities and thoughts (e.g., the profit motive) of an individual.

Critics of life history, such as sociologist Pierre Bourdieu, contend that such an analysis disregards local or personal knowledge and diminishes the role of human agency. Bourdieu would likely contend Dollard's and others' criterion for studying life history "reduces historical agents to the role of 'supporters' (*Träger*) of the structure and reduces their actions to mere epiphenomenal manifestations of the structure's own power to develop itself and to determine and overdetermine [*sic*] other structures."[6] A further problem is that people are not static, the same today as yesterday. People evolve, grow, and change, for better or worse notwithstanding. Nevertheless, while people certainly are not static, admittedly, what is notable in the biographies of the boosters of agriburbs is how consistent they were in pursuing profit throughout their lives.

Finally, the critique that life histories diminish human agency needs to be turned on its head, especially concerning growth machines. Looking at the boosters helps us return to an agency-centered analysis of the growth machine that attempts to overcome the problem critics of life history raise. Far from the old damned if you do, damned if you don't lament, looking at the lives of the individual boosters returns a sense of human agency to the phenomena under analysis. At times, yes, boosters were supporters of the structure—of the growth-machine apparatus and capitalist system. Much of their activities bears that out, and no disregard for life history should come from saying so. At other times, they were clearly interested in much more; they shaped the growth machine as much as they were shaped by it.

Several leading questions prompted the desire to produce, if not full-blown life histories, then short biographies of these boosters. First, *to what extent do the life histories of the boosters both complement and contradict the notion that they were actually members of a growth machine?* Namely, *to what extent do biographies of the boosters reveal local elites engaged in the types of activities attributed to growth machines.* Second, *besides selling their agriburbs, to what extent do these boosters reflect an even broader packaging of place on the metropolitan or regional scales and, if so, what does that mean?* Finally, *besides any economic motivations, what other motivations—be they determined by social structures or indicative of autonomy—are reasonably inferable from the actions of the boosters?*

In answering these questions, the first seems answered already: yes, these boosters' biographies, and the general historic context in which they lived, reveal that they sought profit throughout their lifetimes. About the second, undressing these boosters reveals that suburbs, suburbanization, and growth-machine activity do not take place within a vacuum, but rather upon a metropolitan or regional scale, which connects city, suburbs, and so-called rural hinterlands. Finally, a more complete undressing of the lives and historic context of the boosters aims at something few studies have attempted before as it concerns growth-machine boosters. The goal is to reveal, as best as possible, the motivations of these boosters in developing agriburbs. Their biographies provide a chance to uncover why agriburbs appeared at all, moving beyond—but still including—the profit motive. Rather, the development of agriburbs as suburbs followed the logic of smart business on the one hand and seemingly personal beliefs on the other. Agriburbs were suburbs precisely because that is what the boosters wanted them to be.

ONTARIO'S GROWTH MACHINE

George Chaffey has certainly received his fair share of attention. Recall that Ontario frequently serves as a case study for analyzing Southern California, and Chaffey is the undeniable star. He had his hand in the establishment of several suburbs, from Etiwanda to Ontario and more. Chaffey also receives praise for irrigation projects, especially with the Colorado River. Chaffey was born January 28, 1848, in Brockville, Ontario, Canada. Born to George Sr. and Ann Legoe, Chaffey came of age following the prime years of Kingston along Lake Ontario after the Canadian capital moved from there in 1844, and his family came in 1859. Still, Kingston emerged as an important Great Lakes port and center for shipbuilding and manufacturing.

Chaffey, allegedly a boy of feeble health and a school dropout, engrossed himself in the plethora of engineering books purportedly at the local library. Fascinated with technology, he frequented his father's shipbuilding yard. By 1862, Chaffey apprenticed as a marine engineer. Then, in 1867, he entered the world of banking, working for his uncle Benjamin in Toronto. In 1869, he married Annette McCord, the daughter of Toronto's chaplain, and the couple eventually had three boys. In 1870, he returned to Kingston and collaborated with his father at his shipyard. During these years, Chaffey earned renown as a ship designer, whereby his ship, the SS *Geneva* (one of many boats he would design), built in 1875, graced the cover of the veritable *Scientific American* magazine in 1876, earning the accolade of fastest shallow draught-ship at that time.

Chaffey, remember, begged by his father and brothers who came just a few years before, did not move to Southern California until 1881 to take a shot at real-estate speculation and establish Etiwanda, then Ontario. He helped organize the Etiwanda Water Company, which inspired the creation of the San Antonio Water Company in Ontario.

In addition, recall that Etiwanda has been billed "a community of firsts," including not only the first mutual water company but also the first long-distance telephone call in Southern California and, thanks to Chaffey, the first electric lighting. Chaffey also became the chief engineer in the project to light the streets of downtown Los Angeles for the first time, culminating in becoming president and engineer of the Los Angeles Electric Company in 1884. More importantly, however, this and other endeavors provided him with opportunities to rub elbows with some of Southern California's so-called captains of industry. Besides the other boosters in Ontario, Chaffey's multiple business dealings put him in touch with a regional group of impressive elites.

In establishing Etiwanda, Ontario, and the water companies, Chaffey joined in speculative ventures, whether directly to profit (i.e., real estate sales) or indirectly profit (i.e., water companies or the Chaffey College of Agriculture to entice more subdivision and migration). For example, while Chaffey originally purchased the Etiwanda land from Joseph Garcia, he secured the rights to the Ontario lands via San Francisco investors who had purchased the rights from Garcia as well. Connecting the dots backward, Garcia purchased the land from Isaias W. Hellman, who had bought the 13,000-acre Rancho Cucamonga that comprised most of the Inland Valley. Another connection to Hellman came more directly, however. Hellman, prominent Los Angeles banker and businessman Ozro Childs, and former California governor and businessman John Downey all donated land for the building of the USC Los Angeles campus, putting

FIGURE 19

George B. Chaffey Jr., ca. 1883. Courtesy of the Robert E. Ellingwood Model Colony History Room, Ontario City Library.

him touch with Widney (Chaffey's Ontario partner), while Hellman still owned land that increased in value adjacent to the Chaffey College in Ontario. Hellman is well known in California history as a successful banker (with Downey), loaning the money necessary to Harrison Otis to buy the *Los Angeles Times*, and investing in rail lines, forming the Los Angeles Railway in 1898 and the Pacific Electric Railway in 1901 with mogul Henry Huntington.[7]

By 1886, Chaffey decided to abandon his Ontario and Etiwanda investments and promising irrigation ventures to take a shot in Australia. At the invitation of Australian officials, Chaffey and his family undertook several irrigation projects there, establishing colonies at Renmark and Mildura. Chaffey accepted an invitation to first visit in 1885 after Australian officials had sent a commission to study irrigation in the United States and found Chaffey's work in Ontario impressive. Chaffey ostensibly became so excited about the prospects for community building in Australia that he asked his family to sell their interests in Southern California, come to Australia, and risk it all.

Chaffey's attempts at colonization in Australia were financial failures. Among other reasons, as irrigation provided the keys to Australian colonization, the family failed as they faced local hostility from those who championed water as a public resource and believed that the government, and not private speculation for profit, should oversee it. In fact, succumbing to political pressure, the Chaffeys appeared before a Royal Commission of Inquiry. Though not found guilty of anything, the proceedings left George Chaffey disillusioned. He departed Australia broke in 1897, briefly stopping in Florida before returning to California in 1898. He immediately began working for the San Antonio Water Company in Ontario, helping to increase water flow with a series of wells and a new tunnel. Meanwhile, William and the rest of the Chaffeys (at least for a time) remained in Mildura, Australia, which eventually became successful.

As for the seeming return of the prodigal son to California, in 1900, George Chaffey joined the California Development Company (CDC) to reclaim the lower Colorado Desert. CDC formed in 1896 on the bones of the defunct Colorado River Irrigation Company, which had formed in 1892 but collapsed soon after the maelstrom wreaked by a Depression beginning in 1893. At first looking to tap groundwater, the CDC turned its focus on a project to divert the Colorado River into the Coachella and Imperial Valleys (then known as the Salton Sink) in another profit-seeking venture of irrigating lands and building more subdivisions.

The CDC tapped Chaffey to lead the project, thanks to Luther M. Holt, Chaffey's fellow Ontario booster. Chaffey, in fact, had a notable reputation for his work in Etiwanda and Ontario, as well as Australia (despite any failure). He designed irrigation innovations such as the direct-drive and shaft-driven pumps, earning him election to the veritable Institution of Mechanical Engineers of London. The CDC therefore jumped at the chance to get Chaffey with his engineering expertise and growing financial contacts. Chaffey drew up his own contract with the company, naming himself president, chief financial officer, and chief engineer. He thus seized control (angering some CDC investors). Yet, unbeknownst to him, the company teetered on financial and legal ruin. Why he did not look at the books to find out beforehand is anyone's guess.

The CDC, in short, drowned in debt and did not have full rights to the land. Chaffey, now aware of the fiscal crisis, organized the Delta Investment Company, invested his own money (recovered from his few years back in Ontario), and raised funds from investors to pull the CDC out of the red. From there, Chaffey oversaw the successful completion of the Imperial Canal in two years, effectively conquering the Colorado. Meanwhile, he also organized the Imperial Land Company to sell suburban lots as he did in Etiwanda and Ontario, which laid out Calexico, Heber, Imperial, and Brawley, as well as Mexicali in Mexico.

By 1902, Charles Rockwood, who had long championed the irrigation project but lost control to Chaffey, ousted the man who had saved the company and the project. Concisely, Chaffey and the CDC were shrewd. They sidestepped the rate-fixing authority in California by setting up a Mexican subsidiary that gained ownership of the water as it passed through Baja California before reentering the United States. As it did, the water returned as the technical property of a foreign corporation and hence became exempt from American rates. Secondary canals then transferred the water to thirteen mutual water companies under CDC control that subsequently dispersed it to individual properties. Rockwood slowly obtained control over an increasing number of proxy votes belonging to the mutual water distribution companies. By 1902, Rockwood demanded Chaffey resign or scale back his involvement. Stunned, Chaffey indeed resigned. He sold his interests to Rockwood and his backers for $300,000 in securities, on which he only received $100,000 in cash after declining to push the CDC into bankruptcy. Only a few years later, of course, the Imperial Valley, which Holt suggested Chaffey name to replace the Salton Sink, flourished. Chaffey's stock would have made him millions.

Chaffey continued irrigation work, building more water systems and looking to make money in suburban real estate. In 1902, with his son Andrew, Chaffey oversaw the construction of a hydroelectric plant in San Antonio Canyon, vital to further development along the San Gabriel Mountains. That year he also purchased an interest in the East Whittier & La Habra Water Company, leading to the development of La Habra and Brea. Finally, in 1905, Chaffey purchased land in Owens Valley under his Owens Valley Improvement Company, built a water system, planted fruit trees, and, in 1910, established Manzanar.

Chaffey's financial endeavors were not limited to land and water. He became the founding president of the First Bank of Ontario in 1902. In 1903, Chaffey joined his son Andrew and founded the American Savings Bank and, in 1905, they established the First National Bank of Upland and Sierra Securities. By 1920, they established more than twenty-five banks, culminating in their consolidation that year, along with other banks, to become the California Bank, with Andrew as president and George as the director. At age 80, Chaffey finally retired in 1928, dying at the age of 84 in San Diego.[8]

Chaffey certainly did much to develop Southern California. His pursuit of profit unquestionably drove much of what he did and, through dealings with others, he helped package Southern California for sale, particularly as a suburban oasis. Nevertheless, as his partner Widney makes clearer perhaps, Chaffey's profit motive did not define him alone. If we give any credence to Chaffey's continually stated desires to develop "model" colonies and communities of firsts, he seems to have genuinely been motivated to create utopian-seeming suburbs out of his sincere belief they presented a superior way of life. He believed water would unleash it, and he could be the one to do it.

The other principal partners with Chaffey in Ontario were Robert M. Widney and Luther M. Holt. Widney is also a person not lacking attention when it comes to Southern California. His robust life reveals an individual growth-machine member engaging in myriad attempts at both profit making and, literally, saving souls. His connections in Southern California put him in some rather elite company and, again, provides both faces to and evidence for a growth machine working to cut costs, limit liability, make money, and, ultimately, sell Southern California.

In 1878, Widney wrote *Plan of Creation*, a cobbling together of older works by natural theologians like William Paley in *Natural Theology* (1802). Widney penned his work less than twenty years after Darwin's dangerous idea dropped in 1859 and only several years after *The Descent of Man* in 1871. *Plan of Creation* is mostly a repeat of older arguments, like those of John Ray (1695), first appearing in the Enlightenment age reacting to the emerging geological and astronomical breakthroughs revealing an evolving old earth and universe. What underscored Widney's work was the growing divide between literalists and modernists who accepted or rejected the Bible as a literalist account on one hand, and a metaphor on the other (but still all the word of God). Widney wanted to, like his predecessors, argue that the Bible did not conflict with science and that science provided a creationist account.[9]

Plan of Creation is a fairly pedantically, though pedestrian (which is likely the point), written version of day-age theory mixed with progressive creationism, meaning Widney advocated, with references to geology, astronomy, and biology, an old earth in which the days of creation were not literal days, but epochs of indeterminable length. To account for the diverse fossil record and older, now extinct, animals, say dinosaurs, Widney advocated an old-earth version of French anatomist George Cuvier's catastrophism. He argued for a series of creations in which God created these animals, they went extinct (catastrophes), and then he created new life forms, so on and so on, until he created Adam and Eve (only a few thousand years ago to fit Bishop Usher's famous timeline). In addition, like another French scientist, Marcel de Serres, Widney repeatedly argued that God's plan is a progressive, perfecting one; hence later creations, such as humankind and later generations, such as Widney's own, grew increasingly more perfect. This last point is Widney's major thesis. Moreover, even if implicit, it reveals an individual who repeatedly sought to perfect human life and, as he repeats ad nauseam in *Plan of Creation*, to fulfill His plan, which Widney identifies as increasing "enjoyment" for ever more people. Ontario, the model colony with the "most perfect plan," and the establishment of USC, as we saw, were two such ventures.[10]

Robert Maclay Widney was born in Piqua, Ohio, on December 23, 1838, to John Widney and Arabella Maclay. His maternal uncles were the noted Methodist missionary to China Robert Samuel Maclay and California State Assemblyman and State Senator Charles Maclay. Not long after his father died, in 1857, Widney moved to Santa Clara, California, where his uncle Charles lived. Widney studied law at the University of the Pacific, then in Santa Clara, from 1858 to 1862, earning a B.A. and M.A. He then taught mathematics for several years. Admitted to the bar in 1865, Widney moved to Los Angeles in 1867, marrying Mary Barnes with whom he had five children, and began practicing law. While he practiced law in Los Angeles, he purportedly opened the city's first real estate office, publishing *Real Estate Advertiser* monthly.

In 1871, Widney became judge of the Court of California for Los Angeles and, eventually, San Bernardino counties. Only months after his appointment, on October

FIGURE 20

Robert M. Widney, ca. early 1900s. Courtesy of the Robert E. Ellingwood Model Colony History Room, Ontario City Library.

24, 1871, amid growing hostility about Chinese immigration and labor competition, a mob of over 500 white men stormed Los Angeles's Chinatown, shattering windows, busting doors, and attacking every Chinese person they saw. Some Chinese died by hanging, while others met their fate dragged by the neck. The total number of Chinese murdered remains contested, but most put it around twenty, while some say as many as eighty. Known as the Chinese Massacre of 1871, the murder spree in which white neighbors sought to (and did) kill their Chinese neighbors followed the death of a local white rancher killed in the crossfire of warring Chinese factions (over the abduction of a Chinese woman). Judge Widney reportedly raced to the scene when he heard of the attack, sending word back home for his gun. He helped stop the massacre and protect some Chinese. The gun-wielding judge even once reportedly cleared leather in the courtroom when he felt a witness had disrespected his honor.[11]

As Chicago is the American city of the nineteenth century (and New York for all), Los Angeles in the latter nineteenth century began its rise for becoming the premier American city of the twentieth century. Following the Gold Rush north fueling Sacramento, San Francisco, and Oakland, then a Civil War and a transcontinental railroad line, the 1870s in Los Angeles laid the path for the boom of the eighties, especially as railroad lines and increasing rate competition opened California up to the rest of the nation. In the early part of the decade, the Cerro Gordo silver mine in the Mojave fueled the Los Angeles economy, directly through the influx of the precious metal and indirectly with an increasing population, jobs, and a market they created and fueled. With a then-thriving ranching industry and a growing consortium of real estate speculators, as Widney to Hellman represent, interest in getting a railroad line grew to help add yet more fuel to the proverbial fire.

In 1872 a "Committee of Thirty," composed of several merchants and landowners, organized to entice Southern Pacific Railroad to route its trunk line (i.e., supply route) for long-distance through travel to Los Angeles. Southern Pacific agreed to run fifty miles of its valuable main track if Los Angeles County agreed to cover five percent of its assessed value, or $610,000 (about $11.8 million in 2012 relative value). William Hyde, a member of the Thirty and a Southern Pacific representative, to boot, convinced the County Board of Supervisors to place before the voters a bond proposition granting Southern Pacific the money. This met with local outrage, especially from ranchers who feared a tax increase.

Los Angeles merchants and landowners favored the proposition because they considered the railroad line vital to their interests and worth any cost. Widney emerged as the principal champion of the railroad line, authoring an influential pamphlet, *Los Angeles County Subsidy*, spelling out the case that the line would vastly increase the small city's trade and population by making it a railroad center. "What do we want any railroad for?" Widney asked. Certainly to carry produce to market, yet also attract industry, commuter transportation, and entice migration. Also of issue was whether or not to go with Southern Pacific or another railroad that ran to San Diego, which Widney argued received its supplies from Los Angeles already and to where few Angelenos ever visited or from where migrants departed. Rather, a Southern Pacific line would grant access to San Francisco, the premier Western city and market. Widney and his fellow boosters won. They successfully turned public opinion favorably, and the voters approved the proposition, bringing the railroad to Los Angeles and Los Angeles to the world when, on September 5, 1876, the first train from San Francisco arrived.[12]

No simple Southern Pacific puppet, however, Widney organized Los Angeles's first Chamber of Commerce (which shortly thereafter went defunct until 1888 because of the national Depression in 1883) in his courtroom to unite local business and explore creating a rival railroad or alternate deal when Southern Pacific announced it would tax the transport of silver. Yet, Remi Nadeau, a French Canadian who arrived in Los Angeles in 1861, operated and opened his mule-team freight line to the Cerro Gordo mine, alleviating most fears about the tax with an alternate mode of transportation. The Chamber also took the lead in refuting negative critiques of California by financing and distributing booster publications throughout the nation. Widney and the Chamber included a veritable who's who list of early Los Angelenos. Besides Downey and several others, the chamber included international banker and local politician Solomon Lazard; grocer and banker Herman Hellman; executive and speculator Isaac Lord; lawyer and businessperson M. J. Newmark; executive and Los Angeles mayor from 1874–76 Prudent Beaudry; lumberman and investor John Griffith; and the renowned real-estate mogul, investor, and physician Dr. John Griffin. Widney himself also diversified like these men. He got involved in local public transportation as well. In 1874, he organized the Spring and Sixth Street transit line, a single-track horse car serving downtown. In 1875 he incorporated the East Los Angeles & San Pedro Railway Company, which began construction in 1876 in hopes of reaching a new Southern Pacific depot, but because of low ridership, the company folded after four years and without a line all the way to the depot.

As shared before, Widney drove the establishment of the University of Southern California and, with Chaffey, the Chaffey College of Agriculture in Ontario as a USC branch. Recall his *Plan of Creation*, in which he determined God's plan was the "conferring of enjoyment and happiness. . . . Perfect benevolence would be satisfied only with the greatest enjoyment, for the greatest length of time, the greatest number, with the least suffering to the fewest individuals."[13] With a population capable of massacre, Widney perhaps felt few had found such enjoyment and happiness in Los Angeles. As he asserted that God's plan progressed forward, perfecting people along the way, the time had come to do more perfecting. He also argued in *Plan of Creation* that studying, "investigating and learning," conferred greater enjoyment to a greater number of individuals. USC, already in the works, manifested two years later.[14]

Widney jumped in on several real estate ventures, including Ontario. Speculator William Willmore purchased land in Rancho Los Cerritos in 1880 hoping to establish a thriving subdivision. Lacking resources, in 1888 he turned to Widney, who organized the Long Beach Land and Water Company and bought Willmore's land, establishing the city of Long Beach by 1892, including roads, transportation, and a water system. Widney also joined with his uncle Charles, who purchased a vast amount of acreage in the San Fernando Valley, helping organize more land and water companies, such as the Maclay Rancho Water Company with Widney as a trustee, leading to the establishments of San Fernando in 1874 and Pacoima in 1887.[15]

If not enough, in the early 1890s, Widney delivered a series of addresses he made arguing for a national money system. While the Federal Reserve Act would not pass until 1913, giving the Federal Reserve authority to set monetary policy, Widney concluded decades before, "It is a strange comment on a financial scheme that, to prevent an increase in volume of money, we must destroy the prosperity of a nation and reduce to starvation the laboring classes."[16] Like many farmers, Widney, not surprisingly given nearby silver, was an advocate of the Free Silver Movement, which championed the inclusion of silver with gold backing US currency. In addition, like the Greenbackers in the 1870s and 1880s, he went even further and championed currency, or soft money, not backed by any precious metal.

His advocacy for a national money system that included soft money rested on the desire to see more money put into circulation, believing, "Money is used as a means to carry on business, and varies in demand as business increases or decreases."[17] He continued, "There is a fixed relation between the two which, if disturbed, must cause trouble. As the business, population, and area of our country increases, the volume of money must increase." More money in circulation rested on the idea that it would foster business and spark the overall economy. On the one hand, early advocates like the Greenbackers argued that the inflationary effect would result in the rising of crop prices and hence help farmers make more revenue and climb out of debt. Widney likely thought of his suburban famers. On the other hand, such inflationary hopes also centered on interest rates falling and a subsequent rise in purchasing power among consumers with more money. In turn, production would increase to meet the demand and require the hiring of more workers and a reduction in unemployment. Widney repeatedly made the case that such a monetary policy would grow business as much as people. Whether indeed a good monetary policy or not, he clearly spoke in the language of championing the working class and lifting more and more people out of poverty, perhaps for the opportunity to help increase their "enjoyment."[18]

FIGURE 21

Luther M. Holt, ca. 1890s. Courtesy of the Robert E. Ellingwood Model Colony History Room,
Ontario City Library.

Luther Myrick Holt joined the Chaffeys in Etiwanda and, along with Widney, in
Ontario. Born in 1840 in Michigan and passing away in California in 1920, Holt
emerged as the public relations guru of the team—of Southern California, really.
According to one historian, Holt was "a boomer by temperament and training" and
the leading irrigation journalist in the state.[19] A contemporary newspaper editor
seemed less restrained, hyperbolically describing Holt as "that prince of boomers."[20]
Perhaps a 1922 history of San Bernardino and Riverside counties wins: "Like the
majority of the great army of home and health seekers who laid the foundations for
the popularity and prosperity of Southern California, L. M. Holt was an Eastern
man"; that is, he was white.[21]

Holt came to Sacramento in December 1869 but moved to Los Angeles in 1873.
He had first visited Southern California in Riverside for four weeks in 1872, then
returned north to Healdsburg in Sonoma and organized a company for planting an
orange orchard located near Anaheim. Replaced in the company by 1873, however,
Holt decided to settle in Los Angeles. By 1877, he became editor of the California
Horticulture Society's *Southern California Horticulturist*, later *Rural Californian*,
when it first appeared in September of that year. That society also included a who's
who list, including Nathaniel Carter, another prominent booster involved in the San

Gabriel Valley and the founder of Sierra Madre.²² The journal sold in 1880 on the eve of Holt's involvement in Ontario. Still, the two brash booster publications about Ontario (as well as an earlier one on Etiwanda) appeared under Holt's name: he was listed as editor of the Riverside Press and Horticulturist Steam Print, which were both associated with *Riverside Press and Horticulturist*, the newspaper he took over from James Roe in 1880, who began the paper in 1878. Holt ran it as a tri-weekly evening paper, turning it into a daily in 1886.

Besides his work with Ontario, not to mention running its paper, *The Ontario Fruit Grower*, and the Imperial Land Company, in which he served as the advertising manager, Holt had left the Riverside Press sometime in the 1890s. An anonymous source with the *Riverside Press* newspaper gave a quote for the *Imperial Valley Press* newspaper in 1903 upon Holt's marriage to his second wife, gushing, "He knows western journalism like a book, and has been identified with a number of prominent papers. He was one of the first to recognize the merits of the Imperial country. He is a recognized authority on irrigation and his utterances on all public matters carry considerable weight always."²³ Further, Holt served a few years as the superintendent of circulation for the *Los Angeles Herald* before his Imperial venture.

Besides newspapers, Holt jumped into the Southland's real-estate bonanza. In addition to running publicity for Imperial Land Company, he gets credit for coining *Calexico*, perhaps obviously a mixture of California and Mexico, whereby its border sister city is Mexicali. In addition, Holt assisted in the construction of the Bear Valley Dam, built in 1884, supplying water to Redlands in San Bernardino County. More importantly, for Riverside, he played a vital arbitrary role in relieving tensions between competing stockholder interests, helping the local water company sell out to citizens to form a mutual in 1884, mirroring his work in Etiwanda and Ontario. Still, Holt, like Widney, had been at it for a while. In 1874, after he left his Anaheim orchard, he joined Harry Crow and Thomas Garey. They formed the Los Angeles Immigration and Land Co-Operative, for which Holt served as the secretary, and founded Pomona in 1874 and Artesia in 1875.

Like Chaffey, and to an extent Widney, Holt does deserve some kudos for his work on water systems. Holt often receives credit over Chaffey for having envisioned the mutual water company in Etiwanda and then Ontario, as well as Riverside. Along with the likes of James De Barth Shorb (co-developer in San Marino and Pasadena) and John North (founder of Riverside), Holt led the charge for the passage of the Wright Act by 1887, which allowed for the creation of irrigation districts. Perceptive land speculators in California quickly purchased property along lakes and rivers in hopes of charging ranchers and farmers lavishly high prices for access. Obviously, this hurt the ranchers and farmers' bottom line. Holt, who had helped build entire communities based on the need for water and thus wanted to fill his own pockets, struck back. The Wright Act, originally conceived by a California schoolteacher by the name of Charles Wright, in whose home it appears Holt married his bride in 1903, allowed for the creation of special irrigation districts funded by a tax based on the value of the land, thereby the ranchers and farmers paid only for what they used. The boom of the eighties, therefore, officially got underway. "There is no section," Holt went on to say, "where good cement sidewalks in cities and towns begin to compare with those of Southern California." He continued, "There is no other section where cities and towns have so good a supply and system of domestic water service."[24] Holt also further championed irrigation by organizing the first-ever irrigation convention in California in 1884. Not surprisingly, between 1880 and 1892 alone, and just in the citrus belt east of Los Angeles, fifty-seven irrigation companies organized.[25]

In 1887 Holt also helped organize the first horticultural society in Southern California, the Southern California Horticultural Society. Among their publicity campaigns were some of the earliest citrus and horticultural fairs in the state. Holt, with some of the community's other notable movers and shakers and Californian elites, helped organize the first fair in Riverside in 1879, the Citrus Fair Association. Locals included Elmer Holmes (San Bernardino newspaperman and city official), Prior Russell (nurseryman and uncle to the Riverside Heights Orange Growers' Association founder), Samuel Evans Sr. (father of Riverside's first mayor and a state senator), and Lyman Waite (reportedly a member of twenty-two corporations, from packinghouses to banks throughout Southern California).[26] The more prestigious included future California governor George Stoneman, who had just finished a stint as a railroad commissioner; famed Californian military man, politician, and rancher Mariano Guadalupe Vallejo; and, perhaps lesser known nationally and today, Ellwood Cooper, a Goleta farm producer who for a time had the largest walnut crop in the state. Also, Holt purportedly took the lead in 1886 to ship fruits to Chicago for a fair and again publicize the Southland.

Holt undeniably threw himself into the promotion of his interests. He also threw himself into the politics of the day, rubbing elbows with fellow public relations gurus, politicians, and executives great and small. He even championed seemingly progressive causes, such as subverting the power of land speculators over water and, in Riverside, other liquids, as he led at least one charge to strap liquor sellers with an oppressive payment of $6,000 a year for a license when the mainstream temperance movement there had only sought $100. Holt was also a racist. He led the campaign to expel Chinese residents from Riverside, and he was not shy about using his newspaper.

The real-estate boom fueled anti-Chinese zealotry in Southern California as well as the state in general. Holt emerged as Riverside's most vocal public opponent of Chinese occupants remaining in downtown. Having already moved his Riverside *Press* newspaper away from the town's Chinese Quarter once he purchased the paper, he urged the white power structure to "drive the Chinamen out and tear down their filthy quarters" once a Chinese general store opened near him in the summer of 1885.[27] The town board of trustees then enacted a series of restrictive health ordinances whereby Chinese merchants were arrested and charged with a variety of minor public nuisance violations. The repressive, bigoted regime, which with one breath exalted individual entrepreneurs and private, small businesses, then, within a second breath asked for and received the assistance of the local police to evict Chinese residents, mostly single men from Guangdong Province, "out of crowded shacks and tents they had been occupying in the downtown block."[28] Like that, two dozen laundries and ironing shops, small businesses of individual entrepreneurs who provided essential services within and for the community, disappeared from the downtown business district because of their owners' origins of birth. In early 1886, Holt gleefully reported of the demolition of a local Chinese laundry removed just in time for the construction of the new home of the First National Bank, organized by three local executives and politicians.

With the removal of Chinese people from downtown, many in the community hoped that white labor migrating from the East Coast would replace them. Holt, however, feared the loss of a ready pool of cheap and easily controlled labor that lacked the full rights and protections of citizenship with no chance of change on the horizon. In contrast to the Chinese workers, ethnic white labor (i.e., Jewish and Catholic), however increasingly reviled if not outright abused, at least in theory could receive and expect a modicum of rights and protections based on the color of their skin. While of course facing challenges, they ultimately did have access to citizenship, and they did have access to the ballot box. Therefore, just as capitalist companies and related interests have looked to exploit guest workers and illegal immigrant labor (primarily from Mexico) in the twentieth century to today, Holt and his cohort wanted to maintain a docile workforce of Chinese barely above that of pauper in their time. They wanted this much-maligned workforce to work cheaply in the local service industries and in their farm fields, virtually guaranteeing staving off any unionization attempts by them and others and adversely affecting wage demands or expectations of any white workers looking for work with them as well, with nothing to say of Chinese laborers. "The Chinese are bad enough," Holt concluded, "but what would become of the raisin crop and the coming orange crop were it not for the Chinese to save it?"[29]

Any growth machine is defined by its members or, more correctly, identifiable people who joined with one another in multiple dealings to stimulate growth economically. The Chaffeys, Widney, and Holt, the main members in Ontario, linked to a dizzying array of other landed and commercial interests who sought to grow the Southland and, of course, benefit their bank accounts. As already noted with Chaffey and Widney's link to prominent businesspersons, landowners, and politicians like Hellman, Downey, Childs, and those working on the Imperial Valley project, they also had other impressive links and dealings.

The link between Ontario's boosters and USC gets the point across. As discussed, the emerging school and the new suburb needed and wanted each other. One got a valued institution to help advertise; the other got free land, a cheap building, and more opportunities for increased enrollment and, hence, tuition dollars. While the Chaffeys themselves donated land in Ontario, remember that Hellman, Downey, and Childs also donated land in Los Angeles for the main campus, landing Hellman the role as a regent for nearly forty years. In addition, so-called founding fathers of USC along with Widney and Hellman included another array of impressive executives and politicians. Griffith Compton, for example, founded Compton, CA, in 1887, while Marion Bovard, the university's first president, had a long career in the clergy.[30] Edward Spence had a lengthy career as a successful banker. In 1875, just arriving in Los Angeles, he became a cashier, and later president, at the Commercial Bank of Los Angeles, which was organized by John Hollenbeck (another real estate man). In 1877 he went on to establish Monrovia with John Bicknell (yet another prominent lawyer and land speculator.) Spence joined other prominent local executives to organize the Central Railroad in 1883, which then consolidated with the City Railroad of Los Angeles in 1886 to form the City-Central. He helped form the first electric streetcar line in Los Angeles in 1886, the Los Angeles Electric Railway. Finally, Spence won political office. Already a seasoned state representative and city treasurer for some time up north, he served briefly with the Los Angeles city council in 1880 and 1881, culminating in his election as mayor of Los Angeles from 1885 through 1886.[31]

Joseph Widney, like his brother and some of the other prominent boosters, is a known actor in California, especially Southern California, and the second president of USC. As shared, his brother Robert made use of his climatic studies as he penned the booster pamphlets in Ontario. Born in Ohio like his brother, Joseph graduated from Miami (Ohio) University. Actually, the university also granted him an honorary Doctor of Laws degree later for his *Race Life of the Aryan Peoples* that, as mentioned, forwarded a racialist argument about different races suited for different environments, a thought growing increasingly popular among Social Darwinists and mimicked by Christian clergy, most often to justify their racism.

After a stint in the Civil War, Widney came to California and earned an M.A. at the University of the Pacific and, in a year, received his M.D. from Toland Medical College (later a part of the University of California, San Francisco). After several years as a medical surgeon for the Army, Widney joined his family in the Los Angeles area, opening a medical practice and sharing offices with the founder of East Los Angeles, John Griffin. Widney's medical career, in fact, is pioneer. In 1871, Widney helped start the Los Angeles County Medical Association, another first in California, and in 1884 he helped re-organize the Southern California Medical Society and establish the *Southern California Practitioner* in 1886, serving as the journal's editor in its inaugural years.

Widney also helped create the Los Angeles Library Association and helped write one of the first histories of Los Angeles County, *Centennial History Los Angeles*, in 1876. In fact, this marked Widney's entry into the game of boosterism in Southern California, extolling the embellished virtues of the Southland to entice migration and investment to a region for which he, like his brother, continued to make investments in and seek out speculative ventures. He coauthored in 1888 an influential booster work, *California of the South*, with Walter Lindley, the founder of such institutions as the California Hospital Medical Center, Whittier State School (a reform school for young people), the Los Angeles Orphans' Home, and the College of Medicine at USC. Lindley also served as superintendent for a time of the Los Angeles County Hospital, president of the California State Medical Society, secretary of the California Board of Health, and a member of the Los Angeles Board of Education and Board of Library Directors.[32]

Like the other boosters, Widney became involved in real estate, auxiliary businesses, and politics that further tangled the booster web operating in the Los Angeles area. He began small with several land plots in Wilmington near the San Pedro harbor and San Gabriel Mission, as well as the plot that Los Angeles City Hall soon occupied and much of the Mt. Washington area. In 1885, he purchased 35,000 acres northeast of Los Angeles and formed the Hesperia Land and Water Company to create the suburb, unashamedly named for Hesperus, the Greek god of the West. Joining Widney were his brother Robert, president of the Hesperia Company, and Stephen Mott, secretary and longtime county clerk of Los Angeles; land speculator; and investor in railway transportation, water, gas, and banks throughout the Southland, linking Mott to many of the key players mentioned above.[33] Widney also purchased a hotel and some bathhouses in Santa Fe Springs east of Los Angeles in 1887 before he became a member of the newly (re)formed Los Angeles Chamber of Commerce in 1888, precipitating his booster publication, *California of the South* (1888). In that book and elsewhere, Widney emerged as one of the principal proselytizers of California as a health resort. He also campaigned for harbor improvements to facilitate trade better and boom the region.[34]

SACRAMENTO'S GROWTH MACHINE

Reviewing the lives, activities, and historic context of Sacramento's boosters serves the same purpose as discussing Ontario's boosters. The scale of analysis for discussing boosterism narrows, yet again, as well as to put names and faces on it all. It also specifies a Northern California region not typically covered (besides the Bay Area) when discussing California, agriculture, and suburbanization. Biographies and some general historic context, therefore, show Sacramento's boosters organizing collectively, in fact, as an actual growth machine. These boosters, too, like their Southern Californian counterparts, were adept at reassembling the popular suburban ideal and the California Dream to sell real estate. Likewise, they utilized law, corporations, and popular representations to do the job.

Of all the individuals in Sacramento with a direct investment in the development of agriburbs, in this case Orangevale, Harris Weinstock looms largest. His life and career complicate any narrative that casts boosters as cutthroat businesspersons motivated solely by profit. Weinstock articulated a blend of agrarianism, Populism, Progressivism, racialized Social Darwinism, capitalism, and modernity. His career spanned the late 1870s through the 1920s. He first cut his sociopolitical teeth, however, on local concerns through local organizations before advancing to state, federal, and even international organizations. Weinstock represents a Sacramento businessperson who believed in agrarian democracy and virtue while supporting Progressive reforms involving labor, political corruption, and championing coopera- tives. As a place entrepreneur, he understood the urgency to improve Sacramento's image to enhance the chances of newcomers and investment. Still, through public service, lectures, and crusades against political machines and antilabor violence, and as California's first state market director, he spent his lifetime trying to raise society as much as his own bottom line. He was a quintessential turn of the twentieth-century Progressive who launched his career on the local level.

Born in London, England, in 1854, Weinstock and his family moved to New York later that year. In 1864, Weinstock moved to Sacramento to join his half-brother David Lubin. Together, they opened the Mechanics Store in 1874. Lubin, in fact, more so than Weinstock, perhaps more than anyone in Sacramento, represents what historian Daniel Rodgers has called a *transatlantic Progressive* who culled and dispersed ideas across international borders—though Chaffey qualifies too in Southern California to Australia and back.[35] He was pivotal in the founding of the International Institute of Agriculture in Rome in 1908, which the United Nations absorbed into the Food and Agriculture Organization in 1946. Lubin also took to public service. He played a key role in the development of Sacramento cultural life, helped to start both the California Fruit Union and International Society for the Colonization of Russian Jews, and tirelessly campaigned for subsidies and protection for farmers in California and, eventually, around the globe. These two liberal-minded half-brothers reorganized and incorpo- rated their store as Weinstock, Lubin, & Company in 1888 after emerging as one of the West's largest department stores and mail-order businesses.[36]

Weinstock, with his brother, began his lifelong association with farming when the two acquired 1,200 acres in Colusa County (northwest of Sacramento) in 1884. As a farmer, Weinstock learned the dissimilarity of selling oranges in a store and selling oranges through a commission merchant. From this lesson, he began a lifetime of activity devoted to establishing a better process in the sale, marketing, and distribu- tion of agricultural goods to help farmers dependent on cash crops. Beginning in

FIGURE 22

Harris Weinstock. Courtesy Center for Sacramento History, no. 1996-044-1278.

1885, Weinstock, as well as Lubin, spent nearly half a century devoted to the plight of farmers as producers. Sponsored by the California State Board of Horticulture, formed in 1883, Weinstock and Lubin vigorously participated in the State Fruit Growers' conventions. Weinstock served as the president of a transportation committee that fought to obtain rate reductions and service improvements. In 1885, Weinstock helped organize the California Fruit Union cooperative and, in 1888, he helped start the California Dried Fruit Association. In 1894, he formed and served as president and general manager of the Fruit Growers' and Shippers' Association that brought together growers, growers' organizations, and shippers. While not a marketing association, it did create a Bureau of Information to supply each member with market information so that each could make better shipment decisions. The association also sought to establish auction rooms in each market. Though the association went defunct in 1902, Weinstock continued his advocacy of auction sales and a collective system of distribution so that "the profits, which formerly had gone to shippers and middlemen, would be made by the grower himself."[37]

Weinstock focused on local concerns before joining the California Progressive Movement. He played a key role in framing Sacramento's third city charter, and he hosted political parties, including serving as chair of the reception committee in honor of Governor Henry Cage in 1899.[38] Weinstock's involvement and importance grew as the California Progressives, who organized in 1907 as the Lincoln-Roosevelt League, originally decided on him as their choice for governor in the 1910 election before he deferred to Hiram Johnson. In 1912, Governor Johnson appointed Weinstock to lead a commission to investigate labor crises in Fresno and San Diego involving the Industrial Workers of the World (Wobblies) in which he advocated that the state honor the Wobblies' First Amendment rights. President Woodrow Wilson in 1913 appointed Weinstock to serve as a member of the United States International Relations Commission. In addition, that year, Governor Johnson named Weinstock to a committee to plan a state rural credits system. On the recommendation of the committee, the state established the Colonization and Rural Credits Commission, headed, at Weinstock's suggestion, by Elwood Mead who, not coincidentally enough, had studied the Chaffey Brothers' colonization schemes in Australia that they had first developed in Etiwanda and Ontario. The State Colonization and Rural Credits Commission served as a Progressive advocate for state promotion of rural colonization schemes and aid to small farmers. Finally, in 1916, Weinstock became the first state market director by appointment, once again, of Governor Johnson. As historian Steven Stoll argued, Weinstock thus helped the State of California bring government into the business of agricultural marketing as his bureau—the first of its kind—sought to assist the organization and operation of cooperatives and other associations. According to Stoll, "Weinstock found himself in a position to bring order to the countryside in a way that no country-life reformer could have imagined." "Weinstock's purpose was nothing less than to change the relationship between California and the American economy and to build agriculture on the West Coast into a major industry." Further, "He acted on the premise that what minimized 'the waste and expense of distribution, [worked] to the benefit of the consumers.'"[39]

Weinstock began giving public lectures in the 1880s. He spoke to women's clubs, civic organizations, church groups and synagogues, grammar and college students, and political organizations. Repeatedly he addressed such progressive-minded themes as democratic citizenship, civil liberties, business ethics, moral character, family and home, and opportunities for educated women. In 1903 he served as the first president of the Commonwealth Club. Founded by editorial writer Edward Adam of the *San Francisco Call*, the club created a nonpartisan educational organization to study public affairs. Perhaps of all Weinstock's social advocacies and lectures, his most popular was "Jesus the Jew," which he published in 1902 as *Jesus the Jew: And Other Addresses*. Weinstock, like his brother Lubin, was raised an Orthodox Jew and embraced a progressive Judaism that championed pluralism, modernity, equality, and social justice. He taught that Jesus preached Judaism in its purest form, and he advocated a universal religion with a belief in one God, one unity, and one law for all humankind. He actively participated in the Jewish Publication Society, founded in 1888, which sought to provide children of Jewish immigrants with books about their heritage in English. Weinstock saw himself, and all American Jewry, as white.

Recall that, in his 1905 speech to students in San Francisco, he declared, "Whatever progress the Anglo-Saxon has made beyond that of other races is largely due to his spirit of independence, self-help, and self-reliance; to his power of initiative, and his readiness to assume responsibilities." On the one hand, in his "Jesus the Jew" lecture, he had argued that the republican form of government so apparently beloved by Anglo Americans came from a Jewish tradition thereby, implicit in his view, constituting Jewish inclusion in the whiteness of Anglo Saxondom. On the other hand, in his speech, Weinstock followed up his love of Anglo Saxons with the reasoning that all white Americans were Anglo Saxon. "The fact remains, however, that our language is the Anglo-Saxon, our laws are largely based on the common law of England; our educational methods are, to a great extent, modeled after those of England, and our tone and spirit are preeminently Anglo-Saxon in character." Weinstock (also an Englishman by birth) hence claimed American Jews (and not Jews in all of Europe, the Middle East, or elsewhere) were irreducibly Anglo Saxon and, thereby, white.[40]

Weinstock, as a Progressive, mirrored efforts in not only Sacramento, but also nationally and internationally. In between the end of Reconstruction and World War I, nearly all Americans faced the reality of industrialization as railroad lines and telegraph wires dotted the landscape of the countryside, factories grew in number and size, immigration rose, and many labor disputes became violent. The United States transformed economically and militarily and scarcely a person remained untouched by the changes. With three depressions from the 1870s to 1890s, and the social turmoil they triggered, increasing numbers of Americans, already discontent with the problems of a Gilded Age, came to feel a sense of what one historian has said was "dislocation and bewilderment."[41] According to many, the nation needed to reform if it was to survive. The Progressive movement gained momentum out of this perceived calamity, with the fate of each American seemingly linked with the collective fate of classes, corporations, and nations. While some historians see Progressivism as an extension of the Populist revolt, the continuous struggle of liberalism versus conservatism, or democracy versus aristocracy, Progressivism certainly gained momentum at the turn of the twentieth century. Some historians, on the contrary, see Progressivism as a democratic renaissance and therefore a complete break with the so-called backward-looking republican rhetoric of Populists. Whatever the truth, which will not be settled here, Progressivism gained traction. So, whether a moral crusade to resuscitate older Protestant and individualistic values where the right sort of people (a new middle class) could rule, ease their status anxiety, and bequeath to Americans a bureaucratic structure in the famed search for order, Progressives increasingly turned to the tasks of delivering the American people from what they said was their sin. They sought the eradication of social conflicts, to stand against the worst evils of big business (while maintaining a reverence for capitalism), and devoted themselves to a collectivist, interventionist solution that, at its core, revealed laissez-faire ideology a bankrupt and brutal idiocy built purposefully at the expense of the downtrodden and poor. Sacramento's boosters, like Weinstock, were these Progressives.[42]

On a quick aside, and to be fair, Ontario's boosters echoed the language of many Progressive causes as well. Nevertheless, timing and location do matter. As noted, the land boom in Southern California arose more robustly before the Sacramento area and, as such, many in the north played off the hype. While these boosters overlap in time, the point is that the Ontario boosters did not join in on Progressive institutions as explicitly compared to their Sacramento counterparts. Clearly, the Southland had Progressives, like Charles Dwight Willard, a noted leader of municipal reform and statewide Progressivism. Also clear is the progressive language of Chaffey, Widney, and Holt. Ultimately, the Sacramento boosters simply have a résumé featuring more explicitly progressive reform and institutions—not surprising for they also lived in the State's capital. This is the rationale, whether right or wrong, for a more intense focus on Progressivism now.

Progressive Californians swept to power in 1910 with the election of Hiram Johnson as governor. Progressives in the 1911 state legislature took swift action on economic regulation, challenged the unethical business practices of railroads and utilities, and established agencies and legislation to police banks, assess corporate incomes, and turn property tax collection over to counties. Progressives also advocated political reform combating corruption through such measures as the initiative, referendum, and recall. While many of the Progressive reforms in California and the nation may seem like an anti-business gang tired of politics and politicians, many Progressives, such as Weinstock, were executives themselves who used political offices to advocate change. For these Sacramento boosters, at least, business went hand in hand with their efforts to clean up the image of Sacramento and improve its institutions and infrastructure in hopes of stimulating the economy by attracting new migrants and investors. Consequently, they improved the so-called positive cultural, political, and social reform such new blood and capital allegedly sought.[43]

Reformers, the reform impulse, and the search for order had been growing in Sacramento since the 1870s as local businesspersons and politicians promoted business interests and the creation of a better metropolitan development climate, which also clearly motivated Widney and others in Los Angeles. For example, led by local businesspersons such as Albert Gallatin and Mayor Christopher Green, a Board of Trade came forth in 1873 to promote business. More significantly, in the 1880s, following the mass migration of newcomers into Southern California, Sacramento's boosters increased their efforts to improve and promote the city so as not to miss the wave. At the heart of this promotional and reform impulse, sometimes leading it and sometimes led by it, were the brothers McClatchy of the *Sacramento Bee*. According to one historian, "Both brothers railed incessantly against anything or anybody that stood in their way. Relentlessly they pressed Sacramento to improve its water supply, pave its roads, clean up its politics, eliminate its vice and crime, and beautify its streets by planting trees."[44]

For the McClatchys, as for many of Sacramento's Progressives, the focus was on the marketing of Sacramento. The McClatchys published lavishly illustrated booster pamphlets and were major players in the formation of the Sacramento Chamber of Commerce in 1895 that replaced the Board of Trade and became even more focused on marketing California's "capital city." Sacramento's boosters, Progressive or otherwise, took an expansive approach at fashioning an image of the city as they helped create a frontier myth that celebrated early miners, pioneers, and the days of '49. Sacramento's "who's who" turned to the creation of schools, fraternal and social clubs, as well as the establishment of post offices, new buildings, libraries, beautiful Victorian homes and neighborhoods, and large and beautiful churches such as the Cathedral of the Blessed Sacrament, as well as orphanages, hospitals, and sanitariums. Even Charles K. McClatchy (more often referred to as C. K.) embraced the notion that the rural environment and virtue went together as he became an outspoken proponent of trees and heavily promoted the city's reputation as a "city of trees." Progressives like C. K. held the conviction that cities should copy the moral order of idealized bucolic villages. Urbanites needed to come together somehow as members of a united community linked by shared social and moral values.[45] To accomplish this, reformers of the so-called City Beautiful Movement created the most visible expression of this belief. They assumed that by transforming the urban landscape to mirror a town or village in the countryside, they would complement the expanding reforms in other areas of society.[46] C. K., then, predictably, published front-page obituaries and ran numerous articles concerning felled trees in the *Bee*. According to C. K., "A street joke in Sacramento runneth as follows: 'I see the flag on the *Bee* is at halfmast.' 'Who's dead?' 'Another oak tree.'"[47]

C. K. has garnered the most attention of the brothers when discussing Sacramento. His brother, Valentine S. McClatchy (more often referred to as V. S.), however, also rode prominently across the Sacramento landscape. Sons of James McClatchy, founder of the *Sacramento Bee* (1857), the brothers bought out their father's partner and became the sole owners of the daily newspaper in 1884. V. S. became the business manager of the *Bee*, leaving most of the editorial duties to C. K. In addition to his promotional efforts from his position at the *Bee*, V. S. helped form other booster clubs. He joined the California Citrus Fair Association (of Northern California) in 1892 (which underwrote the San Francisco fair in 1894 to which McClatchy sent Orangevale citrus), served as a Western advisory board member for the Associated Press, and served as a member of the California Promotion Committee (formed in 1902), publishing a periodical and distributing booster pamphlets. While space considerations limit listing all the movers and shakers of these organizations—from non-Californian newspapermen like Victor Lawson in Chicago to Northern California elites all over, like William Gester in Newcastle—V. S.

FIGURE 23

Valentine S. McClatchy, ca. 1880s. Courtesy Center for Sacramento History, no. 82/05/803.

McClatchy had good contacts. Besides land investments in the agriburbs of Orangevale and Fair Oaks (particularly as he helped form both the OVCC in 1887 and the FODC in 1900), he also bought and sold land throughout the Sacramento Valley, including land near Rocklin and Loomis and in Placer County. He became involved in local politics and municipal organizations, helping to form and draft bylaws for the Sacramento Chamber of Commerce. Later V. S. filled offices for various local and state political organizations, including a stint as president of the California State Reclamation Board.[48]

V. S. McClatchy's name most often appears in connection to his agenda as a racist bigot. As president of the California Japanese Exclusion League that helped pass the Alien Land Law in 1920 and the National Origins Act of 1924 and a leader of the California Joint Immigration Committee, McClatchy railed against what he believed a Japanese conspiracy to, as he said, "drive out all Americans" in California. McClatchy, like many Californians and Progressives during the era, targeted the Japanese with a blatant racist zealotry. He bemoaned what he considered the inability of those of Japanese descent (regardless of birthplace or citizenship status) to assimilate and made such statements as "The United States [is] destined to become a Japanese Province unless Japanese immigration is forbidden absolutely." Citing Japanese belligerence in Manchuria and Korea, McClatchy believed California a fifth column for an all-out Japanese takeover. McClatchy's prejudice evokes a Progressive racism in general and against the Japanese in California in particular.

Namely, progress was for whites and, as repulsive as it truly is, this meant restricting opportunities for nonwhites, which mirrored the growing racial science and notions of superiority and savagery. This racism thus reflected both a booster spirit and a white-biased attempt to encode such racialized notions into the organization of the residential landscape.[49]

Like Joseph Widney, Holt, and many Southern California boosters, Sacramento's boosters shared a racist view of the world that mirrored a Progressive and Social Darwinist sense of superiority. In fact, a 1909 Orangevale advertisement in a pamphlet subtitled *Devoted to the Interests of Ideal Country Homes* included a boast of "No Chinese. No Japanese."[50] By the end of the nineteenth century, many California and Sacramento boosters balked against all things Asian, whether Chinese or Japanese, foreign born or not. They fervently embraced the notion of the United States as a "white man's country"—little wonder then that Weinstock counted the American Jewry as members in good standing. In this context, Sacramenteans played a role in building a landscape that was predominantly white and destined for whites (though that made-up category also varied as they worked to do so).[51]

While Weinstock and McClatchy certainly represented two of Sacramento's more dynamic boosters, particularly those involved in Orangevale or Fair Oaks, they had company. Thomas B. Hall, a captain in the California State Militia, served as company president of the OVCC until it dissolved in 1896. He founded the wholesale grocery store Hall, Luhrs, & Company at the age of twenty-three in 1877. Ten years later, he purchased 3,200 acres seven miles northeast of Marysville in Yuba County from his father to rear Holstein cattle and grow wheat. Like McClatchy, Hall became involved with the California Citrus Fair Association in 1892, serving as a founding director. He founded and held controlling interest in Mt. Shasta Mineral Springs Company in 1899, along with future Sacramento Chamber of Commerce leader Frank Miller, Sutter Club president Adam Andrew, and former Sacramento mayor Eugene Gregory. He started and presided over the National and Central Immigration Association, which published more than 20,000 pamphlets of *The Resources of Northern and Central California*. He served as a prominent civic leader in addition to his business efforts. Sacramento leaders sought Hall's help in 1892 to draft Sacramento's third city charter.[52] In the late 1890s, Governor James Budd appointed Hall as a member of the auditing board to the Commissioner of Public Works. The *Bee* praised Hall for devoting "more time, energy, and ability to matters of public enterprise than any other Sacramentean in the few years preceding the publication of this work [1894]."[53] Hall also served on the initial committee to draft bylaws and plan Sacramento's first Chamber of Commerce. In fact, the code supported the Sacramento boosters' growth goals through agriculture, as the Sacramento Chamber was designed "to foster trade, commerce and economic interests of the City and County of Sacramento; to induce immigration and the subdivision of

FIGURE 24

Thomas B. Hall, ca. 1890s. Hall pictured in his California State Militia uniform. Courtesy Center for Sacramento History, no. 82/115/13.

lands, and generally to promote development of agriculture and horticultural resources of Central and Northern California." Perhaps not coincidentally enough, the first office for the Sacramento Chamber was the same office of the OVCC.[54]

The career of Frederick K. Cox also underscores the links between prominent Sacramenteans who played a significant role in the promotion of Orangevale, Fair Oaks, and Sacramento. Cox, a native of England, trekked to the gold-rich region of El Dorado County in 1852. He purchased a meat market and entered into partnership with Crawford Clarke. In the fall of 1854, the two entrepreneurs opened a market in Grass Valley, Nevada County, where they also extended their operations by buying and selling cattle. The latter branch of their business became so extensive that they sold the market and relocated to the Sacramento Valley, where they controlled one of the most extensive cattle ranches on the Pacific Coast. In command of one of the most prolific cattle industries in California, they earned an income that placed them among the wealthiest citizens of Sacramento County. Cox and Clarke took over the "Eureka Ditch" (which ran along the American River west to Orangevale) in 1888 from the American River Ditch Company after orange trees they planted froze during the winter of 1887-88. Beginning in 1888, the North Fork Ditch Company, the name of Cox and Clarke's new company, served the OVCC and extended its services to Fair Oaks and other surrounding areas. Cox fostered other business interests in Sacramento, culminating in his presidency of the California State Bank. He took a profound interest in political affairs too. Elected in 1882, he served as a Democratic state senator for two regular and two extra sessions of the legislature. By appointment of Governor Stoneman, he served for two decades as a member of the State Board of Agriculture, including a stint as president, and he sought to advance the interests of farming classes. He helped draft Sacramento's city charter in 1892. "Applying honest principles in the affairs of life," praised the Standard Genealogical Publishing Company in 1901, Cox "has won the confidence of the business community and in a high degree of the public at large."[55]

The business dealings and political connections of men like Cox highlight the extensive network of organizations and individuals that mark the existence of a Sacramento growth machine, particularly regarding the promotion of Orangevale and Fair Oaks, not to mention greater Sacramento. Cox, for example, helped establish the Sacramento, Fair Oaks, and Orange Vale Railway Company (SFORC), which linked some of Sacramento's most influential executives and politicians and represented an auxiliary business associated with Fair Oaks and Orangevale that precipitated the metropolitan growth goals of Sacramento's boosters. The SFORC formed in July 1895 and signified a financial opportunity that boosters saw could potentially yield profits well after the direct sale of land. "Such corporation," reads the SFORC's articles of incorporation, is "to also have the right to buy, lease, and operate street railways under franchises granted by any incorporated city on or along the line of its railway, and to use any motive power thereof that may be authorized by the franchise of such street railway." With a capital stock of $500,000, the investors of the SFORC included Cox as well as George Mott, Phillip Drescher, William Schaw, and L. T. Hatfield. Mott and Drescher, who also helped establish the OVCC, lent a hand in establishing the Sacramento Chamber of Commerce. Mott had a successful career as the general manager of H. S. Crocker Stationers, while Drescher ran Mebius & Drescher Wholesale Grocers. Schaw, the treasurer of SFORC, helped Hall draft the Chamber of Commerce bylaws and served as vice president in 1899 and president in 1900. Hatfield, a former volunteer (drummer boy) for the Thirty-Ninth Regiment Illinois Veteran Volunteer Infantry during the Civil War, graduated from the law department at Illinois State University in 1871. He moved to Sacramento in 1887 and opened a general civil practice, focusing on corporate and, not surprisingly, real-estate law.[56]

The relationship of these men certainly did link them and their interests to the most prominent of Sacramento's social and political bodies and peoples. In addition to an auxiliary business in Orangevale and Fair Oaks like the SFORC, Sacramento's growth machine members rubbed elbows and organized collectively through such institutions as the Sutter Club and the Sacramento Chamber of Commerce. The Sutter Club emerged as a preeminent local social institution. Thanks to its members and central position in Sacramento, the history of the club mirrored the history of Sacramento's development. The Sutter Club's founders and their successors largely built Sacramento and, in many ways, greater California. They were the leaders of nearly all local commercial and professional fields. They controlled the politics of both parties and established the Sacramento Chamber of Commerce. The association of these men to the Chamber of Commerce also facilitated their endeavors to promote the development of Orangevale, Fair Oaks, and Sacramento. Schaw, also a Sutter Club member as well as Drescher, Hatfield, and Cox's business cohort in SFORC, served as the president of the chamber. As president, he authorized a favorable special investigating committee to look into the Fair Oaks Development Company (headed by V. S. McClatchy), a committee that included a man with a direct financial interest in the success of the company: Drescher. Schaw also presided over the chamber when the Sacramento Board of Supervisors met a delegation of Fair Oaks residents urging construction of a bridge across the American River in 1900. Businesspersons of Sacramento, Schaw said, were in accord with the petitioners, realizing the bridge would be for the mutual benefit of everyone in the metropolitan region. He pointed to the widespread advertising done by the FODC that benefited the entire Sacramento region. The directors of the chamber that summer also included Mott (an investor and original charter member of the OVCC). Not surprisingly, the chamber authorized the construction of the bridge and took the lead role in raising funds not only for the bridge but also for the railway from Sacramento to Fair Oaks.[57]

Brief biographies of the Sacramento boosters clearly reveal both the bonds of a powerful and capable growth coalition and individual place entrepreneurs who dedicated a lifetime of activity to business speculation. Primary among these were Weinstock, McClatchy, Hall, and Cox, all champions of pro-growth political activity and boosterism. Sacramento's boosters approached both their growth goals and their Progressive-driven agendas in private investments and activities and through local organizations and politics—well before they assumed state or even federal offices. They had formed the Sacramento Chamber to facilitate the broader marketing of Sacramento as a regional powerhouse and agricultural metropolis that, in their minds, featured a Progressive spirit and modern outlook. They did not hesitate to put government and organizations to use to serve their needs, which they said represented the best for all.

While the chamber of commerce helped them to market Sacramento and the Sutter Club to network with others, pool resources, and share information, the city government helped them run it like a business. The frequently mentioned third city charter they drafted in 1892 created an independent mayor to run Sacramento like an executive of a company. An expanded board of trustees, a sort of legislative branch, balanced the power of the mayor. Dividing the city into nine wards, the charter allowed each ward to elect its own trustee and its own representative on the board of education. The charter also gave the mayor the right to appoint officers with consent from the board of trustees, including the chief of police, police officers, city surveyor, superintendent of streets, fire chief, firefighters, directors of cemeteries, and employees of the waterworks. The seeming order and efficiency that the third city charter represented, which also signaled management and authority, garnered attention in an 1894 booster publication produced by McClatchy and the *Bee: Sacramento County and its Resources.*[58] Sacramento's boosters formed a powerful working growth coalition that utilized individual talent, business dealings, and social statues, while municipal organizations and government helped them stimulate growth, offset costs, and limit liability.

The development of the agriburb communities of Orangevale and Fair Oaks represented a publicity campaign promoting an entire metropolitan area—or at least aspiring metropolitan area—as much as it represented a means to profit for a few individuals. The Sacramento boosters' growth activities took shape because of their metropolitan desires. While perhaps running the risk of labeling the Sacramento area as metropolitan before its time, placing the suburbanization of the agriburbs within the context of *contributing to and being affected by* the nascent metropolitanization of Sacramento is accurate. The development of Orangevale and Fair Oaks was both a part of and a result of the metropolitanization of Sacramento and a broader publicity campaign to promote the area as a whole to accomplish the elite's place interests.

BOOSTERS AND THE GROWTH MACHINE REVISITED

Orangevale and Fair Oaks were certainly speculative ventures designed to reap profits from the direct sale of land. They were also image builders for an entire aspiring metropolis whereby Sacramento's boosters packaged them as examples of Sacramento's superiority, particularly concerning horticulture and ample supply of suburban homes. A larger conglomerate of Sacramento's boosters hoped to profit from the dreamed-of trickle-down economics fueled by new investors and migrants into Orangevale and Fair Oaks specifically, as well as new investors and migrants to the greater Sacramento area.

The packaging of Orangevale and Fair Oaks as agriburbs also took place within a broader metropolitan context because of both the economic motives and Progressive sensibilities of the individual entrepreneurs. Most histories of Orangevale and Fair Oaks, in fact, mirror the historical account given by one local historian. In "History of Fair Oaks," a local historian surmised, "Fair Oaks, California had its beginnings, as did many California towns, as a speculative promotion whose eastern boosters had one thing in mind: profit."[59] Although the identification of the profit motive is correct, scarce attention goes to the liberal disposition of the Orangevale and Fair Oaks boosters. The local historian further focused on Howard & Wilson in Fair Oaks. This focus is problematic. First, it rehashes an old argument concerning the West. Fair Oaks's genesis, as the argument goes, resembled the beginnings of many other so-called settlements or boomtowns in the Old West. Fair Oaks and other Western settlements were nothing more than mere "colonies" (a complicated term if you recall) under the control of

Eastern influences.[60] The problem here, despite the involvement of the Chicago publishing firm of Howard & Wilson, is that Fair Oaks's development depended heavily upon the activities and influences of local boosters. Likewise, the "oppressed colony" narrative of many Western areas represented more of a cry for attention. It mirrors an invented "legacy of conquest" more than an Eastern dominance analogous to Great Britain's imperialist policies on the eve of the American Revolution.[61] Even with Howard & Wilson, who were far from the equivalent of King George III and George Grenville, Fair Oaks's success depended upon the wider promotion of greater Sacramento and such neighboring communities as Orangevale. The Sacramento Valley, certainly not the domain of Eastern boosters and financiers, grew thanks to a growth machine cohort of local Sacramenteans. Also, whether the focus is on "Eastern boosters" like Howard & Wilson or on a local Sacramento growth machine, economic motives become indistinguishable from any other purpose, particularly any humanitarian motive. Again, while not removing the centrality of the profit motive, understanding the development of Orangevale and Fair Oaks within a metropolitan and even cultural context complicates the too-simplistic profit-motive narrative.

Sacramento's boosters, like Cox and Weinstock, expressed a seemingly genuine concern with the plight of farmers that mirrored national narratives as espoused by farmers and Progressives. The creation of agriburbs, then, based in horticulture, mirrored an attempt to assuage the concerns over the problems faced by farmers and small-farming endeavors. Boosters publicized Sacramento as a modern agricultural empire that possessed the urban amenities, transportation networks, and commercial fortitude to sustain modernized small-farm communities on the outer edges of a metropolis. This perspective is precisely what the boosters had in mind in 1901:

> This means that Sacramento, which has had no accessible show place, will be able to take Eastern excursionists direct to the orange groves, showing them by the way the rich hoplands, orchards, and vineyards of the American River district. . . . It means that the American River district for sixteen miles out of Sacramento City will gradually be utilized for suburban homes, and that the mechanic, for the price of a street car fare, can reach any point along the river within eight or ten miles of the city, and can buy, for less than the cost of a city lot, an acre or two of ground and have his kitchen garden, and orchard, and his cow.[62]

Although the boosters' promotion of an agricultural wonderland does cast their role as one of profit seeking, the men themselves cannot be divorced from their, as they saw it, many endeavors rooted in the greater good. It seems plausible that Sacramento's boosters had no problem—found more or less no contradiction—in their marriage of boosterism for profit and progressive reform. They sought to clean up the city, create idyllic communities for farmers and businessmen alike, and transform greater Sacramento—even California, the nation, and the world—into what they envisioned a more rational, orderly, and functional society devoted to the greater democratization and attainment of equality for most Americans, except, of course, as McClatchy most venomously represented, the nonwhite population.

Also note that the packaging of Orangevale and Fair Oaks, as well as Ontario, as agriburbs took place within a national context as the boosters utilized the lure and appeal of the rural and suburban ideals. Suburbia, remember, represented the perfect marriage of city and country, home and family, rural democracy and urban amenities. The agriburb went a step further to exploit the natural advantages of California. As place-centered resource capitalists, these growth-machine members seized upon a model of suburbia that included agriculture in an area well publicized for horticultural developments.

Besides the agrarian and suburban rhetoric of Ontario's boosters, they too mirrored their Northern California counterparts in reform efforts, whether labeled Progressive in name or not. They too saw no contradiction in pursing profit while looking to reform society or create utopias. Widney is the logical one to spotlight as he emerged as the most vocal in highlighting God, trains, and money in the reform efforts of the Los Angeles area. His brother Joseph, besides writing about race and health, emerged as a stout champion of port and harbor improvements. They both saw USC as a redemptive force for both soul and region. Yet, of course, Holt and Chaffey continually evoked the language of romanticized agrarianism and all their supposed qualities in bringing about a better world, even if encoded grossly in the vocabulary of race, class, and normative gender behavior. Again, as Orsi has argued, these California boosters, both north and south, "evolved in the late nineteenth century in an environment shaped by economic and social turbulence and the frustrated ambitions of Californians." He concluded, "Promoters wrote books, articles, and pamphlets, organized and sent displays of California's products to eastern and European fairs, developed booster organizations, and in other ways worked, not only to augment their private fortunes, but also to strengthen the state's economic and social systems."[63]

A distinction between Northern and Southern California, besides any discussion of Progressivism, is worth noting. Namely, while Sacramento's boosters possessed a metropolitan view that forced me to likewise take a metropolitan view in analyzing them, Ontario's boosters, working out of Los Angeles, had perhaps an even broader view. If calling Sacramento a metropolis by the 1880s and 1890s is tough to swallow, though the argument asserts that boosterism was part of why the area transformed into a metropolis, then so too is Los Angeles from the 1870s through 1880s, carrying through the early twentieth century. In fact, while this could be considered exemplary of a metropolitan view, the boosters in Ontario and throughout the Los

Angeles region took a regional perspective—a regional perspective toward metropolitanization, if you will. In addition, while divisions between Los Angeles, San Diego, and even Santa Barbara are detectable, some in the Southland looked at and operated within all of it. This scenario, of course, already fits in with the established literature whereby numerous scholars have pointed out that the Los Angeles area is a region sprawling over five counties, namely Los Angeles, Orange, San Bernardino, Riverside, and Ventura, with several urban centers, from Los Angeles to Long Beach, Santa Ana, Riverside, Pasadena, and San Bernardino. Therefore, when speaking of Los Angeles, it is easier to speak of regional boosters over metropolitan ones— though the terms can easily be conflated. Yet, in Northern California, Sacramento for example, the boosterism decidedly turned on a singular metropolis, not Northern California as a whole. Put differently, even if a more Northern California, or at least Bay Area, boosterism did eventually emerge, Sacramenteans focused on Sacramento, and not San Francisco, Oakland, or San Jose.

The final picture that emerges from all this is that boosters held both economic and seemingly humanitarian motives in pursuing growth. They also shared a desire to grow more than just their respective, and singular, agriburb, especially as most of them were involved with numerous land deals. This led to a more agency-centered conception of boosterism that also took us out of the heart of the city to realize growth machines operate on vast terrains encompassing suburbs and rural areas, promoting them as well. These men were, well, males, to be sure, but shared common career paths and saw no problem using political offices to accomplish their goals. Yet, there was a divide. Northern California boosters distinctly looked to position the area as superior to Southern California. Namely, these growth machines were in competition with not only, say, the East Coast, Texas, or the Middle West; they also competed against each other. The results might seem schizophrenic, as they were all, at once, local boosters, regional/metropolitan boosters, and statewide boosters. As unsatisfying as that may sound, no rigid lines exist for what qualifies one as a local booster versus what qualifies one as a regional or state booster. Even when positioning themselves against each other, they ultimately succeeded in creating a grander narrative about California, molding the fabled California Dream. Finally, worth noting, this dream was not just a Southern California or just a Los Angeles dream, but, by name, the California Dream, which included Sacramento.

FORGETTING AGRIBURBS

Why do we fail to talk about California's agricultural colonization as suburbanization or colonies as suburbs? Admittedly, the discussion is implicitly present in most works concerning California's agricultural landscape at the turn of the twentieth century. In many ways, case studies about Ontario, Orangevale, and Fair Oaks have simply been a game of connecting the dots. Nevertheless, the lack of discussion concerning the suburban side of agricultural colonies is what reveals a little about the lasting legacy of the boosters themselves. It reveals a particular consequence of the packaging of place as presented by the growth machines of Sacramento and Ontario—one that potentially goes beyond the basic focus on the growth machine outcome of increased taxes, overdevelopment and underdevelopment, and the legitimatization of routinized and organizational systems of greed. It actually reveals much about the power of historical narratives, historical consciousness, sense of place, both individual and community identity, and the nature of memory in suburban communities.

PART THREE

CULTIVATING MEMORY

COMING TO TERMS WITH MEMORY

Men make their own history, but they do not make it just as they please; they do not make it under circumstances chosen by themselves, but under circumstances directly found, given, and transmitted from the past. The tradition of all the dead generations weighs like a nightmare on the brain of the living.

KARL MARX, "THE EIGHTEENTH BRUMAIRE OF LOUIS BONAPARTE," 1852[1]

T HE PACKAGING OF AGRIBURBS served as an essential tool in the boosters' real-estate ventures and reform impulses. This resulted in the development of material objects like roads, bridges, Victorian houses, railroads, and other supposed urban amenities. Boosters thus oversaw the material creation of agriburbs, of second space. Boosters, or growth machine members previously identified by public policy expert John Rennie Short as "regimes of representation," also cultivated first space, or place-based representations, whether as light or shadow narratives, that affected how people came to understand such places, both from within and without. The packaging of agriburbs involved the invention of spatial imageries, of storied spaces, distinguishing agriburbs, and their surrounding areas, from other places so that they might sell more successfully.[2] Ultimately, this is advertising, the commodification of place, resulting in the branding or marketing of place.

The focus so far has been on intensely analyzing California's agricultural colonies and boosterism at various scales and in various places in the mid to late nineteenth century and early twentieth century. The argument centered on the agriburb as a particular suburban type, bequeathed to us by the boosters. The agriburb was, therefore, their legacy. Nevertheless, their legacy goes beyond the establishment of a unique rural suburb. Rather, they cast a long shadow. In creating imageries to sell their suburbs and metropolitan regions, coupled of course with appropriating Romantic suburban imagery and the California Dream, these boosters established the way many people have historically talked about them and, in turn, come to understand them. Put differently, in the spirit of the Pink Floyd quote shared earlier, the metaphor is that they tell you what to dream; or, as Foucault said of "regimes of truth" and Short said of "regimes of representation," they work to construct what (historical) truth is—even if, according to Marx, such construction of truth is a nightmare on the brain of the living and not necessarily a dream. Admittedly, this type of analysis may seem to shift radically from a focus on suburban type, process, boosters, and growth machines. The potential problem such a shift may pose for some readers is understandable. The final two chapters, however, look to understand the enduring consequences of boosterism in California and growth machine activity in agriburbs. It is integral to the story. Namely, the legacies of boosterism have had a much longer effect and influence than many might at first realize or appreciate. The goal here is to chronicle such a legacy.

The reason for focusing on the legacy of land boosterism beyond the creation of a unique suburban type came about from a rather simple question: Why have others analyzing California's agricultural colonies failed to robustly identify the suburban side? Memory studies provide an answer. Namely, the boosters and subsequent historical representations have established a dominant way of representing the past concerning California and specific sites therein that guides—while clouding—subsequent scholarly and local analyses. Therefore, while we often go to the historical record to find answers, the historical record can be problematic as well. Such a focus on historical representations further affords the all-too-rare opportunity to engage suburbanites themselves. It allows for the examination of suburbanites from the proverbial bottom up and helps reveal more fully one aspect of how they attempt to make sense of their own lives in these particular rural suburbs: their conception of what can be called third space, a basis for living in place.

For those not familiar with memory studies, a few words here will help clarify how a memory framework has relevance to understanding the legacies of land boosterism in California. First thing to share, however, is the impossibility of summarizing memory studies in a few pages. It is a large, complicated, multidisciplinary area of research (and that is to its credit), involving fields as diverse as history, sociology, political science, philosophy, art, theology, literary criticism, psychology, anthropology, and even the natural sciences. Because of so many so-called cooks in the kitchen, memory often suffers criticism for being too broad, too incoherent, and not careful enough with the conclusions it portends, especially about individuals. Luckily, several quality works attempt to consolidate memory studies into a coherent field and are great resources for anyone interested in learning more about the historiography in addition to the conceptual foundations of memory, especially as found in Jeffrey Olick, Vered Vinitzky-Seroussi, and Daniel Levy's introduction to The Collective Memory Reader.[3]

Anthropologist James Wertsch wrote that memory is "a term in search of a meaning."[4] That sounds pretentious, but it highlights that memory studies is multidisciplinary and intemperately rolled up in theory. Therefore, much of what is said is bogged down in jargon. Different terms and phrases often appear to discuss the same thing. Yet, to add to the confusion, the same word or phrase often appears across texts to mean different things. Therefore, clarifying terminology is important.

Memory is not as simple to define as one might think. Most people who use the term do indeed mean recalling or remembering the past, a reference to a biological, cognitive process that takes place within individuals and their brains. This last point is the source of much confusion for newcomers to memory studies, the basis for arguments among some practitioners, and a source for rancor and dismissive portrayals from critics. Simply put, individuals remember. Societies and groups do not. While some scholars of memory studies focus on understanding the mental and other processes of remembering by individuals, most—especially within the humanities and social sciences—look to groups. Accordingly, memory is a metaphor for transferring the concept of remembering the past from the individual to the group.

Those looking to memory analyze remembering as something people do as much as a memory they have. More narrowly, the focus is typically on "cultural memory" and "articulate memory." Cultural memory has come, in part, to signify the sociocultural contexts affecting the remembrance of the past of individuals living in groups (hence, it has come to include *social memory*). The idea is that social relationships and phenomena, that culture, ideology, beliefs, and values, all affect the remembrance of the past. Therefore, memory scholars, in the tradition of social and cultural studies, often look to dissect cultural memory as a way to understand something about the society and culture producing said memory. This is the proverbial picture-window approach that contends cultural memory is a viable unit of analysis for understanding any given group or population.

Articulate memory extends this all further by saying that the cultural memory of groups needs to manifest in some tangible way in order for scholars to identify and, subsequently, analyze it.[5] So, rather than just saying culture and societal phenomena affect people's minds and the way they come to understand the past, the idea is that the many various manifestations of memory are what one needs to analyze in order to understand better a group's cultural memory. Put differently, articulations of memory are the products of memory, the so-called cultural texts that scholars can read. Such articulation can come through words, rituals, myths, pageantry, memorialization, tradition, bodily movements, and even gestures. So most scholars look at the various manifestations, or, to use other phrases, articulations, actualizations, objectifications, representations, or vectors of memory, labeled here simply as *memory works* (i.e., manifestations of memory). This is very much an umbrella phrase subsuming distinct modes of remembering the past as divergent as myth, tradition, folklore, textual narratives (e.g., history books), cultural performances, ritual, museum exhibits, etc. Moreover, the phrase *cultural memory* is a simple and easy phrase to deploy to say that (a) individuals living within groups remember the past in socio-cultural contexts, and (b) memory works are what scholars analyze for both dissecting cultural memory and documenting its existence (i.e., identifying and describing cultural memory).

What do such articulations of cultural memory reveal? Those who study groups and cultural memory have come up with a variety of answers. At its most basic, however, analyzing cultural memory narrows on the functional aspect of the remembrance of the past as a (re)construction of groups. More often than not, the argued purpose for groups to (re)produce memory works is that they fashion a shared vision of the past to unite them. The goal is to create a shared likeness among differing, complicated individuals so that the group in which they live is further united and, hence, stable. Obviously, tales of abuse, of power and politics, and the fashioning of hegemony often emerge from such a conceptual framework. Still, while highlighting such phenomena in the next two chapters, the point here is that cultural memory, represented in some way, works to solidify groups, even if that means it simultaneously works to exclude from the group as much as to include—please keep that in mind.

Another reason to study memory works, particularly celebratory ones about the past, however invented or not, is to see how they play a central role in human consciousness and greatly affect the way we think, speak, and behave. People utilize stories and ideas about the past to shape, even manipulate, identity. Identity (a sense of self) is something that is lived in and through activity and so must be conceptualized as it develops in social practices and cultural contexts like those who study cultural memory describe. In other words, identity is a means through which people care and think about what is going on, how they come not only to understand themselves but also others. It further informs their sense of inclusion or not within a group. People thus busily articulate their own identities to each other and to themselves. This activity includes engaging, producing, and/or interacting with stories about the past (i.e., memory works).[6]

This last point brings us back to the level of the individual in some capacity. Memory works are not simply a product of cultural memory. This memory does not create itself. Rather, individuals living within groups actualize cultural memory. Remember, groups do not remember. Individuals within groups do. By producing memory works in whatever capacity, that product or manifestation represents, again, something about the society and culture in which the individual doing the remembering exists. Even those analyzing individual cognitive processes recognize that external factors trigger and shape individual memories as much as internal ones. People, again, remember within sociocultural contexts. Moreover, as individuals look to construct identity, they again pull from representations about the past, among other things of course. Therefore, memory works are not just the products of cultural memory but the products individuals use to further produce and reassemble more memory works, however intentional or conscious notwithstanding. That is, memory works are both the products and mediums of cultural memory.

The goal of this and the next chapter seeks to break down the cultural memory—the remembrance of the past—in agriburbs over time. Doing so accomplishes several things. First, it continues to shine a light on the legacies of boosterism by arguing that the boosters were the first producers of representations about agriburbs that have subsequently dominated conceptions of these communities in later years and, in turn, the (re)production/reassembly of memory works themselves. This bleeds into yet another benefit of memory studies: forgetting. An examination of the many memory works involving agriburbs and California, including academic scholarship, reveals a recurrent, constant, and typical representation dating back to the boosters. A memory study thus advances an argument for why and how the suburban side of these communities' past has evaded more concrete identification and elaboration.

While analyzing the memory works of these communities expands the study of boosterism and growth machines more widely than is typical, it also challenges older, more traditional suburban scholarship. Concisely put, suburbs have notably received scorn over the years, what John Archer has called "the places we love to hate."[7] These feelings of anxiety and disdain, however, are creations. As Archer and new suburban historians have shown, American anxiety and the mostly negative view of suburbs have a context related to modernity, industrialization, and a whole lot more. Regardless of the details, the point is that suburbs are often scapegoats, wrapped in stereotype and mythologies, typically propagated for the purposes of advancing a specific agenda.[8] For example, a common view of suburbia is that it is a white, residential, middle-class community, the banal curse of American consumerism and homogeneity. The agriburb, however, explodes any notion that suburbs are just residential. Indeed, as shared before, new suburban historians have been at the forefront of challenging such narrow visions of suburban types, functions, and demographics. Therefore, to say such a vision is still the dominant one would be a straw-man fallacy.

We still need more, however. Suburbs often receive treatment as placeless and historically rootless. They seem to have little to no connection to the past. Moreover, suburbanites often seem to lack a sense of community, which, as memory scholars remind us, too often comes via a shared sense of history. This is just flat out false. A memory study of agriburbs overturns that. It shows beyond the shadow of a doubt that suburbanites—or, at least, *some* suburbanites—actively engage the past of their communities. Again, this is not a redemptive tale, nor an apology for suburbia. Many less-than-noble features manifest. Still, the point remains: suburban memory exists.

CHAPTER SIX

THE ONGOING LEGACIES OF BOOSTERISM

The seemingly insignificant happenings in the starting of a new settlement
were really of great importance to its growth and development. This is especially
true for the Ontario Colony, for these events laid the foundations
that have persisted to make it truly the Model Colony.

BERNICE BEDFORD CONLEY, 1982[1]

A DOMINANT CULTURAL MEMORY

Ethnographers have previously applied a "themal schemata" to several life histories of people that revealed the use of key ordering concepts, labeled *cognitive templates*.[2] They unearthed the dominance of particulars within life histories. Analyzing these reveal "schematic narrative templates" that represent "generalized functions that characterize a broad range of [specific] narratives"—an underlying pattern that people draw on and/or anticipate both reflexively and nonreflexively.[3] A unitary voice often dominates narratives and other representations.[4] Along similar lines, historian Harold Marcuse discusses "recollective paradigms" whereby "recollective," "recollect," or "recollection" refers to "the social process of sharing information about the past among members of a collectivity."[5] The interest is again in the appearance of recurrent, constant, and typical themes throughout a wide variety of memory works. Marcuse further defines this approach as "reception history," or "the history of the meanings that have been imputed to historical events. . . . [T]he different ways in which participants, observers, and historians and other retrospective interpreters have attempted to make sense of events, both as they unfolded, and over time since then, to make those events meaningful for the present in which they lived and live."[6]

A reception history that utilizes a themal analysis of the many memory works concerning Ontario's, Orangevale's, and Fair Oaks's past reveals a "schematic narrative template"—an overall *dominant cultural memory*. That is the purpose of this chapter: to reveal a dominant cultural memory via its prevalent themes within memory works. Following the lead of those in search of underlying paradigms, patterns, templates, and themes, a dominant cultural memory refers to the presence of common and persistent themes that are manifest within and characteristic of a wide variety of memory works that help shape and are shaped by cultural memory itself. Moreover, memory works, particularly concerning representations about the past, are not limited to texts. Remember, they include a variety of instruments, or cultural texts, that can include television, radio, Internet, newspapers, magazines, film, memoirs, novels, scholarly works, textbooks, classroom instruction, museums, art, laws, monuments, memorials, spectacles, pageantry, and commemorations.[7] The major themes that comprise a dominant cultural memory characterize the various memory works concerning agriburbs like Ontario, Orangevale, and Fair Oaks.

The boosters, again, originally produced the themes that characterize a dominant cultural memory. The themes, in fact, have become fixed and uniform and so continuously highlighted that they drown out most other topics or themes that may be evident within any specific memory work. Boosterism and speculative suburban real-estate ventures, like those concerning agriburbs, have continuing consequences then. They are essential to the formation of a dominant cultural memory. Specifically, the prevailing characteristic of Ontario's, Orangevale's, and Fair Oaks's various memory works has contributed to the suburban side of their agricultural colonization going largely undetected precisely because the themes are, again, rigid and perpetually highlighted. Other consequences are detectable too, including the glossing over of certain historical epochs, phenomena, or, most jarringly, people (e.g., minorities). These are covered in the next chapter.

In this chapter, the purpose is to revisit the original booster literature, on one hand, simply to establish the existence of a dominant cultural memory and its prevalent themes. On the other hand, the idea is to move forward in time to show how the dominant cultural memory and its themes are carried on and manifested in later memory works, marking both the existence of a dominant cultural memory and its continued influence.

A themal analysis of Ontario's, Orangevale's, and Fair Oaks's memory works reveals a dominant cultural memory that is composed of four major themes: (1) the agriburb site as unique; (2) the adoration of agriculture; (3) the agriburb site as innovative; and (4) the glorification of a "self-made man," typically the founder or highly influential and successful businessperson. Once more, these themes comprise a dominant cultural memory that is not only a prevailing one but also one that diverts attention away from the suburban side of these agriburb areas' origins because the themes are so recurrent.[8]

Theme 1: Unique Unto Itself

The argument that most memory works cast Ontario, Orangevale, and Fair Oaks as unique or somehow unparalleled should come as no surprise. The notion that a particular community maintains unique unto itself is a common theme found throughout the United States and the world in general. Yet, as the saying goes, the devil is in the details. Specifically, the ways in which the boosters, suburbanites, and subsequent memory works portray these communities as unique provide further illustrations for how a dominant cultural memory diverts attention away from their suburban heritage.

For clarification, the primary elements of the uniqueness theme are not always exclusively so. In fact, many of the elements for any of the themes within the dominant cultural memory can rightfully overlap and properly receive identification within another theme. For example, the boosters, as well as subsequent memory works, tout electricity as what made Ontario both unique and innovative (the third theme noted above). Nonetheless, the context of how various authors represent electricity overwhelmingly portrays it as innovative. Likewise, citrus made Orangevale and Fair Oaks unique while also representing an adoration of agriculture. Nonetheless, the context of how various writers boast of citrus in Orangevale and Fair Oaks depict it as what explicitly made these communities unique. Accordingly, the elements highlighted here received demarcation within a theme based on both my own interpretation (thus, perhaps rare for a historian, acknowledging my part in the meaning-making process) and a rudimentary calculated effort (an attempt to overcome my own biases no matter how naïve such a noble dream may be). Consequently, for brevity, the ones that manifest most receive attention.

ONTARIO AS UNIQUE

The promotion of Ontario as the "model colony" is by far the foremost element of the *uniqueness* theme. The precise meaning of the term is largely implicit, frequently unarticulated, and without clear-cut definitions. Remember, with the 1883 publicity pamphlet, *Ontario, Located in San Bernardino County, California on the Southern Pacific Railroad*, the boosters stated, "The plan of the colony is of the most advanced and liberal kind."[9] Ontario's superior planning is what thus made it unique. The boosters went on to list irrigation, roadways, and a railway (hence the pamphlet's title) to underscore why the plan "is of the most advanced a liberal kind." No direct statement, however, connects such amenities to "the most advanced" plan. In fact, the actual phrase "model colony" does not seem to have appeared in any booster material aimed at a broader audience until *Los Angeles Times* editor Charles Fletcher Lummis published an article, "Ontario," in his magazine, *Land of Sunshine*, in 1895.[10] Still, the boosters did run an advertisement in *Harper's Weekly* in May 1883, proclaiming "Ontario! The Model

Settlement of Southern California."[11] The boosters published the same ad throughout 1883, beginning in August, in the *Los Angeles Times*.[12] Several local Ontario historians, however, without the use of citations, indicate that the advertising of a "model" settlement or colony began immediately.[13] Nevertheless, regarding the first use of the term *model colony*, it seems to have first occurred in a local advertisement for the December 7, 1884, issue of the *Los Angeles Times*.[14] Regardless, the phrase "model colony," or even "model," whether regarding colony or settlement, did not make any precise connections to what made it model, rather implicitly suggesting that the climate and agriculture, among other things, made it so. Perhaps, later on, some unqualified expressions of Ontario as the "model colony" were simply examples of using the phrase in the title of a work, such as eighth-grader Jane Craig's 1931 essay "The Model Colony" written for a collection compiled by Upland Elementary School students or local historian Ruth Austen's 1990 book *Ontario: The Model Colony*. The title "Model Colony" in both works implies the entire work will reveal why Ontario was such.[15]

Emphasizing—implicitly or explicitly—specific features for what made Ontario a "model" colony or settlement, from those who revere agriculture to those who highlight distinct innovative institutions or infrastructure, is characteristic of Ontario's many memory works. For example, in a 1904 account of Ontario in *Ingersoll's Century Annals of San Bernardino County*, Ontario "was the most perfect plan then formulated for colonization." Once again, various memory works highlight numerous features to suggest why Ontario deserved the distinction of "model colony." In 1981, a local historian referred to the "happenings in the starting of a new settlement" to explain, "these events laid the foundations that have persisted to make it truly the Model Colony."[16] Here, the implication is that superior planning made Ontario unique and truly special.

An Australian journalist's publicity also helped brand Ontario as a "model irrigation colony."[17] Labeling Ontario as such illustrates how some memory works directly cite what made Ontario a model colony. Indeed, when a clear-cut connection to the model colony appears, irrigation is the most typical. Ontario even received the distinction as the "model irrigation colony" when US government engineers erected a scale panorama of Ontario at the St. Louis World's Fair in 1904.[18] In fact, the element of irrigation, as a component of both the uniqueness and innovative themes, further suggests why scholars overlook Ontario's suburban roots. Irrigation is so frequently citied and emphasized within memory works that it receives prominence at the expense of highlighting other things. Irrigation became not only repetitive but also normative.

A more direct set of particulars for why Ontario as the model colony first appeared in the 1884 booster pamphlet authored by Widney, *Ontario: Its History, Description, and Resources; Valuable Information For Those Seeking Homes in Southern California*. Although Widney never called Ontario the "model colony," he did arrogantly call Ontario's colonization "the most perfect plan"—for, as a booster, why would he not? Still, subsequent memory works repeat the set of particulars laid out by Widney to elaborate, though still implicitly, why Ontario began as the model colony. Recall that Widney cited three features for what made Chaffey's plan "matured" and the "most perfect plan ever adopted by a colony in this State": first, the distribution of water for irrigation purposes; second, the construction of a main thoroughfare; and, third, the establishment of the Chaffey College of Agriculture.[19] That the boosters produced pamphlets with such dramatic flair, including accolades of a perfect plan, should come as no surprise. The repeating of such rhetoric in subsequent memory works, which present it as a basic, indispensable, and undisputed historical fact, should astonish some and illustrate the durable power of the original representations and early memory works about Ontario.

One hundred years after Widney, his explanation has endured. "Ontario . . . was based on four principles," concluded prominent California historian Kevin Starr in 1990. The four principles included "water rights, urban planning, an agricultural college, and the prohibition of alcohol."[20] In 1999, a local Ontario historian repeated this.[21] With that said, these works reveal how certain elements of themes can alter, even if subtly, and even weave in new threads. Specifically, Widney, while discussing temperance in Ontario, particularly as it aimed at drawing in the middle class, did

FIGURE 25

WCTU Drinking Fountain. This drinking fountain, homage to the moral upright beginnings of a community, services Ontario in the middle of Euclid Avenue. It was moved from Euclid and Holt Avenue for the Bicentennial Celebration in the 1970s and now rests in front of the Ontario Bandstand, itself homage to a quintessential small-town American ideal that has since evaporated with modernity and urbanization. Photo by author, 2007.

not ascribe temperance to Chaffey's vision for Ontario to become the Model Colony. The addition of temperance to the set of particulars for what made Ontario a perfect plan is the accomplishment of historical development. Author J. A. Alexander included temperance as a particular of the most perfect plan in his 1928 biography of Chaffey. Alexander's book appeared during the great "noble experiment" of national prohibition. His inclusion of temperance as a specific particular is thus understandable and likely reflects his own agenda.[22] The celebration of temperance in Ontario appears in many of the memory works, including a memorial water fountain donated to Ontario by the Women's Christian Temperance Union (WCTU) in 1904, which still serves to quench the thirst of many Ontario residents and visitors today.

ORANGEVALE AND FAIR OAKS AS UNIQUE

Orangevale and Fair Oaks mirror the storied sense of place at work in Ontario. The boosters proclaimed them the best places in California, and thus the nation, to grow fruits and vegetables. Touted as ideal communities with perfect weather, Orangevale and Fair Oaks seemed impeccable. They enjoyed perfect soil, full of potential for a seemingly unbounded national market eager to receive their produce, and they established a rural lifestyle without want of urban amenities, and so on.

According to most memory works shaped from both inside and from outside the communities of Orangevale and Fair Oaks, these places were the best for the growth of citrus. When considering just the memory works not produced locally, the exaltation of Orangevale and Fair Oaks's superior ability to cultivate citrus as compared to any other place, and hence a celebration of their agricultural prowess and past, is what receives the most attention. This thematic representation contributes to the surfeit of information received by most nonlocal researchers and is what potentially directs them to retransmit such information. Attention to some type of suburban planning garners little mention and, regrettably, a process of forgetting sets in (i.e., "structural amnesia" or "collected memory," discussed more in chapter seven).

Orangevale and Fair Oaks, in partial fulfillment of the extraordinary claims made about them, could be proud when it came to the actual growth of citrus. In Orangevale, as shared previously, 2,300 acres were reportedly fenced by 1890, 500 acres of orange trees planted by 1894, and the first crop of oranges came off the trees the following year.[23] Orangevale also had 3,200 acres irrigated by 1913 and, by 1915, had 2,000 acres in orange trees. Orangevale became one of the leading producers of oranges, reaching its peak in 1925.[24] In Fair Oaks, while the numbers did not reach the levels reported in Orangevale, citrus dominated with a reported 1,200 acres of citrus by 1900, but Fair Oaks also had sizeable loads of almonds and olives. The booster booklet of the Fair Oaks Development Company in late 1900 bragged, "There are some navel oranges now in the fourth year, and of these trees there are now . . . a carload and a half, say

30,000 pounds–500 boxes–of fruit which will be shipped between November 15 and January 1, 1901."[25] Moreover, recall that both Orangevale and Fair Oaks purportedly prospered by an "early citrus section" that made their yield not only plentiful and robust but also ready for harvest earlier than in Southern California. This reportedly gave the Orangevale and Fair Oaks citrus growers a commercial advantage of hitting the marketplace early and more often.[26]

The promotion of Orangevale and Fair Oaks, sometimes called "citrus colonies," served to draw investors from out of state and, according to one historian, "burnish" Northern California with the reputation of "a sunshine capital."[27] As a result, citrus became a leading iconographic symbol, a commercial logo, even a brand, in the promotion of California in general and the Sacramento region specifically. Remember that Orangevale and Fair Oaks emerged in numerous contemporary publications in the late nineteenth century and first half of the twentieth century as the most favored and likely sites for the cultivation of citrus in the Sacramento Valley, especially as Sacramento boosters sought to compete with the success of Southern California.[28]

Orangevale and Fair Oaks commonly appeared in booster publications concerning the Sacramento region and advertisements concerning Orangevale and Fair Oaks directly. They received constant praise for being the "best section" or "best district" for the growth of citrus, particularly as the "ideal location for the cultivation of orange

FIGURE 26

Greater Sacramento, cover, 1912. Note the prominent display of oranges, signifying the centrality of citriculture to the imaginary landscape and soil of the Sacramento region. Courtesy Center for Sacramento History, no. 1981/52/07.

trees," and, of course, showed everyone that "no finer looking [orange] groves exist in the State than in these two communities [of Orangevale and Fair Oaks]."²⁹ A picture of a citrus tree or grove in Orangevale or Fair Oaks, particularly an orange one, commonly graced books concerning the Sacramento region, such as the picture "Typical California Bungalow, amid Orange Groves" in Fair Oaks for the 1912 publication of *Greater Sacramento: Her Achievements, Resources and Possibilities.* A picture of a blood orange in Fair Oaks appeared in the 1904 publication of *Fruit Growing is California's Greatest Industry.*³⁰ This image of Orangevale and Fair Oaks as the best places for the cultivation of citrus further received distinction, and, thus, served as additional substantiation of fantastical claims, such as the announcement of good showings and prize-winning efforts at citrus exhibitions.³¹

The lasting power of Orangevale and Fair Oaks as the loci of citrus emerges from the pages of more recent memory works composed in the post–World War II era. The Sacramento Planning Department, for example, in their *Fair Oaks Community Plan* of 1975, determined that citrus had played a major role in the history of the community and its modern character.³² General histories of the region, such as in *Sacramento: Indomitable City,* distinguish Orangevale and Fair Oaks, as well as Citrus Heights, as the primary sites for the growth of citrus. Three out of the five times the historian mentions Fair Oaks and Orangevale, he refers to citrus and fruit growing—the other two refer to expansion after World War II.³³ Other accounts, such as a 1959 article in the *Sacramento Union* and a local history of Orangevale published by a suburbanite in 1962, fondly recalled that Orangevale received its name from cofounder and member of the OVCC, P. C. Drescher, because of "the flourishing citrus groves."³⁴

Also suggestive, in a search in 2005 for a logo to represent the Fair Oaks Historical Society, one entry urged members to select the logo, "Fair Oaks, Home of the Orange," which depicted a well-illustrated orange tree wrapped with the written portion of the logo on a banner. More striking, the logo came from the leading local historian in the community. The local Fair Oaks historian stated, "This logo should reflect the foundation of our community from its birth in 1895." The local historian continued, "Some of you have not had the opportunity to study the origins of our town. None of you were here at the beginning, and the oldest of you were only children at the end of Fair Oaks [*sic*] agricultural Golden Age before the Great Depression." Therefore, in pushing for the orange logo, the local historian concluded it "is incumbant [*sic*] on each of us to choose that symbol which most closely represents why people chose to leave the East and how they struggled to make a living during the early years of our history." They came to "raise agricultural products," the local historian stated, and no "agricultural product was more seductiue [*sic*] to these aspirants than citrus, the orange foremost among the several varieties." Finally, "In selecting the orange as a symbol to represent our society, you will be choosing the very fruit that the earliest developers most used in their promotional material and the fruit that was foremost in the hopes of the earliest colonists." In the end, and likely to the local historian's dismay, another logo, one featuring a giant oak tree (still suggesting and celebrating rurality), won the contest.[35]

Theme 2: The Adoration of Agriculture

The adoration of agriculture found in many memory works concerning Ontario, Orangevale, and Fair Oaks, like the theme "unique," is typical of a considerable number of communities in California. Agriculture is thus a typical and recurrent theme for many communities in California. Such adoration of agriculture, however, diverts attention away from the suburban side of Ontario's, Orangevale's, and Fair Oaks's foundations. It again, though, further reveals the lasting legacies of harvesting suburbs in California because it is also about cultivating memory.

While the adoration of agriculture certainly mirrors a theme of uniqueness in agriburbs, especially Orangevale and Fair Oaks, in that both themes underscore the importance of agricultural produce and production, the unique theme centered more intensely on citrus, at least in Orangevale and Fair Oaks. All the same, while an adoration of agriculture surely does encompass all produce, including citrus, it also includes a larger imagery associated with farming. The adoration of agriculture is much more than a narrative about fruits, nuts, vegetables, and raisins in this case. The people planting the crops and what they have come to symbolize are the significant parts. The issue centers on romantic agrarianism and the ideal of small town and on rural life more than on agriculture or citrus.

The adoration of agriculture concerning Ontario, Orangevale, and Fair Oaks conjures up powerful images of independent farmers cultivating the moral self and family. Agriculture thus represented the beloved image of small-town Americans making a living from the soil, the bedrock of the nation. Musician John Mellencamp expressed this sentiment most vividly when discussing the continued need for Farm Aid—a musical concert and organization devoted to American "farm families" that began in 1985. "We all see what's happening with agriculture, what's happening to our small towns," said Mellencamp. "They are going out of business. That's a direct result of the farm problem. We're still doing Farm Aid because it is contributing. It's doing a job."[36] For Mellencamp and others, then, the "job" is to save some form of a cherished American institution and way of life that people from President Thomas Jefferson to singer Willie Nelson have romanticized.

In her classic, *Town Building on the Colorado Frontier* (1987), historian Kathleen Underwood dissected the small town of Grand Junction, Colorado, to reveal the elements of town-building and social life in so-called frontier towns of the West during the nineteenth century. Among many of her insights, including a detailed social history of what can arguably be called an agriburb outside of California, her commentary on the imagery and romanticization that small towns have come to represent are most appropriate. Beginning with a quote from the 1930s by the noted Yale professor and editor of *Saturday Review of Literature*, Henry S. Canby, Underwood makes clear the power of the small town in American imagination. "It is the small town," said Canby, "that is our heritage." Referencing a 1976 *Time* article, we get a message that the "small town is almost synonymous with community." Mellencamp, as we saw, certainly thought so. On the one hand, like suburbs generally, small towns were simply another alternative to cities. On the other hand, small towns, Underwood reveals, held even more pull as "Americans continued to identify opportunity with small towns at a time when others sought advancement in rapidly growing cities." Indeed, a strong tradition of celebrating the virtues of small towns exists, as does a strong historiography. The point, however, is that small-town imagery related to suburbs (at least at the turn of the twentieth century) emerged as a strong narrative that invoked deep-seated and highly respectable attributes in American culture. An adoration of agriculture in agriburbs, therefore (while focused on numbers and markets as much as farmers), summons this narrative power of small towns to cast these communities as superlative.[37]

ONTARIO AND THE ADORATION OF AGRICULTURE

The enormous "land boom" in Southern California in the 1880s is not a forgotten story. By 1890, Ontario had a population of 683 while the acreage of fruit registered at 7,678. The "major part," of course, belonged to citrus.[38] Earlier, in 1883, Ontario had already shipped 207 train carloads of oranges and lemons and 104 carloads of deciduous fruits and raisins to market.[39] The agricultural growth in Ontario following the boom of the eighties receives much attention. The point of such attention, again, is not to get lost in the numbers but to realize the focus has a purpose, an appeal. Nevertheless, let us look at what appears.

"It would be an impossibility for a person to remain more than a few minutes within the limits of Ontario without realizing that here oranges are grown," asserted the *Ontario Record* in 1907.[40] Again, as memory works recall repeatedly, thriving agriculture in Ontario grew dramatically with the completion of several railroad lines. We also learn that several cooperative associations and packing companies formed too, such as the Mitchell and Butterfield packinghouse and the Ontario Fruit Exchange. Ontario also began to establish and participate in other agricultural "fairs," reportedly a creation of the booster Luther M. Holt. The growth contrasted with Ontario's industrial progress, particularly with the establishment of Hotpoint in 1903, which produced electric appliances (later for General Electric). The enduring result of Ontario's meteoric rise and lasting viable agricultural production from the end of the nineteenth century through the first half of the twentieth century is a (rightful) celebration and recollection of such. Still, while a stunning number of figures favorably receive attention in the memory works—such as how many carloads of grapes shipped out in 1926 (3,300 to be exact)—Ontario's production and growth proportions dominate, which mirrors the exaltation of agriculture in the pantheon of California history in general.[41] These are not just good small-town agricultural sites, but, of course, the best ones as the numbers and other memory works make clear.

The conception of agriculture, specifically horticulture, as the foundation for suburban planning, however, loses some credibility when vague notions of "colony" guide most memory works chronicling Ontario's beginnings as the model colony. While such memory works about Ontario generally recognize the role that agriculture played in the community's foundation, they understand it in terms of *colony* and then quickly move to describe the exceptional number of urban amenities Ontario developed. In this plot line, the true legacy of agriculture in Ontario is its rising production, development, and economic importance, not its paramount role in the establishment of the community (though it is the basis for respecting it). Focusing on the suburban side of Ontario's origins turns that legacy on its head to reinterpret the significance of agriculture in the planning of a unique suburban type. Indeed, the plethora of urban amenities accompanying the suburbanization of Ontario—as opposed to developing regardless—is what set the foundation and created the necessary infrastructure and institutions necessary to foster the rise of agricultural production. Such infrastructure also paved the way for remarkable industrial growth, ultimately leading to the accelerating urbanization of Ontario following World War II.

THE ADORATION OF AGRICULTURE IN ORANGEVALE AND FAIR OAKS

The adoration of agriculture present in memory works about Orangevale and Fair Oaks also mirrors Ontario and other boosters' praise of California's fertile soil. In the Sacramento region, unsurprisingly, one could pick up such titles as *Fruit Growing is California's Greatest Industry: Sacramento County is the Very Heart of its Greatest Production* (ca. 1904); *Fair Oaks, Sacramento County: In the Heart of the Fruit-Growing Section of California* (1900); or *Sacramento, California: The World's Garden Valley* (1925).

Agriculture and its growth in Sacramento County do deserve notice. By 1910, the US Census Bureau had recorded the value of just fruits and nuts in Sacramento County at $2,265,690.00 (roughly $53.6 million in purchasing power in 2010). In 1920, the valuation of fruits and nuts jumped to $6,346,873.00 (roughly $69.1 million in purchasing power in 2010; thus, from 1910 to 1920 the annual percentage growth rate was about twenty-nine percent in terms of 2010 relative value).[42] Orangevale and Fair Oaks, in the years leading up to 1910 and 1920, as well as through the 1920s, thus ignited agricultural growth in Sacramento. Nevertheless, in conjunction with their agricultural proficiency, Orangevale and Fair Oaks also represented a *colonization enterprise* that subdivided the land into small-town lots to allow migrants to enjoy a farming lifestyle without the sacrifice of supposed urban comforts.

Colonization enterprises, such as Orangevale and Fair Oaks, reflected what early boosters described as "choice subdivisions" and areas of "productiveness." They were for "fruit-raising" and, when not called agricultural colonies, citrus colonies, or even irrigation colonies, the boosters and subsequent researchers called them *fruit colonies*.[43] Ultimately, such communities retained their association with Sacramento, and as one observer noted in 1999, "newer 'commuter farm' communities like Orangevale, Fair Oaks, and Carmichael, had crops on small acreages" because of the "the strong public interest in all things agricultural." In fact, the image of farming in the area made it seem effortless while robust and lucrative at the same time. According to historian Joseph McGowan, "Advertising throughout the nation," boosters "hoped to profit from the land sales while the purchasers thought all they had to do was to sit on the front porch and watch the fruit grow. Orangevale, Fair Oaks, Rio Benito, Thermolito, and the Maywood Colonies (Corning) were some of the better-known schemes."[44]

Orangevale and Fair Oaks were not just any fruit colony or colonization enterprise; they were, like citrus, hyped as the best "fruit districts," with "fertility of soil," best "topography," best climate in the area for early ripening, without extreme heat or extreme cold, and blessed with the perfect amount of rainfall.[45] Orangevale and Fair Oaks, as one anonymous writer stated in 1899, "Has been demonstrated, as nowhere else, that all of the fruits, of whatever name or character, can be raised side by side in the soil."[46] In *Farm, Field and Fireside*, the Howard & Wilson Publishing Company praised Fair Oaks because the "report of the California State Horticultural Society for 1892, on page 191, says of this section that it is 'one of the foremost sections of the State, and from a horticultural point of view, the foremost section.'"[47] Orangevale and Fair Oaks had received such recurrent publicity as places of such exceptional quality that the Sacramento Chamber of Commerce purportedly took one prominent visitor, Benjamin Franklin Bush, president of Gould Lines (Western Pacific Railroad), on a trip to Fair Oaks and Orangevale in 1913.[48] The reason for such a trip, to be sure, was clear enough, for in Orangevale and Fair Oaks, idyllic beauty and weather awaited, as the OVCC made clear in 1894. "Shut in and sheltered from the cold winds and fogs of the coast, and protected, by chains of intervening hills and mountains from the chilly blasts of the higher altitudes, here is found a spot free from killing frosts, where flowers bloom and tender plants thrive the year round, in an atmosphere clear and bright, and under a practically cloudless sky."[49] So, no wonder that in 1988 the locally produced *Fair Oaks Guide* printed the lyrics to a song, "The Home of Fruit and Beauty," with the chorus:

Fair Oaks, Fair Oaks, we render her our duty.
We love her well, her praise we'll tell.
The Home of Fruit and Beauty.[50]

Most accounts that deal with the history of Orangevale and Fair Oaks typically close, or at least reach a climax before a quick end, with the freeze of 1932.[51] This freeze, as shared before, effectively wiped out Orangevale and Fair Oaks as major fruit producers. Many growers were unenthusiastic about replanting because of the unforgiving economy and fickle consumer tastes (i.e., Florida oranges for orange juice expanded). In Orangevale, for example, the orange acreage, once at 2,000, dropped drastically to 879 in 1935 and then to 473 in 1940. Yet, as illustrated by the *Fair Oaks Guide* in 1988 and the Fair Oaks Historical Society's contest for a logo, the importance and self-image of these communities as loci of agricultural activity and prowess dominate. What is more striking is that agriculture, while the basis for these communities and what, in reality, provided for the further establishment of institutions and infrastructure congruent with their development as suburban types, perhaps pales to the impact of growth in population and infrastructure after World War II. This is particularly true of histories produced during and after the 1960s, as the size of these communities, examined in more detail later, boomed. Their agricultural heritage, while essential in their establishment, is only a part of the story, and not the whole story.

Theme 3: Agriburbs as Innovative (Ahead of Their Time)

The perpetual dominance of innovative institutions and infrastructure in many memory works concerning Ontario, Orangevale, and Fair Oaks also diverts attention from their suburban roots. The plethora and multivariate nature of the actual institutions and infrastructure are striking in the context of Ontario's, Orangevale's, and Fair Oaks's memory and early self-image as agricultural colonies. The self-image and ongoing representation of these communities' origins as agricultural colonies contrast with the modern urban amenities they developed early on. For some historians, particularly local, this element demonstrates why Ontario was a community with all the amenities of a city without the city—the ideal small town. Indeed, Widney counted a main thoroughfare as the second of three particulars marking Ontario's "perfect" plan. Historian Kevin Starr, however, identified it as *urban planning*.[52] Conversely, the conception of Ontario, Orangevale, and Fair Oaks as having urban amenities without the city is largely why they were in fact suburbs and, ironically, likely the most glaring reason why scholars fail to identify these communities' suburban roots.

ONTARIO AS INNOVATIVE

The specific institutions and infrastructure highlighted in various memory works include, among others, clubs, irrigation, electricity, and transportation. Churches and schools also receive a fair amount of attention, as does the mule car (streetcar/

tram), which emerged more prominent in comparison by the end of the twentieth century, especially because of the allocation of public space and memorialization of the mule car with an exhibit in the middle of Euclid Avenue. Likewise, the Chaffey College of Agriculture now ranks above churches and schools because (aside from secularization, perhaps) of its prominence in early memory works and its connection with Chaffey and the other boosters. Nonetheless, no other institution or infrastructure receives as much praise and mention throughout the entirety of Ontario's memory works as Euclid Avenue, the "world famous" and "beautiful" street. The typical narrative concerning Euclid Avenue claims Chaffey conceived of the thoroughfare as part of his most-perfect plan. Euclid provided residents of Ontario with a quality road and an attractive thoroughfare lined with eucalyptus trees. The City Planning Commission of Ontario successfully nominated Euclid Avenue for inclusion on the National Register of Historic Places in August 2005.[53]

A 1997 Historic American Buildings Survey/Historic American Engineering Record (HABS/HAER), conducted before improvement on California State Route 30 (present-day I-210), captures the sense of history related to Euclid as well. The survey record opens:

Euclid Avenue is significant in three areas: community planning, landscape architecture, and transportation. Each reflect the vision of George and William Chaffey, who designed the avenue and oversaw its construction—a vision continued by citizens of the communities of Upland [formerly North Ontario] and Ontario.[54]

More than 100 years earlier, the first booster pamphlet in 1883 announced, even before the completion of the thoroughfare, "Euclid Avenue is the name of a beautiful double drive . . . being a great benefit to the entire settlement." With the 1884 pamphlet, Euclid Avenue rose prominently to serve as a major advertising point along with irrigation, health, profit, and home ownership on the title page. Widney immortalized "the main thoroughfare" in his three sets of particulars of the most-perfect plan. Euclid, lined with "beautiful evergreens," also served as the thoroughfare where the streetcar system, including the mule car, ran from north to south and connected with the Southern Pacific depot in the heart of downtown Ontario. In 1890, the Lewis Publishing Company's *An Illustrated History of Southern California* found Euclid worth mentioning along with irrigation and railroads. In 1895, Charles Lummis's *Land of Sunshine* determined that Euclid Avenue was "now the finest boulevard in California." In 1903, *The Ontario Record* featured a picture of the now "Famous Euclid Avenue" on the front page, which rhetorically asked, "Why is it the Model Colony." In 1907, *Sunset* magazine featured an article "A City of Ten-Acre Lots," which compared Euclid to "Cleveland's world famous street [Euclid]."[55]

FIGURE 27

Euclid Avenue, ca. 1920s. Courtesy of the Robert E. Ellingwood Model Colony History Room,
Ontario City Library.

When Chaffey biographer J. A. Alexander told the Euclid Avenue story in 1928, he addressed its "beauty," even its "exotic beauty." "To-day Euclid Avenue is almost a little bit of Australia set in the heart of California," claimed Alexander. He continued, "If more Australians knew the serene beauty of Euclid Avenue, with its variegated evergreen tints, there would be fewer imported trees in their home boulevards." Euclid Avenue thus receives a sort of creation myth, in terms of naming, at least. Alexander claims Chaffey (an engineer) named Euclid Avenue "after his favorite study and recreation," which referred to Euclid—the most prominent mathematician of Greco-Roman antiquity.[56]

The continuous attention to Euclid has remained throughout Ontario's history. Specifically, Euclid Avenue appears in most memory works, from local student essays in the 1930s to other local histories in the 1950s, 1970s, 1990s, and today.⁵⁷ Such admiration culminated in Euclid Avenue's designation on the National Register of Historic places in 2005. Still, Euclid Avenue, antipodal to agriculture in an "urban/rural interplay" schematic popularized by historians, represents "urban amenities" (even "urban planning" for Starr).⁵⁸ As noted before in the introduction, such urban amenities, like Euclid Avenue, are represented as innovative in that they developed regardless of Ontario's beginnings as an agricultural colony. On the one hand, it was said that the urban amenities are part of a utopian, garden-city ideal. At worst, urban amenities within a humble agricultural colony seem fantastic and deserve embellishment. Yet neither scenario opened the door for a conception of Ontario as a suburb. This seems so striking precisely because such amenities reveal Ontario began as a planned suburb.

ORANGEVALE AND FAIR OAKS AS INNOVATIVE

An image of a city without the city, to be sure, constituted an important aspect to the promotion of agriburbs such as Ontario, Orangevale, and Fair Oaks. But bridges, good roads, libraries, social clubs, stylish buildings, numerous schools, and village areas—commercial districts or downtowns, that is—were not symptoms and conditions of isolated, backward-looking, rural areas supposedly characteristic of the Great Plains and elsewhere, but signs and symbols of modernity, progress, sophistication, and even refinement. As reviewed in chapter one, they were hallmarks of romantic suburbs, of bourgeois utopias. They also marked these communities as middle class. Remarkably, most of the infrastructure, such as roads and bridges, were built because of the capital investment made by the original boosters. Because of speculative real-estate capitalism, the innovation that largely marked these communities resulted from nothing less than suburban planning on the part of a local growth machine.

Much of the innovation that marked Orangevale and Fair Oaks as cutting edge was tied to agriculture, namely through colonization enterprises, as "Sacramento's Suburban Site for Little Farms."⁵⁹ Orangevale and Fair Oaks combined community life with agriculture and were a "striking illustration of self supporting small farms." Fair Oaks, according to the subtitle of *Fair Oaks* (1900), was *The Paradise of the Fruit Grower, Health Seeker and Tourist*. In fact, colonization enterprises, as the word enterprise suggested, meant that the colonies' so-called founding fathers had taken great pains to make investments in improvements for the community, such as, in Orangevale, "a church, school, and hotel . . . and the work of beautifying." An early bridge, for example, "eliminated the community's [Fair Oaks's] isolation" according to a 2005 history of the area and made it easier not only to get fruit to market but also to commute to Sacramento and other surrounding areas. The plethora of so-called innovations that demarcated and then proved that Orangevale and Fair Oaks were not your traditional backwards farm areas included beautiful houses, churches, clubs, schools, irrigation and a water company, transportation infrastructure, and commercial businesses.[60]

At the turn of the twentieth century, the single-family house had become the embodiment of the middle-class ideal for domestic life, and, accordingly, the lure of home ownership figured prominently in the booster literature of Orangevale and Fair Oaks. Indeed, comparable to the rhetoric of Romantics, Sacramento's boosters positioned the homes of Orangevale and Fair Oaks in a semi-rural environment away from the city but full of modern conveniences. Orangevale's and Fair Oaks's homes thus seemed innovative for being located in a rural environment. As early as 1900, for example, the Fair Oaks Development Company promised a "charming home made there for the wife and babies." They promised a suburb:

> For the home it offers you, under the cloudless skies of Fair Oaks, the sub-urban residence district of Sacramento, in the heart of California, while sheltered by magnificent oaks and looking, as far as the eye can reach, over picturesque swells of orchards of orange, olive, and all kinds of deciduous fruits, and vineyards of Flame Tokay, yet offers all the conveniences of a developed and settled community, in fine residences, water piped under pressure to the door, educational facilities, postal delivery, suburban com-munication with a large city, etc.[61]

In Orangevale, as in Fair Oaks, boosters offered "self-supporting" homes and "comfortable cottages." Orangevale and Fair Oaks receive distinction in subsequent literature, most of it locally produced, for offering the "prettiest suburban homes" and "handsome residences" that added an "attractiveness that is ideal." Moreover, remember that other regionally based booster booklets often used a picture of an "orchard home" in Orangevale or Fair Oaks to promote the Sacramento area.[62]

As the boosters in Orangevale and Fair Oaks were busy "planting orchards" and "beautifying" the area, they were also, according to the Orangevale boosters in 1894, "laying out streets and avenues, building roads and bridges." Sacramento's boosters hence emerged narratively as designing innovative rural-seeming, small-town communities that included transportation infrastructure. Orangevale's and Fair Oaks's appeal was their "rural communication with that [Sacramento] city" through the creation of local "good roads" and avenues. On the one hand, bridges—including the Fair Oaks, Thomas B. Hall (Orangevale), Orangevale Avenue, and Rainbow bridges (Orangevale), in addition to later bridges of the mid-twentieth century (Hazel Avenue and Sunrise Boulevard in Fair Oaks)—are fondly remembered because of the "communication" they allowed locals with Sacramento and other surrounding areas. The bridges, particularly the Fair

Oaks Bridge, connected to a railroad line, in what the *Sacramento Bee* in 1901 called "A Suburban Railroad to Fair Oaks," which "means suburban homes." Bridges "eliminated the community's isolation." Maps ordered by the boosters to stimulate migration and investment prominently featured them. One article about Orangevale in 1893 highlighted connections with Sacramento. Three locals from Orangevale made the trip to the "big city" of Sacramento to see a lovable country hayseed travel to the big city of New York in (the now famous) *The Old Homestead* play in which they "expressed themselves as amply repaid for their jaunt." In Fair Oaks, bridges connected residents to the department stores, such as Weinstock and Hall's own stores, among others. On the other hand, bridges provided access to market, which was essential to carrying on a lucrative farming endeavor. Without this access, then, even the least cynical of minds would find it hard to swallow the boosters' many claims. Given the importance of bridges, and the railroads with which they connected, they predictably became the symbols of these communities, as they connected them to a larger Sacramento saga, and, by implication, a national story.[63]

Among the roads one can still travel in Orangevale and Fair Oaks are Fair Oaks Boulevard, Winding Way, Main Avenue, and Greenback Lane (Orangevale Avenue).[64] In addition to being the major thoroughfares of these communities, these roads served as leading elements of the boosters' advertising campaigns. Early suburban designers' focus on good roads and well-planned streets and avenues (recall chapter one)—of curvilinear design (such as Winding Way in Fair Oaks)—further mark Orangevale and Fair Oaks as suburban types. With that said, rather paradoxically (and despite the occasional "suburb" reference), the focus on these roads in the booster literature and subsequent memory works is how incredible they were. Orangevale Avenue, for example, was "the approach to this model colony." Promoters and subsequent interpreters claimed Orangevale and Fair Oaks were modern and not merely rural farms because the roads and avenues were "arranged" and "thoroughly planned."[65]

Essential to "thoroughly planned" and innovative communities like Orangevale and Fair Oaks were other public amenities such as water and irrigation. Indeed, water ensured the cultivation of the soil while churches, schools, and clubs helped, purportedly, cultivate community members' hearts, minds, and souls. Orangevale and Fair Oaks in that case could truly blossom, which eventually required even more services that only commercial businesses could provide. Such services included, among many others, blacksmiths, dry goods stores, and "mail facilities" to reach the outside world. Water, irrigation, and piping receive constant promotion in representations concerning Orangevale and Fair Oaks because they brought life to the communities. In addition, the piping and water company mutual scheme also signified progress. This technological and business progression signaled the modern amenities of these

FIGURE 28

Winding Way, Fair Oaks, ca. early twentieth century. Winding Way, a major "good road" in Fair Oaks for over a century, emulated the curvilinear roads (to imply rurality in contrast to the urban grid pattern) imagined by, and designed by, suburban image-makers, architects, and planners, such as Olmsted and Vaux, in the nineteenth century. Courtesy Center for Sacramento History, Paul Sandul Collection, no. 2006/030/312.

areas while the celebration of churches, libraries, clubs, and schools marked these communities as ethical and intellectual communities. They were modern but not at a sacrifice to tradition. Indeed, one regionally produced 1915 source stated, "Rural high schools," like those in Fair Oaks, for instance, "[were] equal to high schools in large cities." The source also noted that students from rural high schools in the Sacramento area often went on to the esteemed University of California, Berkeley, to "study any branch of higher learning desired."[66]

Institutions and the buildings they occupied are also important in representations of the past and other reproductions of cultural memory in Orangevale and Fair Oaks. They are particularly so in recent years because many of these buildings that housed early businesses, such as the Murphy-Scott Building in Fair Oaks (ca. 1901), still stand and service the community. Indeed, the Orange Vale Water Company still exists after 100 years and provides for Orangevaleans (the company's building is located off Central Avenue). The presence of these businesses and their long-used buildings provide locals with a sense of continuity with the past. Nonetheless, these institutions represent a specific past: the past of a small semi-rural community never without. They, despite being "colonies," had modern businesses, executives, investment, and structures so important to their constitution.

Theme 4: The Glorification of Forward-Looking Entrepreneurs

Memory works concerning Ontario, Orangevale, and Fair Oaks incessantly brag about the presence of perceptive and smart businesspeople and locals from the early days of the communities. These supposed pioneers linked locals and the local story to a national saga saturated in themes of nation building, social civilization, and material progress. The story and success of Ontario, Orangevale, and Fair Oaks, in this context, are not just local success stories, but further proof of an advanced and perfecting evolutionary trajectory of the American mind and spirit in general. The men, and, to an extent, the women, of Ontario, Orangevale, and Fair Oaks were cast as entrepreneurial enough to seize the good life and laid-back enough to enjoy it in a cherished small-town American community. They were, as others have represented them, quintessentially American. This form of ancestral worship is typical of many smaller communities throughout the United States.[67] Realizing that their rural, small-town character has faced and still faces dramatic changes as the United States continually becomes transformed, modernized, and urbanized—or, more rightfully, suburbanized—these communities have made more of an effort to commemorate ancestors and whom they call pioneers of their rural past.

THE GLORIFICATION OF GEORGE CHAFFEY IN ONTARIO

The glorification of George Chaffey ranks high among the themes composing a dominant cultural memory in Ontario. Specifically, Chaffey has become the George Washington or Christopher Columbus of Ontario. Unquestionably so, a statue of him has been erected (in Upland, once part of Ontario), and the Ontario Museum of History and Art offers a lecturing tour in which they visit local schools, part of the George Chaffey School District, and teach about his life and the founding of Ontario. This is salient because others, such as his brother William, Widney, Holt, and even later booster Charles Frankish, had as much to do with the development and growth of Ontario as Chaffey.

The focus on George Chaffey rose gradually. In fact, he received recognition along with his brother William in both the 1883 and 1884 booster pamphlets, usually referencing them collectively as the "Chaffey Brothers," because, perhaps, that was a name of one of their companies. This remained the principal way to discuss George until Alexander's *Life of George Chaffey* in 1928. George had steadily been acquiring more attention, however, at least in comparison to William, by the first decade of the twentieth century, likely because of his return to California to work on the irrigation project in the Imperial Valley and his homecoming to Ontario in 1898, while William remained in Australia (remember they established Mildura). While Alexander discusses William, the focus of his biography, George, steals the show. Graduate student Beatrice Paxton Lee also gives William substantial attention in her 1929 master's thesis, "The History and Development of Ontario," as do local Upland elementary students in a collection of historical essays written in 1931. George died in 1932, and five years later the students of Lois Griffin's class announced Ontario was "George Chaffey's Model Colony." Indeed, his death sparked a moment of memorialization and memory work in and out of Ontario.[68]

On March 1, 1932, Chaffey died in San Diego at the age of 84. A March 5, 1932, article in the Los Angeles Times, "George Chaffey Buried after Simple Services," remarked on the importance of Chaffey as a "pioneer founder" and that "a picked group of singers from Chaffey Junior College sang three hymns." The Times continued, "The service was simple. No eulogy was spoken. The landmarks left by the pioneer founder speak his eulogy," which included a school and, of course, Euclid Avenue. Here, within the immediate aftermath of his death, mourners, or at least an anonymous contributor to the Times, directly conceived of Chaffey's contributions to Ontario as nothing less than "landmarks." On March 10, Chaffey, this time as "A Real Empire Builder," received yet another honor in the Times, with Ontario as well as Etiwanda and Upland now "monuments to his genius." A little over a year later, in November 1933, the Chaffey Union High School began planning a memorial library in honor of their beloved founder, though also mentioning William, and discussed efforts "to have it erected through a $100,000 trust fund." The next year, in a Los Angeles Times article, Chaffey emerged alongside Leland Stanford, Collis P. Huntington, Charles Crocker, and Mark Hopkins, a.k.a. Southern Pacific's "The Big Four," as well as other prominent Western executives, such as James J. Hill and Edward Harriman, as "Giants of the West." On September 19, 1935, the Chaffey Memorial Library at Chaffey Union High School opened its doors with an evening of celebration and keynote speakers. The Times ran the same article, "What He Gave/His Monument" on January 28, 1936, 1938, 1940, and 1941 (the birthday anniversary of George Chaffey) and noticeably excluded William, as well as Holt and Widney, by stating, "The citizens of Ontario have paid tribute to the city's benefactor by dedicating the Chaffey Memorial Library to his [George's] memory." (To be fair, in Ontario, Luther M. Holt has a street and auto mall named after him.) By 1951, the Chaffey Historical Room appeared in the Chaffey Civic Auditorium (again, with no mention of the others), and Chaffey Day was declared on January 28, 1952, the 104th anniversary of George Chaffey's birth. Within twenty years, Chaffey's legacy sharpened and grew, and commemorative efforts moved from a living memorial (the library and history room), among others, to a public event in which the community allocated a day to commemorate him.[69]

The memory works that glorify Chaffey continued. Perhaps most striking among them is the local 1976 Bicentennial Commission's publication in which he appears

FIGURE 29

George Chaffey and George Washington, Founding Fathers, *A Bicentennial Salute.* In the 1976 *A Bicentennial Salute* by the Ontario City Council, George Chaffey is featured side by side with George Washington. The booklet is about 11 inches wide and 8 inches high. Therefore, when you turn to page 2, featuring Washington, George Chaffey appears directly across from him on page 3. Both images are the courtesy of the Robert E. Ellingwood Model Colony History Room, Ontario City Library.

as the founder of Ontario alongside George Washington as the founder of the United States. Chaffey's legacy continues to this day as various memory works persist in highlighting the "founding pioneer" of Ontario.[70] He receives both a creation myth, as a pioneer founder, and a social role, as a community builder. Chaffey became a model citizen of the model colony. He founded the colony, with the "most perfect plan," engineered incredible irrigation projects, and even started educational facilities and ensured the construction of "beautiful," "world famous" roads. Chaffey's plan of an agricultural colony with urban amenities and modern technologies is often correlated with progress.[71] Chaffey's legacy moved from that of one of several founders to an important pioneer who typified a larger national spirit of patriotic nation-building in the West: the entrepreneurial "self-interested man" or "self-made man."[72] Chaffey, therefore, as a local pioneer, was linked to a national story and placed within a structure of patriotism, what sociologist Diane Barthel has called "the saga of social progressivism."[73]

THE GLORIFICATION OF PROGRESSIVE MEN
IN ORANGEVALE AND FAIR OAKS

The homes and people of Orangevale and Fair Oaks, filled with more than one "charming home" of "wife and babies," lay adjacent to Sacramento and surrounding communities, a metropolitan patchwork of suburbs, hinterlands, and a growing urban center.

Orangevale and Fair Oaks, as one observer boasting of the quality of life in Fair Oaks in 1895 proclaimed, were near "a great metropolis in the future." Even more telling was that Orangevale and Fair Oaks, as the boosters and subsequent authors remind us, were full of not only faraway colonists but also local, even the "best," businesspeople of the city. "For the people of intelligence, or refinement," the FODC stated in 1900, "particularly if they have families . . . invest[ed] in cheap lands of this [Orangevale's and Fair Oaks's] description." The boosters thus created Orangevale and Fair Oaks, they said, "with the purpose of settling" them "with people who would become tributary to, and add to the material prosperity of, Sacramento." Orangevale, for example, was "for practical businessmen of shrewdness and independence." Fair Oaks had "attracted prominent men from the East, and particularly from Boston." Fair Oaks had also become "a favorite with Chicago people and a number of wealthy men of that city have built fine homes there." By 1911, one observer concluded, "Both these districts [Orangevale and Fair Oaks] are settled mostly by progressive, energetic Eastern farmers and their success has been phenomenal." Orangevale, as well as Fair Oaks, constituted business investments, filled with progressive, even shrewd, businessmen who, according to the *Bee* in 1894, were a "better class of colonists." They were also, supposedly, of an urbane, not necessarily urban, East Coast aristocracy, the successful of Boston and Chicago. (As noted before, this was turn-of-the-twentieth-century code for saying "white people.") Orangevale and Fair Oaks, at that time, supposedly attracted "only the most desirable class of residents." They were not only moral, but also filled with the spirit of progressivism and business understanding.[74]

Recall that Orangevale and Fair Oaks did not shun those who, while not rich, were willing to work hard. "The man with modest means can," said the boosters of Fair Oaks, "with brains and energy, make and maintain at Fair Oaks an attractive home as readily as a millionaire." In Orangevale, "Not the least important feature of the enterprise is that a person with only a few hundred dollars as a beginning can, by laying aside each month a small portion of his salary or earnings, soon become the owner of a tract in Orange Vale, and thereafter secure freedom from all other occupations, if desired, except the supervision of this property." This focus on "working men" making it in Orangevale and Fair Oaks echoed loudly in a local 2001 account that concluded with a celebration of the evolution of "working men" by stating that "to earn a profit on his small farm, the Colonist needed new knowledge—of scientific methods of land development."[75]

The celebration of "working men," "settlers," "better class of colonists," and "people of intelligence, or refinement" has been a key defining feature of memory works focusing on Orangevale and Fair Oaks. On the one hand, the highlighting of such so-called settlers, such as in an 1893 article in the *Folsom Telegraph* or a 1944 Sacramento Chamber of Commerce publication (*Hub of Western Industry*), served as further publicity material for boosters to point out that these communities, and the metropolitan region in general, represented progress.[76] On the other hand, a focus on "pioneers" and early successful and prominent "settlers" was yet again a form of hero worship and continuity with the past for locals in Orangevale and Fair Oaks, as well as for Chaffey regarding Ontario. They articulated a sense of themselves through narrating the identities of their ancestors. As their "pioneer" forebearers built (or had built by others) institutions, tilled the soil, and linked these communities to a national story, subsequent generations celebrated their "progress[ive] spirit and executive powers." According to one regional historian in the 1920s, these communities had, like W. W. Hinsey of Fair Oaks, who came in 1898, "a stimulating effect upon business activity and growth in general."[77] The pioneers of Orangevale and Fair Oaks had taken a celebrated errand into the iconic American wilderness whereby they dutifully built an all-American small town for an all-American family that, while rooted in an agrarian past, looked to a progressive future. Subsequent generations, who then fondly remember, memorialize, and even worship these early pioneers, see themselves as benefactors and trustees of such a heritage. Shaped by it, they have a sense of maintaining it, and now, particularly through the reproduction of memory works, they see it as their task, their errand, and their legacy to carry it forward.

CONCLUSION

The four major themes of a dominant cultural memory deflect attention away from Ontario's, Orangevale's, and Fair Oaks's suburban roots and reveal the long-lasting influence and legacy of boosterism. Celebrating these sites as *unique* underscored what made them the "Model Colony" or the "best" places for growing citrus. Rather than highlighting suburban planning in the conception of the "Model Colony" or "colonial enterprises," these communities came to represent many implicit things, from some generic form of planning a colony to innovative institutions manufactured to supply urban amenities without the city.[78] Again, the implicit argument here is that suburban planning had little to do with California's residential and suburban experience. The precise way memory works celebrate agriculture in Ontario, Orangevale, and Fair Oaks, which focuses on an abstract notion of *colony*, improvement, and production, pays more attention to the rural side of agriculture and not to the suburban side of urban. The focus on their innovative institutions and infrastructure stressed how remarkable such accomplishments were for places that originated as "agricultural colonies." Such representations demote the role institutions and infrastructure contributed in the suburban planning of these communities. The glorification of entrepreneurs and founders directs a remembrance of pioneers who connect to a celebratory national story. Consequently, the boosters' planning of these communities emerges not as suburban by design, but rather as that of a "model colony" or "fruit colony"—colonies that began simply as rural, small-town communities amid a dry, barren land.

Taken together, the many memory works focusing on Ontario, Orangevale, and Fair Oaks do indeed do much to redirect attention away from the suburban side of their past. Yet, as this review demonstrates, they can paradoxically at times provide the information needed to recognize the suburban heritage of these communities. Larger trends and themes in state, regional, and national histories coalesced with and legitimized a conception of Ontario, Orangevale, and Fair Oaks as agricultural colonies, and are un-suburban. In general, the lack of a general definition of suburbs, as a form, and suburbanization, as a process, contribute to the lasting power of memory works to divert attention away from potential suburban types and a larger understanding of suburbanization as a process. By seeking to expand on suburbanization, find new suburban sites, and critically analyze memory works, scholars can hope to increase the understanding of suburbia and mold a more definitive understanding of America's suburban experience.

Lastly, as case study sites, Ontario, Orangevale, and Fair Oaks tell some about the nature of cultural memory in (formerly) small-town, rural-seeming communities (in and out of California) that have an agricultural past tied to horticulture. Long-lasting cultural costs came with the original boosters' packaging of place at the end of the nineteenth century. Citizens of Ontario, Orangevale, and Fair Oaks were (and are) directed to remember their community's history similarly. This has resulted in legitimizing a dominant cultural memory.

This scenario is mapped out in more detail in the next chapter. Specifically, more memory works exist, particularly in the post–World War II era of these communities' history. Again, tracing them advances the argument that a dominant cultural memory exists and that boosterism has had a robust and prolonged legacy. Therefore, the next chapter proceeds in much the same way: by breaking down memory works, connecting them to prevalent themes, and speculating on their meaning. Nevertheless, two things are worth noting that make the next chapter different. First, while suburbanites' memory works constituted many of the sources analyzed in this chapter, they take center stage in the next chapter—the reason being suburbanites produced more following World War II (a phenomenon explained). Second, the consequences (i.e., legacy) of boosterism and the establishment of a dominant cultural memory go beyond masking the suburban side of these communities' past. Rather, even more is at stake. As discussed further, cultural memory helps shape selfhood, community identity, and can even reflect the existence of power structures, of proverbial winners and losers. It can help reveal, and maintain, cultural hegemony. In turn, as the voices of hegemony get their due, the voiceless, those absent in memory works, stand out more glaringly. Their absence consequently has meaning. The next chapter attempts to tease out that meaning.

CHAPTER SEVEN

COLLECTED MEMORY AND THE CONTINUED LEGACIES OF BOOSTERISM

The past is past, but this section of Fair Oaks with the winding streets, hills and Carmel-like setting, still holds charm.

DICK HILL, "FAIR OAKS VILLAGE," 1988[1]

HISTORIAN MICHAEL KAMMEN ONCE OBSERVED, "Societies in fact reconstruct their pasts rather than faithfully record them, and that they do so with the needs of contemporary culture clearly in mind—manipulating the past in order to mold the present."[2] Although his observation sounds rather ominous, a dominant cultural memory, or what some like Foucault have called a "dominant tradition," concerning the past provides the building blocks for the construction and reconstruction of memory works in Ontario, Orangevale, and Fair Oaks. The process by which these agriburbs (re)constructed their past occurred within (and contributed to) a process of formalization and ritualization. The depiction of the past in them resulted from routinization as much as it did from some purposeful—and, even worse, deceitful—manipulation of the past.[3] The themes of Ontario's, Orangevale's, and Fair Oaks's foundations as laid out by their boosters became authoritatively common as they emerged to shape a dominant cultural memory. The narratives and representations of both the boosters and those who since have reconstructed the past is certainly a teleological story that positions the agriburbs, not to mention the residents, as forward-looking but traditional, backward-looking but modern, and forever on a course of progress, the foundation for what famed philosopher Friedrich W. Nietzsche called "monumental history."[4]

Nietzsche noted that interpreters of history are, and have been, affected by the sheer volume and weight of history. Accounts of the agriburbs and their past provided by the boosters became the resources of others, whose memory works then became the resources of others, and so on. This resulted in "collected memory" as memory works became Ontario's, Orangevale's, and Fair Oaks's main archival resource when seeking to (re)construct a historical understanding about their past. A dominant cultural memory, then, played a role in a long history of directing people to remember in similar ways, favoring some themes while discarding others, favoring certain people while silencing others, and fostering a template that influences how these communities, as well as scholars, reassemble the past in the present. Ontario, Orangevale, and Fair Oaks, in other words, got branded, hot for historical consumption. A unitary voice emerged that became authoritative, if only by repetition and as persuasive discourse. As a consequence, any silencing, marginalization, or errors in historical fact were passed down through the years and through various memory works, which then made and make them all the more difficult to overturn.

If communities do manipulatively reassemble the past, as Ontario, Orangevale, and Fair Oaks did (and still do) then they do so out of an inherited dominant cultural memory that they further (re)make and further legitimize through the continued production of memory works. This phenomenon in Ontario, Orangevale, and Fair Oaks is comparable to what sociologist Paul Connerton labels "structural amnesia." Specifically, structural amnesia, like collected memory, suggests that what is available concerning the past, such as memory works, affects how communities and individuals remember and forget or advance and discard historical information. The historical representations about agriburbs hence became standardized, making it easier to forget their suburban origins.[5]

In Ontario, Orangevale, and Fair Oaks, the use of the past has been to reify and diffuse a dominant cultural memory that resulted in a "monumental" history. This monumental history provides an element of local community identity. Moreover, it constitutes the basis for the grander formation of an "imagined community," that famed phrase and conception of Benedict Anderson's to highlight the power of narratives and other representations to anchor the maintenance of groups—what centers solidarity and likeness in the Durkheimian tradition.[6] This relates to another famous phrase and idea, that of "invented tradition," which, according to historian Eric Hobsbawn, "is taken to mean a set of practices, normally governed by overtly or tacitly accepted rules and of a ritual or symbolic nature, which seek to inculcate certain values and norms of behavior by repetition, which automatically implies continuity with the past."[7]

Indeed, as explored in works by the likes of Barraclough, Berglund, Deverell, Glassberg, Kropp, Norkunas, Otero, and Stanton (see the introduction), the invention of tradition and the shaping of an imagined community imply some serious consequences, ranging from inculcating individual values and societal norms, to the formation and upholding of community. Moreover, memory works, which constitute the invention of tradition (i.e., a dominant cultural memory), are part of sustaining an imagined community. In agriburbs, we have already seen what invented tradition looks like, as well as its cost: forgetting the suburban side of their origins. Nonetheless, other costs and consequences are detectable.

The costs of a dominant cultural memory in agriburbs are also weighed in the continued silencing and marginalizing of ethnoracial minorities and women in these communities. In this context, historian Blake McKelvey provides a somber warning: "Escape from the past is scarcely more possible for a community than for an individual." He continued, "New growth is ever occurring but generally as an outgrowth of vital [invented] traditions or latent capacities. . . . [T]he community's [invented] tradition (its own story, its history) is then part of its character."[8] Looking to memory works is thus a good way to dissect a community's character or, as Hobsbawn pointed out, its values and norms. Again, doing so might not tell us the whole story, but it still tells us plenty. It provides a snapshot into the soul of a community, what they value through what they choose to preserve and present as factual and as history. It is in this context, then, that the affirmation of suburban memory's existence is decisive. Yet there is no pretense that such a memory is present and accounted for and embraced by every suburbanite in these communities. Still, as this chapter shows, a dominant cultural memory clearly still prevails as evidenced by the continued production of memory works, most of which take place at the local, suburban scale.

Taking note of the fact that ethnoracial minorities are not a part of any agriburbs' dominant cultural memory is important for several reasons and hence figures prominently in reviewing memory works in this chapter. First, it tells us a lot about who does and who does not have power and influence in these communities (a glimpse of cultural hegemony in practice), at least regarding who produces the memory works at the local level. Second, because of the first, it may be tempting to throw our hands up and shout "racists!" Yet, as notions of collected memory and cultural memory make clear, that would be too simple. The intent is not to say this is true in any way, nor false in any way; no doubt, champions of social justice live in agriburbs. Rather, the intent is to say that by reviewing why and in what ways memory works exclude ethnoracial minorities, we can further dissect the many meanings of a dominant cultural memory, particularly for those who continue to spread it. Ultimately, what emerges is a dominant cultural memory continuing to divert attention from the suburban origins, admittedly, but it is also a memory most meaningful and useful to a white middle class, perhaps validating Kammen's assertion about the manipulation of historical representations.

FIGURE 30

George Chaffey Statue, erected in 2005. The statue sits in front of Upland City Library (formerly North Ontario and formerly Ontario) on Euclid Avenue. The Chaffey statue is a 13-foot-bronze depiction of the founder standing firm on an outcropping of rocks (San Gabriel Mountains) looking gallantly out on the San Gabriel Valley as he holds a compass in one hand and a surveyor's scope in the other. Behind Chaffey is a cactus carving as they both rest atop a circular base of gliding fish. The statue's plaque states, "George Chaffey, Jr. / 1848–1932 / Man of Vision / Land, Water and Power / Father of The Model Colony." Photo taken by author, 2007.

Trends in public memory works since World War II receive attention for chronicling the prevalence of a dominant cultural memory, bringing it up to the more recent past and in more recent mediums, like the Internet. The goal of studying the preponderance of a dominant cultural memory in the postwar era is to highlight memory works produced by suburbanites themselves, which typically take us beyond textual memory works into elements such as pageantry and historic preservation, conclusively revealing how suburbanites themselves aid in propagating a dominant cultural memory. Finally, by explicitly pointing out the gross marginalization and erasure of minorities from the dominant cultural memory espoused in agriburbs, deeper meanings of dominant cultural memory emerge, specifically as they relate to issues of race and class. As discussed in the introduction, however, the perhaps ironic result of my analysis is the further marginalization and erasure of minorities by not digging up their history in these pages. The aim below, however unsatisfying or not, is to explore as fully as possible the words and deeds of those who were able or had the means to talk about the agriburbs and then to break down what they were actually saying. Doing so provides another way for understanding the continued legacies of boosterism in these suburbs.

   One of the more outstanding examples of the constant influence of a dominant cultural memory in Ontario returns us to a discussion of George Chaffey, the celebration of him as a pioneer, and the erection of a statue to him.[9] On October 15, 2005, 200 people gathered in front of Upland City Hall on North Euclid Avenue for the unveiling of a statue to Chaffey. Upland, as noted, had once been a part of Ontario, founded by Chaffey and others in 1882.[10] Behind Chaffey is a cactus carving, both of them at rest atop a circular base of gliding fish. The statue's plaque states, "George Chaffey, Jr. / 1848–1932 / Man of Vision / Land, Water and Power / Father of The Model Colony." Six bronze reliefs also adorn the statue's pedestal showing the SS *Geneva*, long-distance telephone, Chaffey College of Agriculture, Euclid Avenue, hydroelectricity, and a recreational vehicle. Chaffey's statue memorializes him as an entrepreneur ahead of his time.

Conveying how many others have remembered and exalted George Chaffey and the establishment of Ontario, Susan Chaffey Powell, great-granddaughter of the "Man of Vision," commented to the crowd during the statue's unveiling, "Not only do you care about your past but you care enough to do something."[11] Former mayor of Ontario, Robert E. Ellingwood, in an effort "to remember Ontario's most prominent citizen with a proper tribute," stated, "Rancho Cucamonga has its Jack Benny statue, and San Dimas its Jedediah Smith statue; surely Chaffey's amazing life and contributions to Ontario and Southern California deserve similar recognition."[12] Earlier he had guessed the statue would cost $80,000 and recognizing city governments (i.e., Upland and Ontario) could not fund it all, Ellingwood imagined private donations sufficient, including "hopes the children will respond by saving their pennies."[13]

Interpretation of the statue can vary, but clear themes do emerge that reveal Chaffey, and by implication Ontario (and Upland), is considered exceptional and discernibly modern for the era in which he lived. The base of fish, for example, represents Chaffey's irrigation efforts and maritime love, while the bronze carvings depict "Chaffey's accomplishments" and memorialize his role in building up the community through the consortium of Euclid Avenue (good roads), Chaffey School of Agriculture (education), and telephone service and electricity (modern technologies). Novel topics are depicted as well, including his connection to the SS *Geneva*—the fastest ship of the day—and the growing popularity of recreational vehicles, with one plaque stating: "First RV, 1920."[14]

The statue that local children donated pennies for thence seems priceless. The statue's sculptor, John Edward Svenson, who had virtually channeled Chaffey sitting under some trees, stated, "I hope they look at this as representing a man who had a vision for what this area could and did become."[15] His statement again illustrates how the Chaffey statue, as well as other memory works concerning Ontario, celebrates progress. Chaffey stands in front of a cactus and majestically on a mountaintop, holding a scientific tool, looking down upon a land in need of improvement. His legacy in Ontario and the region is that of an entrepreneur who improved upon what he had found, particularly through irrigation, as the cactus represents a dry, barren land.

A celebration of progress also affects how minorities are remembered in Ontario's past and, by implication, how they are largely thought of in the present and future. A focus on material improvements and social civilization forgets the presence and role of minorities. Instead, the focus is on so-called civilization and progress, which repeats the nomenclature of white middle-class America at the turn of the twentieth century. While some recent historical narratives have highlighted minorities in Ontario, most concentrate on minorities' early role as laborers and not community fellows or, more to the point, co-benefactors. Native Americans therefore receive attention so that progress and civilization can arrive. Likewise, Mexicans, Chinese, Japanese, etc., and their descendants only receive mention when toiling in the fields or operating factory devices. They are distinguished only for their service to the so-called progress and advancement

FIGURE 31

Bronze Reliefs, Chaffey Statue. These six bronze reliefs adorn the pedestal of the statue showing Chaffey's so-called visionary "accomplishments." They are (top, L to R): Chaffey College; a recreational vehicle; (middle, L to R) Euclid Avenue; Hydro-electricity; (bottom, L to R) long-distance telephone; and *S.S. Geneva*. Photos by author, 2007.

of Ontario, whether harvesting citrus or grapes, shaping irons at Hotpoint, or performing domestic work for Ontario's "best class of people."[16]

Recent preservation efforts in Ontario, in fact, ignore the potential places and sites possibly important to minorities, particularly a growing—and vast majority—Mexican-American population (69 percent as of 2010; up from 59.9 percent in 2000), as well as African Americans (6.4 percent) and Asian Americans (5.2 percent).[17] Ontario's preservation efforts show one representation of the past—a white, mainly male, middle-class conception of a rural Garden of Eden. Recall that Euclid Avenue, "the most beautiful" and "famous" street, was Ontario's latest National Register nomination. Other sites include the Frankish Building (listed on the National Register of Historic Places in 1980) and Hofer Ranch (listed on the National Register in 1993). Both receive recognition because of their connections with the early growth and development of Ontario. Specifically, the Frankish Building links with early businessperson Charles Frankish's commercial astuteness in early Ontario. Representatively, he provides Ontario with a sophisticated business core again remarkable for a booming "agricultural colony."[18] The Hofer Ranch links to Ontario's agricultural heritage and, according to the nominator of Hofer Ranch to the National Register, "stand[s] out in a rapidly urbanizing landscape." Neither structure, needless to say by this point, represents women or minorities, nor do they account for a suburban past.[19]

When researching for this book, the Ontario Planning Commission had developed six historic districts featuring mostly bungalows and other homes occupied primarily by the middle class in Ontario's past.[20] The districts are within the older downtown, and the Planning Commission, at the time, hoped to expand on these while also creating six more nearby.[21] Implicit here is the primacy of middle-class conceptions of aesthetic value and history. While interest in minority workers in Ontario's early years exists, few memory works have materialized. Most striking is the silence of minority voices and counter memories. To be clear, a focus on silence here does not affix blame or point fingers at Ontario's commission officials and staff as if they are members of some Gramscian-bourgeois capitalist elite who are consciously villainous and purposely deceitful in controlling and holding down minorities. Rather, the silence of minorities—or the deafness of others—reveals the saliency of middle-class sensibilities and historical consciousness, both present in various memory works characteristic of Ontario's dominant cultural memory. Nonetheless, the activities of the commission, most notably its drive for the creation of historic districts in a historically white middle-class downtown area, illustrates the pervasiveness and dominance of a white middle-class perception of history that seemingly yearns to preserve the rural, nonindustrial side of its past. If not clear by now, it reveals the power of the original boosterism.

FIGURE 32

Mule Car Exhibit along the grass of the double-drive of Euclid Avenue. Also added to the main image is (on the left) one of the plaques outside the exhibit, atop the stone marker and (on the right) a panel about the Mule Car that sits inside the exhibit, which is just to the right of the mule in the main photo. Photos by author, 2007.

While not capturing the voices of past minorities, some questions with them in mind suggest ways in which Ontario's memory works ignore many of its citizens and diverse ethnic and cultural history. To start, where did most of the Mexican American and Chinese Americans live? Some sources cite communities in Upland.[22] And what places would Mexican Americans and Chinese Americans, who likely built Ontario's railroad lines and spurs, Euclid Avenue, and street railway, consider worth preserving? Even if they did not live in the Ontario city limits, would they have traveled the street railway or faced restrictions? For those who labored in the orchards and vineyards, provided laundry services, or worked as servants, which places had aesthetic value or provided a sense of history? Did (a) particular community center(s) or gathering place(s) exist where the working class and ethnically and racially diverse minorities could meet, converse, and exchange information? Such places may have been crucial in developing a sense of self for these groups, as well as a sense of collective identity. Even if such places are gone, commemoration and memorialization creates public spaces, especially in that they do more than simple plaques or texts in a museum, as Ontario has done.[23] Likewise, the mule car, in operation for a scarce nine years, prominently stands protected today in a glass showcase in the center of Euclid Avenue, praising the work of two mules in a public space. One may wonder where the public-space commemorations of Ontario's hundreds, to eventual thousands, of agricultural and even early industrial laborers, are. Perhaps allotments of public spaces could establish some form of celebration of Mexican field workers who toiled on Ontario's many farms, or of Chinese Americans who, in the agricultural and domestic industry, serviced the fantasies of a "better class of people."

While the planning commission seeks political support for the preservation of Ontario's heritage, one has to ask whose heritage they attempt to preserve.[24] Playing cards produced by the commission to educate the public about architecture and preservation underscore this point. Four architectural types are highlighted, one for each suit. Each suit contains a photo for visual representation, lists the years of principal construction, and briefly describes "common features." The types are Neoclassical Revival (1905–1920), Craftsman (1895–1920s), Mediterranean Bungalow (1900–Present), and Colonial Revival Bungalow (1890–1915). The houses listed are ones usually occupied by the middle class and represent, for the most part, a small window of time in Ontario's history. Note, however, other than the Hofer Ranch, no agricultural homesteads receive attention, not to mention prefabricated or self-built houses popular among working-class people.[25] Implicit here is what the commission considers architecture: buildings built only by professionally trained architects for a well-to-do consumer. Indeed, the

FIGURE 33

Ontario Planning Commission's "City of Ontario, CA Celebrates Historic Preservation" Playing Cards. These playing cards were created by the Ontario City Planning Department's Historic Preservation Commission to help "educate" the public about the "historic and cultural resources" in Ontario. Cards in possession of author.

commission's mission statement for historic preservation asserts, "The program seeks to preserve & protect the significant architectural, historical, & cultural resources, which reflect Ontario's unique character & heritage."[26] Architecture in this context does not represent all buildings in Ontario, as evidenced by what the department has sought to preserve. Likewise, historical and cultural resources reflect physical and conceptual boundaries reserved for the white middle class—their exclusive character and heritage. Based on what they have preserved already, as well as what the commission hopes to preserve in the future, "significant architectural, historical, & cultural resources" are those that are significant to a middle-class notion of an idealized rural past. This point underscores the saliency of the historical narrative as first established by the boosters. The adoration of agriculture and urban amenities directs citizens and other interpreters to narrow their preservation efforts and memory works to the homes of the more affluent and white residents of Ontario's past.

Expanding preservation efforts to include the broader cultural and ethnic landscape and history of Ontario could provide the political and public support the commission desires. For example, reinterpreting the importance of downtown to include

FIGURE 34

Packing citrus in Upland, ca. early twentieth century. This rare photo of minority laborers, besides the white driver, shows Asian workers, likely Chinese, Japanese, Filipino, or some mixture thereof, picking and packing produce for the Upland Citrus Association. Remember, Upland was not only once a part of Ontario, but also, according to several local sources, where most minorities that worked in Ontario lived. Courtesy of the Robert E. Ellingwood Model Colony History Room, Ontario City Library.

a more diverse cultural and ethnic landscape would be prudent. Downtown Ontario served as a business center and the culmination of Ontario's middle-class aspirations. It is doubtful that downtown provided jobs to white middle-class men only. Further, one has to wonder if any women or minorities ran businesses. If so, perhaps Ontario could honor, recognize, and commemorate these aspects of the community, including the creation and dedication of public spaces. If not, perhaps Ontario could reinterpret existing places or a general area to appeal to a more diverse audience today. For example, a public mural placed in the middle of Euclid, or possibly near the run-down Hotpoint factory, could feature information and works of art devoted to Mexican Americans, explaining their role in the growth and development of the community.

Preservation reflects the needs of the present, and preservation efforts in Ontario ought to reflect the needs of a present community whose majority population is Hispanic, as well as address the contributions of women and other minorities.[27] Admittedly, more questions arise than answers. Still, the underlying point is that Ontario's memory works continue to perpetuate a white middle-class perception of history. Public commemoration and memory works in Ontario, in fact, further tease

FIGURE 35

Sponsor Plaques, Chaffey Statue. Markers such as these surround the Chaffey statue and show the various names of sponsors and their "levels" of support. "Benefactors," as well as "Executive" and "Corporate" sponsors also receive recognition. Such sponsor plaques signify investment into the culture and history of the community and, possibly, signal to others that any given sponsor deserves special recognition for participation and investment. Photo by Author, 2007.

out the nature of political power and beg the question of who exercises it. The building of the Chaffey statue with markers devoted to highlighting donors underscores this point. The statue and the markers reinforce a sense of community among the donors and designate their special position in the community as keepers of the cultural memory. Preservation efforts in Ontario underscore the same thing. Middle-class (mainly) white people are deciding on the use of public resources to preserve a white middle-class sense of history. Because the political power belongs to them, their heritage graces plaques, appears in marble, and receives protection—as collected memory.

A noticeable lack of memory works is a symptom of Orangevale's recent, post–World War II memory activities. While not entirely absent, there has been a dearth of memory works, which may have a lot to do with the fact that Orangevale's population from 1990 to 2010 actually slowed in comparison to earlier years. It did grow 0.30 percent per year since 1990, from 26,266 to 33,960, but it grew astoundingly at 0.76 percent per year from 1960 to 1990, almost doubling the population from 11,722 to 20,585. Moreover, Orangevale remains a largely white community with 87.4 percent of the population recorded as white in the 2010 census, with 10.2 percent Hispanic or Latino, 3.1 percent Asian, and 1.4 percent Black or African American. Economically, Orangevale, according to the 2010 census, had a median household income of $71,136 as compared to the national average of $60,833. In contrast, Sacramento County—which does not include all the areas of the Sacramento metropolitan area,

TABLE 5

Population and Growth Rate of Orangevale and Sacramento County, 1950–2010

ORANGEVALE			SACRAMENTO COUNTY		
Year	Population	Growth Rate from Previous Decade	Year	Population	Growth Rate from Previous Decade
1950	1,600	n/a	1950	277,140	0.63
1960	11,722	6.25	1960	502,778	0.81
1970	17,222	0.48	1970	634,373	0.26
1980	20,585	0.20	1980	783,381	0.23
1990	26,266	0.28	1990	1,041,219	0.33
2000	26,705	0.02	2000	1,223,499	0.18
2010	33,960	0.27	2010	1,418,788	0.16

SOURCES: *For all of Orangevale's population numbers and Sacramento's following 1980, see endnote no. 28 for this chapter. For Sacramento County, 1950-1980, see U.S. Census Bureau, Table 2, Land Area and Population: 1930 to 1980, Characteristics of the Population, vol. 1, Number of Inhabitants, ch. A, California, part 6, 1980 Census of Population (Government Printing Office, Washington, D.C.: U.S. Department of Commerce and Bureau of the Census, issued March 1982).*

such as the rapidly growing areas of Roseville and Rocklin and their more than 1750,000 residents—experienced a per-year growth rate of approximately 0.36 percent from 1990 to 2010—1,041,219 to 1,418,788—with 57.5 percent white, 21.6 percent Hispanic or Latino, 14.3 percent Asian, and 10.4 percent Black or African American. The median household income for the county came in at $56,439.[28]

The relatively limited growth of Orangevale over the past twenty years compared to a boom earlier, as well as its racial homogeneity, particularly when contrasted with its location within a larger diverse and growing metropolitan region, is suggestive. With little change in demography, not to mention economic trends, infrastructure, and political culture, nothing has fundamentally posed a significant threat to the historically salient cultural, economic, political, or social hierarchies and power structures in Orangevale.[29] Because Orangevale has retained a white, conservative, middle-class makeup and power structure, the need of this particular social group to affirm its place atop the local power structure, which would include the production of memory works, is minimal. Not many minorities or other groups outside the dominant white middle-class population have moved in or made their presence felt in any overtly public forums or ways. "It is always possible," wrote Sigmund Freud, "to bind together a considerable number of people in love, so long as there are other people left over to receive the manifestations of their aggressiveness."[30] The lack of any great outpouring of memory works in Orangevale may be simply a result of the lack of pressure to do so, or it could be due to the relative—nonobjective—sense of satisfaction with contemporary community identity and the stability of various mechanisms of the dominant power structure. In Freudian terms, then, the need to bind together, and, for our purposes, to create memory works that could foster the creation and maintenance of imagined community, is lacking because there is an absence of someone—or some group(s) of people—to hate or feel anxious about.

Despite no largesse of memory works in Orangevale in more recent years, it would be wrong to say that none exists. The influence of a dominant cultural memory is still evident in events, community organizations, and cultural-resources management reports. This moves us beyond (but still includes) literary texts, toward a look at the activities of suburbanites themselves. Indeed, Orangevale holds an annual community celebration called the Orangevale Pow Wow Days. The name itself is suggestive, as it references a Native American gathering and festivity. As one historian put it, "[P]laying Indian is a persistent [white American] tradition."[31] Native Americans are often treated "like parts of the natural landscape—like antelopes and cougars, if you will, sometimes threatening and sometimes benign . . . [i]t is this very naturalizing that leads a lot of White Americans to claim some Native ancestry" (usually to a female Cherokee). In a postindustrial and postmodern world, white Americans often appropriate Native American customs and rituals, or at least what they believe are such

FIGURE 36

Orangevale Pow Wow Days. This picture provides a small glimpse into some of the meanings attached to Pow Wow Days. The image is from the Pow Wow Days parade in 1969 and reveals a bit about what parade participants have looked like over the years, and how Pow Wow Days and parades encompass and disseminate (romantic) representations of scenes from history, particularly through rich costumes. Notice how the image shows a woman and girl dressed as "pioneers," complete with bonnets and flowing dresses, a wagon train, participants marching with the American flag, all while they traverse a paved road with palm trees and shrubbery and power lines. Courtesy Center for Sacramento History, Drawer 85, Row 6, Neibaur, May 1969, no. 12/17/1969.

(including genealogical claims), because being "Native American, unlike to be Black, is to be naturally, primordially part of America."[32] Being Native American or to correlate a community gathering to a Native-American gathering is somehow being more authentically American. Pow Wow Days started in 1963 as Chuck Wagon Days—another quintessentially American reference, this time to a romanticized westward movement that echoed the theme of Manifest Destiny. That Pow Wow Days/Chuck Wagon Days began in 1963 should not surprise. From 1950 to 1960, Orangevale had just experienced its largest period of growth, with an increase of about 6.5 percent per year (1,600 to 11,600).[33] In 1964 the name Chuck Wagon Days fell to Fiesta Days (perhaps homage to California's Spanish, Mexican, and Californio past—and thus a naturalizing claim to the California landscape). Fiesta Days then fell out of use to Pow Wow Days in 1965.[34]

During Pow Wow Days, locals and visitors gather for several days of games, shows, food, horse shows, and carnival rides. One of the highlights of the Pow Wow Days celebration is a parade. Beginning with the inaugural celebration in 1963, the route traversed one of Orangevale's historic "good roads," Central Avenue, also the location of the historic Orangevale Water Company, ending at the Orangevale Youth Center on Hazel Avenue, arguably Orangevale's second largest thoroughfare. The parade route moved to the main thoroughfare of Greenback Lane by 1965 to likely accommodate larger crowds and then to Oak Avenue in 1971, returning to its current route on Greenback Lane in 1974. Parade members have included an astonishingly large amount of variety, including representatives from local clubs, emergency services, schools, sports clubs, and children. While the parade features many notable older clubs, organizations, and services, the celebration is the result of cultural memory and a cultural performance of how the community of Orangevale has narrated its past, what it imagines itself to be in the present, and what it fantasizes about being in the future. Specifically, through Pow Wow Days, Orangevale projects a self-image of an archetypal American small town that is semirural and values community cohesion (real or imagined), neighborliness, and, seemingly, an aura of "traditional" simplicity. Like one observer said in a 1972 *Sacramento Union* article, "Show me a man with a pickup truck, a gun rack, a cowboy hat and a pair of boots, and I'll show you the spirit of Orangevale." The observer concluded, "If the man doesn't live there, he probably wishes he did."[35]

As suburbia's critics—from Frederick Lewis Allen to William H. Whyte to Betty Friedan—have made clear, the "Orangevale spirit" could not be further from the so-called negative images of suburbia. The "spirit of Orangevale" is a romanticized American ideal of a rural community where one could pass through old streets, stop and buy fruit and get a story from old Mr. Tomich just off Greenback Lane, and visit local shops where locals gather to gossip. Forget, for the moment, that SUVs, baseball hats and visors, Nikes, and cell phones long ago replaced pickup trucks, cowboy hats, boots, and gun racks. Never mind, for the moment, that Orangevale sits within a large metropolitan community of about 1.5 million people (twenty-eigth largest in the nation). In fact, if one extends the area to include the Roseville area, which the US Census Bureau does, then, according the 2000 census, the Sacramento metropolitan region was the twenty-seventh largest metropolitan area in the United States, with 1,796,857 people; twenty-sixth in 2007, with 2,091,120; and twenty-fourth in 2010, with 2,149,127.[36] Moreover, if one extends the area to run east to include the Gardnerville Ranchos area in Nevada and north to include the Yuba City area in California, which the US Census Bureau does, then the region, with 2,461,780 people according to the 2010 US Census Bureau, is the eighteenth largest combined statistical area in the United States.[37] It is this growth bordering Orangevale that has given traction to the celebration of small-town America, of Orangevale as a semi-rural community amid an incessantly mounting urban and metropolitan jungle. Indeed recall that in 1976 the Sacramento Community Planning Department drafted a report for planned growth and zoning in Orangevale that stated two goals for the community: (1) "To protect and enhance the high quality rural lifestyle available in the Orangevale area"; and (2) "To provide opportunity for bona fide agricultural pursuits in the Orangevale community."[38] At all costs, then, and despite suspicions to the contrary, Orangevale needed to remain rural and middle class, steeped in fantasies of renewed agricultural prowess. This fantasy and self-image, perhaps, are contributing reasons to why Orangevale has failed to grow much in terms of human population—including diversity. Putting aside other seemingly obvious factors as real-estate prices and location vis-à-vis place of work, Orangevale's "rural lifestyle," which encompasses Orangevale's white middle class sense of history, in an otherwise budding metropolitan area of considerable diversity, may not appeal to many people. Specifically, it may not appeal to anyone other than a white middle class who are in search of a "rural lifestyle" among a predominantly white community that celebrates, overtly, white-middle-class conceptions of the past.

Performance is not the only way cultural memory is sustained and further disseminated in Orangevale. Memory works are, by definition, diverse and dynamic. Institutions deeply rooted in a celebratory past in Orangevale help sustain cultural memory as well. Longtime community organizations also remain vibrant and active in Orangevale and provide the community with a sense of continuity with the past. Of the many organizations, perhaps none (besides several churches and schools) seem as vibrant and important to the community as the Orangevale Water Company, the Woman's Club, and the Grange. These organizations dominate historical publications and, as such, deserve attention as the premier institutional and popular representations offered up by locals and meant to characterize their community both to themselves and to any potential reader.

The Water Company began in 1896 under the leadership of George Katzenstein, a member of the OVCC, and still services the community today. It has also published two impressive historical accounts concerning Orangevale: *Information Bulletin* and *One Hundred Years of Service*. The Woman's Club, still in existence as well, began in 1913 when locals met at the home of Mary Alice Calder to discuss the formation of a club that, they said, put their talents toward building up the community. The Orangevale Grange organized in 1910. Among other things, the Grange has been an indispensable champion of the development of Orangevale, assisting in bringing a library to the area, sponsoring local youth groups, such as the Boy Scouts, helping Orangevale become part of the Citrus Heights Fire District, awarding scholarships to local students, and supporting local events. Together, the Water Company, the Woman's Club, and the Grange, not to mention churches and schools, such as the Orangevale Open Elementary School (established in 1890), provide community members with a sense of continuity with the past.

But again, they represent a particular past. With the Grange, continuity is rooted in an agrarian past, lifestyle, and the adoration of agriculture. With the Woman's Club, continuity stems from middle-class values. Moreover, despite being one of the most clear and uniquely historically rooted organizations planned and maintained by and for women in an otherwise masculine landscape, the club is an organization largely devoted to, and characterized by, service. With the Orangevale Water Company, there is continuity with the so-called colonizers and innovation, with modern technology and business savvy that seems innovative in an otherwise small, semi-rural community. Other institutions such as the Orangevale Library (established in 1912) and churches, such the Orangevale Methodist Church (established in 1890), convey and project themes of innovation, refinement, and "traditional" morality as well.

Another manifestation of cultural memory in Orangevale concerns historic preservation. Again, cultural memory manifests through a variety of mediums and in a variety of situations and sociocultural practices. Specifically, looking at performance and institutional representations, and now preservation, reveals that history books alone clearly do not embody cultural memory. Certainly many books (or least coverage within books) exist about Orangevale. Nevertheless, deconstructing cultural memory as is appears in other types of memory works underscores the depth to which cultural memory exists within this particular suburb. With that said, it would be a gross error to slight the many local and even academic—"outsider"—history books. Rather, especially with preservation in mind, history books help sustain the dominant themes, institutions, and even people covered or accounted for in cultural performances, institutional representations, and in preservation. These other manifestations of memory both result from each other and, in turn, contribute to the manifestation of each other. This marks the duality of memory works, certainly, but also the dynamism of cultural memory as that much more powerful.

Perhaps obviously, the above also represents moments of transmission when cultural memory is indeed open to some kind of change or alteration. That the dominant cultural memory mostly does not alter much, if at all, from memory work to memory work thus reveals the emotive staying power of a dominant cultural memory not in just Orangevale, but also Fair Oaks and Ontario. Preservation efforts reviewed below have focused on institutions, individuals, or dominant themes that have also characterized the coverage within history books. The themes originated with the original boosterism but have remained present in locally produced historical representations, as well as in historical works produced by outsiders—most often as such are part of larger pieces of scholarship, typically those about metropolitan Sacramento. The point is that preservation concerns follow the lead of previously written history books and other memory works by narrowing in on what these previous works have marked as historically significant. Moreover, outsiders have led these preservation efforts, which points to the influence locally produced memory works have had on affecting perceptions of what is historical and thus revered concerning Orangevale. So looking to the work of outsiders is really another way of highlighting the spread of locally constructed cultural memory, which, again by implication, circles back into maintaining a memory meaningful to locals.

The context for the preservation efforts in Orangevale follows the suburb's growth from the mid-1970s to 1990, a rise of about 18,000 people in 1975 to 26,266 in 1990. Orangevale also experienced material growth in terms of buildings, houses, commercial businesses, and infrastructure, such as road expansions. As a result, and concerning national laws (Section 106 of the National Historic Preservation Act) and state laws (Section 15065 of the California Environmental Quality Act), this material growth required historic surveys to determine if any historic connection to the past would be adversely affected and potentially cause a great cultural loss to the community. Of those surveys that are on file, three places were reviewed. There are two main reasons these places stood out. First, historical narratives, especially within history books, continually mention them. Second, preservationists took a particular interest in these three locales as opposed to others because of their susceptibility to being threatened by growth projects.

In 1990, at the close of Orangevale's last significant population growth spurt, the Sacramento-based firm of Historic Environmental Consultants surveyed the Warhaftig House, the Villa, and the Serve Our Seniors Complex. The Warhaftig House, which included a packing shed nearby, was one of the original houses built by the OVCC in 1888. In fact, according to the survey's author, ". . . it was one of the

FIGURE 37

Villa, ca. 1894. This rough image actually comes from a booster publication about the entire Sacramento region, *Sacramento County and its Resources*, published by the *Sacramento Bee* (1894), underscoring the use of rural suburbs like Orangevale as crucial elements in selling a metropolis. Courtesy Center for Sacramento History.

first four constructed by the company in its initial development and promotional activities." In addition, the house may have served as a local headquarters for the OVCC. By the late 1890s, Sol (Peter) Warhaftig assumed ownership of the house, and the family remained there, even using it as an office for their own fruit packing endeavors, until 1960. The house's importance, according to the survey, was in its connection to the OVCC and the Warhaftig family itself, particularly Peter. The family was "prominent in the development and growth of the Orange Vale Colony and its surrounding area," particularly as they ran a fruit packing business, which employed local women and girls in addition to family members, and because of Peter's service to the Orangevale Water Company from 1924 to 1951. In the end, the survey concluded that the Warhaftig House merited listing on the National Register of Historical Places because it "is an important remnant of its [the OVCC's] existence and influence, and represents a principle aspect of the area's settlement. . . . [A]nd [it] represents the theme of settlement." The house also has historical significance because of Peter Warhaftig, "an influential and important figure in the growth and development era of the community" (though the 1950s were far more explosive in terms of actual growth and development). Warhaftig's chief importance was attached to his connection with the Orangevale Water Company, which "allowed" for Orangevale's "extensive agricultural development." Finally, the deteriorating packing shed nearby got marked as historically significant for its association with early agricultural activity.[39] The Warhaftig House's importance, then, lay in its connection to the celebrated and revered colonization company and its founders, to an early pioneer, to agriculture, and to innovation.

The Villa, a stick-style structure built about 1888, originally stood along the bluffs overlooking the American River. The OVCC's investors and clients used it to entertain before a later owner moved the house to Greenback Lane in 1916, and it became a private residence. The Villa again moved and currently rests on Oak Avenue under private ownership. While the survey concluded that the Villa warranted importance for its association to the colonization company and "settlement" of the area, it did not get listed on the National Register for such (because it moved). Nevertheless, because the Villa represented "a particularly fine example" of a stick-style structure rarely found in the Sacramento area, yet alone in a "rural" area, the Villa receives demarcation as historically significant. Indeed, stick-style architecture grew from the picturesque Gothic ideals of famed landscape designer Andrew Jackson Downing (who was, recall, a key figure in popularizing the Romantic suburban ideal) and flourished in house pattern books of the 1860s and 1870s, peaked in construction in the 1880s, but fell out of fashion by the 1890s with the rise of the Queen Anne movement. A structurally sound balloon-framed house, elaborate stick work and ornamentation that served no structural purpose distinguished the stick style— favorably and unfavorably. Ultimately, stick-style houses were the quintessential

TABLE 6

Population and Growth Rate of Fair Oaks and Sacramento County, 1960–2010

FAIR OAKS			SACRAMENTO COUNTY		
Year	Population	Growth Rate from Previous Decade	Year	Population	Growth Rate from Previous Decade
1960	1,622	n/a	1960	502,778	0.81
1970	11,256	6.10	1970	634,373	0.26
1980	22,602	1.01	1980	783,381	0.23
1990	26,867	0.19	1990	1,041,219	0.33
2000	28,008	0.04	2000	1,223,499	0.18
2010	30,912	0.10	2010	1,418,788	0.16

SOURCES: *For all of Fair Oaks, as well as Sacramento County from 1990-2010, see endnote no. 42 for this chapter. For Sacramento County, 1950-1980, see U.S. Census Bureau, Table 2, Land Area and Population: 1930 to 1980, 1980 Census of Population.*

favorites of middle-class audiences and tastes at the time that Downing himself had helped fuel. In Orangevale, then, a stick-style house such as the Villa emerges as unique—innovative and remarkable of course—in an otherwise rural community, not to mention it goes back to the early founders.[40] In fact, upon reviewing the Serve Our Seniors Complex, originally a residence, built in the 1910s, preservationists determined the structure had limited historical significance. Nonetheless, because the property the house stood on had been associated with the early founders and subsequent development of the area, it merited review for potential preservation.[41]

Fair Oaks has been far more active in the reproduction of memory works as compared to Orangevale. As with Orangevale, the answer perhaps emerges from glancing at the census data. In 1960, Fair Oaks reportedly had 1,622 people and grew by an astounding 6.1 percent per year until 1970 when the population reached 11,256, while Sacramento County grew at a rate of 0.26 percent (502,778 to 634,373). While the growth per year dropped to 1.01 percent per annum from 1970 to 1980, the population nonetheless more than doubled from 11,256 in 1970 to 22,602 in 1980, while Sacramento County grew at only a 0.23 percent rate per year (634,373 to 783,381). In the thirty years since, Fair Oaks has grown modestly with growth rates of 0.19 percent from 1980 to 1990, 0.04 percent from 1990 to 2000 (28,008), and 0.10 percent from 2000 to 2010 (30,912). During the same time span, Sacramento County, as noted before, grew at a rate of 0.36 percent (from 1990 to 2010). As of 2010, Fair Oaks's population was 85.7 percent white, 9.6 percent Hispanic or Latino, 4.2 percent Asian, and 2.4 percent Black or African American, and the median household income was $73,583 as compared to the national average of $60,833.[42]

While one can easily get lost in the numbers, the data reveals some suggestive information that can help explain why Fair Oaks experienced a greater outpouring of memory works as compared to Orangevale. Specifically, while Orangevale only experienced a growth rate of 0.20 percent from 1970 to 1980, adding just more than 3,000 people (17,222 to 20,585), Fair Oaks actually doubled in size, from 11,256 to 22,602 and grew at a rate of 1.01 percent per year.

The epoch of growth is what makes this increase seem significant. As historian John Bodnar has chronicled so well, the lead-up to and culmination of the bicentennial celebration in 1976 resulted in an outpouring of not only national attention and celebrations of the past, but also local memory works that exalted both the national story and the local story as it connected to larger national themes such as early pioneers cast as patriots and the adoration of small-town America.[43] Against this backdrop, the Fair Oaks Historical Society formed in the spring of 1975 for preserving and presenting Fair Oaks's history. At a time in which Fair Oaks experienced growing pains, a nationwide spread of nostalgia and patriotism soared. For some, the community ties that bind, the security of localized relations and mechanisms of power, seemed under threat, or at least potentially threatened, by a doubling of the local population. Specifically, this occurred during a patriotic era when many Americans looked to the past for meaning in the present. A surge in memory works resulted in Fair Oaks to seemingly counter, alleviate, or cope, or some combination thereof, with an explosion in population that could potentially threaten to transform, even dismantle, localized power structures in a time of reverent nostalgia. Some local Fair Oaks residents, it seems, decided to turn to the production, organizational manipulation, and memorialization of the past to maintain some semblance of the status quo and social order. They seized control of the culture and, more importantly, the cultural production process in Fair Oaks. In the years between 1960 and 1980, the growth rate reached 12.94 percent (1,622 to 22,602). During that time, Fair Oaks suburbanites published the most circulated and frequently cited memory work, *Fair Oaks and San Juan Area Memories,* in 1960, a collection of newspaper articles featuring tales about "settlement" from original "colonists" and "pioneers." They also formed the most powerful organization devoted to (re)producing representations concerning the past: the Fair Oaks Historical Society (FOHS) in 1975.

Some recent activities of the FOHS reveal the continued effect of a dominant cultural memory. Besides running the History Center (a repository and museum that has moved around several times in the past few years in search of a permanent home), the FOHS published a book, *Fair Oaks: The Early Years,* organized a walking tour, and strengthened and updated the organization with collections management policies and training and archival cataloging guides and practices. Society members received computer and software instruction, and they have created and maintained a vibrant website: www.fairoakshistory.org. At the website, a visitor can print out the walking tour map and guide and peruse society newsletters; a history of Fair Oaks by a local historian; historic photographs and images both from primary and secondary sources; as well as a detailed index, *Fair Oaks and San Juan Area Memories* (which I found very useful of course). The "History of Fair Oaks," found on the FOHS website, the walking tour, and the "Old Homes of Fair Oaks" section in the society's newsletter reveal just what the FOHS considers "historical," particularly as its mission focuses on the "collecting, preserving and presenting [of] the historical record of Fair Oaks and its inhabitants."

In the "History of Fair Oaks," written by a local historian, Fair Oaks' "history," as with the walking tour and "Old Homes of Fair Oaks" newsletter piece, is distinctly limited in time, roughly the 1890s to 1930s, and in scope—a celebration of agriculture, local pioneers, and early infrastructure and buildings predominantly important to a white middle class. The "History" does begin with a single sentence on the local Native Americans, the Maidu, who occupied the land "for at least 10,000 years we are told." While Maidu use of the land, 10,000 years' worth, receives acknowledgment, such a scant reference unfortunately trivializes it (not to mention further dismisses it with the phrase "we are told"). Representations like this can seem obligatory and marginalize the historical actors, effectively recasting

FIGURE 38

The Murphy-Scott Building. Originally built in the early 1900s, this building has served Fair Oaks as a store building and public hall where Fair Oaks residents have, over the years, been able to buy groceries, visit a doctor, get ice cream, socialize, buy hardware, purchase insurance, and down a cold beer at Stockman's bar. Photo taken by author before going to Stockman's bar, 2006.

them as caricatures familiar in the histories of most places in the United States. Furthermore, the reference seems more to serve the purpose of establishing a basis from which to highlight and measure Fair Oaks's Anglo-American growth—the now-familiar narrative of the triumph of American social civilization and material progress as brought to fruition by Fair Oaks's so-called pioneers. The "History" is largely devoted to the "colonization" story, the arrival of "colonists," the establishment and maintenance of farms, the construction of houses, and the creation of the "physical and cultural needs" of the community, such as a merchant store, churches, and schools. One sentence, presumably in an attempt at equity, informs the reader that much of the labor came from minority groups.

"History" ends with that "devastating freeze" in 1932, which, if you recall, destroyed most of the crops in Fair Oaks. "So[,] Fair Oaks life changed forever," the author concluded. "But if one takes a slow walk around town, one can see the vestiges of the orange groves, [and] the olive and almond orchards. Some original buildings hide under several layers of remodeling. A lucky visitor might meet some [white] folks who were born in the 1920s and 1930s and who can tell tales first hand of what life was like when Fair Oaks was fulfilling its original design." Otherwise stated, if visitors were "lucky," they could visit a quaint semi-rural community steeped in a past of agriculture, which, ultimately, was its "original design."[44]

FIGURE 39

The Fair Oaks Fruit Packing Plant and Workers, ca. early 1900s. This image shows a rare glimpse inside the Fair Oaks Fruit Packing Plant, also known as Pioneer, which often employed female Japanese immigrants to help sort, pack, and ship produce. Courtesy Center for Sacramento History, Paul Sandul Collection, no. 2006/030/553.

The walking tour, a self-guided one, and the "Old Homes of Fair Oaks" section of the newsletter reveal not only what the FOHS considers "historical" but also "architecture." One critic of the tour, a graduate student, concluded in a thesis, "[T]he walking tour is a good addition to the publications of the society, but it still covers too many places of interest for a quick tour through town."[45] Indeed, the tour consists of forty-seven "places of interest," all of which are located primarily, though not entirely, in the Fair Oaks "Village" area. The observation has merit. The forty-seven sites are perhaps too much for even the most stalwart of Fair Oaks history enthusiasts to take in—at least within a short amount of time. Even more telling, the forty-seven sites run the gamut from a cemetery to old buildings and commercial sites important to the early years of Fair Oaks's so-called colonization to schools, churches, and houses. (To view the walking tour map and descriptions, visit the FOHS website at http://www.fairoakshistory.org/.)

Noticeably absent from the tour is any potential site(s) important to minorities, particularly those who toiled in the fields, worked the packing sheds, and served in domestic roles. There are at least a few images and family stories, such as those of the Dewey family, that document and thus show the presence and roles of minorities in Fair Oaks. For example, Fair Oaks had Chinese and Japanese laborers, like the Chinese immigrant Jim Gee who worked for and lived with the Dewey family, domestic servants for the celebrated local "pioneer" Buffum family, and female Japanese immigrants or those of Japanese ancestry who worked at the Fair Oaks Fruit Packing Plant of Pioneer.[46] Admittedly, FOHS and others may not know of any sites that were of possible significance to Fair Oaks's forgotten residents and laborers, who themselves could have likely told a "lucky visitor" of tales from when Fair Oaks fulfilled its "original design." In addition, it is likely that no such sites remain or are in good condition. Nevertheless, FOHS, through its walking tour, still managed to demarcate the sites of buildings, houses, and even a tennis court that are no longer there. Indeed, it may seem striking, on the surface of things, that the walking tour memorializes a tennis court while no ethnoracial site, even presence, is mentioned. When we consider the power of collected memory and of a dominant cultural memory, however, which celebrates Fair Oaks as, among other things, cutting edge in an otherwise rural landscape, the celebration of a defunct and departed tennis court is not at all that striking. It distinctly represents a white middle-class heritage working to preserve a white middle-class legacy.

Regardless of the dismissive tendency of the dominant cultural memory, there are ways alternate to actual preservation efforts for communities to celebrate minority and other forgotten groups. For example, public art could easily be produced and could supplement, or fill in, for the lack of physical structures. Museum exhibits, more attention in publications, and lectures, which the FOHS sponsors at annual society meetings, could all enhance the current dearth of attention paid to minority groups in Fair Oaks. At the least, Fair Oaks and the FOHS could be more blunt and honest to the public about its failures and lack of knowledge concerning minority groups, including women not part of the local women's organization—the Woman's Thursday Club—or some early "pioneer" families.[47] Indeed, the Hermitage site of President Andrew Jackson's plantation in Nashville took this approach in recent years. They informed visitors, through publications, word of mouth, and billboards on the ground at the Hermitage, that they had failed to represent slaves and slave life of the Hermitage adequately and were, finally, excavating so they could thoroughly represent this reality to future visitors.[48]

The "Homes of Fair Oaks" piece in the FOHS newsletter began in January 2005. According to the newsletter, "A committee has been formed to record the old homes of Fair Oaks from 1920 through the 1940 [sic]." All the "homes" (not merely houses, mind you) have been of a dominant white middle class and do not include houses or "homes" or at least possible gathering places to which minority groups were somehow connected. The houses include a colonial (built in 1928); bungalow (1928); cottage (1921); farm house (1906, outside the originally stated period of focus); other bungalows built in 1907–11, 1921, and 1922; folk houses (ca. 1895 and 1890s); Payday Shack (1898); prairie style (after 1907); craftsman prairie ("after 1910"); pioneer (1894); and craftsman (1915–20). There was even a section on homes that burned down, but none included a home of anybody not white. Even if a home associated with a minority family still stands, it did not receive attention like the so-called old homes that burned to the ground. Without exception, each home belonged to a white family, often associated with cultural leaders in the community, such as "Farmer Bob," a long-time beloved figure and citizen of Fair Oaks; business owners, such as the home of a local florist; and FOHS members. Such a reality, however, is not such a surprise, as the "Homes of Fair Oaks" simply appears in a newsletter designed and intended for group members of a particular club. Nevertheless, the failure to remember—or more appropriately, the successful effort to forget—"homes" of those outside the dominant white middle class, or at least sites important to them, further marginalizes the presence and significance of minority groups in Fair Oaks. Moreover, and perhaps most striking, the memorialization of middle-class homes is yet another example of how paradoxical an agriburb's representation and celebration of the past can be. Specifically, this seems so striking and paradoxical because such middle-class houses further demonstrate that these communities actually began as planned suburbs.[49]

In Ontario, Orangevale, and Fair Oaks, memory works have shaped cultural memory, and in turn, cultural memory further shapes memory works (this is the duality of cultural memory). The dominant cultural memory of agriburb communities encompasses four major themes that, as collected memory, direct people to remember, and forget, the histories of these communities in similar ways. Foremost among the things, people, and developments forgotten is the suburban side of these communities' origins. This further demonstrates the power and lasting consequences of the original boosterism whereby boosters, spurred by market strategies, or perhaps humanitarian motives, created narratives that have cast a long shadow. Specifically, they created an imagery and narrative template for talking about, thinking of, and representing the past in the present. As more memory works came about, and took their cues from the original packaging of place, a retransmission of a dominant cultural memory reified, legitimized, and sanctified the original boosters' conception of place.

The cultural cost of a dominant cultural memory, amplified when a larger pool of memory works mostly works in concert to disseminate it, to emerge as collected memory, manifests in numerous ways. Of those highlighted, the continued influence on the production of memory works in more recent decades reveals the importance of local history and representations of the past to a community and, more importantly, to at least some of the individuals residing within. A surfeit of information, as embodied in more than a hundred years' worth of memory works in agriburbs, can further work to marginalize, even trivialize, minority groups not typically represented, if at all, in current understandings of the past. Much of this might result from a willed or intended action, while much of this might also result from the desire of those who produce memory works to satisfy their own understandings of the past, as a possible investment in cultural and/or social capital. The result may be no less unsatisfactory, at least regarding remembering the role of minority groups and the suburban side of agriburb communities' past. Nevertheless, the results might not be the sole result of some purposeful, even malicious (or racist or sexist), attempt to misrepresent the past, forget historical phenomena and factual details, and dominate those on the lower levels of the power hierarchy. Perhaps more tragically, the devil is in the details. A dominant cultural memory and its continued dissemination and influence suggests it has become institutionalized, that it works to direct people to represent the past likewise. To produce counter narratives, then, becomes not impossible but that much more difficult to do, particularly when facing over a century of productions and reproductions of the past that portrays it in strikingly similar ways. This, then, is a legacy of boosterism.

HARVESTING SUBURBS, CULTIVATING MEMORY

It combines the positive cultural, physical, and financial characteristics from both the urban and rural ends of the land use spectrum to create an entirely new designation.

AGRIBURBIA, 2010[1]

I N A 2009 BLOG-ARTICLE titled "Agriburbia Takes Hold in Colorado," land planner Matthew "Quint" Redmond described his vision of mixing suburban land use with agriculture in ways jarringly similar to nineteenth-century boosters and suburban real-estate speculators in California. "We are trying to figure out a way to facilitate a more Jeffersonian type of living style for people so they can do multiple things," he said. Redmond continued, "You can be a computer programmer, but you still own a steward lot in an Agriburbia subdivision and produce fruits and vegetables for commercial reasons or for your own use."[2] Agriburbia, the brainchild of Redmond and his wife Jennifer, is a multidimensional vision of agricultural development within suburbia. Clearly, and in no consultation with me (or I them), the Redmonds' conception of Agriburbia is highly comparable to the rural suburban model of "agriburbs." It reveals, in fact, a continued belief and imagining that such a design still appeals to American consumers and/or homeowners and, hence, makes for a good business opportunity.

Agriburbia came about in the mid-2000s, an auxiliary of the Redmonds' TSR Group, Inc. planning company formed in Golden, Colorado, in 1997, more recently joined by another auxiliary company known as Agristruction, a "professional full service agricultural construction and operation firm."[3] The Redmonds seem uniquely qualified to promote Agriburbia. Quint holds a B.S. degree in geology and two master's degrees, one in urban land planning and one in landscape architecture. Jennifer holds a B.S. degree in biology and a master's degree in urban land planning. If these credentials are not impressive enough, the couple touts Jennifer's upbringing on a farm. To round out the group, their staff includes an array of educated specialists, such as an architect/engineer; an environmental designer; a "sustainability and code/ zone researcher"; permaculturists; and communications personnel; not to mention a "morale builder," a creative writer, an economist, and a real estate agent.[4]

The idea for Agriburbia is simple: transform nonagricultural land in suburbs into "prime farmland." TSR offers a variety of mechanisms and schemes in which an individual homeowner to an entire neighborhood development can contract with the group to make a profit. First, of course, the land needs to undergo "agricultural conversion insuring success," and the group, (i.e., Agristruction) will come in; access the site; and, depending on what is needed, landscape, make soil amendments, and/ or set up drip irrigation. After these tasks, the client, which for TSR can include individuals, school districts, utilities, homeowner's associations, and municipalities, can look to contract with the group. One can either pay for maintenance or lease land in a sharecropping scheme. Paying for maintenance is just as it sounds. An individual landowner or entity pays the group the annual maintenance on a time and materials basis in exchange for the "harvested bounty" of their Agriburbia farm. The idea here is that the individual can consume the food or sell it locally, perhaps to a local restaurant, caterer, or farmer's market. The Agriburbia website boasts of a variety of examples and testimonials from local restaurants and chefs in Colorado that purchase Agriburbia produce. The implication is that a demand exists. The sharecropping/lease scheme is also just as it sounds. An individual contracts with the group to manage and farm their land at "a negotiated price per square foot of cultivated ground."[5]

As for targeting school districts, utilities, and municipalities, the group looks to duplicate the above schemes, targeting each entity in a specific strategy. For example, schools have a lot of unused land: by converting it to a farm (they discuss lettuce), the school makes a profit while also presenting the kids with a good teaching exercise, and if that's not enough, it cuts down on lawn watering and mowing expenses. For municipalities or utilities, as well as private businesses, why not take land not heavily used (such as under power lines), if at all, and likewise convert it to make a profit (e.g., grow spinach)? Good for a city or county in need of some cash, to be sure, not to mention businesses looking to diversify or simply profit in whatever way they can.[6]

Agriburbia also proposes the development of entire suburban communities. Besides plans for a development in North Carolina, dubbed Farmstead, the group has been planning the Platte River Village in Milliken, Colorado, for a while as a community of more than 600 acres that would feature nearly 1,000 living spaces, ranging from "multi-family town homes to horse lots." They also plan to include twenty-four acres of mixed-use "neighborhood and commercial" space, counting, they highlight, a fire station and reserved land for future parks and playfields.⁷

Agriburbia and places like the planned Platte River Village certainly echo the themes and model of agriburbs in California more than a century before. Still, the whys and how's of it all may sound even more familiar. The significance of Agriburbia is twofold: it promotes the suburban farm as a viable type for developers to market and therefore turn a profit, and it reveals the remarkable saliency of the rhetoric, language, and even vocabularies used both then and now in conceiving of and selling such places.

Of particular notice in the sales materials and press concerning Agriburbia is the anxiety they reflect. Specifically, just as the turn-of-the-twentieth-century boosters in California's agriburbs deployed hyperbolic demagogy concerning the ill effects of modernization, industrialization, and dramatic demographic change in the wake of increased immigration, Agriburbia does not hide its discontent with twenty-first century America (even the world) as a means to package its product. "In today's climate of soaring gas prices, international conflicts, and concerns about food availability and quality," reads an opening paragraph on the Agriburbia website, "there are highly profitable opportunities for merging sustainable land development."⁸ Elsewhere on the website they state, "Because transportation is becoming ever more expensive and wasteful, there is a real need to grow food close to the population base."⁹ In another online report concerning several similar ventures, Agriburbia seems direly needed precisely because "sprawl-pattern development endangers food supplies and other resources, as well as the health, wealth, and survival prospects of individuals and even whole communities."¹⁰ Whatever the legitimate case may be about the modern world progressing unsustainably and that a real threat exists (and it does), the point is that a return to the farm seems, then as now, the best cure for what ails us.

Contrasted with this shadow narrative of contemporary society is the light narrative of Agriburbia: the appeal of the suburbs, farming, and a middle-class lifestyle, the existence of which are touted within the promotional material. Also explicit is the familiar rhetoric of a planning type and design that are innovative and cutting edge, reflective of both the developers' intelligence as well as the individual consumer's astuteness. First, as might be expected, Agriburbia comes across as perfect porridge. Agriburbia is a "'truly' sustainable initiative [that] improves the quality of life by combining the best qualities of rural living with the advantages of urban conveniences and culture." One can imagine Olmsted's and Beecher's approval. "The result," the Agriburbia boosters say, "is improved agriculture, enhanced development practices, and the enrichment of the residents, tenants, and guests within these Agriburbia mixed-use developments." This blend of rural and urban is a blend of the best parts of each. "Agriburbia is [a] design movement and economic model that advocates for private development and re-development which integrates aspects of Agrarianism, along with contemporary design methods and other environmentally sound principles of real estate development." Further, "It combines the positive cultural, physical, and financial characteristics from both the urban and rural ends of the land use spectrum to create an entirely new designation." This "new designation," while not so new, "changes how we think about land use" because, "[i]n the past, land was thought of as either agricultural or non-agricultural." With Agriburbia, as with agriburbs, it is both. In addition, "in the past," Agriburbia's boosters say, you were "either a city mouse or a country mouse—but not both."[11]

The people who choose to defy the constricted labels of city dweller or country dweller show intelligence. They are not willing to go without, but they are willing to shun what many might see as the negative side of any land use. They are looking to tap into agricultural production on the suburban homestead. Not only does one proverbially return to the land as a farmer, but one also reclaims—or at least transforms—the land to be farmed. In this way, life in Agriburbia presents a dual purpose, allowing food production both for self-use and for sale at the local market. Perhaps the "local" aspect here is too rich to ignore. It plays off powerful feelings and images of local farm produce—locally produced anything—as being superior to anything made far away. Recent campaigns about buying local have further enhanced the narrative power of the local theme. In the case of Agriburbia, it implies not just freshness but also healthy decision making by the consumer.

As already suggested, transforming one's land into farmland, or moving into an entire Agriburbia development, shows progressive thinking. It shows an investment in a sacred notion of agriculture and an investment in the use of modern innovations. This portends a smart way to go about making money by selling to local chefs or restaurants, saving money by cutting costs on purchasing groceries, and doing so in a world and era in which, if you recall the dire warnings above about sustainability (or the lack thereof), such seems direly needed. The purchaser of Agriburbia land or services, by implication, looks both backward and forward. Besides being touted as innovative, the Agriburbia design is further an appeal for incorporating so-called sound principles. "Agriburbia incorporates," the website says, "the current set of sustainable practices such as alternative energy, natural storm water management, and pedestrian focus and adds a new element that is the re-interpretation of food production directly within the living environment."[12] Agriburbia, while further playing off the modern power of "sustainability" hype (encompassing the concepts of "green" or "smart growth"), offers plenty of advice, and has qualified staff ready to come and help; or you can hire one to do the work for you. If you choose to do most the farming yourself, however, Agriburbia envisions that you can hire locals, perhaps "over 55-retirees, teens or kids."[13]

Agriburbia would not be complete without an appeal to homes and lifestyle. According to boosters, the sustainability, agrarianism, and "urban conveniences" rhetoric qualify Agriburbia as a superlative lifestyle choice as much as a sound financial decision. In looking to develop entire communities, Agriburbia's boosters make sure to give proper due to "housing diversity." They claim, "It is generally accepted as good development practice to provide a variety of housing product type [*sic*] across a project." They continue, "This diversity provides some security in sales as part of the real estate process [and thus is smart to do]. In Agriburbia, however, it is a necessity to have this variety [to] include high quality affordable housing." The neighborhood design, like that of the Platte River Village in Milliken, Colorado, or the Farmstead in North Carolina, features parks and promises of mixed-use commercial spaces for the development of businesses and services, as well as the pursuit of "infrastructure," like good roads. Like boosters in California's agriburbs more than a century before, Agriburbia's boosters envision providing everything one could possibly need "to host a 'micro-farm.'"[14]

Agriburbia is not necessarily new, of course. Besides obvious links to agriburbs, in many ways Agriburbia belongs to the family of *new urbanism* design that promotes *agricultural urbanism, new ruralism*, or any other label used to parade forth a planned agrarian suburb or urban-like community.[15] Seaside, Florida, dating back to the early 1980s, is perhaps the most famous of the new urbanism communities. With that said, while agriculture and local produce are hyped in Seaside, recent developments like Hampstead in Montgomery, Alabama, more explicitly appeal to local farming.[16] In these communities, not everyone is a farmer, but rather buys shares into a local farm via community-supported agriculture (CSA), whereby boxes of vegetables or fruits are delivered to customers each week throughout the season.

The method of fashioning and selling the combined image of urbanity and rurality has become an essential aspect of the so-called new urban politics and new urbanism marketing strategies in many post-industrial and post-colonial cities and areas, and it is often called *urban entrepreneurialism*.[17] While a condition of the post-industrial and post-colonial world, this method's roots go back to real-estate capitalism as practiced since the mid to late nineteenth century. Boosters with an interest in agriburbs transformed place by constructing material objects and narrating a sense of place, attributing to them emotionally and symbolically charged signs and signifiers. This practice helped them better sell their agriburbs and promote the metropolitan region. Agriburbs represented both physical places and a state of mind. The development of agriburbs relied on the interplay between spaces and imaginations. Agriburbs were actual physical environments on one hand (i.e., second, or material, space) and spaces experienced in popular culture, photographs, art, architecture, politics, and ideology on the other (i.e., first, or imagined, space).[18] More recently, Agriburbia and other communities like Hampstead are much the same.

Agriburbs were unquestionably a mixture of city and country, a core element of the suburban ideal. As such, they were semi-autonomous enclaves that provided many of the amenities, institutions, and infrastructure to allow them to remain less dependent on cities in comparison to many later subdivisions, and they surely predate the planning, or evolution, of the new urbanism and so-called *super suburbs, megaburbs, technoburbs*, Agriburbia, or edge cities and/or edge nodes of the late twentieth and early twenty-first centuries.[19] Nevertheless, places like Hampstead and Agriburbia remind us of the power and appeal of a suburban farm and agriculture when attached to perceived urban amenities. They display the longer history of combining rural and urban aesthetics as a powerful tool for selling and packaging places.

A leading contention of this work has been that boosters constructing the California Dream largely appropriated the Romantic suburban ideal of the nineteenth century to package the Golden State. In many ways, this explicit suburban focus is an alternate interpretation of the California Dream—if not altogether new, then at least refocused and enlarged. Whatever the case, expanding the geographic scope to locate agriburbs outside California, as we saw, is possible. Certainly, other horticultural communities in California, such as those outside Fresno, Runnymede in the Bay Area, or several Little Landers colonies, mirror the promotion and development of Ontario, Orangevale, and Fair Oaks in the early twentieth century.[20] Nevertheless, many other areas outside California, particularly recent developments like Hampstead and the Agriburbia design, indicate the agriburb model and idea can surface elsewhere.

A Colorado consortium of entrepreneurs founded Agriburbia. Their plans for a model "village," the Platte River Village, are in Colorado (Milliken). Colorado is thus as good as a place as any to see if agriburbs existed in the past as well as the present. Still, I would be remiss by not mentioning that in states such as Florida, New Jersey, New York, North Carolina, Oregon, Texas, and Washington—where we also saw the rise of "horticultural pursuits" and rural or agricultural colonization at the turn of the twentieth century—an agriburb hunt could likewise be, well, fruitful. The agriburb model laid out here can serve as a point of comparison for many other areas outside California, and from within, where horticulture served as a primary means to advertise, promote, and otherwise develop semi-rural-seeming communities that included urban amenities.

Concerning California, however, an understanding of agriburbs as a unique rural suburban type reconceptualizes growth in the Golden State at the turn of the twentieth century. It establishes growth, as historian Glenn Dumke once said of just the Southland, as a largely "suburban phenomenon" decades before speculative suburban real estate ventures in the 1920s or 1950s ever materialized. In many ways, the California Dream signified the suburban ideal by the end of the nineteenth century. California's boosters deliberately echoed the language and design of nineteenth-century Romantic suburban image-makers. While much of this understanding was built upon other impressive works concerning California, particularly those by Carl Abbott, Matt Garcia, Richard J. Orsi, Douglas C. Sackman, Kevin Starr, and David Vaught, the suburban side of California's agricultural colonization and, hence, California's true suburban legacy had rarely been so thoroughly dissected at the turn of the twentieth century.[21]

An understanding of California's agriburbs also deepens an appreciation for the diversity of suburban types across the United States. Recall that recent historical literature concerning suburbia, or the *new suburban history*, has concluded that earlier suburban historians sketched out a restrictive, narrow vision of suburbia. In short, they have challenged earlier depictions of suburbia for their omissions about industry, multifamily or non-single family housing, and the presence of working class and minorities in suburbs. They also challenged the notion that all suburbs were for whites only, affluent, and almost exclusively residential in character.[22] Agriburbs, as a unique rural suburban type, simply pile on more evidence in the ongoing new suburban history challenge to the traditional narrative of what constitutes a suburb.

An understanding of the suburban side of California's agricultural colonization has, as mentioned, also shown the lasting effects of boosterism. Examining the influence of booster narratives exposes much about the nature of memory in these suburban communities specifically and suburbia generally. It shows the importance and lasting influence of older booster narratives and other memory works on present-day memory works and public representations of the past (i.e., the legacies of boosterism). It also contributes to the deeper historiography concerning suburbia by revealing how some suburbanites actively utilize the past in the present to construct (or at least mold) some sense of history and historical understanding. These suburban communities' public history works, memorials, ceremonies, and public spectacles without question show the lasting influence of the original booster narrative and the suburban use of the past. This real sense of suburban memory, as shown in part III, counters the more traditional image of suburbanites as uninterested in narratives about the past as it concerns their suburban locales.

Perhaps another way to come at suburban memory is an ethnographic approach similar to earlier suburban studies, like those of William H. Whyte and Herbert Gans, and much in the vein of more recent works like Mary Patillo-McCoy's *Black Picket Fences: Privilege and Peril among the Black Middle Class*.[23] Indeed, looking at "Groveland," a black middle-class suburb in the Chicago metro area, Patillo-McCoy unpacks a story of middle-class black life and the fragility of class- and race-based statuses and identities. In a good ethnographic tradition, Groveland's black suburbanites themselves are her informants and her evidence. In fact, an ethnographic approach to the study of memory works in agriburbs would help measure how much suburbanites themselves truly appropriate the themes of, and identify with, a dominant cultural memory.

The evidence of the continued production of memory works in these communities—that repeatedly espouse the dominant cultural memory themes—is conclusive of some level of appropriation of cultural memory by suburbanites. Suburban cultural memory exists. With that said, what is still absent is exactly why and how suburbanites find meaning in the history of their suburban communities. In seeking to tell the story of land boosterism and its continued legacy via the production and reproduction of a dominant cultural memory, I have offered a representational history aimed at dissecting the various memory works, to thematically unpack them and suggest what they mean. An ethnographic approach could go further. It could help unravel the meaning of history at a personal, individual level and could verify how pervasive a dominant cultural memory is or is not and if cultural hegemony is present or not.

Suburban places, such as agriburban communities like Ontario, Orangevale, and Fair Oaks, do seem to represent places that are what some scholars have called *theatres of memory, storehouses of memory,* or *sites of memory.* In agriburbs, public recollections about the past have stood against both a flood of place images articulated in memory works and the actual material landscape of these places, which encompassed historic sites, memorials, museums, historic preservation projects, and spectacles. As agriburb boosters packaged place, they imparted a sense of place—they branded it. In turn, subsequent reproductions of place, of memory works, served to reify and legitimize the original production of place. The historical dominant cultural memory concerning agriburbs thus resulted from place making and in turn became an agent in place making.

While fleshing out a palpable sense of memory in suburban areas like the rural suburbs of Ontario, Orangevale, and Fair Oaks, it would be a mistake to say the results are entirely positive. Admittedly, the primary reasons for analyzing the cultural memory of Ontario, Orangevale, and Fair Oaks were intentionally twofold. First, it revealed some of the lasting influences of the original boosters' packaging of place. Second, it paradoxically revealed a dominant cultural memory that, while serving well to divert attention away from these rural suburban communities' origins, further revealed that these communities were indeed unique suburban types: agriburbs. The focus narrowed on making a case for Ontario, Orangevale, and Fair Oaks representing unique rural suburbs. Suburban communities like agriburbs subsequently emerged as rather complex and dynamic places in which individuals looked to use as they fashioned a sense of self and community. This all seems to complicate simple depictions of suburbs as negative, bland, placeless, and lacking cultural memory that seem to dominate our popular culture and even scholarly tradition—what, as referenced to before, John Archer has called "The Places We Love to Hate."[24] While far from being a suburban apology, particularly because a dominant cultural memory in agriburbs has grossly misrepresented factual details and marginalized minorities, suburbs like agriburbs suggest that maybe, just maybe, suburbs are not as lacking as many suburban critics like to say. It seems as if a unitary voice dominates most accounts of suburbia and has had the effect of becoming collected memory, directing subsequent interpreters to adopt similar views and perspectives.

It would be a mistake to imply suburbs are entirely wonderful. I share in many of the complaints about suburbs and suburbanization as detrimental to the environment (though so are cities). They do seem to foster a segregated residential landscape (though popular media and entertainment do so as well—which can also be contributing to some bland uniformity, I suspect). Suburbs do seem to contribute to the way in which resources do, or do not, flow in certain areas spread across a broad metropolitan landscape. The point, then, is not to present suburbs as entirely positive, to produce some type of counter or light narrative to the more typical negative or shadow narratives. Rather, the point is to raise concerns about representing suburbs as simply harbingers of placelessness and blandness—as historically rootless. Suburbs may indeed be responsible for many less-than-admirable phenomena; however, suburbs are also dynamic and complex forms of social and territorial organization. It is best, then, that we treat them as such.

In Ontario, Orangevale, and Fair Oaks, many individuals and organizations appear to take an active role in representations of the past. They seem to find a sense of community and particular meaning in it, even if the result is to divert attention from their communities' suburban origins and to marginalize minorities. Nevertheless, agriburbs, as suburban types, suggest that there is such a thing as suburban memory—good, bad, or ugly. Historical narrative certainly played a central role in this phenomenon, particularly textual narratives, but so too did museums, memorials, walking tours, historic preservation, and cultural performances like Orangevale's Pow Wow Days. In fact, these were the mediums, the vectors of cultural memory, which coalesced to form a dominant cultural memory and privileged specific remembrances of the past. But regardless of who is doing it or what the results are, it does seems that more attention can be paid to the suburbs as dynamic, and doing so does not necessarily need to fall back on simplistic narratives of suburbs as bland, lacking memory, placeless, and altogether terrible. Individuals, even in suburbs, give the impression of taking a lot of pride and investing a lot of themselves in reproducing historical narratives and representing the past to a public audience (even if it is wrapped up in dynamics of social and/ or cultural capital). Suburbanites, just like many others, find a sense of community and identity in the history of their communities, and many take an active role in doing so.

Perhaps overcoming a decidedly antisuburban rhetoric in historical narratives is where suburban history, as a field of study, needs to go if it is not already doing so. Another new direction could include the production of counter-memory works to include the history of more minorities in these suburbs. That might be easier said than done. Historian Lydia R. Otero's recent study about Tucson in *La Calle* (2010) has a similar story about the consequences of a dominant cultural memory. Specifically, she traced the fashioning and continued domination of a "Spanish fantasy past" that worked to erase Tucson's Hispanic history. Such a narrative marginalized and displaced Tucson's Hispanic population (historically called *tucsonense*). At the same time, Otero also documented how such phenomena conversely led to a revival of historical consciousness among the *tucsonense* population precisely because they had fallen under attack and had such somber ramifications for the community. She revealed a counter-reaction to the forces of cultural and economic elitism. It triggered a more robust historical consciousness within and about the *tucsonense* community. While losing many of the battles, though, they eventually succeeded in raising the consciousness of others.

Herein is a message, then, for many historians and others, especially public historians. Otero spotlighted the power of historical narrative and the production of history. I have tried to do so as well. Indeed, a vast and booming literature on the topic exists in addition to Otero's work.[25] In fact, public historian Anne Petersen, in a review of Pheobe Kropp's work about the fashioning of a cultural memory about the Spanish past in Southern California, noticed serious implications for public historians too:

> Kropp's analysis of the inherent politics of control and domination in these preservation projects contains some discomfiting implications for public history. Public historians would like to see our own work as distinct from the more unsavory aspects of the cultural projects of our predecessors, but our projects are also intimately connected to larger cultural, economic, and political trends. As professionals who often work closely with communities to identify, study, preserve, and protect the buildings, landscapes, and stories that make up their pasts, we are consistently faced with choices that determine, to some extent, what that past will look like in the present and the future. Every time we design a walking tour, landmark a building, or identify the subject of an oral history, we employ the notion of authenticity . . . . Public historians produce great projects when guided by a recognition that the cultural power of what we do comes from its potential for openness and inclusiveness. Kropp's dissection of a historical rhetoric used by . . . boosters in large part to decorate, organize, control, exclude, and ignore should inspire public historians to create projects that acknowledge, complicate, illuminate, and empower.[26]

In my own review of Otero's *La Calle*, I tried to say the same thing, perhaps not as well. Citing Otero's focus on boosters and subsequent movers and shakers in Tucson who shaped and circulated an exclusionary historical narrative, I noted, "Public historians need to be aware of their potential membership within growth machine apparatuses, particularly those who work for local governments and powerful local organizations." I continued, "Often, if not outright members, public historians are the everyday foot soldiers in the growth machine army. Indeed, public historians are about the business of helping craft a community's sense of place and imaginary landscape through narratives about the past. To what ends and purposes such narratives are put to use are not inconsequential either. Public historians can thus play a vital (or even corrective) role in sustaining, molding, and uplifting community for the benefit, use, and enjoyment of all."[27]

The message is that public historians and public history practitioners appear uniquely situated to both flesh out cultural memory and do something about any possible errors or misrepresentations. About the first: public historians occupy an obvious position to document the existence of suburban memory by the mere fact that many work in, consult with, or evaluate (suburban or otherwise) museums, historic sites, and memorials, among other things. About the second: public historians are also in a prime position to recraft cultural memory itself—to counter it. This is a noble dream, one that, perhaps, is not objective.

Such a goal has come under fire, however, especially in Richard Handler and Eric Gable's *New History in an Old Museum* and Cathy Stanton's *The Lowell Experiment*.[28] They point out the social agenda and activism that pervades the work and mind-set of some public historians. While I am not going to challenge such an essentialist depiction of public historians, their point remains compelling. They document a tragic irony in which contemporary public historians often work to fashion a more inclusive history while contributing to the marginalization of minorities in the present. Public historians, it seems, often betray their better angels. It is a warning to take to heart.

A similar call about reshaping memory and history comes from Michael Frisch in his influential *A Shared Authority* (1990). Frisch wrote, "What is most compelling about oral and public history is a capacity to redefine and redistribute intellectual authority, so that this might be shared more broadly in historical research and communication rather than continuing to serve as an instrument of power and hierarchy."[29] Shared authority concerning public history, and oral history for that matter, thus embodies collaboration between professionals and community members about interpreting the past, what and who to interpret, and how. This is exactly the kind of approach Petersen called for, that I have suggested, and that others like Stanton have reviewed. Nevertheless, critiques and concerns abound. Reservations concerning not just shared authority, but also, generally, the purposeful production of counternarratives, are many, with a few standouts.[30]

First, critiques focus on how sharing authority or producing counternarratives can push too much in one direction. Counternarratives can too easily tumble over into uncritical and celebratory "monumental history."[31] Too relentless a focus on, say, race or ethnicity overlooks internal divisions within any such historically marginalized group, particularly along class and gender lines. A determined emphasis on history from the proverbial bottom up can neglect the top-down influences and actions of the rich and powerful. Second, shared authority and counternarratives too often result in too narrow of a vision. The charge is that localism too easily leads to provincialism that slights big-picture developments. A third critique is that a too-narrow or even unidirectional focus can actually contribute to the further marginalization of minority groups traditionally left out. For example, this argument manifests itself in critiques that say erecting a statue to a Black civil-rights leader in a historically segregated neighborhood signals her and, by implication, the Black community's continued second-class citizenship by the mere fact that the leader, and they, are not well represented in more prominent or official community spaces and histories.

All these arguments have merit. Yet they fail to recognize the importance of each small step. This is what shared authority looks like and how it contributes to the creation of both a counternarrative and a *historic bloc*. Working with community members, especially those who represent marginalized groups, public historians can begin to share authority and function as what theorist Antonio Gramsci referred to as "organic intellectuals." Gramsci felt that dominant social groups exert power as much through ideological hegemony (dominance over others) as through physical force (say a long reign of racial violence), and he charged that "traditional intellectuals," e.g., the white elite producing memory works in agriburbs, reinforce social hierarchies by serving as "experts in legitimation." Gramsci also pointed out that subdued groups have their own intellectuals, too, who attempt to pose "counter-hegemony" by producing counter memory works subversive of existing power relations. Organic intellectuals, in contrast to traditional, therefore, attempt to build a historic bloc—a coalition of oppositional groups unified around counter-hegemonic ideas.[32]

Perhaps attempts at sharing authority and purposefully producing so-called counternarratives about suburbs, while imperfect and small steps, can reflect the struggle to assemble a historic bloc capable of challenging the ideological hegemony of white cultural domination. Nevertheless, despite any critiques, these would only be first steps. Necessary first steps. To speak the language of spatial theorists again, this is an attempt to "poach" power—a "schemata for action"—no matter how small or how fleeting; to redefine and to push at the shape and structure of third, lived, or practiced space.[33] The goal is to work toward building a stronger community, which is precisely what helps overcome the larger problems of shared authority and the dearth of memory works about and for minority groups in suburbia. I suspect the problems inherent in shared authority do not outweigh the potential benefits. The problems of too narrowly focusing in one direction, of concentrating on so-called minor history projects that supposedly risk marginalizing oppressed groups further, overlooks their importance in establishing community and awareness in the first place. In lieu of any charismatic authority, in light of a long history of racial tensions, in spite of a lopsided existent memorial landscape, attention needs to center on the construction of a historic bloc in the first place more than on any singular outcome.

We also risk dismissing another vital component to the creation and maintenance of a more accurate, diverse, and meaningful memory: the real power of public history and counter-memory works. Borrowing from oral historians like Paul Thompson, Michael Frisch, Alessandro Portelli, and many others, oral history, like any memory work in general, is often a viable tool in the inaugural formation of unified communities.[34] Conducting oral histories with ethnoracial suburbanites, for example, could help fashion new, more inclusive memory works, or just memory works about the community broadly, and can aid in the formation of a unified community, as they will have participated in the creation of historical narratives. Therefore, whether or not any particular effort at shared authority or the production of counter narratives is fraught with problems, the real concern is on the formation of a community in the first place. Acknowledging it will be imperfect, work toward community building is the first step to challenge better cultural hegemony and dominant cultural memory. In that context, I easily imagine an awesome role for public historians in helping reshape the memory of any community, let alone agriburbs like Ontario, Orangevale, and Fair Oaks. In tune with the purpose for writing this book (as well as its own dominant theme), I think that would be a tremendous new legacy.

ENDNOTES

INTRODUCTION

1 Ralph Waldo Emerson, 1844 journal entry, in *Journals of Ralph Waldo Emerson*, vol. 6, ed. Edward Waldo Emerson and Waldo Emerson Forbes (Boston: Houghton Mifflin, 1910), 506.

2 Joseph Alexander, *The Life of George Chaffey: A Story of Irrigation Beginnings in California and Australia* (Melbourne, Australia: Macmillan, 1928), 42–43. For others' recounting of this moment, see Glenn Dumke, *The Boom of the Eighties in Southern California* (San Marino: Huntington Library, 1944), 106–8; Matt Garcia, *A World of Its Own: Race, Labor, and Citrus in the Making of Greater Los Angeles, 1900–1970* (Chapel Hill: University of North Carolina Press, 2001), 28–33; Carey McWilliams, *Southern California: An Island on the Land* (New York: Duell, Sloan & Pearce, 1946), 154–56; Kevin Starr, *Material Dreams: Southern California Through the 1920s* (New York: Oxford University Press, 1990), 14–19; and Ian Tyrrell, *True Garden of the Gods: Californian-Australian Environmental Reform, 1860–1930* (Berkeley: University of California Press, 1999), 141–43.

3 Geographer George Henderson calls this a narrative of "rural realism" in California. George Henderson, *California and the Fictions of Capital* (New York: Oxford University Press, 1999).

4 Alexander, *Life of George Chaffey*, 42.

5 "Orangevale," *Sacramento Union* (May 8, 1888), 3.

6 See Carl Abbott, *How Cities Won the West: Four Centuries of Urban Change in Western North America* (Albuquerque: University of New Mexico Press, 2008), 96–99; José M. Alamillo, *Making Lemonade out of Lemons: Mexican American Labor and Leisure in a California Town, 1880–1960* (Urbana: University of Illinois Press, 2006); Garcia, *A World of Its Own*; Gilbert Gonzalez, *Labor and Community: Mexican Citrus Worker Villages in a Southern California County, 1900–1950* (Urbana: University of Illinois Press, 1994); Becky Nicolaides, "'Where the Working Man is Welcomed': Working-Class Suburbia in Los Angeles, 1900–1940," *Pacific Historical Review* 68, no. 4 (November 1999): 517–59; and Paul Rhode, "Learning, Capital Accumulation, and the Transformation of California Agriculture," *Journal of Economic History* 55, no. 4 (December 1995): 773–800.

7 For more on exurbs, especially in California, see James Vance, "California and the Search for the Ideal," *Annals of the Association of American Geographers* 62, no. 2 (June 1972): 185–210; and, generally, John Stilgoe, *Borderland: Origins of the American Suburb, 1820–1939* (New Haven: Yale University Press, 1989).

8 *Ontario Record Twenty-Fifth Anniversary Edition* 22, no. 47 (November 1907): 8.

9 Richard Walker, *The Conquest of Bread: 150 Years of Agribusinesss in California* (New York: New Press, 2004), 57.

10 A good review of this literature is provided for by Douglas Sackman in the Bibliographic essay at the end of the University of California's reprint of Carey McWilliams's *Factories in the Field: The Story of Migratory Labor in California* (1935, reprint, Berkeley: University of California Press, 1999), 335–42.

11 McWilliams, *Southern California*, 12, 206, 216–17.

12 Kevin Starr, *Americans and the California Dream, 1850–1915* (New York: Oxford University Press, 1973), 192, 416.

13 Starr, *Material Dreams*, 15–17. See also Starr's *California: A History* (Kevin Starr, [New York: Modern Library, 2005], 151) whereby he characterized the agricultural development of California as one that "brought a new kind of agriculturalist—the intensive farmer, educated, middle class, capable of making a living on forty acres—and an aesthetic reshaping of the landscape."

14 Richard J. Orsi, "Selling the Golden State: A Study of Boosterism in Nineteenth-Century California," dissertation, University of Wisconsin (1973), 498.

15 Steven Stoll, *The Fruits of Natural Advantage: Making the Industrial Countryside in California* (Berkeley: University of California Press, 1998), 34; and Garcia, *A World of Its Own*, 31. Other examples of historians comparing agriculture in California to suburbs, or at least suburban-like characteristics, include Cletus E. Daniel, David Vaught, and Douglas Sackman. Daniel, for example, identified a "small farm" ideal that spurred the original development of agriculture in California. According to Daniel, some lofty expectations accompanied the small-farm ideal, including "an increase in diversified farms that still had the capacity to generate a modest cash income from the sale of the fruits whose cultivation was especially suited to California's mild climate." In short, the agrarians hoped the change would at last introduce into the state's rural society a conviction that farming ought to be a way of life rather than simply an instrument of capitalistic enterprise and profit. See Cletus E. Daniel, *Bitter Harvest: A History of California Farmworkers, 1870–1941* (Berkeley: University of California Press, 1981), 20, 32. David Vaught has argued that California's farmers "advanced . . . [a] horticultural ideal within a framework that blended both agrarian and capitalistic perspectives." This horticultural ideal represented "a place where educated, land-owning families lived on small, orderly, and prosperous orchards and vineyards in close proximity to one another." This practical horticulture, like agricultural colonies and irrigation colonies, included social urban advantages such as churches, schools, and even hotels. See David Vaught, *Cultivating California: Growers, Specialty Crops, and Labor, 1875–1920* (Baltimore, MD: Johns Hopkins University Press, 1999), 2 *(see also 3)*, 10, 34, 31. Douglas Sackman has also concluded that many growers believed that a way of life focused on growing fruit would be supremely rewarding—culturally, fiscally, and physically. For Sackman, the "grower was a clean, efficient, gentlemanly, and yet modern businessman imbued with the aesthetic sensibility of an artist, the pragmatism of an engineer, and the spirit of a civic leader." Linking city and country, he quoted from a 1903 edition of *Out West*: "The horticulturist combines city life with country pleasure and his occupation is one requiring rather more brains than of hard labor." See Douglas Sackman, *Orange Empire: California and the Fruits of Eden* (Berkeley: University of California Press, 2005), 26, 40, 41–42.

16 This list is indeed remarkable: For "a world of their own," see McWilliams, *Southern California*, 207. For "Arcadia," see Vance, "California and the Search for the Ideal," 199, 202; for "agricultural colonies," see Dumke, *Boom of the Eighties*, 106; Sackman, *Orange Empire*, 40; Kevin Starr, *Inventing the Dream: California Through the Progressive Era* (New York: Oxford University Press, 1985), 46–47, 166; and Vance, "California and the Search for the Ideal," 200. For "agricultural empire," see Starr, *Inventing the Dream*, 134. For "agricultural wonderland," see McWilliams, *Southern California*, 214. For "blend of rural and suburban," see Stoll, *Fruits of Natural Advantage*, 34. For "boom towns," see Dumke, *Boom of the Eighties*, 77, *passim*. For "citrus belt," see McWilliams, *Southern California*, 207. For "citrus colony" and "citrus districts," see Alamillo, *Making Lemonade*, 12, 13, 15. For "citrus suburbs," see Garcia, *A World of Its Own*, 17. For "citrus towns," see Abbott, *How Cities Won the West*, 94; Garcia, *A World of Its Own*, 2, 28. For "colonies," see Abbott, *How Cities Won the West*, 96; Dumke, *Boom of the Eighties*, 6, 70, 106; Garcia, *A World of Its Own*, 28; Robert Hine, *California's Utopian Colonies* (San

Marino, CA: Huntington Library, 1953); McWilliams, *Factories in the Field*, 21; Donald Pisani, *From the Family Farm to Agribusiness: The Irrigation Crusade in California and the West, 1850–1931* (Berkeley: University of California Press, 1984), 17–8, 121–28; Sackman, *Orange Empire*, 25; Starr, *Americans and the California Dream*, 408; Starr, *Inventing the Dream*, 46–47, 166–68; Starr, *Material Dreams*, 15–16; Stoll, *Fruits of Natural Advantage*, 34–35; Vance, "California and the Search for the Ideal," 200; and Clifford Zierer, "The Citrus Fruit Industry of the Los Angeles Basin," *Economic Geography* 10, no. 1 (January 1934): 54–55. For "eclectic mixes of rural and urban," see Garcia, *World of its Own*, 27–28. For "family farms," see Daniel, *Bitter Harvest*, 16–23; Pisani, *From the Family Farm to Agribusiness*, 11; and Starr, *Inventing the Dream*, 165. For "farms," see Daniel, *Bitter Harvest*, 16–19. For "fruit colony," see Alamillo, *Making Lemonade*, 14. For "garden cities," see Abbott, *How Cities Won the West*, 88–99. For "gentleman-farming" districts of areas, see Laura Barraclough, *Making the San Fernando Valley: Rural Landscapes, Urban Development, and White Privilege* (Athens: University of Georgia Press, 2011), 25, 59. For "horticultural settlements," see Daniel, *Bitter Harvest*, 35–36; Stoll, *Fruits of Natural Advantage*, 40; and Vance, "California and the Search for the Ideal," 199. For "horticultural wonderland," see Sackman, *Orange Empire*, 35. For "irrigation cities," see Abbott, *How Cities Won the West*, 90–93. For "irrigation colony," see Pisani, *From the Family Farm to Agribusiness*, 121; Starr, *Material Dreams*, 16; and Vaught, *Cultivating California*, 15–19. For "irrigation district," see Dumke, *Boom of the Eighties*, 241–42; Stephanie Pincetl, *Transforming California: A Political History of Land Use and Development* (Baltimore: Johns Hopkins University Press, 1999), 11; and Pisani, *From the Family Farm to Agribusiness*, 129–58. For "irrigation settlement," see Dumke, *Boom of the Eighties*, 104; and McWilliams, *Southern California*, 194. For "neither country nor urban," see McWilliams, *Southern California*, 207. For "never-never land," see Vance, "California and the Search for the Ideal," 204. For "orange empire," see McWilliams, *Southern California*, 216; and Sackman, *Orange Empire*, 35. For "orchards," see H. Vincent Moses, "'The Orange-Grower in not a Farmer': G. Harold Powell, Riverside Orchardists, and the Coming of Industrial Agriculture, 1893–1930," *California History* 74, no. 1 (Spring 1995): 34; Stoll, *Fruits of Natural Advantage*, 37; and Vaught, *Cultivating California*, 10. For "progressive rural communities," see Vaught, *Cultivating California*, 52. For "quasi-utopian experiments," see Starr, *Inventing the Dream*, 46. For "rurban," see McWilliams, *Southern California*, 12. For "small farms," see Daniel, *Bitter Harvest*, 16–19, 32; Pisani, *From the Family Farm to Agribusiness*, 73; and Starr, *Inventing the Dream*, 165. For "small rural-seeming communities," and for "specialized form of urban settlement," see Vance, "California and the Search for the Ideal," 200, 205. For "subdivisions," see Dumke, *Boom of the Eighties*, 8; McWilliams, *Southern California*, 122, 216; Starr, *Americans and the California Dream*, 202; and Starr, *Inventing the Dream*, 15. For "suburban and plantation-like," see Anthea Hartig, "'In a World He Has Created': Class Collectivity and the Growers' Landscape of the Southern California Citrus Industry, 1890–1940," *California History* 74, no. 1 (Spring 1995): 100. For "suburban estate," see McWilliams, *Southern California*, 211. For "suburb," see Dumke, *Boom of the Eighties*, 10, 41, 76, 131; and Vance, "California and the Search for the Ideal," 186. For "urban/rural interplay," see Starr, *Material Dreams*, 17. For "utopian settlements," see Hine, *California's Utopian Colonies*; and Vance, "California and the Search for the Ideal," 200–202. For "vineyards," see, among many others, Vaught, *Cultivating California*, 10.

17 Indeed, the people of California's agricultural colonies and farms have been called many things, such as: "Agrarians," see Daniel, *Bitter Harvest*, 29; Moses, "The Orange-Grower in not a Farmer," 24; and Pisani, *From the Family Farm to Agribusiness*, 11–12. For "agriculturalists," see Starr, *California*, 151; and Starr, *Inventing the Dream*, 168. For "better class of people," see Carey McWilliams, *California: The Great Exception* (1949, reprint, Berkeley: University of California Press, 1999), 69; and Stoll, *Fruits of Natural Advantage*, 42–46. For "bourgeois horticulturists," see Starr, *Americans and the California Dream*, 202. For "citrus industrialists," see Hartig, "In a World He Has Created," 105. For "citrus

scientists," see Sackman, *Orange Empire*, 33. For "farm fascists," see McWilliams, *Factories in the Field*, 9. For "farmers," see Daniel, *Bitter Harvest*, 15; Sackman, *Orange Empire*, 50; Starr, *California*, 151; and Starr, *Inventing the Dream*, 165. For "gentleman farmers," see McWilliams, *Southern California*, 211. For "growers," see Dumke, *Boom of the Eighties*, 14; Carey McWilliams, "Farmer Gets Tough," *American Mercury* 33 (October 1934): 245; Sackman, *Orange Empire*, 41–44; Starr, *Inventing the Dream*, 142; Stoll, *Fruits of Natural Advantage*, 32–46; and Vaught, *Cultivating California*, 2. For "horticulturists," see Dumke, *Boom of the Eighties*, 107; Sackman, *Orange Empire*, 42; Starr, *Americans and the California Dream*, 202–3; Starr, *California*, 151; Starr, *Inventing the Dream*, 142; and Stoll, *Fruits of Natural Advantage*, 42. For "industrial agriculturalists," see Hartig, "In a World He Has Created," 106. For "innovative," see Starr, *Material Dreams*, 15. For "an intelligent class of people," see Sackman, *Orange Empire*, 41; and Stoll, *Fruits of Natural Advantage*, 41. For "Jeffersonian," see Daniel, *Bitter Harvest*, 15; Garcia, *A World of Its Own*, 19; Moses, "The Orange-Grower in not a Farmer," 24; and Starr, *Inventing the Dream*, 170. For "middle-class horticulturist," see Starr, *Inventing the Dream*, 46; and Starr, *Material Dreams*, 17. For "orchard capitalists," see Moses, "The Orange-Grower is not a Farmer," 24; and Stoll, *Fruits of Natural Advantage*, 32. For "producers," see McWilliams, *California*, 112–13. For "revolutionary capitalists," see Moses, "The Orange-Grower is not a Farmer," 26. For "scientific farmer," see Starr, *Americans and the California Dream*, 202.

18 Ideals those people coming to California have been in search of include: "Agrarian," see Daniel, *Bitter Harvest*, 32; Garcia, *A World of Its Own*, 19–22; Pisani, *From the Family Farm to Agribusiness*, 11–12; Sackman, *Orange Empire*, 56; and Stoll, *Fruits of Natural Advantage*, 16. For "agricultural," see Daniel, *Bitter Harvest*, 21; Starr, *Americans and the California Dream*, 192; and Starr, *Inventing the Dream*, 45, 83, 134. For "Californian," see Starr, *Americans and the California Dream*, 417; and Starr, *Inventing the Dream*, 3. For "communal," see Starr, *Americans and the California Dream*, 145–54. For "family farm," see Daniel, *Bitter Harvest*, 21–23. For "the geography of the ideal," see Vance, "California and the Search for the Ideal," 202. For "horticultural," see Vaught, *Cultivating California*, 10. For "Jeffersonian," see Daniel, *Bitter Harvest*, 21–23; Moses, "The Orange-Grower is not a Farmer," 24; Starr, *Americans and the California Dream*, 192; and Starr, *Inventing the Dream*, 170. For "middle class," see McWilliams, *Southern California*, 96–97; Pisani, *From the Family Farm to Agribusiness*, 73; Moses, "The Orange-Grower is not a Farmer," 24; Starr, *Americans and the California Dream*, 201; Starr, *California*, 133–34, 146, 154; and Starr, *Inventing the Dream*, 46–47, 138, 142. For "rural," see Sackman, *Orange Empire*, 29; Starr, *Inventing the Dream*, 134–42; and Vaught, *Cultivating California*, 197. For "small farm," see Daniel, *Bitter Harvest*, 32; and Starr, *Inventing the Dream*, 165. For "suburban," see Starr, *Americans and the California Dream*, 416.

19 McWilliams, *Southern California*, 234–35; Garcia, *A World of Its Own*, 25; and Abbott, *How Cities Won the West*, 98.

20 For discussions on suburban revisionism, or what also is referred to as the "new suburban history," as it is distinguished from an earlier cohort (e.g., Kenneth T. Jackson and Robert Fishman) also sometimes called "new suburban history," see Kevin Kruse and Thomas Sugrue, eds., *The New Suburban History* (Chicago: University of Chicago Press, 2006), 1–10; Matthew Lassiter, "The New Suburban History II: Political Culture and Metropolitan Space," *Journal of Planning History* 4, no. 1 (February 2005): 75–88; Margaret Pugh O' Mara, "Suburbia Reconsidered: Race, Politics, and Prosperity in the Twentieth Century," *Journal of Social History* 39, no. 1 (Fall 2005): 229–44; Becky Nicolaides and Andrew Wiese, eds., *The Suburb Reader* (New York: Routledge, 2006), 5–11; Amanda Seligman, "The New Suburban History," *Journal of Planning History* 3, no. 4 (November 2004): 312–33; and Mary Corbin Sies, "North American Urban History: The Everyday Politics and Spatial Logics of Metropolitan Life," *Urban History Review/Revue d'histoire* 32, no. 1 (Fall 2003): 28–42. Recent examples of suburban revisionist works have grown large, perhaps too large to sufficiently list; thus, here are some names of the many scholars who have produced some seminal works: Dolores Hayden, Matthew Lassiter, Robert Harris, Robert Lewis, Lisa McGirr, Sylvia Murray, Becky Nicolaides, Robert Self, Christopher Sellers, and Andrew Wiese.

21 Kenneth Jackson's *Crabgrass Frontier* (1985), together with works by John Archer, Henry Binford, Michael Ebner, Robert Fishman, Ann Durkin Keating, Margaret Marsh, and John Stilgoe, usually receive demarcation as the founding literature of either the "orthodox" suburban history or, idiosyncratically, the old "new suburban history." John Archer, "Country and City in the American Romantic Suburb," *Journal of the Society of Architectural Historians* 42, no. 2 (May 1983): 139–56; Henry Binford, *The First Suburbs: Residential Communities on the Boston Periphery, 1815–1860* (Chicago: University of Chicago Press, 1985); Michael Ebner, *Creating Chicago's North Shore: A Suburban History* (Chicago: University of Chicago Press, 1988); Robert Fishman, *Bourgeois Utopias: The Rise and Fall of Suburbia* (New York: Basic Books, 1987); Kenneth Jackson, *Crabgrass Frontier: The Suburbanization of the United States* (New York: Oxford University Press, 1985); Ann Durkin Keating, *Building Chicago: Suburban Developers and the Creation of a Divided Metropolis* (Columbus: Ohio State University Press, 1988); Margaret Marsh, *Suburban Lives* (New Brunswick: Rutgers University Press, 1990); and Stilgoe, *Borderland*. To be clear, with the exception of Sam Bass Warner Jr.'s 1962 *Streetcar Suburbs: The Process of Growth in Boston, 1870–1900* (1962, reprint, New York: Athenaeum, 1976), Jon Teaford's 1979 *City and Suburb: The Political Fragmentation of Metropolitan America, 1850–1970* (Baltimore: Johns Hopkins University Press, 1979), and, to a lesser extent, Lewis Mumford's 1961 *The City in History: Its Origins, Its Transformations, and Its Prospects* (New York: Harcourt, Brace & World, 1961), the old "new suburban historians" delivered a more intense examination of suburbs than previously given by historians. Three groupings thus emerge, regardless of their label: (group A) Mumford and Warner—Teaford is in reality not mentioned very often (though footnoted a lot), (group B) Archer, Binford, Ebner, Fishman, Keating, Jackson, Marsh, and Stilgoe, and (group C) Harris, Lassiter, Lewis, Nicolaides, McGirr, Rome, Self, and Wiese.

22 A large body of works has focused on African Americans, minorities, industrial deconcentration, and working suburbs. These works not only challenge the stereotype that suburbs are for the middle class, but also demonstrate a trend in examining nonwhite suburbs that the new suburban historians claim an earlier cohort reified. See, Margaret Crawford, *Building the Workingman's Paradise: The Design of American Company Towns* (New York: Verso, 1995); Timothy Fong, *The First Suburban Chinatown: The Remaking of Monterey Park, California* (Philadelphia: Temple University Press, 1994); Garcia, *A World of Its Own*; Richard Harris, *Unplanned Suburbs: Toronto's American Tragedy, 1900 to 1950* (Baltimore: Johns Hopkins University Press, 1996); Richard Harris and Robert Lewis, "The Geography of North American Cities and Suburbs, 1900–1950: A New Synthesis," *Journal of Urban History* 27, no. 3 (March 2001), 262–93; Dolores Hayden, *Building Suburbia: Green Fields and Urban Growth, 1820–2000* (New York: Vintage Books, 2003), 97–127; Greg Hise, *Magnetic Los Angeles: Planning the Twentieth-Century Metropolis* (Baltimore: Johns Hopkins University Press, 1997); Wei Li, "Building Ethnoburbia: The Emergence and Manifestation of the Chinese Ethnoburb in Los Angeles' San Gabriel Valley," *Journal of Asian American Studies* 2, no. 1 (February 1999): 1–29; Robert Lewis, ed., *Manufacturing Suburbs: Building Work and Home on the Metropolitan Fringe* (Philadelphia: Temple University Press, 2004); Becky Nicolaides, *My Blue Heaven: Life and Politics in the Working-Class Suburbs of Los Angeles, 1920–1965* (Chicago: University of Chicago Press, 2002); Mary Pattillo-McCoy, *Black Picket Fences: Privilege and Peril among the Black Middle Class* (Chicago: University of Chicago Press, 1999); Thomas Sugrue, *The Origins of the Urban Crisis: Race and Inequality in Postwar Detroit* (Princeton University Press, 1996); Alexander von Hoffman, *Local Attachments: The Making of an American Urban*

Neighborhood, 1850–1920 (Baltimore: Johns Hopkins University Press, 1994); Andrew Wiese, *Places of Their Own: African American Suburbanization in the Twentieth Century* (Chicago: University of Chicago Press, 2004); and William Wilson, *Hamilton Park: A Planned Black Community in Dallas* (Baltimore: Johns Hopkins University Press, 1998).

23 Lewis, *Manufacturing Suburbs*, 16.

24 Harlan Douglass, *The Suburban Trend* (New York: Century, 1925). See also Graham Taylor, *Satellite Cities: A Study of Industrial Suburbs* (New York: Appleton, 1915) and, providing a good review of the literature and phenomena, Christopher Sellers, *Crabgrass Crucible: Suburban Nature and the Rise of Environmentalism in Twentieth-Century America* (Chapel Hill: University of North Carolina Press, 2012), 11–24.

25 Lewis, *Manufacturing Suburbs*.

26 Taylor, *Satellite Cities*. Andre Sorensen's article "Subcentres and Satellite Cities" is a concise and quality review of the definition of satellite cities, complete with a useful bibliography. See Andre Sorensen, "Subcentres and Satellite Cities: Tokyo's 20th Century Experience of Planned Polycentrism," *International Planning Studies* 6, no. 1 (2001): 9–32.

27 Alamillo, *Making Lemonade;* Garcia, *A World of Its Own;* Jerry Gonzalez, "'A Place in the Sun': Mexican Americans, Race, and the Suburbanization of Los Angeles, 1940–1980," doctoral dissertation, history department, University of Southern California (2009); Gonzalez, *Labor and Community.* Nicolaides, "Where the Working Man is Welcomed," 531; and Abbott, *How Cities Won the West*, 96.

28 Pisani, *From the Family Farm to Agribusiness*, 11–12. See also, Patricia Nelson Limerick, *The Legacy of Conquest: The Unbroken Past of the American West* (New York: Norton, 1987), 130–31; Henry Nash Smith, *Virgin Land: The American West as Symbol and Myth* (Cambridge: Harvard University Press, 1950), 138–50; and Donald Worster, *Rivers of Empire: Water, Aridity, and the Growth of the American West* (New York: Oxford University Press, 1985), 96–125.

29 Pisani, *From the Family Farm to Agribusiness*, 73. For a coeval primary source, see California State Agricultural Society, "Transactions, 1874" (Sacramento: [n.p], [1875]) *in* California Legislature, *Appendix to the Journals of the Senate and Assembly of the 21st Session of the Legislature of the State of California*, vol. 1 (Sacramento: State Printing, 1876), 201.

30 Pisani, *From the Family Farm to Agribusiness*, 73, 120–21,122–27. See also, Abbott, *How Cities Won the West*, 88–99.

31 Indeed, urban historian Carl Abbott highlighted colonies like Fresno, Ontario, and others in Southern California in a chapter titled "Garden Cities" in *How Cities Won the West*, 88–99.

32 See Worster, *Rivers of Empire*, 83–96. For more on garden cities, see Daniel Schaffer, *Garden Cities for America: The Radburn Experience* (Philadelphia: Temple University Press, 1982); and Peter Hall and Colin Ward, *Sociable Cities: the Legacy of Ebenezer Howard* (Chichester: John Wiley & Sons, 1998).

33 Abbott, *How Cities Won the West*, 88–99.

34 Alan Michelson and Katherine Solomonson, "Remnants of a Failed Utopia: Reconstructing Runnymede's Cultural Landscape," in *Shaping Communities: Perspectives in Vernacular Architecture IV*, ed. Elizabeth Cromley and Carter Hudgins (Knoxville: University of Tennessee Press, 1997), 4, 6. Runnymede is part of the Little Landers Movement begun by William Smythe in 1909 outside San Diego. By 1916 five Little Lander Colonies that mixed small farms with the advantages of city culture existed in California, from Smythe's outside San Diego to Runnymede to Hayward Heath in Alameda County, and colonies in the San Fernando Valley and at Cupertino in San Jose. For more on the Little Landers, see Hine, *California's Utopian Colonies*, 145–49; and Laurence Lee, "The Little Landers Colony of San Ysidro," *Journal of San Diego History* 21, no. 1 (Winter 1975): 26–48.

35 Robert Self, *American Babylon: Race and the Struggle for Postwar Oakland* (Princeton: Princeton University Press, 2003), 25.

36 Garcia, *A World of Its Own*, 17–46.

37 Nicolaides and Wiese, *Suburb Reader*.

38 John Archer, "The Place We Love to Hate: The Critics Confront Suburbia, 1920–1960," in Klaus Stierstorfer, ed., *Constructions of Home: Interdisciplinary Studies in Architecture, Law, and Literature* (New York: AMS Press, 2010), 45–82.

39 Fishman, *Bourgeois Utopias*.

40 Vaught, *Cultivating California*, 10–15.

41 Charles Howard Shinn, "Social Changes in California," *Popular Science Monthly* 38, no. 6 (April 1891), 798.

42 William Cronon, *Nature's Metropolis: Chicago and the Great West* (New York: W. W. Norton, 1991), 46.

43 Abbott, *How Cities Won the West*, 8 (emphasis added).

44 David Hamer, *New Towns in the New World: Images and Perceptions of the Nineteenth Century Urban Frontier* (New York: Columbia University Press, 1990); and Orsi, "Selling the Golden State."

45 Michel Foucault explains a "regime of truth" in connection to systems of power, "which produce and sustain it, and to effects of power which it induces and which extend it." In short, a regime of truth reflects a structure and relation of power that establishes "truth" and disseminates it. Michel Foucault, *Power/Knowledge: Selected Interviews and Other Writings, 1972–77*, ed. Colin Gordon (New York: Pantheon, 1980), 131–33 (quote from 131).

46 "A History of Fair Oaks," Fair Oaks: Fair Oaks Historical Society, 2005, accessible at the Fair Oaks Historical Society's website, www.fairoakshistory.org.

47 Upland Elementary School, *Historical Essays*, collection of essays written by students of Upland Elementary School (Ontario: privately printed, 1931), housed at the Robert E. Ellingwood Model Colony History Room, Ontario City Library, Ontario, CA (hereafter referred to as Model Colony History Room); Ontario Diamond Jubilee Committee, *Ontario Diamond Jubilee: Historical Review: Pictures and Events of Ontario and Surrounding Communities* (Ontario: Ontario Diamond Jubilee Committee, 1957), Model Colony History Room; Ontario Bicentennial Commission, *A Bicentennial Salute: An Historical Review of Ontario, California and Our Nation, 1776–1976* (Ontario: Ontario City Council, 1976); and Michael Rounds, *Ontario: The Gem of the Foothills* (Carlsbad, CA: Heritage Media Corp., 1999).

48 Rounds, *Ontario*, 45–63.

49 The list of outstanding works concerning the process of suburbanization is large. See the following for examples: John Archer, *Architecture and Suburbia: From English Villa to American Dream House, 1690–2000* (Minneapolis: University of Minnesota Press, 2005); Fishman, *Bourgeois Utopias*; Hayden, *Building Suburbia*; Jackson, *Crabgrass Frontier*; Lewis, *Manufacturing Suburbs*; Nicolaides and Wiese, *Suburb Reader*; and Jon Teaford, *The American Suburb: The Basics* (New York: Routledge, 2008).

50 See Mike Wallace, *Mickey Mouse History and Other Essays on American Memory* (Philadelphia: Temple University Press, 1996), 20–21; and Pierce F. Lewis, "The Future of the Past: Our Clouded Vision of Historical Preservation," *Pioneer America* 7 (July 1975), 1–20.

51 Harvey Molotch, "The City as a Growth Machine: Toward a Political Economy of Place," *American Journal of Sociology* 82, no. 2 (September 1976), 309–22. See also David Harvey, *Social Justice and the City* (Baltimore: Johns Hopkins University Press, 1973); Andrew E. G. Jonas and David Wilson, eds., *The Urban Growth Machine: Critical Perspectives Two Decades Later* (Albany: State University of New York Press, 1999); Henri Lefebvre, *The Production of Space* (1974; repr., Oxford, UK: Blackwell, 1991); John Logan and Harvey Molotch, *Urban Fortunes: The Political Economy of Place* (Berkeley: University of California Press, 1987); John Logan, Rachel Bridges Whaley, and Kyle Crowder, "The Character and Consequences of Growth Regimes: An Assessment of Twenty Years of Research," *Urban Affairs Review* 32 (May 1997): 603–31; and David Rusk, "The Sprawl Machine," in *Inside Game, Outside Game: Winning Strategies for Saving Urban America* (Washington, D.C.: Brookings Institution, 1999), 82–100.

52 The literature on spatial theory is vast, perhaps too vast, but useful in discussing space as something more than a material landscape (sometimes called material space or second space) and includes how space is something that can be represented, even imagined (often called imagined space, storied space, or first space), as well as lived and experienced (sometimes called lived space, practiced space, or third space). See Michel de Certeau, *The Practice of Everyday Life* (Berkeley: University of California Press, 1984); Steven Feld and Keith Basso, eds., *Senses of Place* (Santa Fe: School of American Research Press, 1996); Dolores Hayden, *The Power of Place: Urban Landscapes as Public History* (Cambridge: MIT Press, 1996); Lefebvre, *Production of Space*; Gyan Prakash and Kevin Kruse, eds., *The Spaces of the Modern City: Imaginaries, Politics, and Everyday Life* (Princeton: Princeton University Press, 2008); Edward Soja, *Thirdspace: Journeys to Los Angeles and Other Real-and-Imagined Places* (Cambridge: Blackwell, 1996); and Yi-Fu Tuan, *Space and Place: The Perspective of Experience* (Minneapolis: University of Minnesota Press, 1977).

53 Michel Foucault, *Psychiatric Power* (Basingstoke, England: Macmillan, 2008), 16.

54 Foucault, *Power Knowledge*, 197.

55 Barbara Berglund, *Making San Francisco American: Cultural Frontiers in the Urban West, 1846–1906* (Lawrence: University Press of Kansas, 2010); John Bodnar, *Remaking America: Public Memory, Commemoration, and Patriotism in the Twentieth Century* (Princeton: Princeton University Press, 1992); William Deverell, *Whitewashed Adobe: The Rise of Los Angeles and the Remaking of its Mexican Past* (Berkeley: University of California Press, 2004); David Glassberg, *Sense of History: The Places of the Past in American Life* (Amherst: University of Massachusetts Press, 2001); Harvey Graff, *The Dallas Myth: The Making and Unmaking of an American City* (Minneapolis: University of Minnesota Press, 2008); Hayden, *Power of Place*; Phoebe S. Kropp (now Phoebe S. K. Young; all references and citations to Kropp), *California Vieja: Culture and Memory in a Modern American Place* (Berkeley: University of California Press, 2007); James Lindgren, *Preserving Historic New England: Preservation, Progressivism, and the Remaking of Memory* (New York: Oxford University Press, 1995); McWilliams, *Southern California*; Martha Norkunas, *The Politics of Public Memory: Tourism, History, and Ethnicity in Monterey, California* (Albany: State University of New York Press, 1993); Lydia Otero, *La Calle: Spatial Conflict and Urban Renewal in a Southwest City* (Tucson: University of Arizona Press, 2010); Cathy Stanton, *Lowell Experiment: Public History in a Postindustrial City* (Amherst: University of Massachusetts Press, 2006); Patricia West, *Domesticating History: The Political Origins of America's House Museums* (Washington, DC: Smithsonian Institution Press, 1999); and Chris

Wilson, *The Myth of Santa Fe: Creating a Modern Regional Tradition* (Albuquerque: University of New Mexico Press, 1997). See also, David Hamer, *History in Urban Places: The Historic Districts of the United States* (Columbus: Ohio State University Press, 1998); Prakash and Kruse, *Spaces of the Modern City*; Michel-Rolph Troillot, *Silencing the Past: Power and the Production of History* (Boston: Beacon Press, 1995); and Stephen Ward, *Selling Places: The Marketing and Promotion of Towns and Cities, 1850–2000* (New York: Routledge, 1998).

56 Deverell, *Whitewashed Adobe*, 4–5.

57 Barraclough, *Making the San Fernando Valley*, 25, 59, and, in *passim*, 2.

58 Kropp, *California Vieja*, 15.

59 Berglund, *Making San Francisco American*, 30; see also 219.

60 McWilliams, *Southern California*, 71.

61 I say near monopoly as historian David Vaught has done a keen job looking around Davis, also near Sacramento, and the central valley, as has Donald Pisani. See, Pisani, *From the Family Farm to Agribusiness*; and Vaught, *Cultivating California*. I also do not mean to slight many quality histories focusing on the San Francisco Bay Area and its fruit culture running down to San Jose. See Gray Brechin, *Imperial San Francisco: Urban Power, Earthly Ruin* (Berkeley: University of California Press, 2006); Glenna Matthews, *Silicon Valley, Women, and the California Dream: Gender, Class, and Opportunity in the Twentieth Century* (Palo Alto: Stanford University Press, 2002); David Naguib Pellow and Lisa Sun-Hee Park, *The Silicon Valley of Dreams: Environmental Injustice, Immigrant Workers, and the High-Tech Global Economy* (New York: New York University Press, 2002); and Stephen Pitti, *The Devil in Silicon Valley: Northern California, Race, and Mexican Americans* (Princeton: Princeton University Press, 2004).

62 Theodore Hershberg, "The New Urban History: Toward an Interdisciplinary History of the City," *Journal of Urban History* 5, no. 1 (November 1978): 3–40; Setha Low, "The Anthropology of Cities: Imagining and Theorizing the City," *Annual Review of Anthropology* 25 (1996), 384.

63 Bruno Latour, *Reassembling the Social: An Introduction to Actor-Network Theory* (New York: Oxford University Press, 2005), 12.

Part 1

MARKET REVOLUTION

1 George Rogers Taylor coined the phrase "transportation revolution" in *The Transportation Revolution, 1815–1860* (New York: Rinehart, 1951). For the market revolution see Daniel Walker Howe, *What Hath God Wrought: The Transformation of America, 1815–1848* (New York: Oxford University Press, 2007), 525–69; Scott Martin, ed., *Cultural Change and the Market Revolution in America, 1789–1860* (Lanham, MD: Rowman and Littlefield, 2005); Charles Sellers, *The Market Revolution: Jacksonian America, 1815–1846* (New York: Oxford University Press, 1991); and Melvyn Stokes and Stephen Conway, eds., *The Market Revolution in America: Social, Political, and Religious Expressions, 1800–1880* (Charlottesville: University Press of Virginia, 1996).

2 The literature on demographic characteristics, immigration, slavery and cotton, urbanization, and westward movement is enormous. For immigration, see Kathleen Conzen, *Immigrant Milwaukee, 1836–1860: Accommodation and Community in a Frontier City* (Cambridge: Harvard

University Press, 1976); Oscar Handlin, *The Uprooted* (Boston: Little, Brown, 1973); Noel Igna-tiev, *How the Irish Became White* (New York: Routledge, 1995); and Kerby Miller, *Emigrants and Exiles: Ireland and the Irish Exodus to North America* (New York: Oxford University Press, 1985). For transportation and communication, see Albert Fishlow, *American Railroads and the Trans-formation of the Antebellum Economy* (Cambridge: Harvard University Press, 1965); and Robert Fogel, *Railroads and American Economic Growth: Essays in Econometric History* (Baltimore: Johns Hopkins University Press, 1964); and Taylor, *Transportation Revolution*. For business, technolo-gies, and law, see Alfred Chandler, *The Visible Hand: The Managerial Revolution in American Business* (Cambridge: Belknap Press, 1977); Thomas Cochran, *Business in American Life: A History* (New York: McGraw-Hill, 1972); and Morton Horwitz, *The Transformation of American Law, 1780–1860* (Cambridge: Harvard University Press, 1977). For factories and the working class, see Mary Blewett, *Men, Women, and Work: Class, Gender, and Protest in the New England Shoe Industry, 1780–1910* (Urbana: University of Illinois Press, 1988); Herbert Gutman, *Work, Culture, and Society in Industrializing America: Essays in American Working-Class and Social History* (New York: Knopf, 1976); David Roediger, *The Wages of Whiteness: Race and the Making of the American Working Class* (New York: Verso, 1999); and Sean Wilentz, *Chants Democratic: New York City & the Rise of the American Working Class, 1788–1850* (New York: Oxford University Press, 1984). For society, culture, and urbanization, see Stuart Blumin, *The Urban Threshold: Growth and Change in a Nineteenth-Century American Community* (Chicago: University of Chicago Press, 1976); Timothy Gilfoyle, *City of Eros: New York City, Prostitution, and the Com-mercialization of Sex, 1790–1920* (New York: Norton, 1992); Eric Monkkonen, *America Becomes Urban: The Development of U.S. Cities & Towns, 1780–1980* (Berkeley: University of California Press, 1988); Christine Stansell, *City of Women: Sex and Class in New York, 1789–1860* (New York: Knopf, 1986); and David Thelen, *Paths of Resistance: Tradition and Dignity in Industrial-izing Missouri* (New York: Oxford University Press, 1986). For slavery, see Ira Berlin, *Many Thousands Gone: The First Two Centuries of Slavery in North America* (Cambridge: Belknap Press, 1998); David Eltis, *The Rise of African Slavery in the Americas* (Cambridge: Cambridge University Press, 2000); Eugene Genovese, *Roll, Jordan, Roll: The World the Slaves Made* (New York, Pantheon Books, 1974); and Walter Johnson, *Soul by Soul: Life Inside the Antebellum Slave Market* (Cambridge: Harvard University Press, 1999).

3 For transportation, communications, and newspapers, see Clarence Brigham, *History and Bib-liography of American Newspapers, 1690–1820*, 2 vols. (Worcester: American Antiquarian Society, 1947); Colleen Dunlavy, *Politics and Industrialization: Early Railroads in the United States and Prussia* (Princeton: Princeton University Press, 1994); Carter Goodrich, *Government Promotion of American Canals and Railroads, 1800–1890* (New York: Columbia University Press, 1960); David Paul Nord, *Communities of Journalism: A History of American Newspapers and their Readers* (Urbana: University of Illinois Press, 2001); Jeff Pasley, *The Tyranny of Printers: Newspaper Politics in the Early American Republic* (Charlottesville: University Press of Virginia, 2001); Ronald E. Shaw, *Canals for a Nation: The Canal Era in the United States, 1790–1860* (Lexington: University Press of Kentucky, 1990); Carol Sheriff, *The Artificial River: The Erie Canal and the Paradox of Progress, 1817–1862* (New York: Hill and Wang, 1996); Stover, *American Railroads*; and Taylor, *Transportation Revolution*. For factories and mills, see Blewett, *Men, Women, and Work*; David A. Hounshell, *From the American System to Mass Production, 1800–1932: The Development of Manufacturing Technology in the United States* (Baltimore: Johns Hopkins University Press, 1984); and Barbara Tucker, *Samuel Slater and the Origins of the American Textile Industry, 1790–1860* (Ithaca: Cornell University Press, 1984). For agriculture and farming, see Joyce E. Chaplin, *An Anxious Revolt: Agricultural Innovation and Modernity in the Lower South, 1730–1815* (Chapel Hill: University of North Carolina Press, 1993); David Danbom, *Born in the Country: A History of Rural America*, 2nd ed. (Baltimore: Johns Hopkins University Press, 2006); R.

Douglas Hurt, *American Agriculture: A Brief History*, rev. ed. (West Lafayette, IN: Purdue University Press, 2002); and Peter McClelland, *Sowing Modernity: America's First Agricultural Revolution* (Ithaca: Cornell University Press, 1997).

4 For more on the rural ideal, see David Allmendinger Jr., *Ruffin: Family and Reform in the Old South* (New York: Oxford University Press, 1990); Archer, "Country and City," 139–56; Daniel Boorstin, *The Lost World of Thomas Jefferson* (New York: H. Holt, 1948); Chaplin, *An Anxious Revolt*; William Cronon, "The Trouble with Wilderness," *New York Times Magazine*, August 14, 1995, 46–47; Danbom, *Born in the Country*, 65–69; Clarence Danhof, *Change in Agriculture: The Northern United States, 1820–1870* (Cambridge: Harvard University Press, 1969); Fishman, *Bourgeois Utopias*, 53–54, 127; Garcia, *A World of Its Own*, 17–22; Hurt, *American Agriculture*, 72–77; Jackson, *Crabgrass Frontier*, 57; Marsh, *Suburban Lives*, xiii, 5; Leo Marx, *The Machine in the Garden: Technology and the Pastoral Ideal in America* (New York: Oxford University Press, 1964); McClelland, *Sowing Modernity*; J. John Palen, *The Suburbs* (New York: McGraw-Hill, 1995), 70, 93–94; Morrill Peterson, *The Jefferson Image in the American Mind* (New York: Oxford University Press, 1960); Smith, *Virgin Land*; Warner, *Streetcar Suburbs*, 11–12, 14, 45, 90; and Raymond Williams, *The Country and the City* (New York: Oxford University Press, 1973).

5 Hurt, *American Agriculture*, 72.

6 Danbom, *Born in the Country*, 65, 66.

7 See Joyce Appleby, *Inheriting the Revolution: The First Generation of Americans* (Cambridge: Belknap Press, 2000); Stuart Blumin, *The Emergence of the Middle Class: Social Experience in the American City, 1760–1900* (New York: Cambridge University Press, 1989); Karen Halttunen, *Confidence Men and Painted Women: A Study of Middle-Class Culture in America, 1830–1870* (New Haven: Yale University Press, 1982), 35–40; and Mary Ryan, *Cradle of the Middle Class: The Family in Oneida County, New York, 1790–1865* (New York: Cambridge University Press, 1981), 230–42.

8 See Appleby, *Inheriting the Revolution*; and Michael Kimmel, *Manhood in America: A Cultural History* (New York: Free Press, 1996).

9 See George Chauncey, *Gay New York: Gender, Urban Culture, and the Makings of the Gay Male World, 1890–1940* (New York: Basic Books, 1994), 111–14; Elliott Gorn, *The Manly Art: Bare-Knuckle Prize Fighting in America* (Ithaca: Cornell University Press, 1986), 187–206; David Pugh, *Sons of Liberty: The Masculine Mind in Nineteenth-Century America* (Westport, CT: Greenwood Press, 1983), 23–35; and E. Anthony Rotundo, *American Manhood: Transformations in Masculinity from the Revolution to the Modern Era* (New York: Basic Books, 1993), 249.

10 Henry Ward Beecher, *Lectures to Young Men on Various Important Subjects* (1846 repr., New York: M. H. Newman; 1849), 26–27.

11 Thorstein Veblen, *The Theory of the Leisure Class: An Economic Study in the Evolution of Institutions* (New York: Macmillan, 1899); and Pierre Bourdieu, *Distinction: A Social Critique of the Judgment of Taste* (Cambridge: Harvard University Press, 1984), 1, 7, 91.

12 Katherine Chaison, "Plot Development, or E. F. Beadle's Adventures in Building Suburban Homes in Late Nineteenth-Century New York," *New York History* 81, no. 1 (Winter 2007): 55–60; Clifford Edward Clark, Jr., *The American Family Home, 1800–1960* (Chapel Hill: University of North Carolina Press, 1986), 16; Katherine Grier, *Culture and Comfort, Parlor Making and Middle Class Identity, 1850–1930* (Washington, D.C.: Smithsonian Press, 1988), 5; Fishman, *Bourgeois Utopias*, 3–9, 88, 118–19; Hayden, *Building Suburbia*, 25; Jackson, *Crabgrass Frontier*, 50, 91; Mumford, *City in History*, 484; Linda Smiens, *Building an American Identity, Pattern*

Book Homes and Communities, 1870–1900 (Walnut Creek, CA: Altamira Press, 1999), 86; Warner, *Streetcar Suburbs*, 34, 48, 53, 64, 155; Gwendolyn Wright, *Building the Dream: A Social History of Housing in America* (New York: Pantheon Books, 1981), 113; and Gwendolyn Wright, *Moralism and the Model Home: Domestic Architecture and Cultural Conflict in Chicago, 1870–1913* (Chicago: University of Chicago Press, 1980), 55.

13 For a more direct connection of the rural ideal to the development of historical consciousness, see Peter Fritzsche, *Stranded in the Present: Modern Time and the Melancholy of History* (Cambridge: Harvard University Press, 2004), 49–50.

CHAPTER I

1 Andrew Jackson Downing, *A Treatise on the Theory and Practice of Landscape Gardening* (New York: George Putnam, 1850), ix.

2 See Allmendinger, *Ruffin*; Archer, "Country and City," 139–56; Boorstin, *Lost World of Thomas Jefferson*; Cronon, "The Trouble with Wilderness"; Danbom, *Born in the Country*, 65–69; Danhof, *Change in Agriculture*; Fishman, *Bourgeois Utopias*, 53–54, 127; Hurt, *American Agriculture*, 72–77; Jackson, *Crabgrass Frontier*, 57; Marx, *Machine in the Garden*; McClelland, *Sowing Modernity*; Warner, *Streetcar Suburbs*, 11–12, 14, 45, and 90; and Williams, *Country and the City*.

3 James Manchor, *Pastoral Cities: Urban Ideals and the Symbolic Landscape of America* (Madison: University of Wisconsin Press, 1987), 158.

4 For more on Romantic suburbs, see Archer, *Architecture and Suburbia*, 204–38; Archer, "Country and City"; Fishman, *Bourgeois Utopias*, 121–33; Hayden, *Building Suburbia*, 45–70; Jackson, *Crabgrass Frontier*, 73–86; and Nicolaides and Wiese, *Suburb Reader*, 2–3.

5 Marx, *Machine in the Garden*.

6 Andrew Jackson Downing, *Architecture of Country Houses: Including Designs for Cottages, Farm Houses, and Villas, with Remarks on Interiors, Furniture, and the Best Modes of Warming and Ventilating* (New York: Appleton, 1850; reprint, New York: De Capo, 1968), 269.

7 "Virtuous citizen" quoted from Downing, *Architecture of Country Houses*, 270; see also xiv, xxiii, 257, 264, 267, and 286; Archer, *Architecture and Suburbia*, 308, 349, and 403; Archer, "Country and City," 147; and Jackson, *Crabgrass Frontier*, 65–66.

8 Jefferson, Query XIX, *Notes on the State of Virginia*, 170–71. For more on suburbs and their relationship to democracy, republicanism, citizenship, and civic participation, see Archer, *Architecture and Suburbia*, 173–202; Clark, *American Family Home*, 24; Jackson, *Crabgrass Frontier*, 65–66; Marsh, *Suburban Lives*, 5; and Warner, *Streetcar Suburbs*, 158.

9 Olmsted, Vaux, and Co., "Letter to the Riverside Improvement Company," September 1, 1868, in *Building the Nation: Americans Write About Their Architecture, Their Cities, and Their Landscape*, ed. Steven Conn and Max Page (Philadelphia: University of Pennsylvania Press, 2003), 266; Samuel Sloan, *City Homes, Country Houses, and Church Architecture* (Philadelphia: Claxton, Remsen, and Haffelfinger, 1871), 746–47; and Calvert Vaux, *Villas and Cottages* (1857; repr., New York: Da Campo Press, 1968), 22, emphasis original.

10 Henry Morgan, *Boston Inside Out! Sins of a Great City! A Story of Real Life, Tenth Thousand, Revised and Enlarged* (Boston: Shawmut Publishing Company, 1880), excerpted in Ivan D. Steen,

Urbanizing America: The Development of Cities in the United States From the First European Settlements to 1920 (Malabar, FL: Krieger, 2006), 144.

11 *Suburban Homes on the West Jersey Railroad* (Philadelphia: Allen, Lane, and Scott Printers, 1881), in Conn and Page, *Building the Nation*, 270; and Catharine Beecher and Harriet Beecher Stowe, *The American Woman's Home: or, Principles of Domestic Science; Being a Guide to the Formation and Maintenance of Economical, Healthful, Beautiful, and Christian Homes* (1869; repr., New York: Arno, 1971), 43–44.

12 Archer, *Architecture and Suburbia*, 149, 155; Randall Bartlett, *The Crisis of America's Cities: Solutions for the Future, Lessons from the Past* (Armonk: M.E. Sharpe, 1998), 13–14; Fishman, *Bourgeois Utopias*, 120; Howard Frumkin, Lawrence Frank, and Richard Jackson, *Urban Sprawl and Public Health: Designing, Planning, and Building for Healthy Communities* (Washington, D.C.: Island Press, 2004), 44–64; Jackson, *Crabgrass Frontier*, 57–70; Marsh, *Suburban Lives*, 5; Marx, *Machine in the Garden*, 235–36; and Warner, *Streetcar Suburbs*, 12.

13 Thomas Jefferson, letter to Benjamin Rush (1800), quoted in Jackson, *Crabgrass Frontier*, 68; Ralph Waldo Emerson, quoted in Marx, *Machine in the Garden*, 235–36; Henry McMurtie, *Sketches of Louisville and its Environs* (Louisville: S. Penn, Jr., 1819), 114; and Henry David Thoreau, quoted in Jackson, *Crabgrass Frontier*, 68.

14 Thomas Jefferson, quoted in Charles Glaab and A. Theodore Brown, *A History of Urban America* (New York: Macmillan, 1967), 55; Henry David Thoreau, "Walking," in *The Writings of Henry David Thoreau*, Walden Edition, vol. 5, *Excursions and Poems* (New York: AMS Press, 1968), 205; and Ralph Waldo Emerson, *Nature: Addresses and Lectures*, Concord Edition (1849; repr., Boston: Houghton Mifflin, 1903), 16. For more on the English influence, see Archer, "Country and City," 140–45; Fishman, *Bourgeois Utopias*, 9, 24, 53, 88, 120–21; Jackson, *Crabgrass Frontier*, 13, 63; and Vincent Scully, *The Shingle Style and the Stick Style: Architectural Theory and Design from Downing to the Origins of Wright* (New Haven: Yale University Press, 1971).

15 Mumford, *City in History*, 483; Gervase Wheeler, *Homes for the People, in Suburb and Country* (New York: Scribner, 1855), 69; and Anonymous, *Suburban Homes on the West Jersey Railroad*, 269–70.

16 Olmsted, Vaux, and Co., *Preliminary Report upon the Proposed Suburban Village at Riverside, near Chicago* (New York: Sutton, Browne and Co., 1868), 7; see also 24 (Vaux makes a similar statement in his *Villas and Cottages*, 267); Frederick Law Olmsted, et al., *Report of a Preliminary Scheme of Improvements*, submitted to the Staten Island Improvement Commission (New York: James Sutton, 1871), 9; Olmsted, Vaux, and Co., *Preliminary Report*, 7; and Frederick Law Olmsted, letter to Henry H. Elliott, August 27, 1860, in *The Papers of Frederick Law Olmsted*, ed. Charles Beveridge and David Schuyler, vol. 3, *Creating Central Park* (Baltimore: Johns Hopkins University Press, 1983), 264; Olmsted, letter to Elliott, August 27, 1860, *Papers of Frederick Law Olmsted*, vol. 3, 264; Olmsted, Vaux, and Co., *Preliminary Report*, 28; and Olmsted, Vaux, and Co., *Preliminary Report*, 5. For more on Olmsted, see Archer, "Country and City," 140–45; Clark, *American Family Home*, 24–30; Fishman, *Bourgeois Utopias*, 126–48; Hayden, *Building Suburbia*, 61–64; Jackson, *Crabgrass Frontier*, 79–81; Laura Wood Roper, *FLO: A Biography of Frederick Law Olmsted* (Baltimore: Johns Hopkins University Press, 1977); Roy Rosenzweig and Elizabeth Blackmar, *The Park and the People: A History of Central Park* (Ithaca, NY: Cornell University Press, 1992); and Elizabeth Stevenson, *Park Maker: A Life of Frederick Law Olmsted* (New York: Macmillan, 1977). For more on Vaux, see William Alex, *Calvert Vaux: Architect & Planner* (New York: Ink, 1994); Francis Kowsky, *Country, Park, & City: The Architecture and Life of Calvert Vaux* (New York: Oxford University Press, 1998); Rosenzweig and Blackmar, *Park and the People*; Witold Rybczynski, *A Clearing in the Distance: Frederick Law Olmsted and America in the Nineteenth Century* (New York: Scribner, 1999), chapters 20–44.

17 For more on family, see Philippe Ariès, *Centuries of Childhood: A Social History of Family Life* (New York: Knopf, 1962), particularly 8–12; Carl Degler, *At Odds: Women and the Family in America from the Revolution to the Present* (New York: Oxford University Press, 1980), 3–25; Joseph Hawes and Elizabeth Nybakken, eds., *Family and Society in American History* (Urbana: University of Illinois Press, 2001), particularly part III, "The Nineteenth Century"; Kirk Jeffrey, "The Family as Utopian Retreat from the City: The Nineteenth-Century Contribution," *Soundings* 55 (1972): 21–41; and Steven Mintz and Susan Kellogg, *Domestic Revolutions: A Social History of American Family Life* (New York: Free Press 1987), 43–66.

18 William G. Eliot, Jr., *Lectures to Young Women* (New York: Crosby, Nichols, and Company, C. S. Francis, 1854), 55; and Beecher and Stowe, *American Woman's Home*, 23–24.

19 Catharine Beecher, *A Treatise on Domestic Economy, for the use of Young Ladies at Home, and at School* (1841; repr., New York: Source Book Press, 1970), 251.

20 Warner, *Streetcar Suburbs*, 156.

21 Eric Avila, *Popular Culture in the Age of White Flight: Fear and Fantasy in Suburban Los Angeles* (Berkeley: University of California Press, 2006); Barraclough, *Making the San Fernando Valley*; David Freund, *Colored Property: State Policy and White Racial Politics in Suburban America* (Chicago: University of Chicago Press, 2007); Matthew Lassiter, *The Silent Majority: Suburban Politics in the Sunbelt South* (Princeton: Princeton University Press, 2006); George Lipsitz, *The Possessive Investment in Whiteness: How White People Profit from Identity Politics* (Philadelphia: Temple University Press, 1998); and Self, *American Babylon*. See also Mike Davis, *City of Quartz: Excavating the Future in Los Angeles* (London: Verso, 1990); Setha Low, *Behind the Gates: Life, Security, and the Pursuit of Happiness in Fortress America* (New York: Routledge, 2003); Evan McKenzie, *Privatopia: Homeowner Associations and the Rise of Residential Private Government* (New Haven: Yale University Press, 1994); and Sugrue, *Origins of the Urban Crisis*.

22 Henry Holly Hudson, *Modern Dwellings in Town and Country* (New York: Harper and Brothers, 1878), 22; Olmsted, Vaux and Co., *Preliminary Report*, 26; and Beecher and Stowe, *American Woman's Home*, 455.

23 For more on domesticity and women in the early nineteenth century, see Clark, *American Family Home*, particularly chapters 1–3; Nancy Cott, *The Bonds of Womanhood: "Woman's Sphere" in New England, 1780–1835* (New Haven: Yale University Press, 1977), 63–100, 200; David Handlin, *The American Home: Architecture and Society, 1815–1915* (Boston: Little, Brown, 1981), particularly chapters 2–4; Jeffrey, "The Family as Utopian Retreat," 21–41; Marsh, *Suburban Lives*, 1–22; and Wright, *Building the Dream*, particularly chapters 5–6.

24 Sarah Josepha Hale, "Domestic Economy: No. III," *Godey's Lady's Book* 20 *(April 1840):* 154.

25 For more on Beecher, see Archer, *Architecture and Suburbia*, 197–200; Hayden, *Building Suburbia*, 35–42; Dolores Hayden, *Grand Domestic Revolution: A History of Feminist Designs for American Homes, Neighborhoods, and Cities* (Cambridge: MIT Press, 1981), 53–69; Jackson, *Crabgrass Frontier*, 62–64; Marsh, *Suburban Lives*, 12–45; and Kathryn Kish Sklar, *Catharine Beecher: A Study in American Domesticity* (New Haven: Yale University Press, 1973).

26 Beecher and Stowe, *American Woman's Home*, 84.

27 Beecher and Stowe, *American Woman's Home*, 455–59; see also Catharine Beecher, "A Christian Neighborhood," *Harper's New Monthly Magazine* 34, no. 203 (April 1867): 573–84.

ENDNOTES * 235

28 Although not an exhaustive list, some of Beecher's other writings are pertinent as well, such as "American People Starved," *Harper's New Monthly Magazine* 32, no. 192 (May 1866): 762–72; *The Duty of American Women to Their Country* (New York: Harper & Brothers, 1845); "How to Redeem Woman's Profession," *Harper's New Monthly Magazine* 31, no. 186 (November 1865): 710–16; *Letters to Persons who are Engaged in Domestic Service* (New York: Leavitt & Trow, 1842); *Letters to the People on Health and Happiness* (New York: Harper & Brothers, 1855); and *Principles of Domestic Science; as Applied to the Duties and Pleasures of Home; A Text-book for the Use of Young Ladies in Schools, Seminaries, and Colleges*, with Harriet Beecher Stowe (New York: J. B. Ford, 1870).

29 Frederick Jackson Turner, "Architecture Through Oppression," *University Press* 15, June 21, 1884, in Conn and Page, *Building the Nation*, 23.

30 For more on house and home, see Archer, *Architecture and Suburbia*; Clark, *American Family Home*, particularly chapters 1–2; Handlin, *American Home*; particularly chapters 1–4; Hayden, *Grand Domestic Revolution*; Hayden, *Building Suburbia*, particularly chapters 1–4; Jackson, *Crabgrass Frontier*, particularly chapter 3; and Wright, *Building the Dream*, particularly chapters 5–6.

31 H. W. Cleveland and W. S. Backus, *Village and Farm Cottages* (New York: D. Appleton, 1856), 3.

32 "Domestic Architecture," *The New-England Magazine* 2, no. 1 (January 1832): 32–33.

33 Downing, "Our Country Villages," June 1850, in *Rural Essays*, 242, emphasis original; Downing, "Hints to Rural Improvers," July 1848, in *Rural Essays*, 111; and Downing, *A Treatise on the Theory and Practice of Landscape Gardening*, ix; Downing, *Treatise*, ix; Downing, *Treatise*, viii–ix; Andrew Jackson Downing, "The Horticultural Festival at Faneuil Hall," *Horticulturist* 3 (November 1848): 235; and Downing, *Architecture of Country Houses*, 258; Downing, *Architecture of Country Houses*, v; and Downing, *Architecture of Country Houses*, v–vi. For more on Downing, see Archer, *Architecture and Suburbia*, 177–241; George William Curtis, foreword, and George Tatum, introduction, Downing, *Rural Essays*; Arthur Channing Downs, Jr., "Downing's Newburgh Villa," *Bulletin of the Association for Preservation Technology* 4, no. 3–4 (1972): 1–113; Handlin, *The American Home*, 29–40; Hayden, *Building Suburbia*, 25–35; David Schuyler, *Apostle of Taste: Andrew Jackson Downing, 1815–1852* (Baltimore: Johns Hopkins University Press, 1996); Scully, *The Shingle Style*, 25–50; Stilgoe, *Borderland*, 86–93, 102–10, 118–22, 212–19, 314–18; Adam W. Sweeting, *Reading Houses and Building Books: Andrew Jackson Downing and the Architecture of Popular Antebellum Literature, 1835–1855* (Hanover: University Press of New England, 1996); and George B. Tatum and Elisabeth Blair MacDougall, eds., *Prophet with Honor: The Career of Andrew Jackson Downing, 1815–1852* (Washington, D.C.: Dumbarton Oaks Research Library and Collection, 1989).

BOOSTERISM

1 Lee M. A. Simpson, "Boosters and the Selling of the American West," *Journal of the West* 42, no. 4 (Fall 2003): 6. For more works on boosters and boosterism, see Carl Abbott, *Boosters and Businessmen: Popular Economic Thought and Urban Growth in the Antebellum Middle West* (Westport, CT: Greenwood Publishing Group, 1981); Cronon, *Nature's Metropolis*; Hamer, *New Towns in the New World*; Richard J. Orsi, "Selling the Golden State: A Study of Boosterism in Nineteenth-Century California," dissertation, University of Wisconsin, 1973; Special Issue, "Boosterism in the West," *Journal of the West* 42, no. 4 (Fall 2003); and Ward, *Selling Places*.

2 Lizabeth Cohen, *A Consumers' Republic: The Politics of Mass Consumption in Postwar America* (New York: Knopf, 2003).

3 Roy Bird, "What Pioneers Read," *Journal of the West* 42, no. 4 (Fall 2003): 3–5.

4 Pamela Walker Laird, *Advertising Progress: American Business and the Rise of Consumer Marketing* (Baltimore: The Johns Hopkins University Press, 1998), 1–9.

5 Jackson Lears, *Fables of Abundance: A Cultural History of Advertising in America* (New York: Basic Books, 1994), 1.

6 Lears, *Fables of Abundance*, 1–13; and Laird, *Advertising Progress*, 1–9. See also, Roland March-and's celebrated *Advertising the American Dream* (Berkeley: University of California Press, 1985).

7 Thorstein Veblen, *The Theory of the Leisure Class* (New York: Oxford University Press, 2009).

8 John Rennie Short, "Urban Imagineers: Boosterism and the Representations of Cities," in Jonas and Wilson, *The Urban Growth Machine*, 38.

9 Short, "Urban Imagineers," 40–42.

CHAPTER 2

1 "Going to California," song by Led Zeppelin from the album *Led Zeppelin IV*, released November 8, 1971, by Atlantic Records. While the song has more to do with youthful love and earthquakes, admittedly, it is a rare opportunity to quote Led Zeppelin in a scholarly work and yet still provide a quote so concisely and powerfully expressing the feelings of many who have made their way to California.

2 Shinn's body of work is large. Most of his titles can be found at the California State Library, Sacramento, California. His papers and correspondence are also housed at the Bancroft Library, Charles Howard Shinn Papers, 1890–1923, Bancroft Library, Berkeley, California.

3 Richard B. Rice, William A. Bullough, and Richard J. Orsi, eds., *The Elusive Eden: A New History of California*, third edition (Boston: McGraw Hill, 2002), 332–33; Joseph McGowan, *History of the Sacramento Valley* (New York: Lewis Historical Publishing, 1961), vol. 1: 380–83, and vol. 2: 5; and Rhode, "Learning, Capital Accumulation, and the Transformation of California Agriculture," 773–800.

4 For all data, except Sacramento's population totals, see Historical Census Browser, from the University of Virginia Geospatial and Statistical Data Center, http://fisher.lib.virginia.edu/collections/stats/histcensus. For Sacramento's population totals, see California Department of Finance, "Population Totals by Township and Place for California Counties: 1860 to 1950," compiled by Campbell Gibson, 2005, available online at the California Department of Finance webpage: www.dof.ca.gov. See also United States Census Bureau, "Population of the 100 Largest Cities and Other Urban Places in the United States: 1790–1990," complied by Campell Gibson, Population Division, U.S. Bureau of the Census, Washington, D.C., June 1998, Population Division Working Paper No. 27, available online at www.census.gov/population/www/documentation/twps0027/twps0027.html.

5 Alamillo, *Making Lemonade;* Garcia, *A World of Its Own;* Gonzalez, "A Place in the Sun"; and Gonzalez, *Labor and Community.* For more on early agricultural development in California, see Robert Cleland, *The Cattle on a Thousand Hills: Southern California, 1850–1870* (San Marino: Huntington Library, 1941); Gilbert Fite, *The Farmers' Frontier, 1865–1900* (New York: Holt, Rinehart and Winston, 1966); Paul Gates, *California Ranchos and Farms, 1846–1862* (Madison: State Historical Society of Wisconsin, 1967); Claude Hutchison, ed., *California Agriculture* (Berkeley: University of California

Press, 1946); Lawrence J. Jelinek, *Harvest Empire: A History of California Agriculture* (San Francisco: Boyd & Fraser, 1982); and Pisani, *From the Family Farm to Agribusiness.*

6 Henry George, *Our Land and Land Policy: National and State* (San Francisco: White & Bauer, 1871), 14. See also McWilliams, *Factories in the Field*, 24; Pincetl, *Transforming California*, 7; Pisani, *From the Family Farm to Agribusiness*, 7; and Starr, *Americans and the California Dream*, 133–41.

7 Paul Gates, *Land and Law in California: Essays on Land Policies* (Ames: Iowa State University Press, 1991), 267–68; McWilliams, *Factories in the Field*, 17; and Pincetl, *Transforming California*, 6–7.

8 David Phillips, *Letters from California: Its Mountains, Valleys, Plains, Lakes, Rivers, Climate and Productions* (Springfield: Illinois State Journal Co., 1877), 126–27.

9 *California, State Agricultural Society, Transactions, 1882* (Sacramento: [n.p.], [1883]), 29–30.

10 Robert W. Waterman, report to the State Board of Agriculture, February 1, 1888, in *California State Agricultural Society, Transactions, 1888* (Sacramento: [n.p.], [1889]), 12–13.

11 Starr, *Americans and the California Dream*, 21.

12 William Robert Garner, "Letters from California, 1846, to the Editors of the *North American*," *The Magazine of History* 26 (extra no. 103): 221, quoted in Starr, *Americans and the California Dream*, 14.

13 Orsi, "Selling the Golden State," 39–40.

14 Quoted in Orsi, "Selling the Golden State," 21–22.

15 Hinton Helper, *The Land of Gold: Reality Versus Fiction* (Baltimore: Hinton Helper, 1855), 21.

16 Mark Twain, *Roughing It* (Hartford: American, 1872), 409, 412.

17 Orsi, "Selling the Golden State," 25–26.

18 Quoted in Orsi, "Selling the Golden State," 28.

19 Quoted in Orsi, "Selling the Golden State," 30.

20 Orsi, "Selling the Golden State," 30–33.

21 Noah Brooks, "Personal Reminiscences of Lincoln," *Scribner's Monthly* 15, no. 5 (March 1878): 681.

22 Sackman, *Orange Empire*, 8–9, 26; and Vaught, *Cultivating California*, 45–48, 53.

23 Shinn, "Southern California," 448.

24 B. N. Rowley, in *California Fruit Grower*, August 17, 1889, quoted in Vaught, *Cultivating California*, 47.

25 J. G. Whittier, "Eldorado: Adventures in the Path of Empire," *The International Magazine of Literature, Art, and Science* 1, no. 3 (July 15, 1850): 77.

26 "Progress of Democracy, vs. Old Fogy Retrograder," *The United States Democratic Review* 30, no. 166 (April 1852): 303.

27 Jefferson, Query XIX, *Notes on the State of Virginia*, 176.

28 Garcia, *A World of Its Own*, 21. See, among many of their works, Karl Marx and Friedrich Engels, *Manifesto of the Communist Party* (1848), in Robert C. Tucker, ed., *The Marx-Engels Reader*, 2nd edition (New York: W. W. Norton, 1978), 490; George, *Our Land and Land Policy*, particularly chapter 3, "Land and Labour"; Henry George, *Progress and Poverty* (New York: J. W. Lovell, 1882), particularly book 3, chapter 1, "The Inquiry Narrowed to the Laws of Distribution"; Harvey, *Social Justice and the City*, 314; Lefebvre, *Production of Space*, 336–38; and Logan and Molotch, *Urban Fortunes*, 280–81.

29 Richard Dana, *Two Years before the Mast* (1840; repr., Boston: Houghton Mifflin, 1911), 216.

30 Edward Wickson, *California Fruits and How to Grow Them*, Seventh Edition (San Francisco: Pacific Rural Press, 1914), 355 (first edition 1889).

31 Sackman, *Orange Empire*, 61–62; Vaught, *Cultivating California*, 46–48; Starr, *Inventing the Dream*, 31–32; and Horace Bell, *Reminiscences of a Ranger; or, Early Times in Southern California* (Los Angeles: Yarnell, Caystile & Mathes, 1881), 49, 73.

32 Bernard Marks, *Fresno Daily Evening Expositor*, March 30, 1892, quoted in Vaught, *Cultivating California*, 21; Southern Pacific Company, *Catalogue of the Products of California* (New Orleans: Press of W. B. Stansbury, 1886), quoted in Sackman, *Orange Empire*, 41; and Southern Pacific Company, *California Industries: Personal Testimonies of Experienced Cultivators* (San Francisco: Southern Pacific Company, 1902), 7.

33 Charles Fletcher Lummis, quoted in McWilliams, *Southern California*, 150.

34 Starr, *Inventing the Dream*, 90; Daniel, *Bitter Harvest*, 23; Garcia, *A World of Its Own*, 5; and Pisani, *From the Family Farm to Agribusiness*, 73.

35 Avila, *Popular Culture*; Bruce Haynes, *Red Lines, Black Spaces: The Politics of Race and Space in a Black Middle-Class Suburb* (New Haven: Yale University Press, 2001); Jackson, *Crabgrass Frontier*, 190–230; Lipsitz, *Possessive Investment in Whiteness*; and Wiese, *Places of Their Own*.

36 Edward Wickson, *California Garden-Flowers, Shrubs, Trees and Vines* (San Francisco: Pacific Rural Press, 1915), 8; and William Andrew Spalding, *The Orange: Its Culture in California* (Riverside: Press and Horticulturist Steam Print, 1885), quoted in Starr, *Inventing the Dream*, 142–43.

37 Benjamin Truman, *Homes and Happiness in the Golden State of California: Being a Description of the Empire State of the Pacific Coast, Its Inducements to Native and Foreign-born Emigrants, Its Productiveness of Soil and its Productions, Its Vast Agricultural Resources, Its Healthfulness of Climate and Equability of Temperature, and Many Other Facts for the Information of the Homeseeker and Tourist* (San Francisco: Passenger Department of the Central Pacific Railroad Company, 1883), 12.

38 M. B. White, *Yearbook of the United States Department of Agriculture, 1904* (Washington, D.C.: Government Printing Office, 1905), 169–72.

39 Charles Postel, *The Populist Vision* (New York: Oxford University Press, 2007), 15, 38; Daniel, *Bitter Harvest*, 41–42; McWilliams, *Southern California*, 215; Sackman, *Orange Empire*, 33, 38–42, 47–49, 53, 60; Starr, *Americans and the California Dream*, 90, 201; Starr, *Inventing the Dream*, 142–43; and Stoll, *Fruits of Natural Advantage*, 16, 19, 42, 45–46.

40 McWilliams, *Southern California*, 207–213; and Starr, *Inventing the Dream*, 140.

41 Spalding, *The Orange*, in Starr, *Inventing the Dream*, 142; Shinn, "Southern California," 448; and Josephine Clifford, "Tropical California," *Overland Monthly* 7, no. 4 (October 1871): 11, quoted in Imre E. Qualstler, "American Images of California Agriculture," Ph.D dissertation, Department of Geography, University of Kansas, 1971, 212.

42 Quoted in Charles Nordhoff, *California for Health, Pleasure and Residence* (New York: Harper & Brothers, 1882), 130–31.

43 Alamillo, *Making Lemonade.*

44 McWilliams, *Southern California*, 216; Starr, *Inventing the Dream*, 134; and Sackman, *Orange Empire*, 35.

45 David Berry, letter to Thomas Elliott, September 18, 1873, quoted in Dumke, *Boom of the Eighties*, 14.

46 Garcia, *A World of Its Own*, 25–28; McWilliams, *California*, 83, 102; McWilliams, *Southern California*, 231; Sackman, *Orange Empire*, 52; Starr, *Inventing the Dream*, 165; Stoll, *The Fruit of Natural Advantage*, 34; and Vaught, *Cultivating California*, 20.

47 Llewellyn, "Pomona," 412; Harry Ellington Brook, *Los Angeles: The City and County*, revised edition (Los Angeles Chamber of Commerce: Home Printing, 1911), 37 (first edition 1893); and Phillips, *Letters from California*, 126–27.

48 Benjamin Truman, *Semi-Tropical California: Its Climate, Healthfulness, Productiveness, and Scenery* (San Francisco: A. L. Bancroft, 1874), 48; and Truman, *Homes and Happiness*, 12; Charles Reed, *Presidential Address, 1869*, in California State Agricultural Society, *Transactions, 1868–1869* (Sacramento: [n.p.], [1870]), 161; and California, State Agricultural Society, *Transactions, 1874*, 201.

49 Bernard Marks, *Small-Scale Farming in Central California* (San Francisco: Crocker, 1882), 2.

50 Wickson, *California Fruits*, 358; and California Immigrant Union, *Memorial and Report of the California Immigrant Union to the Legislature of the State of California* (Sacramento: T. A. Springer, 1872), 13. Family homes and home ownership were dominant themes for promoters throughout the state, as numerous local and statewide publications make clear: *Homes in Los Angeles City and County* (1873); *Plain Reasons Why Home Seekers Should Purchase Homes in the Northern Portion of San Joaquin County, California* (1887); *Butte County, California: Its Resources and Advantages for Home Seekers* (1888); *Homes* [in Madera, Fresno County] (1890); *Placer County California: Facts and Figures for Homeseekers* (1891); *The Counties of California: A Guide for Home-Seekers, Settlers and Investors; Containing an Accurate Description of Each County in the State* (1895); and *The Sacramento Valley of California: Its Resources, Industries and Advantages, Scenery, Climate and Opportunities; Facts for the Investor, Home-maker and Health-seeker* (1904). All these titles are available at the California History Room, California State Library, Sacramento, CA (hereafter referred to as California History Room). For more on Immigration associations, see Orsi, "Selling the Golden State," especially chaps. 6 and 7.

51 *The Weekly Call, California as It Is* (San Francisco: San Francisco Call, 1881), 29.

52 Oscar Winther, "The Use of Climate as a Means of Promoting Migration to Southern California," *The Mississippi Valley Historical Review* 33, no. 3 (December 1946): 411.

53 McWilliams, *Southern California*, 96.

54 Linda Nash, *Inescapable Ecologies: A History of Environment, Disease and Knowledge* (Berkeley: University of California Press, 2007), 2.

55 A. C. Fish, *The Profits of Orange Culture*, 2nd edition (Los Angeles: Semi Tropic Land and Water Company, 1890), 25; Theodore Van Dyke, *Southern California: Its Valleys, Hills and Streams; Its Animals, Birds, and Fishes; Its Gardens, Farms and Climate* (New York: Fords, Howard & Hulbert, 1886), 189; and Nordhoff, *California For Health*, 130.

56 Dumke, *Boom of the Eighties*, 29–30; McWilliams, *Southern California*, 96–97, 110; and Sackman, *Orange Empire*, 18–41.

57 Cronon, "The Trouble with Wilderness," 46–47.

58 William Bishop, *Old Mexico and Her Lost Provinces* (New York: Harper, 1883), 436; and Charles Warner, "The Golden Hesperides," *Atlantic Monthly* 61, no. 363 (January 1888): 50–51.

59 Walter Lindley and Joseph Widney, *California of the South: Its Physical Geography, Climate, Resources, Routes of Travel and Health-Resorts, Being a Complete Guide-Book to Southern California* (New York: Appleton, 1888), 22; and Charles Howard Shinn, "Our Duty and Destiny," in Oscar Shuck, ed., *California Anthology; or, Striking Thoughts on Many Themes; Carefully Selected from California Writers and Speakers* (San Francisco: Barry & Baird, 1880), 380–81. Kevin Starr's treatment of the Mediterranean metaphor in *Americans and the California Dream* is the best treatment on the subject (chapter 12, "An American Mediterranean," 365–414).

60 Charles Fletcher Lummis, quoted in Starr, *Inventing the Dream*, 83.

61 For more on California and health, see John Baur, *Health Seekers of Southern California, 1870–1900* (San Marino, CA: Huntington Library, 1959); Billy Jones, *Health-Seekers in the Southwest, 1817–1900* (Norman: University of Oklahoma Press, 1967); McWilliams, *Southern California*, 96–112; Nash, *Inescapable Ecologies*; Starr, *Americans and the California Dream*, 365–414; and Vance, "California and the Search for the Ideal," 196–98. For example, beyond mere page after page of text devoted to the subject, some boosters felt strongly enough to parade forth the healthfulness of their particular site, along with the such obviously related matters of home ownership, leisure, profit motive, and tourism, in the subtitle of their publications: George Wharton James, *B. R. Baumgardt and Co.'s Tourists' Guide Book to South California: For the Traveler, Invalid, Pleasurist and Home Seeker* (Los Angeles: B. R. Baumgard, 1895); *San Diego "Our Italy": Illustrative and Descriptive of the Natural Resources, Developments and Prospects of San Diego County; Containing Information for the Capitalist, Home Seeker, Tourist and Invalid*, compiled under direction of the San Diego Chamber of Commerce by the Literature Committee, John Young, et al. (San Diego: San Diego Chamber of Commerce], 1895); Jerome Madden, *Southern Pacific Company, California: Its Attractions for the Invalid, Tourist, Capitalist, and Homeseeker, with General Information on the Lands of the S.P.R.R. Co.* (San Francisco: Crocker, 1890); and Southern California Bureau of Information, *Southern California: An Authentic Description of Its Natural Features, Resources, and Prospects; Containing Reliable Information for the Homeseeker, Tourist, and Invalid* (Los Angeles: Bureau of Information Print, 1892).

62 Gregg Mitman, "Geographies of Hope: Mining the Frontiers of Health in Denver and Beyond, 1870–1965," *Osiris* 19 (2004): 93–111.

63 Truman, *Semi-Tropical California*, 33–34.

64 Andrew Jackson Downing, "Cultivators,—The Great Industrial Class of America," June 1848, *Rural Essays*, 386; "Introductory," July 1846, *Rural Essays*, 5; "Influence of Horticulture," July 1847, *Rural Essays*, 13; "On the Mistakes of Citizens in Country Life," January 1849, *Rural Essays*, 123–24; "How to Choose a Good Site for a Country Seat," December 1847, *Rural Essays*, 161; "Moral Influence of Good Houses," February, 1848, *Rural Essays*, 210; "Moral Influence of Good Houses," 210; "Our Country Villages," June 1850, *Rural Essays*, 238; and "How to Choose a Good Site for a Country Seat," 161.

65 *Oxford English Dictionary Online*, s.v. "Horticulture." http://www.oed.com.

66 "Annual Review, 1888–1889," *California Fruit Grower*, August 17, 1889, 5.

67 Vaught, *Cultivating California*, 31, 45. See Daniel, *Bitter Harvest*, 32; Richard Orsi, *Sunset Limited: The Southern Pacific Railroad and the Development of the American West, 1850–1930* (Berkeley: University of California Press, 2005); Sackman, *Orange Empire*, 26–27; Starr, *California*, 151; Starr, *Inventing the Dream*, 45–46; and Stoll, *Fruits of Natural Advantage*, 40–41.

68 Vaught, *Cultivating California*, 10.

69 *Yolo Weekly Mail*, January 1, 1892, quoted in Vaught, *Cultivating California*, 39.

70 Vaught, *Cultivating California*, 53. See also, Starr, *Inventing the Dream*, 45–46.

71 Sackman, *Orange Empire*, 26. See Fishman, *Bourgeois Utopias*; Hayden, *Building Suburbia*; Jackson, *Crabgrass Frontier*; and Warner, *Streetcar Suburbs*.

72 Wickson, *California Fruits*, 355.

73 Daniel, *Bitter Harvest*, 32. See also, Sackman, *Orange Empire*, 27.

74 Frederick Cox, quoted in Daniel, *Bitter Harvest*, 37.

75 See Cronon, *Nature's Metropolis*; Limerick, *Legacy of Conquest*; and Worster, *Rivers of Empire*.

76 Abbott, *How Cities Won the West*, 95–96; Sackman, *Orange Empire*, 34.

77 Alamillo, *Making Lemonade*; Albert Camarillo, *Chicanos in a Changing Society: From Mexican Pueblos to American Barrios in Santa Barbara and Southern California, 1848–1930* (Cambridge: Harvard University Press, 1996), especially 53 for *barrioization*; Garcia, *A World of Its Own*; Gonzalez, "A Place in the Sun"; Gonzalez, *Labor and Community*; Nicolaides, "Where the Working Man is Welcomed," 531; and Abbott, *How Cities Won the West*, 96. See also George Sanchez's seminal work *Becoming Mexican American: Race, Ethnicity, and Identity in Chicano Los Angeles, 1900–1945* (New York: Oxford University Press, 1993). Finally, as Jerry Gonzalez's work is a dissertation ("A Place in the Sun"), his review of this scholarship is very helpful (see his "Introduction" 1–27).

78 René Maunier, *The Sociology of Colonies: An Introduction to the Study of Race Contact*, 2 vols. (London: Routledge and Paul, 1949).

79 Glenn Dumke, "Colony Promotion during the Southern California Land Boom," *The Huntington Library Quarterly* 6, no. 2 (February 1943): 238.

80 Oscar Winther, "The Colony System of Southern California," *Agricultural History* 27, no. 3 (July 1953): 94–103.

81 William Bishop, "Southern California," *Harper's New Monthly Magazine* 65, no. 390 (November 1882): 863–82; Dumke, "Colony Promotion"; Winther, "Colony System"; McWilliams, *Southern California*, 215; Orsi, "Selling the Golden State"; Pisani, *From the Family Farm to Agribusiness*, 122; Stoll, *Fruits of Natural Advantage*, 34–35; Vaught, *Cultivating California*, 17–22; and Garcia, *A World of Its Own*, 29–32.

82 James Guinn, *A History of California and an Extended History of Los Angeles and Environs*, vol. 1 (Los Angeles: Historic Record Company, 1915), 297.

83 Zierer, "Citrus Fruit Industry," 55; Vance, "California and the Search for the Ideal," 199; and Starr, *Inventing the Dream*, 46.

84 See Garcia, *A World of Its Own*, 29–32; Pisani, *From the Family Farm to Agribusiness*, 73, 119, 120–22. See also, McWilliams, *Southern California*, 215; Starr, *Inventing the Dream*, 166–67; Starr, *Material Dreams*, 17; and Vaught, *Cultivating California*, 19–22.

85 Bodnar, *Remaking America*, 24; Appleby, *Inheriting the Revolution*; Percy Miller, *Errand Into the Wilderness* (Cambridge: Belknap Press of Harvard University Press, 1956).

Part 2

SUBURBAN DEFINITIONS, ARCHETYPES, AND LIMITATIONS

1 James Howard Kunstler, "Books by James Howard Kunstler," Kuntsler's website/blog, www. kunstler.com/books.php (accessed June 5, 2013).

2 Ranulf Higden, *Prolicionycion* (ca. 1342), translated into English as *Polychronicon Ranulphi Higden Monachi Cestrensis, Together with the English Translations of John Trevisa and of an Unknown Writer of the Fifteenth Century*, vol. 4, Joseph Rawson Lumby, ed. (London: Longman, 1872), 211; Thomas Blount, *Glossographia: or a Dictionary, Interpreting all such Hard Words* (1656 repr., Meston, England: Scolar Press, 1969), s.v. "Suburbian"; *A Facsimilation of Noah Webster's 1828 Edition of An American Dictionary of the English Language* (New York: Johnson Reprint Corporation, 1970), vol. 2, s.v. "Suburb"; *Webster's Student Dictionary* (New York: American Book Company, 1953), s.v. "Suburb"; *Webster's New World Dictionary of the American Language, College Edition* (Cleveland: World Publishing Company, 1966), s.v. "Suburb"; *Webster's New World Dictionary and Thesaurus of the American Language* (New York: World Publishing Company, 1970), s.v. "Suburb"; and *Webster's II: New Riverside University Dictionary* (Boston: Riverside Publishing, 1984), s.v. "Suburb." For more examples of suburbs being defined in juxtaposition to the city, see Geoffrey Chaucer, who mentioned "the suburbs of a town" in "The Canones Yeoman's Tale," *Canterbury Tales* (ca. 1386), chapter 48, line 104, available online through the Electronic Literature Foundation, www. thegreatbooks.org; and John Kersey's 1708 *Dictionarium* recorded for suburb, "that part of a City or Town, which lies without the Walls" (John Kersey, *Dictionarium Anglo-Britannicum* [1708 repr., Meston, England: Scolar Press, 1969]) s.v. "Suburb."

3 See Todd Gardner, "The Slow Wave: The Changing Residential Status of Cities and Suburbs in the United States, 1850–1949," *Journal of Urban History* 27, no. 3 (March 2001): 296–99; Hayden, *Building Suburbia*, 249; Nicolaides and Wiese, *Suburb Reader*, 2; Palen, *The Suburbs*, 11–12; and U.S. Bureau of Census, *Census of Population and Housing: 2000*, vol. 1, *Summary of Population and Housing Characteristics*, pt. 1 (Washington: Government Printing Office, 2002), Appendix A–16. See also, Myron Orfield, *American Metropolitics: The New Suburban Reality* (Washington, D.C.: Brookings Institution Press, 2002); Peter Dreir, John Mollenkopf, and Todd Swanstrom, *Place Matters: Metropolitics for the Twenty-first Century* (Topeka: University of Kansas Press, 2002); Bruce Katz and Robert Lang, eds., *Redefining Urban and Suburban America: Evidence from Census 2000* (Washington, D.C.: Brookings, 2003). About shopping and job location, see Palen, *The Suburbs*, 5; William Sharpe and Leonard Wallock, "Bold New City or Built-Up 'Burb? Redefining Contemporary Suburbia," *American Quarterly* 46, no. 1 (March 1994): 2; and Harris and Lewis, "Geography of North American Cities and Suburbs," 263.

4 A letter to the King of Persia in 539 BCE represented "the first extant expression of the suburban ideal," according to Kenneth Jackson. It read: "Our property seems to me the most beautiful in the world." The author continued: "It is so close to Babylon that we enjoy all the advantages of the city, and yet when we come home we are away from all the noise and dust" (quoted in Jackson, *Crabgrass Frontier*, 12). References to suburbs with a town or city—at least in some translations—even appear in the Hebrew Bible. In *I Chronicles* (450–435 BCE) the author mentioned, "The suburbs thereof round about" Judah and other places to conclude, "And the children of Israel gave to the Levites these cities with their suburbs" (*I Chronicles* 6:55–64).

5 Monkkonen, *America Becomes Urban*, 53–58. Despite citing a "New World" legacy different from Europe, Monkkonen still subscribed to the dominance of a city center, what he called the "tyranny of the center" (58). See also, Sam Bass Warner Jr., *The Private City: Philadelphia in Three Periods of its Growth* (Philadelphia: University of Pennsylvania Press, 1968), especially 3–11, 14–21.

6 Jackson, *Crabgrass Frontier*. See also Fishman, *Bourgeois Utopias*; and Archer, *Architecture and Suburbia*.

7 See Harris and Lewis, "Geography of North American Cities and Suburbs"; Richard Harris and Robert Lewis, "Constructing a Fault(y) Zone: Misrepresentations of American Cities and Suburbs, 1900–1950," *Annals of the Association of American Geographers* 88, no. 4 (1998): 622–41; and Lewis, *Manufacturing Suburbs*.

8 Crawford, *Building the Workingman's Paradise*; Fong, *First Suburban Chinatown*; Garcia, *A World of Its Own*; Harris, *Unplanned Suburbs*; Harris and Lewis, "Geography of North American Cities and Suburbs"; Hayden, *Building Suburbia*, 97–127; Hise, *Magnetic Los Angeles*; Li, "Building Ethnoburbia"; Lewis, *Manufacturing Suburbs*; Nicolaides, *My Blue Heaven*; Pattillo-McCoy, *Black Picket Fences*; Sugrue, *Origins of the Urban Crisis*; von Hoffman, *Local Attachments*; Wiese, *Places of Their Own*; and Wilson, *Hamilton Park*.

9 Peter Blake, *God's Own Junkyard: The Planned Deterioration of America's Landscape* (New York: Holt, Rinehart and Winston, 1964); and Mumford, *City in History*. See also Frederick Lewis Allen, "Suburban Nightmare," *The Independent* 114 (June 13, 1925) in *Suburb Reader*, ed. Nicolaides and Wiese, 228–30; Andres Duany, Elizabeth Plater-Zyberk, and Jeff Speck, *Suburban Nation: The Rise of Sprawl and the Decline of the American Dream* (New York: North Point Press, 2000); Robert Fogelson, *Bourgeois Nightmares: Suburbia, 1870–1930* (New Haven: Yale University Press, 2005); Betty Friedan, *The Feminine Mystique* (New York: W. W. Norton, 1963); Jane Jacobs, *Dark Age Ahead* (New York: Random House, 2004); Jane Holtz Kay, *Asphalt Nation: How the Automobile Took Over America, and How We Can Take It Back* (New York: Crown, 1997); and James Kunstler, *The Geography of Nowhere: The Rise and Decline of America's Man-Made Landscape* (New York: Simon & Schuster, 1993).

10 Robert Park, *Human Communities: The City and Human Ecology* (New York: Free Press, 1952), 170; and Bourdieu, *Distinction*, 171.

11 For suburbia as cultural practice, see Archer, "Country and City," 139–56; Fishman, *Bourgeois Utopias*, 8–9; Hayden, *Building Suburbia*, 3, 8; Mary Corbin Sies, "Moving Beyond Scholarly Orthodoxies in North American Suburban History," *Journal of Urban History* 27, no. 3 (March 2001): 355–61; and Mary Corbin Sies, "The City Transformed: Nature, Technology, and the Suburban Ideal, 1877–1917," *Journal of Urban History* 14, no. 1 (November 1987): 81–111. Also, for reviews of popular cultural representations of suburbia, see Robert Beuka, *SuburbiaNation: Reading Landscape in Twentieth-Century American Fiction and Film* (New York: Palgrave, 2004); Catherine Jurca, *White Diaspora: The Suburbs and the Twentieth-Century American Novel* (Princeton: Princeton University Press, 2001); and Lynn Spigel, *Make Room for TV: Television and the Family Ideal in Postwar America* (Chicago: University of Chicago Press, 1992).

12 Frederick Lewis Allen, "The Big Change in Suburbia, Part I," *Harper's Magazine* 208, no. 1249 (June 1954): 21–28.

13 Two recent volumes of collected works make clear the antipathy toward suburbs over history: Conn and Page, *Building the Nation*; and Nicolaides and Wiese, *Suburb Reader*.

14 Jackson, *Crabgrass Frontier*, 6.

CHAPTER THREE

1 *Ontario, Located in San Bernardino County, California on the Southern Pacific Railroad* (Riverside: Press and Horticulturist Press, 1883), 7.

2 David Allen, "With his RV, Chaffey jumped on the bandwagon," *Inland Valley Daily Bulletin*, December 17, 2005, accessed via LexisNexis, http://web.lexis-nexis.com/universe.

3 Bernice Bedford Conley, *Dreamers and Dwellers: Ontario and Neighbors; An Offering of the Years of Research into the Beginnings of the Model Colony and its Neighbors in the Boom Years of Southern California* (Privately Published: Stump Printing & Services, 1982), 102–81.

4 Alexander, *Life of George Chaffey*, 43.

5 Reyner Banham, *Los Angeles: The Architecture of Four Ecologies* (Berkeley: University of California Press, 2000), 147–50; Dumke, *Boom of the Eighties*, 106–8; Garcia, *A World of Its Own*, 28–33; McWilliams, *Southern California*, 154–56; Starr, *Material Dreams*, 14–19; and Tyrrell, *True Garden of the Gods*, 141–43. See also, Alexander, *Life of George Chaffey*, 42–69; *An Illustrated History of Southern California: Embracing the Counties of San Diego, San Bernardino, Los Angeles and Orange, and the Peninsula of Lower California, from the Earliest Period of Occupancy to the Present Time; together with Glimpses of their prospects* (Chicago: Lewis Publishing, 1890), 473–75; Ruth Austen, *Ontario: The Model Colony, An Illustrated History* (Chatsworth, CA: Windsor Publications, 1990), 28–37; Conley, *Dreamers and Dwellers*, 1–2, 22–40; John Brown and James Boyd, eds., "Ontario," in *History of San Bernardino and Riverside Counties*, vol. 1 (Chicago: Lewis Publishing, 1922), 229–37; Eleanor Freeman, "History of Ontario," in Luther Ingersoll, ed., *Ingersoll's Century Annals of San Bernardino County, 1769–1904* (Los Angeles: Ingersoll, 1904), 565–81; Jack Frankish, "Some Early History of Ontario," *Pomona Valley Historian* 4, no. 4 (October 1968): 176–80; James Guinn, "Ontario and Upland," in *A History of California and an Extended History of Its Southern Coast Counties, also Containing Biographies of Well-known Citizens of the Past and Present*, vol. 1 (Los Angeles: Historical Record Company, 1907), 451–53; "Ontario," *Land of Sunshine*, 247–50; and Rounds, *Ontario*, 45–63.

6 George Chaffey, quoted in interview with Charles Booth, Nov. 23, 1925, quoted in Conley, *Dreamers and Dwellers*, 25.

7 Dumke, *Boom of the Eighties*, 106–8; Garcia, *A World of Its Own*, 28–33; McWilliams, *Southern California*, 154–56; Starr, *Material Dreams*, 14–19; and Tyrrell, *True Garden of the Gods*, 141–43. See also, Alexander, *Life of George Chaffey*, 42–69; *An Illustrated History of Southern California*, 473–75; Austen, *Ontario*, 28–37; Conley, *Dreamers and Dwellers*, 22–40; Brown and Boyd, *History of San Bernardino and Riverside Counties*, 229–37; Freeman, "History of Ontario," 565–81; Frankish, "Some Early History of Ontario," 176–80; Guinn, *A History of California*, 451–53; "Ontario," *Land of Sunshine*, 247–50; and Rounds, *Ontario*, 45–63.

8 Alexander, *Life of George Chaffey*; Austen, *Ontario*, 27; Conley, *Dreamers and Dwellers*, 25; and Rounds, *Ontario*, 46.

9 Robert MacDougall, "The Wire Devils: Pulp Thrillers, the Telephone, and Action at a Distance in the Wiring of a Nation," *American Quarterly* 58, no. 3 (September 2006): 737–38.

10 Robert Widney, *Ontario: Its History, Description, and Resources; Valuable Information for Those Seeking Homes in Southern California* (Riverside: Press and Horticulturist Steam Printing House, 1884), 5.

11 Widney, *Ontario*, 7.

12 *Ontario, Located in San Bernardino County*, 47; and Widney, *Ontario*, 15–17. See also, Austen, *Ontario*, 34–36; Conley, *Dreamers and Dwellers*, 24; Dumke, *Boom of the Eighties*, 235–36; Garcia, *A World of Its Own*, 28; McWilliams, *Southern California*, 155; Rounds, *Ontario*, 53; and Starr, *Material Dreams*, 16.

13 *Ontario, Located in San Bernardino County*, 32; Widney, *Ontario*, 20–23.

14 *Ontario, Located in San Bernardino County*, 28. For railroad lines, see Austen, *Ontario*, 41; Conley, *Dreamers and Dwellers*, 3–5; and Rounds, *Ontario*, 62.

15 *Ontario, Located in San Bernardino County*, 7; and Widney, *Ontario*, 14.

16 Widney, *Ontario*, 20; *Ontario, Located in San Bernardino County*, 28; *Ontario, Located in San Bernardino County*, 29; see also 30–31; *Ontario, Located in San Bernardino County*, 40; and Widney, *Ontario*, 14.

17 For population numbers, see California, Department of Finance, "Population Totals by Township and Place for California Counties: 1860 to 1950." See also Conley, *Dreamers and Dwellers*, 98; Bank of America Economic Department, *Economic Growth and Development in the San Bernardino – Riverside – Ontario Area* (n.p.: [Bank of America], 1961), 5; and California Department of Finance, Budget Division, *Report to the City of Ontario on its Population Growth* (Sacramento, CA: California Department of Finance, 1959), 1. For the expanding acreage of Ontario, see Austen, *Ontario*, 30–40; Brown and Boyd, *History of San Bernardino and Riverside Counties*, 229–37.

18 Colton had an area of 4.1 square miles, or 2,624 acres, listed in 1940 and a population of 1,315 in 1890 (320.1 people per sq mi according to 1940 land size); 1,285 in 1900 (313.4 per sq mi); 3,980 in 1910 (970.1 per sq mi); 4,282 in 1920 (1044.4 per sq mi); 8,014 in 1930 (1,954.6 per sq mi); 9,686 in 1940 (2,362.4 per sq mi); and 14,465 in 1950 (3,528 per sq mi). Redlands had an area of 16.5 square miles, or 10,560 acres, listed in 1940 and a population of 1,904 in 1890 (115.4 people per sq mi according to 1940 land size); 4,797 in 1900 (290.7 per sq mi); 10,449 in 1910 (633.27 per sq mi); 9,571 in 1920 (580.1 per sq mi); 14,177 in 1930 (859.2 per sq mi); 14,324 in 1940 (868.1 per sq mi); and 18,429 in 1950 (1,116.9 per sq mi). See California Department of Finance, "Population Totals by Township and Place for California Counties: 1860 to 1950."

19 For a more detailed discussion on the literature and theories of suburbanization as a process of decanting the core, see Richard Walker and Robert Lewis, "Beyond the Crabgrass Frontier: Industry and the Spread of North American Cities, 1850–1950," *Journal of Historical Geography* 27, no. 1 (January 2001): 3–5. This article is also republished in Lewis, *Manufacturing Suburbs*.

20 Harris and Lewis, "Geography of North American Cities and Suburbs," 263. For more works that provide invalidating evidence of decentralization, see Harris and Lewis's review in "The Geography of North American Cities and Suburbs," particularly endnote 3. Mary Corbin Sies also provides a good review in "North American Urban History," 30–34. For more on railroad suburbs in the 1830s and 1840s, see Binford, *First Suburbs*, especially 18–44; and Jackson, *Crabgrass Frontier*, 101.

21 See Garcia, *A World of Its Own*, 17–46; Marx, *Machine in the Garden*; McWilliams, *Southern California*, 205–6; Starr, *Inventing the Dream*; Starr, *Material Dreams*; Vance, "California and the Search for the Ideal"; and Warner, *Streetcar Suburbs*.

22 *Ontario, Located in San Bernardino County*, 28.

23 *Ontario, Located in San Bernardino County*, 14, 47; *Ontario*, 37–38; "Ontario," *Land of Sunshine*, 248. See also, George B. Chaffey Jr., "Letter to J. W. Lee," Toronto, Canada, November 24, 1883,

Chaffey Letters, Book II, in Chaffey Letters, Binder 2, transcription complied by Ron Baker and transcribed by M. Tikfesi, Book 2: November 14, 1883 to September 4, 1885, letters 176–486, Model Colony History Room.

24 *Ontario, Located in San Bernardino County*, 14; and Widney, *Ontario*, 37–38.

25 McWilliams, *Southern California*, 207; 213; Dumke, *Boom of the Eighties*, 107; McWilliams, *Southern California*, 206–9; R. Louis Gentilcore, "Ontario, California and the Agricultural Boom of the 1880s," *Agricultural History* 34, no. 2 (April 1960): 87; F. W. Hart, *Ontario Colony* (Ontario, CA, 1885), quoted in Gentilcore, "Ontario, California," 87; Bank of America, *Economic Growth and Development*, 12 (Hotpoint was established in 1903 as the Pacific Electric Heating Company and, after becoming Hotpoint in 1908, merged into General Electric in 1918); and *The Ontario Record Twenty-Fifth Anniversary Edition*, November 1907, 3.

26 Downing, "Our Country Villages," June 1850, *Rural Essays*, 242, emphasis original; and Downing, *Treatise*, ix.

27 *Ontario, Located in San Bernardino County*, 27, 29.

28 *Ontario, Located in San Bernardino County*, 45; 38; Widney, *Ontario*, title page, 7.

29 *Ontario, Located in San Bernardino County*, 7 (investment dollar amount from Widney, *Ontario*, 14); Widney, *Ontario*, 5; and Widney, *Ontario*, 7. For just a few examples of those who quote this line without citation to Widney, see Starr, *Material Dreams*, 16; Garcia, *A World of Its Own*, 29; and Alexander, *Life of George Chaffey*, 47.

30 *Ontario, Located in San Bernardino County*, 15–17; and Widney, *Ontario*, 14, 33.

31 *Ontario, Located in San Bernardino County*, 30.

32 Austen, *Ontario*, 28–30; Garcia, *A World of Its Own*, 31; Rounds, *Ontario*, 48–50; Starr, *Material Dreams*, 15. For some early sources referring to Ontario's electricity, see *An Illustrated History of Southern California*, 472; Emma Jolliffe, "Ontario," *Rural Californian* 7 (November 1884): 247–50; Ontario Land and Improvement Company, *Ontario, California: The City that Charms* (Ontario: Ontario Publishing Company, 1908), Model Colony History Room; Ontario Land and Improvement Company, *Ontario, Gem of the Foothills of Southern California* (Ontario: Ontario Land and Improvement Company, 1897), California History Room; "Ontario," in *San Bernardino City and County Directory, 1887*, 177–90 (Los Angeles: F. L. Morrill, 1887); "Ontario," *San Bernardino City and County Directory, 1891* (Riverside: George Bagot, 1891), 256–73; *The Ontario Record Industrial Review Edition*, (1903); *The Ontario Record Industrial Souvenir Edition* (1905); Sherrill B. Osborne, *Ontario Colony, California* (Ontario: Ontario Chamber of Commerce, 190–?), Model Colony History Room; and Bertha Smith, "A City of Ten-Acre Lots: Something about the Orange Grove Prosperity of Ontario, California," *Sunset* 19, no. 1 (May 1907): 65–69.

33 Olmsted, Vaux, *Preliminary Report*, 4–5, 28.

34 Frederick Law Olmsted, quoted in Hayden, *Building Suburbia*, 64.

35 Norris Hundley, Jr., *The Great Thirst: Californians and Water, A History, Revised Edition* (Berkeley: University of California Press, 2001); Hutchison, *California Agriculture*; Jelinek, *Harvest Empire*; McWilliams, *Southern California*; Pisani, *From the Family Farm to Agribusiness*; Sackman, *Orange Empire*; and Vaught, *Cultivating California*.

36 *Ontario, Located in San Bernardino County*, 20–27; and Widney, *Ontario*, 44.

37 Lawrence Friedman, *A History of American Law*, Third Edition (New York: Simon & Schuster, 2005), 390–403; Morton Horwitz, *The Transformation of American Law, 1870–1960: The Crisis of Legal Orthodoxy* (New York: Oxford University Press, 1992), 73–74; and Martin Sklar, *The Corporate Reconstruction of American Capitalism, 1890–1916* (New York: Cambridge University Press, 1988), 1–40.

38 Horwitz, *Transformation of American Law, 1870–1960*, 73–74.

39 Widney, *Ontario*, 19–27. For more on USC, particularly the Widney years and its formation, see Guinn, *History of California*, 415; Rockwell Hunt, ed., *California and Californians*, vol. 4 (Chicago: The Lewis Publishing Company, 1932), 98; Rockwell Hunt, *California in the Making: Essays and Papers in California History* (Caldwell, ID: The Caxton Printers, 1953), 199–204; and Starr, *Inventing the Dream*, 90.

40 Horwitz, *Transformation of American Law, 1870–1960*, 80–84. Concerning Wickson's speech at the Chaffey College of Agriculture cornerstone-laying celebration, see *Ontario Fruit Grower*, March 22, 1883; and Widney, *Ontario*, 20.

41 Widney, *Ontario*, 25–27.

42 For more on climate and health in California, see Bauer, *Health Seekers of Southern California*; McWilliams, *Southern California*, 96–112; Nash, *Inescapable Ecologies*; Starr, *Americans and the California Dream*, 25, 172–209; Vance, "California and the Search for the Ideal," 196–200; and Winther, "The Use of Climate."

43 Vance, "California and the Search for the Ideal."

44 Beecher and Stowe, *American Woman's Home*, 43–44; and Olmsted, Vaux, and Co., "Riverside, Progress Prospectus," 1869, in Nicolaides and Wiese, *Suburb Reader*, 25. For more on nature and health concerning suburbia, see Archer, "Country and City," 139–56; Hayden, *Building Suburbia*, 21–44; Mumford, *City in History*, 484–87; and Warner, *Streetcar Suburbs*, 11–12, 45, 90.

45 Emerson, *Nature: Addresses and Lectures*, 16.

46 Starr, *Inventing the Dream*, 46.

47 *Ontario Record Industrial Souvenir Edition*, publisher's note page, [i].

48 Chaffey Brothers, Etiwanda, letter to O. T. Dyer, Riverside, September 10, 1882, Chaffey Letters, Book 1, in Chaffey Letters, Binder 1. See also, Chaffey Brothers, Ontario, letter to W. M. Wilkes, March 26, 1883, in Chaffey Letters, Book 1, Binder 1; George B. Chaffey Jr., letter to "Friend Burns," October 23, 1883, Chaffey Letters, Book 1, Binder 1; Chaffey Brothers, letter to T. C. Hollway, Toronto, Canada, November 22, 1883, Chaffey Letters, Book II, in Chaffey Letters, Binder 2; Chaffey Brothers, letter to Wm. L. Buxton, Powesheek Co., Iowa, December 3, 1883, Chaffey Letters, Book II, in Chaffey Letters, Binder 2; Chaffey Brothers, letter to Dr. C. R. Sykes, Chicago, December 17, 1883, Chaffey Letters, Book 2, in Chaffey Letters, Binder 2; George B. Chaffey Jr., letter to L. M. Holt, Riverside, January 29, 1884, Chaffey Letters, Book II, in Chaffey Letters, Binder 2; and Chaffey Brothers, letter to Chas. H. Howland, Lambton Mills, Ontario, Canada, February 8, 1884, Chaffey Letters, Book II, in Chaffey Letters, Binder 2.

49 Starr, *Inventing the Dream*, 90.

50 *Ontario, Located in San Bernardino County*, 17.

51 Widney, *Ontario*, 42, 45.

52 While attention to minority workers in Ontario's early years exists, little actually does so. For some discussion of where minorities, particularly Chinese and Mexican, lived, see Austen's *Ontario* and Rounds's *Ontario*, who locate minority communities in Upland (North Ontario).

53 For 1890 population numbers, see *Ontario Record*, July 9, 1890; and Conley, *Dreamers and Dwellers*, 98. For 1950s population numbers, see Bank of America Economic Department, *Economic Growth and Development in the San Bernardino*, 5. The 2010 census lists Ontario's population at 163,924, with 51 percent white, but just 18.2 percent as "white persons not Hispanic," 69 percent as "persons of Hispanic or Latin origin," 6.4 percent Black, and 5.2 percent Asian. See U.S. Census Bureau, "State and County Quick Facts," Ontario City, California, Census 2010, U.S. Census Bureau website, www.census.gov.

54 For more on class and the agricultural landscape in California, see Sackman, *Orange Empire*, 40–44, 61–62; Starr, *Inventing the Dream*, 31–32; and Vaught, *Cultivating California*, 19–22, 46–48.

55 Robert Wiebe, *The Search for Order, 1877–1920* (New York: Hill and Wang, 1967).

56 *Ontario, Located in San Bernardino County*, 35.

57 Limerick, *Legacy of Conquest*, 130–31.

58 Peter Filene, *Him/ Her/ Self: Sex Roles in Modern America*, 2nd ed. (Baltimore: Johns Hopkins University Press, 1986), 73. See also, Blumin, *Emergence of the Middle Class*, 258–97; Chauncey, *Gay New York*, 111; Jackson Lears, *No Place of Grace: Antimodernism and the Transformation of American Culture, 1880–1920* (New York: Pantheon, 1981), 60; and Rotundo, *American Manhood*, 247–51.

59 Chauncey, *Gay New York*, 111, 114; Rotundo, *American Manhood*, 249; and Lears, *No Place of Grace*, 60. "Overcivilization" and "feminization" references to the notion that men at the turn of the twentieth century faced the dangers of "overcivilization" in which American manhood, and thus American culture, actually faced the dangers of women's civilizing influence and the effeminization, i.e. feminization, of men.

60 Margaret Marsh, "Suburban Men and Masculine Domesticity," *American Quarterly* 40, no. 2 (June 1988): 165–86.

61 *Ontario, Located in San Bernardino County*, 38–41.

62 *Ontario, Located in San Bernardino County*, 28. See also George B. Chaffey Jr., letter to Charles E. Green, San Francisco, May 22, 1883, Chaffey Letters, Book I, in Chaffey Letters, Binder 1.

63 Chaffey Brothers, letter to A. H. Burney, Collins Bay, Ontario, Canada, May 25, 1883, Chaffey Letters, Book 1, in Chaffey Letters, Binder 1.

64 Chaffey Brothers, letter to Hutchins, October 22, 1883, Chaffey Letters, Book 1, in Chaffey Letters, Binder 1.

65 *Ontario, Located in San Bernardino County*, 29, emphasis added.

66 See Blumin, *Emergence of the Middle Class*; Fishman, *Bourgeois Utopias*; Hayden, *Building Suburbia*, Jackson, *Crabgrass Frontier*; Ryan, *Cradle of the Middle Class*, 230–42. See also Appleby, *Inheriting the Revolution;* and Halttunen, *Confidence Men and Painted Women*, 35–40.

67 Widney, *Ontario*, 14.

68 See Garcia, *A World of Its Own*, 29–32; Pisani, *From the Family Farm to Agribusiness*, 73, 120–22; and 119. See also, McWilliams, *Southern California*, 215; Starr, *Inventing the Dream*, 166–67; Starr, *Material Dreams*, 17; and Vaught, *Cultivating California*, 19–22.

69 Widney, *Ontario*, 20; *Ontario, Located in San Bernardino County*, 41.

CHAPTER 4

1 "Orangevale: A Sacramento Fruit Colony Enterprise," *Sacramento Union*, May 8, 1888, 3.

2 *History of Sacramento County, California with Illustrations Descriptive of Its Scenery, Residences, Public Buildings, Fine Blocks, and Manufactories* (Oakland: Thompson & West, 1880).

3 *History of Sacramento County, California; Sacramento: The Commercial Metropolis of Northern and Central California* (Sacramento: A. J. Johnston & Company, 1888); James McClatchy & Company, *Sacramento County and its Resources: A Souvenir of the Bee* (Sacramento: H. S. Crocker, 1894); William Bryan, *Souvenir of the Capital of California: Sacramento City and Country as seen through the Camera*, issued by the *Sacramento Union* (San Francisco: Stanley-Taylor, 1901); Sacramento Chamber of Commerce, *Resources of Sacramento County, California* (Sacramento: H. S. Crocker, 1903); Sacramento Chamber of Commerce, *Sacramento and its Tributary County* (Sacramento: Sacramento Chamber of Commerce, [1904?]); *Greater Sacramento: Her Achievements, Resources and Possibilities* (Sacramento: Kelman, 1912); and *Sacramento Valley and Foothill Counties of California*, compiled and edited by Emmett Phillips and John Miller, under the direction of the Sacramento Valley Exposition (Sacramento: Sacramento Valley Exposition, 1915). See also, among others, *Sacramento Union, Suburban Sketches* (Sacramento: *Sacramento Union*, 1873); Winfield Davis, *An Illustrated History of Sacramento County, California: Containing a History of Sacramento County from the Earliest Period of its Occupancy to the Present Time* (Chicago: Lewis Publishing, 1890); *Sacramento City and County Directory, 1893* (Dallas: R. L. Polk, 1893); Sacramento Board of Supervisors and Sacramento Chamber of Commerce, *Resources of Sacramento County, California* (Sacramento: Sacramento Board of Supervisors and Sacramento Chamber of Commerce, [1899]); *Sacramento City and County Directory, 1901* (Dallas: R. L. Polk, 1901); Douglas White and William Lawson, "Northern California: The Story of the Sacramento Valley," *Harper's Weekly* 47, no. 2453 (December 26, 1903): 2099–103; Sacramento Chamber of Commerce, *Fruit Growing is California's Greatest Industry: Sacramento County is the Very Heart of its Greatest Production; Possesses a Climate Unsurpassed for its Equilibrity* (Sacramento: Sacramento Chamber of Commerce, [1904]); Winfield Davis, *Sacramento County, California: Its Resources and Advantages* (Sacramento: Board of Supervisors, 1905); William Willis, *History of Sacramento County, California* (Los Angeles: Historic Record Company, 1913); and Sacramento County Board of Supervisors, *Sacramento County in Heart of California* (Sacramento: Alvord & Young, [1915]). All titles are at the California History Room or the Sacramento Room, Central Library, Sacramento (hereafter referred to as Sacramento Room).

4 Bryan, *Souvenir of the Capital*, 3.

5 McWilliams, *Southern California*; Davis, *City of Quartz*; and Hise, *Magnetic Los Angeles*.

6 *Sacramento: The Commercial Metropolis*, 35; and *Sacramento and its Tributary County*, 5.

7 *Sacramento and its Tributary County*, 5; Bryan, *Souvenir of the Capital*, 7; Bryan, *Souvenir of the Capital*, 14; and *Sacramento: The Commercial Metropolis*, 26. For more on "narratives of triumph," see William Cronon, "A Place for Stories: Nature, History, and Narrative," *Journal of American History* 78, no. 4 (March 1992): 1347–76.

8 *Sacramento: The Commercial Metropolis*, 11, 47, 11.

9 McClatchy & Company, *Sacramento County and its Resources*, 34.

10 *Greater Sacramento*, [7]; and White and Lawson, "Northern California," 2099–100; *Greater Sacramento*, [2]; *Sacramento: The Commercial Metropolis*, 48; and *Greater Sacramento*, [25].

11 White and Lawson, "Northern California," 2099; and *Souvenir of the Capital*, 14.

12 *Souvenir of the Capital*, 15; *Sacramento: The Commercial Metropolis*, 38; *Sacramento and its Tributary County*, 3; *Greater Sacramento*, [40]; and *Sacramento: The Commercial Metropolis*, 18, 38, 18. See also McWilliams, *Southern California*, 151, 194.

13 *Souvenir of the Capital*, 11–12; *Sacramento and its Tributary County*, 2; *Souvenir of the Capital*, 7, 13, 3; and *Sacramento: The Commercial Metropolis*, 47; and McClatchy & Company, *Sacramento County and its Resources*, 34.

14 *Sacramento Valley and Foothill Counties*; and McClatchy & Company, *Sacramento County and its Resources*, 60.

15 Besides general county histories and histories of the Sacramento region in whole already cited, see the following for more on the history of Orangevale: "Orangevale: A Sacramento Fruit Colony Enterprise," *Sacramento Daily Union*, May 8, 1888, 3; "Wake Up Sleepy Folsom," *Sacramento Union*, May 28, 1889, 2; "Orange Vale's Water System," *Sacramento Union*, July 27, 1889, 5; Orange Vale Colonization Company (hereafter referred to as the OVCC), *Map of Sacramento County Showing Location of Orange Vale: Property of The Orange Vale Colonization Company, Sacramento County, Cal., comprising 3,200 acres cultivated land* ([Sacramento: The Company, 1892]), California History Room; "Orange Vale: An Excursion to the Sacramento Colony Near Folsom," *Sacramento Union*, June 16, 1890, 1; "Orange Vale: Making Rapid Progress," *Folsom Telegraph*, February 18, 1893, 2; OVCC, *A Souvenir of Orange Vale* (Sacramento: Orange Vale Colonization Co., 1894); California History Room; Orange Vale Water Company Papers (Orangevale: The Company, [1896]), Sacramento Room; Orange Vale Water Company, *Information Bulletin* (Orangevale: Orange Vale Water Company, 1958); Selden Menefee, Patricia Fitzgerald, and Geraldine Fitzgerald, eds. (hereafter referred to as Menefee and Fitzgeralds), *Fair Oaks and San Juan Area Memories* (Fair Oaks: San Juan Record Press, 1960); Mary Laucher, *History of Orangevale* (n.p., 1962), California State University, Sacramento Library; Sheila LaDuke, *The History of Orangevale* ([Orangevale]: Vintage Typographics, 1980) Orangevale Public Library, Orangevale, CA; Catherine Hack, *A History of the Orangevale Community* (n.p., 1990), California History Room; Orange Vale Water Company, *One Hundred Years of Service* (Orangevale: Orange Vale Water Company, 1996); Carol Anne West, "*Northern California's First Successful Colony: The Orange Vale Legacy*" ([Orangevale, CA]: Carol Anne West, 2001), California History Room; Gary Pitzer, *150 Years of Water: The History of the San Juan Water District* (Granite Bay, CA: San Juan Water District, 2004); and Paul J. P. Sandul and Tory D. Swim, *Orangevale* (Charleston: Arcadia, 2006).

16 *Sacramento County and its Resources*, 60.

17 "Orangevale," *Sacramento Union*, May 8, 1888, 3.

18 "Orangevale," *Sacramento Union*, May 8, 1888, 3; Steven Avella, *Sacramento: Indomitable City* (Charleston: Arcadia, 2003), 75; *Sacramento County and its Resources*, 151; Sandul and Swim, *Orangevale*, 17; "Orange Vale: An Excursion to the Sacramento Colony Near Folsom," *Sacramento Union*, June 16, 1890, 1; Leigh Hadley Irvine, *A History of the New California: Its Resources and People* (New York: Lewis Publishing Co., 1905), 436–38; Orangevale Water Company, *Information Bulletin*, 2, 10; see also Buckley and Taylor (Sacramento, California), *Abstract of title to the San Juan tract, Sacramento County, California: on which is located the Farm, Field and Fireside's Sunset Colonies, Fair Oaks and Olive Park* (Sacramento: Buckley and Taylor, 1895).

19 SCRC, Articles of Incorporation of Orange Vale Colonization Company, case file no. 505, Center for Sacramento History, Sacramento (hereafter referred to as only Center for Sacramento History), 1.

20 Sadie Cable, "Orangevale Resident Tells of Early People, Events and Area Growth," in Menefee and Fitzgeralds, *Fair Oaks and San Juan Area Memories*, 28–30; Ella Landis and Anthony Landis, "Longest Resident Family in Orangevale Gives Historical Account of Area," in Menefee and Fitzger-alds, *Fair Oaks and San Juan Area Memories*, 38–39; G. Early McNeely, "Orangevale Man, Formerly Big League Ball Player, Tells of Vale Growth," in Menefee and Fitzgeralds, *Fair Oaks and San Juan Area Memories*, 58–59; L. K. Jordan, "Engineer of the North Fork Ditch Tells Lore of the Early Days," in Menefee and Fitzgeralds, *Fair Oaks and San Juan Area Memories*, 59–60; O. H. Close, "Early Area Resident Tells History of San Juan Union High School," in Menefee and Fitzgeralds, *Fair Oaks and San Juan Area Memories*, 64–65; Guy Van Maren, "Van Marens Served on Sylvan School Board for 42 Years Altogether," in Menefee and Fitzgeralds, *Fair Oaks and San Juan Area Memories*, 62–63; and Howard Greenhalgh, "Long Time Vale Resident Remains Active in Business, Public Affairs," in Menefee and Fitzgeralds, *Fair Oaks and San Juan Area Memories*, 63–64.

21 For the history of Fair Oaks, in addition to the county histories and general histories of the Sacramento region, see the following: Howard & Wilson Publishing Company, *Heart of California* (Chicago: Howard & Wilson, 1897); Howard & Wilson Publishing Company, *Sunset Colonies: Fair Oaks and Olive Park, In Heart of California/Farm, Field and Fireside and Western Rural, Colony Department* (Chicago: Farm, Field and Fireside and Western Rural, Colony Dept., 1896); Fair Oaks Development Company (hereafter referred to as FODC), *Fair Oaks, Sacramento County: In the Heart of the Fruit-growing Section of California* (Sacramento: FODC, 1900); Menefee and Fitzgeralds, *Fair Oaks and San Juan Area Memories*; Sacramento County Planning Department (SCPD), *The Fair Oaks Community Plan* (Sacramento: Sacramento County Board of Supervisors, Resolution no. 75–12, January 8, 1975); *Fair Oaks Guide*, contributing writers Judy Kemper, Hugh Gorman, Maggie Upton (Fair Oaks: P. D. Willey, 1984), California History Room; Fair Oaks Woman's Thursday Club, *Fair Oaks*; *The History of St. Mel's Catholic Church, Fair Oaks, California, 1921–1985* (Tappan: Custombook, 1985) on file at the Fair Oaks Library; Fair Oaks Historical Society, *Fair Oaks: The Early Years* (Fair Oaks: Fair Oaks Historical Society, Centennial History Book Committee, 1995); and Lee M. A. Simpson and Paul J. P. Sandul, *Fair Oaks* (Charleston: Arcadia Publishing, 2006).

22 Buckley and Taylor, *Abstract of Title to the San Juan Grant*, 44.

23 Charles Howard, "The American Farmer in Relation to Economic Conditions," 3, speech, no date, Chares Henry Howard Collection, Articles and addresses, diaries, clippings, notes, etc., 1808–1957, folder 51, George Mitchell Department of Special Collections & Archives, Bowdoin College Library, Brunswick, Maine; James W. Wilson, *Farm, Field, and Fireside's Financial Cat-echism* (Chicago: Howard & Wilson, [1896]); James Wilson, *Wilson's Financial Catechism* (Chicago: Howard & Wilson, 1898), available on microfiche at the University of Chicago Library, Chicago, Illinois; and Buckley and Taylor, *Abstract of Title to the San Juan Grant*, 44–45. See also Howard & Wilson, "A Natural Fruit Country," *Farm, Field and Fireside* (May 25, 1895): 744; Grant Vail Wallace, "Memories of Fair Oaks," in Menefee and Fitzgeralds, *Fair Oaks and San Juan Area Memories*, 85.

24 Buckley and Taylor, *Abstract of Title to the San Juan Grant*, SCPD, *Fair Oaks Community Plan*, 2; and Howard & Wilson, *Heart of California*, 37–38.

25 James Wilson, "Among the Cowboys—the Land of Blue Skies and Magnificent Sunsets," *Farm, Field and Fireside* (May 25, 1895): 756; James Wilson, "The Sunset California Excursion—What Members of the Party Think of Fair Oaks and Olive Park," *Farm, Field and Fireside* (June 8, 1895): 820–21; "The San Juan Colony," *Sacramento Union*, April 23, 1895, 5; "Sunset Colonies," *Sacramento Union*, September 10, 1895, 12; and Howard & Wilson, *Heart of California*.

26 Wilson, "Among the Cowboys," 756. See Howard & Wilson, *Heart of California,* 37–38, 45; Wilson, "Among the Cowboys," 756–57; James Wilson, "Among the Fair Oaks of Sunset Colony," *Farm, Field and Fireside* (June 1, 1895)," 788–89; Wilson, "The Sunset California Excursion," 820–21; "Sunset Colonies," *Sacramento Union,* September 10, 1895, 12; J. Murray Broadley, "Broadley Family Arrives in Fair Oaks with Father from Canada in 1897," in *Fair Oaks and San Juan Area Memories,* ed. Menefee and Fitzgeralds 12; SCPD, *Fair Oaks Community Plan,* 2.

27 Howard & Wilson, *Heart of California,* 3–10, 43–57; FODC, *Fair Oaks,* 21; John E. Holst, "Tales of the Early Days: Fair Oaks in Retrospect," in *Fair Oaks and San Juan Area Memories,* ed. Menefee and Fitzgeralds, 91–93; Stephen Kieffer, "Fair Oaks: A Factor in a New Empire," (December 1902), in *Fair Oaks and San Juan Area Memories,* ed. Menefee and Fitzgeralds, 81; Wallace, "Memories of Fair Oaks," 86; SCPD, *Fair Oaks Community Plan,* 2.

28 V. S. McClatchy, Sacramento, CA, letter to F. E. Linnell, Orangevale, CA, December 8, 1899, in V. S. McClatchy, *V. S. McClatchy Letter Books,* 389–90, Eleanor McClatchy Collection, Center for Sacramento History (hereafter referred to as the *McClatchy Letter Books*). See also V. S. McClatchy, Sacramento, letter to F. E. Linnell, Orangevale, January 9, 1900 and V. S. McClatchy, Sacramento, letter to E. Hoffner, Orangevale, January 31, 1900, *McClatchy Letter Books,* 415, 431.

29 McClatchy, Sacramento, letter to Linnell, January 9, 1900, *McClatchy Letter Books,* 415; V. S. McClatchy, Sacramento, letter to Captain Thomas Hall, Sacramento, February 9, 1900, *McClatchy Letter Books,* 438; V. S. McClatchy, Sacramento, letter to Kohler & Van Bergen, Sacramento, April 24, 1900; V. S. McClatchy, Sacramento, CA, letter to Wheeler & Rennie, Natoma, April 24, 1900; V. S. McClatchy, Sacramento, letter to Westfall Bros., Sacramento, April 24, 1900, V. S. McClatchy, Sacramento, letter to Schnabel Bros., Roseville, April 24, 1900; V. S. McClatchy, Sacramento, letter to F. A. Peltier, Sacramento, April 24, 1900; V. S. McClatchy, Sacramento, letter George Katzenstein, Sacramento, April 24, 1900, *McClatchy Letter Books,* 485–88.

30 V. S. McClatchy, Sacramento, letter to Thomas Hall, Sacramento, January 19, 1900, *McClatchy Letter Books,* 424; V. S. McClatchy, Sacramento, letter to Messengers of Wood, Curtis, & Co., Sacramento, January 19, 1900, *McClatchy Letter Books,* 424.

31 Thomas Hall, et al., Sacramento, letter to L. H. Landis, et al., November 10, 1899, *McClatchy Letter Books,* 337.

32 V. S. McClatchy, Sacramento, agreement contract for the sale of Clarke and Cox lands, April 1900, *McClatchy Letter Books,* 489–500.

33 McClatchy, agreement contract, April 1900, *McClatchy Letter Books,* 489, 495, 496.

34 SCRC, Articles of Incorporation of the FODC, case file no. 828, California State Archives, Sacramento, California; FODC, *Fair Oaks,* 40. Please note: Adam Andrew, a Sutter Club President, originally signed as a charter member for the FODC on the Articles of Incorporation. Likewise, Walter Raymond is absent from mention on the Articles of Incorporation. Nonetheless, when the promotional pamphlet for Fair Oaks came out in November 1900, only two months after the formation of the company, Andrew is absent as a member, and Raymond is present. Likewise, when McClatchy discusses the company in his letter books, he mentions Raymond, not Andrew.

35 FODC, *Fair Oaks,* 40; *Sacramento City and County Directory, 1901,* 304; and *Who's Who in the Pacific Southwest: A Compilation of Authentic Biographical Sketches of Citizens of Southern California and Arizona* (Los Angeles: Times-Mirror Print & Binding House, 1913), 309; *Sacramento City and County Directory, 1901,* 413.

36 V. S. McClatchy, Sacramento, rough draft of leaflet for the FODC, *Fair Oaks*, October 1900, *McClatchy Letter Books*, 208–26, 228–34, 240–47.

37 FODC, *Fair Oaks*, 3.

38 FODC, *Fair Oaks*, 8, 8–9, 4, 9. For more on department stores and their appeal to women, see Elaine Abelson, *When Ladies Go A-Thieving: Middle-Class Shoplifters in the Victorian Department Store* (New York: Oxford University Press, 1989).

39 FODC, *Fair Oaks*, 26, 27.

40 V. S. McClatchy, Sacramento, letter to Charles Dickinson, Brookline, MA, October 7, 1901, *McClatchy Letter Books*, 444; and V. S. McClatchy, Sacramento, agreement contract between the North Fork Ditch Company and Charles Dickinson, April 1900, *McClatchy Letter Books*, 500.

41 SCPD, *Fair Oaks Community Plan*, 23; 11; FODC, *Fair Oaks*, 16; and California, Department of Finance, "Population Totals by Township and Place for California Counties: 1860 to 1950."

42 For other examples, see Harris and Lewis, "Geography of North American Cities and Suburbs," 263; Harris and Lewis, "Constructing a Fault(y) Zone," 622–39; Lewis, *Manufacturing Suburbs*; and Walker and Lewis, "Beyond the Crabgrass Frontier," 3–5. Earlier suburban historians Binford and Jackson also acknowledged the existence of noncontiguous suburbs (Binford, *First Suburbs*, 18–44; and Jackson, *Crabgrass Frontier*, 101).

43 See Vance, "California and the Search for the Ideal." See also, Allmendinger, *Ruffin*; Archer, "Country and City"; Boorstin, *Lost World of Thomas Jefferson*; Cronon, "The Trouble with Wilderness," 46–47; Danbom, *Born in the Country*, 65–69; Danhof, *Change in Agriculture*; Garcia, *A World of Its Own*, 17–22; Hurt, *American Agriculture*, 72–77; Marsh, *Suburban Lives*, xiii, 5; Marx, *Machine in the Garden*; McClelland, *Sowing Modernity*; Palen, *The Suburbs*, 70, 93–94; Peterson, *Jefferson Image*; and Williams, *Country and the City*.

44 Wilson, "Among the Fair Oaks of Sunset Colony," 788; Howard & Wilson, *Heart of California*, 18–43.

45 "A New Deal at Fair Oaks," *Sacramento Union*, May 31, 1900, 4.

46 FODC, *Fair Oaks*, 9, 24; and "Orangevale: A Sacramento Fruit Colony Enterprise," *Sacramento Union*, May 8, 1888, 3.

47 FODC, *Fair Oaks*, 9–10.

48 FODC, *Fair Oaks*, 24.

49 McClatchy & Company, *Sacramento County and its Resources*, 59, 62; and *Sacramento Valley Sunbeam*.

50 FODC, *Fair Oaks*, 3–4.

51 "Orange Vale," *Sacramento Union*, July 16, 1890, 1; and FODC, *Fair Oaks*, 12–15.

52 FODC, *Fair Oaks*, 3; "Orange Vale," *Sacramento Union*, July 16, 1890, 1; McClatchy & Company, *Sacramento County and its Resources*, 62; "Orangevale," *Sacramento Union*, May 8, 1888, 3; "Orangevale," *Sacramento Union*, May 8, 1888, 3; "A New Deal at Fair Oaks," *Sacramento Union*, May 31, 1900, 4; Broadley, "Broadley Family Arrives in Fair Oaks With Father From Canada in 1897," 13; and Howard & Wilson, *Heart of California*, 7.

53 FODC, *Fair Oaks*, 10; "Orange Vale," *Sacramento Union*, July 16, 1890, 1; McClatchy & Company, *Sacramento County and its Resources*, 59–62; "Orangevale," *Sacramento Union*, May 8, 1888, 3; Orange

Vale," *Sacramento Union*, July 16, 1890 1; "Orange Vale's Water System," *Sacramento Union*, July 27, 1889, 5; "Waking Up Sleepy Folsom," *Sacramento Union*, May 28, 1889, 3; "Orange Vale: Making Rapid Progress," *Folsom Telegraph*, February 18, 1893, 2; "A New Deal at Fair Oaks," *Sacramento Union*, May 31, 1900, 4; Howard & Wilson, *Heart of California*; FODC, *Fair Oaks*, 16; McClatchy & Company, *Sacramento County and its Resources*, 60, 63 (see also 62); and "Orangevale," *Sacramento Union*, May 8, 1888, 3. For "luxuries" and "conveniences" extolled by Olmsted and other suburban image-makers, see Olmsted, Vaux, *Preliminary Report*, 7; and Downing, *Architecture of Country Houses*, 269.

54 Emma Bramhall, "Young Chicago Man Was First Doctor To Practice Here, 1902," in *Fair Oaks and San Juan Area Memories*, ed. Menefee and Fitzgeralds, 6; and Kieffer, "Fair Oaks," 82.

55 FODC, *Fair Oaks*, 24

56 FODC, *Fair Oaks*, 24, 4, 18; and McClatchy & and Company, *Sacramento County and its Resources*, 62.

57 McClatchy & and Company, *Sacramento County and its Resources*, 60.

58 FODC, *Fair Oaks*, 6, 17.

59 "Orangevale," *Sacramento Union*, May 8, 1888, 3.

WELCOME TO THE GROWTH MACHINE

1 Elvin Hatch, *Biography of a Small Town* (New York: Columbia University Press, 1979), 259–60.

2 Molotch, "The City as a Growth Machine," 309–22.

3 Logan and Molotch, *Urban Fortunes*, 30.

4 See Avila, *Popular Culture*; Davis, *City of Quartz*; Low, *Behind the Gates*; Nancy MacLean, *Freedom Is Not Enough: The Opening of the American Workplace* (New York: Russell Sage Foundation, 2006); McKenzie, *Privatopia*; Self, *American Babylon*; and Sugrue, *Origins of the Urban Crisis*.

5 See Carl Abbott, *Metropolitan Frontier: Cities in the Modern American West* (University of Arizona Press, 1993); Cronon, *Nature's Metropolis*; William Leach, *Country of Exiles: The Destruction of Place in American Life* (New York: Pantheon Books, 1999); Adam Ward Rome, *Bulldozer in the Countryside: Suburban Sprawl and the Rise of American Environmentalism* (Cambridge: Cambridge University Press, 2001); and Worster, *Rivers of Empire*.

6 See Avila, *Popular Culture*; Howard Gillette, *Camden After the Fall: Decline and Renewal in a Post-Industrial City* (Philadelphia: University of Pennsylvania Press, 2005); Self, *American Babylon*; and Stanton, *Lowell Experiment*.

7 Sam Bass Warner Jr. made this argument in several works, including *Private City*; *Streetcar Suburbs*; and *Urban Wilderness: A History of the American City* (New York: Harper & Row, 1972).

8 Lewis, *Manufacturing Suburbs*; Monkkonen, *America Becomes Urban*; and Arthur Meier Schlesinger, *Rise of the City, 1878–1898* (New York: Macmillan, 1933).

9 Lee M. A. Simpson, *Selling the City: Gender, Class, and the California Growth Machine, 1880–1940* (Palo Alto: Stanford University Press, 2004).

10 Orsi, "Selling the Golden State"; and Orsi, *Sunset Limited*.

11 See Schlesinger, *Rise of the City*; and Robert Wiebe, *Self-Rule: A Cultural History of American Democracy* (Chicago: University of Chicago Press, 1995). For more works that focus on the role of ideas, particularly concerning moral uplift and social control, see, among others, Peter Baldwin, *Domesticating the Street: The Reform of Public Space in Hartford, 1850–1930* (Ohio State University Press, 1999); Paul Boyer, *Urban Masses and Moral Order in America, 1820–1920* (Cambridge: Harvard University Press, 1978); Amy Bridges, *Morning Glories: Municipal Reform in the Southwest* (Princeton University Press, 1997); and Rosenzweig and Blackmar, *Park and the People.*

12 This characterization of the growth machine borrows from historian Paul Sonnino's characterization of Michel Foucault's work in *Discipline and Punish* (1975) in "A Young Person's Guide to Postmodernism," *Praesidium: A Journal of Literate and Literary Analysis* 4, no. 2 (Spring 2004): 22–32.

13 Simpson, "Boosters and the Selling of the American West," 6.

14 Warner, *Streetcar Suburbs*, 156–57.

15 Hatch, *Biography of a Small Town*, 259–60; and Warner, *Streetcar Suburbs*, 156–57.

16 While many critics have surfaced, the list drawn here comes primarily from Jonas and Wilson's *Urban Growth Machine.*

CHAPTER 5

1 Pink Floyd, "Welcome to the Machine," *Wish You Were Here*, 1975, Pink Floyd Music Publishers Ltd.

2 Harris Weinstock, "Observation as a Commercial Asset," a lecture to the students of the College of Commerce, February 20, 1905, reprint from the *University Chronicle* 8, no. 3: 210–14, California History Room.

3 David Harvey, *Limits to Capital* (Chicago: University of Chicago Press, 1982), 346, see also 12. For more on the commodification of space/place, see Jean Baudrillard, *The Mirror of Production* (St. Louis: Telos Press, 1975); Glassberg, *Sense of History*; Hayden, *Power of Place*; Lefebvre, *Production of Space*; Logan and Molotch, *Urban Fortunes*; and John Urry, *Consuming Places* (New York: Routledge, 1995).

4 For more on the importance of placing events within the experience of an individual's lifetime and issues concerning "life history," see James Clifford, *The Predicament of Culture: Twentieth-century Ethnography, Literature, and Art* (Cambridge: Harvard University Press, 1988), 21–54; John Dollard, *Criteria for the Life History* (New Haven: Yale University Press, 1935), 1–36; and M. McCall and J. Wittner, "The Good News about Life History," 46–89, in *Symbolic Interaction and Cultural Studies*, ed. H. Becker and M. McCall, (Chicago: University of Chicago Press, 1990).

5 Dollard, *Criteria for the Life History*, 27–28.

6 Pierre Bourdieu, *The Logic of Practice* (Palo Alto: Stanford University Press, 1990), 41.

7 For biographical information on Isaias W. Hellman, see Robert Glass Cleland and Frank B. Putnam, *Isaias W. Hellman and the Farmers and Merchants Bank* (Berkeley: University of California Press, 1980); and Frances Dinkelspiel, *Towers of Gold: How One Jewish Immigrant Named Isaias Hellman Created California* (New York: St. Martin's Press, 2008).

8 There is a vast amount of literature on George Chaffey, particularly as it relates to irrigation, specifically in Etiwanda, Ontario, the Imperial Valley in California, and Australia. All research should begin with the amazing collection at the Robert E. Ellingwood Model Colony History Room

in the Ontario City Library, Ontario, California. For just a few sources, see Alexander, *Life of George Chaffey;* "The Greater Chaffey," *FASTI,* Ontario High School Yearbook, 1912, on file at the Chaffey High School, Ontario, CA; Guinn, *History of California,* vol. 1, 415–16; Dumke, *Boom of the Eighties,* 106, 205–6, 235–36; Hunt, *California and Californians,* 98; Hunt, *California in the Making,* 199–204; Garcia, *A World of Its Own,* 28–32; W. H. Hutchinson, *California: Two Centuries of Man, Land, and Growth In the Golden State* (Palo Alto: American West Publishing Company, 1969), 219; "Irrigation of the Delta of the Colorado," *Scientific American* 85, no. 23 (December 7, 1901): 358; Frederick Kershner Jr., "George Chaffey and the Irrigation Frontier," *Agricultural History* 27 (October 1953): 115–22; Bede Nairn and Geoffrey Serle, eds., *Australian Dictionary of Biography, Volume 7: 1891–1939, A–Ch* (Carlton, Victoria, Australia: Melbourne University Press, 1979), 599–601; Andrew F. Rolle, *California: A History* (New York: Thomas Y. Crowell Company, 1969), 362–63; Tyrrell, *True Garden of the Gods;* Starr, *Material Dreams,* 14–29; and Edward White, "The Drift Wealth to Los Angeles," *Banke* 72, no. 6 (June 1906): 872. For William Chaffey, see Nairn and Serle, *Australian Dictionary of Biography, Volume 7,* 599–601.

9 For more on the evolutionary debates and various reactions to them, especially modernists and fundamentalists, see Edward Larson, *Evolution: The Remarkable History of a Scientific Theory* (New York: Modern Library, 2004).

10 Robert M. Widney, *The Plan of Creation* (Los Angeles: Robert M. Widney, 1881).

11 For more on the Chinese Massacre of 1871, and even Widney's drawing of a gun in the courtroom, see Scott Zesch, *The Chinatown War: Chinese Los Angeles and the Massacre of 1871* (New York: Oxford, 2012), 27, 139–44.

12 Robert M. Widney, *Los Angeles County Subsidy: Which Shall I Vote For, or Shall I Vote Against Both?; Discussed From a Business Standpoint* (Los Angeles, 1872), reprinted in *The Historical Society of Southern California Quarterly* 38, no. 4 (December 1956): 347–62.

13 Widney, *Plan of Creation,* 50.

14 Widney, *Plan of Creation,* 141.

15 For information on Charles Maclay, see the Robert M. Widney biographical works listed below, as well as Marc Wanamaker, *San Fernando Valley* (Charleston: Arcadia, 2011), 13–16.

16 Robert M. Widney, "A National Currency," p. 6 in "A National Money System Addresses," Los Angeles, collection of speeches given in the early 1890s, donated to the University of California, also available online through the Hathi Trust Digital Library at http://catalog.hathitrust.org/api/volumes/oclc/28733959.html.

17 Widney, "A National Currency," 6.

18 For biographical information concerning Widney, see Hubert Bancroft, *History of California, Volume 7: 1860–1890,* vol. 24 of *The Works of Hubert Howe Bancroft* (San Francisco: The History Company, 1890), 250; Dumke, *Boom of the Eighties,* 7, 71–72, 246–47; Robert Fogelson, *The Fragmented Metropolis: Los Angeles, 1850–1930* (Cambridge: Harvard University Press, 1967), 55, 113; Guinn, *History of California,* vol. 1, 415–16; Hunt, *California and Californians,* 96–99; Hunt, *California in the Making,* 199–204; "Long Beach," *Los Angeles Times,* July 10, 1893, 3; Los Angeles Public Library Bio File for Robert M. Widney, Los Angeles Public Library, Los Angeles, CA; Remi Nadeu, *City-Makers: The Men Who Transformed Los Angeles from Village to Metropolis During the First Great Boom, 1868–76* (Garden City: Doubleday, 1948); and "Robert M. Widney," *Los Angeles Times,* November 16, 1929, A4.

19 Elmer Holmes, *History of Riverside County, California: With Biographical Sketches of the Leading Men and Women of the County Who Have Been Identified with its Growth and Development from the Early Days to the Present* (Los Angeles: Historic Record Company, 1912), 58.

20 "To Honor Memory of Town Builder," *Los Angeles Times*, August 16, 1920, II3.

21 Brown and Boyd, *History of San Bernardino and Riverside Counties*, 436.

22 For Carter, see Orsi, "Selling the Golden State," 473–74.

23 "Proud—Holt," wedding announcement, *Imperial Valley Press*, February 21, 1903, 9.

24 Luther M. Holt, quoted in McWilliams, *Southern California*, 122.

25 McWilliams, *Southern California*, 122.

26 Holmes, *History of Riverside County*, 57.

27 Luther M. Holt, quoted in Mark Howland Rawitsch, *The House on Lemon Street: Japanese Pioneers and the American Dream* (Boulder: University Press of Colorado, 2012), 43.

28 Quoted in Rawitsch, *House on Lemon Street*, 44.

29 Quoted in Rawitsch, *House on Lemon Street*, 44. For biographical information on Holt, see "To Honor Memory of Town Builder II3; Alexander, *Life of George Chaffey*, in *passim*; Brown and Boyd, *History of San Bernardino and Riverside Counties*, 436–37; Dumke, *Boom of the Eighties*, 104–06, 120, 235–36, 241, 264; Holmes, *History of Riverside County*, 58–60, 74; Kershner, "George Chaffey and the Irrigation Frontier," 116; "Proud—Holt," 9; Rawitsch, *House on Lemon Street*, 43–44; and Starr, *Material Dreams*, 14–25.

30 Dumke, *Boom of the Eighties*, 247–48; and "Marion M. Bovard," About USC, University of Southern California Los Angeles, online at http://about.usc.edu/presidents/marion–m–bovard/ (accessed May 19, 2013).

31 Dumke, *Boom of the Eighties*, 79, 249; and Los Angeles Public Library Bio File for Edward Spence, Los Angeles Public Library, Los Angeles, CA.

32 For Walter Lindley, see James Guinn, *History of California and an Extended History of Los Angeles and Environs*, vol. 2 (Los Angeles: Historic Record Company, 1915), 384–87.

33 For Stephen Mott, see Lewis Publishing, *An Illustrated History of Los Angeles County, California; Containing a History of Los Angeles County from the Earliest Period of Its Occupancy to the Present Time, Together with Glimpses of Its Prospective Future* (Chicago: Lewis Publishing, 1889), 771.

34 For Joseph Widney, see Dumke, *Boom of the Eighties*, 33, 72, 248; Glenn Dumke, "Joseph Pomeroy Widney," in *Dictionary of American Biography* 12 (New York: Charles Scribner's Sons), 715–16; McWilliams, *Southern California*, 65–69; and Starr, *Americans and the California Dream*, 443.

35 Daniel Rodgers, *Atlantic Crossings: Social Politics in a Progressive Age* (Cambridge: Harvard University Press, 1998). Rodgers argues that reform efforts in the United States, in fact, originated out of a much broader and connected attempt in Britain, Denmark, France, and Germany. The impetus for this era of reform intertwined with these nations' population explosion, urban growth, rising poverty, and mass migrations. Consequently, reformers in the United States looked across the Atlantic for inspiration and guidance.

36 For more on Harris Weinstock, as well as David Lubin, see, first, biographical information from scrapbooks in the Harris Weinstock Papers, 1878–1922, Judah L. Magnes Museum, Western

Jewish History Center, Berkeley, CA (WJHC 1969.035); and Harris Weinstock, *Scrapbooks: A Collection of Newspaper Clippings* ([s.n.]1893–1922), available at the Bancroft Library, Berkeley. See also Edward Adams and C. E. Grunsky, *Memorial to Harris Weinstock: First President of the Commonwealth Club of California, 1903–1907, Born, September 18, 1854, Died, August 22, 1922*, issued by the Commonwealth Club of California, ([San Francisco]: The Club, 1922); Avella, *Sacramento*, 72–75; Grace Larsen, "A Progressive in Agriculture: Harris Weinstock," *Agricultural History* 32, no. 3 (July 1958): 187–93; Sandul and Swim, *Orangevale*, 8, 11, 16; Stoll, *Fruits of Natural Advantage*, 64–80; "Weinstock Succumbs After Fall, Former State Market Commissioner Dies of Fractured Skull," *Los Angeles Times*, August 23, 1922, I11. For Weinstock's writings, see Harris Weinstock, *Jesus the Jew: And Other Addresses* (New York: Funk & Wagnalls, 1902); Weinstock, "Observation as a Commercial Asset"; Harris Weinstock, *The Nation's Chief Need of the Hour* ([San Francisco: Harris Weinstock], 1907); Harris Weinstock, California, Special Labor Commissioner, *Report on the Labor Laws and Labor Conditions of Foreign Countries in Relation to Strikes and Lockouts* (Sacramento: Superintendent State Printing, 1910); Harris Weinstock, *Report of Harris Weinstock, Commissioner to Investigate the Recent Disturbances in the City of San Diego and the County of San Diego, California* (Sacramento: Superintendent of State Printing, 1912); Harris Weinstock, *Statement of Harris Weinstock, State Market Director, in answer to the criticisms of Senator Wm. E. Brown of Los Angeles relative to the administration of the California state market law* (San Francisco: [Harris Weinstock], 1917); Harris Weinstock, California, State Market Commission, *The Burden for Better Marketing Rests with the Farmer and Not with the State* ([Sacramento: State Market Commission, 1918]); and sixteen of Weinstock lectures are available in the University of California Office of the President Records, 1914–1958, CU–5, Series 2, Bancroft Library, Berkeley.

37 Weinstock, quoted in Stoll, *Fruits of Natural Advantage*, 65.

38 McClatchy & Company, *Sacramento County and its Resources*, 127; and "Brilliant Ball at the State Capitol," 8.

39 Stoll, *Fruits of Natural Advantage*, 78.

40 Some scholars have contended that Jewish Americans have been racialized as something other than white, particularly because they argue the United States defined itself as essentially a Christian nation (see, Matthew Frye Jacobson, *Whiteness of a Different Color: European Immigrants and the Alchemy of Race* [Cambridge: Harvard University Press, 1998]; and Karen Brodkin, *How Jews Became White Folks and What That Says About Race in America* [New Brunswick, NJ: Rutgers University Press, 1998]). Be that as it may, other historians, such as Paul Spickard, argue that Jews, while undeniably facing malicious anti–Semitism, were still perceived as white, though at the "nether edges of whiteness," particularly regarding the purposes of naturalization law and the prominence of Jews in the inner circles of American politics and business (see, Paul Spickard, *Almost All Aliens: Immigration, Race, and Colonialism in American History and Identity* [New York: Routledge, 2007], 247). In fact, the "difference" in Jewish whiteness rests on another issue: The racialization of religion. In this context, Weinstock embraced and articulated a vision of Progressive Judaism and of "Jesus the Jew" that sought to marginalize his Jewishness, as a religion, in favor of his whiteness through a perceived heritage of Anglo–Saxonism. Regardless whether Jews were (or are), in fact, white is irrelevant (especially as biologists and geneticists tell us race is extremely complicated). The important point is that Weinstock believed that Jews were white and Anglo–Saxon regardless of their religion.

41 Wiebe, *Search for Order*, 12.

42 Richard McCormick, "Public Life in Industrial America, 1877–1917," in *The New American History, Revised and Expanded Edition*, ed. Eric Foner, (Philadelphia: Temple University Press,

1997), 107–32; and "The Progressive Movement: Elitist or Democratic?," 176–78, in *Interpretations of American History; Patterns and Perspectives, Vol. 2: From Reconstruction*, Seventh Edition, edited by Francis Couvares, Martha Saxton, and George Billias (New York: Free Press, 2000).

43 William Deverell, *Railroad Crossing: Californians and the Railroad, 1850–1910* (Berkeley: University of California Press, 1994); William Deverell and Tom Sitton, *California Progressivism Revisited* (Berkeley: University of California Press, 1994); George Mowry, *California Progressives* (Berkeley: University of California Press, 1951); Gerald D. Nash, *State Government and Economic Development: A History of Administrative Policies in California, 1849–1933* (Berkeley: Institute of Governmental Studies, University of California, 1964); Spencer Olin, *California Politics, 1846–1920* (San Francisco: Boyd & Fraser, 1981); Spencer Olin, *California's Prodigal Sons: Hiram Johnson and the Progressives, 1911–1917* (Berkeley: University of California Press, 1968); Orsi, *Sunset Limited*; and R. Hal Williams, *The Democratic Party and California Politics, 1880–1896* (Palo Alto: Stanford University Press, 1973).

44 Avella, *Sacramento*, 68.

45 For Progressive attitudes like this, see Boyer, *Urban Masses and Moral Order*, vii.

46 Thomas Hines, "The Imperial Mall: The City Beautiful Movement and the Washington Plan of 1901–02," in *The Mall in Washington, 1791–1991* (Washington: National Gallery of Art, 1991), 95.

47 Charles K. McClatchy, *Private Thinks by C. K.* (New York: Scribner, 1936), quoted in E. Gregory McPherson and Nina Luttinger, "From Nature to Nurture: The History of Sacramento's Urban Forest," *Journal of Arboriculture* 24, no. 2 (March 1998): 77.

48 *Sacramento City and County Directory*, 1893, 340; "Northern–Belters," *Los Angeles Times*, Feb 26, 1892, 4; "Western Advisory Board," *Los Angeles Times*, May 22, 1896, 1; *San Francisco Call*, May 17, 1908, 27 (for more on the California Promotion Committee, see Irvine, *A History of the New California*, 221–28); V. S. McClatchy, Sacramento, letter to George E. Mitchell, Assessor, Placer County, May 17, 1900, *McClatchy Letter Books*, 16; V. S. McClatchy, Sacramento, letter to McAfee Bros., Sacramento, September 23, 1898, *McClatchy Letter Books*, 20; and Myrtle Shaw Lord, *A Sacramento Saga: Fifty Years of Achievement—Chamber of Commerce Leadership* (Sacramento: Sacramento Chamber of Commerce, News Publishing Company, 1946), 10.

49 V. S. McClatchy, "Overruled by Editors," *Los Angeles Times*, Apr 24, 1913, I1; and V. S. McClatchy, *The Germany of Asia: Japan's Policy in the Far East; Her "Peaceful Penetration" of the United States; How American Commercial and National Interests are Affected* (Sacramento: [V. S. McClatchy], 1919), 21. For more on McClatchy's efforts against Japanese and Japanese Americans, see Roger Daniels, *Asian America: Chinese and Japanese in the United States since 1850* (Seattle: University of Washington Press, 1988), 119, 146–49; 194–95; Gordon Chang, ed., *Asian Americans and Politics: Perspectives, Experiences, Prospects* (Palo Alto: Stanford University Press, 2001), 19–33; Eithne Luibhéid, *Entry Denied: Controlling Sexuality at the Border* (Minneapolis: University of Minnesota Press, 2002), 62–73; and Mae M. Ngai, *Impossible Subjects: Illegal Aliens and the Making of Modern America* (Princeton: Princeton University Press, 2004), 47–49, 109, 116–17.

50 *Sacramento Valley Sunbeam: Devoted to the Interests of Ideal Country Homes* (Sacramento: B. F. Hullings, 1909).

51 What some have called a "spatiality of racism" or a "spatiality of whiteness," suburban communities, while not always white in fact, reflect and reflected a construction of identity based on place and imagination whereby suburbia became a generic, but still key defining characteristic, of what it has meant and still means to be white in America. See, Avila, *Popular Culture*; Lipsitz, *Possessive Investment in Whiteness*; Self, *American Babylon*.

52 An expert on law, Hall had just published a work on patent law in 1888, followed by another in 1893. For more on Hall, see *Sacramento Bee*, January 10, 1899, 8; *Sacramento City and County Directory, 1893*, 409; McClatchy & Company, *Sacramento County and its Resources*, 151–52; Thomas Hall, *Treatise Patent Estate, Comprehending Nature, Conditions and Limitations of Interest in Letters Patent* (Cleveland: Ingham, Clarke, 1888); Thomas Hall, *The Infringement of Patents: For Inventions, Not Designs: With Sole Reference to the Opinions of the Supreme Court of the United States* (Cincinnati: Robert Clarke, 1893); Irvine, *A History of the New California*, 364–66; "Shasta Retreat & Shasta Mineral Springs, Siskiyou, California," in "Summer Holidays Among The Hills," *Sunset Magazine* 1, no. 2 (June 1898): 21–24.

53 McClatchy & Company, *Sacramento County and its Resources*, 152.

54 Lord, *Sacramento Saga*, 10–18. For biographical information on Hall, see Unidentified newspaper article, February 16, 1920, in "Hall, Thomas" Bio Info File at California History Room. See also, Sacramento County Recorder Collection (hereafter referred to as SCRC), Articles of Incorporation of the Orange Vale Colonization Company, case file no. 505, Center for Sacramento History; "Brilliant Ball at the State Capitol in Honor of Governor Henry T. Cage," *Sacramento Bee*, January 16, 1899, 8; McClatchy & Company, *Sacramento County and its Resources*, 127, 150–60; Frank Millard, *History of the San Francisco Bay Region*, vol. 2 (Chicago: American Historical Society, 1924), 124; *Sacramento Bee*, January 10, 1899, 8; *Sacramento City and County Directory, 1893*, 409; "Shasta Retreat & Shasta Mineral Springs, Siskiyou, California," in "Summer Holidays Among The Hills," *Sunset Magazine* 1, no. 2 (June 1898): 21–24; Lord, *Sacramento Saga*, 10–18; *A Volume Of Memoirs And Genealogy of Representative Citizens Of Northern California, Including Biographies of Many of Those who have Passed Away* (Chicago: Standard Genealogical Publishing Co., 1901), 204–06; Orange Vale Water Company, *Information Bulletin*, 2–3; California State Library, "Clarke, Crawford W.," Bio Info File, 1–2, California History Room; Pitzer, *150 Years of Water*, 21–29.

55 *A Volume Of Memoirs And Genealogy of Representative Citizens Of Northern California*, 204–6; McClatchy & Company, *Sacramento County and its Resources*, 150, 160–161; Orange Vale Water Company, *Information Bulletin*, 2–3.

56 SCRC, Articles of Incorporation of the Sacramento, Fair Oaks and Orange Vale Railway Company, case file no. 690, Center for Sacramento History, 1, 4; Lord, *Sacramento Saga*, 10, 18, 20; "Chamber of Commerce Elects Officers," *Sacramento Bee*, January 10, 1899, 8; and McClatchy & Company, *Sacramento County and its Resources*, 149–50.

57 Timothy Comstock, *The Sutter Club: One Hundred Years* (Sacramento: The Sutter Club, 1989), 1, 10–26; Lord, *Sacramento Saga*, 250–51; and "A Suburban Railroad to Fair Oaks," *Sacramento Bee*, March 1, 1901, 4.

58 Avella, *Sacramento*, 75–76.

59 "History of Fair Oaks," www.fairoakshistory.org.

60 Bernard DeVoto, *The Course of Empire* (Boston: Houghton, Mifflin, 1952); and Norman Graebner, *Empire on the Pacific* (New York: Ronald Press, 1955).

61 Limerick, *Legacy of Conquest*, 78–83. See also Worster, *Rivers of Empire*, 262–64; and Chris Friday, "Where to Draw the Line? The Pacific, Place, and the US West," in *A Companion to the American West*, ed. William Deverell (Malden, MA: Blackwell, 2004), 276–77.

62 "A Suburban Railroad to Fair Oaks," *Sacramento Bee*, March 1, 1901, 4.

63 Orsi, "Selling the Golden State," 39.

Part 3

COMING TO TERMS WITH MEMORY

1 Karl Marx, "The Eighteenth Brumaire of Louis Bonaparte," 1852, in *The Collective Memory Reader*, ed. Jeffrey Olick, Vered Vinitzky-Seroussi, and Daniel Levy (New York: Oxford University Press, 2011), 89.

2 David Harvey, *The Condition of Postmodernity* (Oxford: Blackwell, 1989), 295.

3 Olick, Vinitzky-Seroussi, and Levy, *Collective Memory Reader*, 3–62. Among other summaries and reviews, I have found anthropologist James Wertsch's discussion of collective memory in *Voices of Collective Remembering* very helpful, as well as the introduction to Astrid Erll and Ansgar Nunning's *A Companion to Cultural Memory Studies*. See James Wertsch, *Voices of Collective Remembering* (New York: Cambridge University Press, 2002); and Astrid Erll and Ansgar Nunning, eds., *A Companion to Cultural Memory Studies* (New York: De Gruyter, 2010), 1–15. A list of works concerning memory is large; nevertheless, besides the above, the following have shaped my thoughts the most: Robert Archibald, *A Place to Remember: Using History to Build Community* (Walnut Creek, CA: AltaMira Press, 1999); James Fentress and Chris Wickham, *Social Memory* (Oxford: Blackwell, 1992); Glassberg, *Sense of History*; Hayden, *Power of Place*; Eric Hobsbawm and Terence Ranger, eds., *The Invention of Tradition* (New York: Cambridge University Press, 1983); Iwona Irwin-Zarecka, *Frames of Remembrance: The Dynamics of Collective Memory* (New Brunswick: Transaction, 1994); Michael Kammen, *Mystic Chords of Memory: The Transformation of Tradition in American Culture* (New York: Knopf, 1991); Edward Linenthal, *Preserving Memory: The Struggle to Create America's Holocaust Museum* (New York: Viking, 1995); Sanford Levison, *Written in Stone: Public Monuments in Changing Societies* (Durham, NC: Duke University Press, 1998); Harold Marcuse, *Legacies of Dachau: The Uses and Abuses of a Concentration Camp, 1933–2001* (New York: Cambridge University Press, 2001); Daniel Walkowitz and Lisa Maya Knauer, eds., *Memory and the Impact of Political Transformation in Public Space* (Durham: Duke University Press, 2004); and L. O. Zamora, *The Useable Past: The Imagination of History in Recent Fiction of the Americas* (Cambridge: Cambridge University Press, 1998).

4 Wertsch, *Voices of Collective Remembering*, 30.

5 Marcuse, *Legacies of Dachau*, 14; and Wertsch, *Voices of Collective Remembering*, 17. See also, Jay Winter and Emmanuel Sivan's *War and Remembrance in the Twentieth Century*, as they prefer the term *collective remembrances* whereby "Collective remembrance is public recollection. It is gathering pieces of the past and joining them together in public." Jay Winter and Emmanuel Sivan, eds., *War and Remembrance in the Twentieth Century* (New York: Cambridge University Press, 1999), 6. For "articulate memory," see Fentress and Wickham, *Social Memory*, 47.

6 Jerome Bruner, *Actual Minds, Possible Worlds* (Cambridge: Harvard University Press, 1986); Hayden White, *The Content of the Form: Narrative Discourse and Historical Representation* (Baltimore: Johns Hopkins University Press, 1987); and D. Holland, W. Lachicatte Jr., D. Skinner, and C. Cain, eds., *Identity and Agency in Cultural Worlds* (Cambridge: Harvard University Press, 1998), 5.

7 Archer, "The Place We Love to Hate," 45–82.

8 Kruse and Sugrue, *New Suburban History*, 1–10; Lassiter, "The New Suburban History II," 75–88; O' Mara, "Suburbia Reconsidered," 229–44; Nicolaides and Wiese, *Suburb Reader*, 5–11; Seligman, "New Suburban History," 312–33; and Sies, "North American Urban History," 28–42.

CHAPTER 6

1 Conley, *Dreamers and Dwellers*, 22.

2 Mark Luborsky, "Analysis of Multiple Life History Narratives," *Ethos* 15, no. 4 (December 1987): 369; and Michael Agar, "Stories, Background, Knowledge, and Themes: Problems in the Analysis of Life History Narrative," *American Ethnologist* 7, no. 2 (May 1980): 231.

3 Wertsch, *Voices of Collective Remembering*, 60.

4 Wertsch, *Voices of Collective Remembering*, 74–76.

5 Harold Marcuse, "Memories of World War II and the Holocaust," in *A Companion to Europe 1900–1945*, ed. Gordon Martel, (Oxford: Blackwell, 2006), 488.

6 Harold Marcuse, "Reception History: Definition and Quotations," Harold Marcuse Faculty website at University of California, Santa Barbara," available online at http://www.history.ucsb. edu/faculty/marcuse/receptionhist.htm.

7 As in hermeneutics, the concept of "cultural texts" entails extending "texts" beyond written documents to include any number of objects subject to interpretation, such as historic sites, museums, and commemorations. See Hobsbawm and Ranger, *Invention of Tradition*; Norkunas, *Politics of Public Memory*; Wertsch, *Voices of Collective Remembering*; and Henry Russo, *The Vichy Syndrome: History and Memory in France since 1944* (Cambridge: Harvard University Press, 1991).

8 A themal analysis of several hundred distinct memory works concerning Ontario, Orangevale, and Fair Oaks caused me to conclude that these memory works divert attention away from their suburban roots. For clarification, I primarily—but not exclusively—focused on memory works that discussed, in whatever capacity, these areas' early foundational and developmental years (Ontario: 1882–87; Orangevale: 1887–96; Fair Oaks: 1895–1902). While these specific memory works cover a wide range of years, particularly as more time passes, these years of focus are designed to correlate with the years in which these areas' promoters planned, promoted, and developed the agriburb. Important themes, which comprise a dominant cultural memory, such as the adoration of agriculture, are rather salient and are certainly not limited to the principal years of foundation and early development. A spotlight on such a period, however, is what accounts for the determination and characterization of a dominant cultural memory. For the precise sources that constitute the memory works I analyzed, see the bibliography. For Ontario, see "Ontario's Collected Memory." For Orangevale and Fair Oaks, see "Orangevale and Fair Oaks' Collected Memory."

9 *Ontario, Located in San Bernardino County*, 7.

10 "Ontario," *Land of Sunshine*, 250. The phrase "model colony" coincides with the arrival of an Australian delegation, which came to Ontario to inspect the irrigation project set up by Chaffey and the landed boosters in 1885. J. L. Dow, an Australian journalist who accompanied the delegation, described Ontario as a model for what Australia could do in Victoria and South Australia in a May 2, 1885, edition of the Melbourne *Age*—the *Land of Sunshine* article appeared in October 1895. See Starr, *Material Dreams*, 17; and Tyrrell, *True Garden of the Gods*, 143.

11 "Ontario," display ad, *Harper's Weekly* 27, no. 1379 (May 26, 1883): 336.

12 See the *Los Angeles Times*, p. 0_1, classified ad, August 10, 1883; August 11, 1883; September 6, 1883; September 7, 1883; October 23, 1883; October 26, 1883; and October 30, 1883.

13 Rounds, *Ontario*, 53; and Austen, *Ontario*.

14 "Ontario," classified ad, *Los Angeles Times*, December 7, 1884, 0_3.

15 Austen, *Ontario*; and Jane Craig, "Model Colony," in Upland Elementary School, *Historical Essays*, 29–34, Model Colony History Room.

16 Freeman, "History of Ontario," 569; and Conley, *Dreamers and Dwellers*, 22.

17 Tyrrell, *True Garden of the Gods*, 143.

18 See, among many others, *The Ontario Record*, January 17, 1903; Alexander, *Life of George Chaffey*, 55; Starr, *Material Dreams*, 16; and Rounds, *Ontario*, 78. To be exact, the government decided to present the colony as a model irrigation type in 1903. The model then appeared at the 1904 World's Fair in St. Louis.

19 Widney, *Ontario*, 7.

20 Starr, *Material Dreams*, 16.

21 Rounds, *Ontario*, 50.

22 Alexander, *Life of George Chaffey*, 47.

23 Peter Hayes, ed., *The Lower American River: Prehistory to Parkway* (Carmichael, CA: American River Natural History Association, 2005), 98.

24 Hack, *History of Orangevale*, 34, 35, 45, and 54; and Sandul and Swim, *Orangevale*, 23.

25 FODC, *Fair Oaks*, 34–35.

26 Sacramento Valley Development Association, *Sacramento Valley, California* (San Francisco: Sunset Magazine Homeseekers' Bureau, [1911]), 43; *Greater Sacramento*, no page number; and Sacramento Chamber of Commerce, *Sacramento, California: The World's Garden Valley* (Sacramento: Anderson Printing, 1925), 5.

27 Hayes, *Lower American River*, 99; McGowan, *History of the Sacramento Valley*, vol. 1, 410; and Avella, *Sacramento*, 81.

28 *Greater Sacramento*, no page number; McClatchy & Company, *Sacramento County and its Resources*, 24; OVCC, "A Map of Sacramento County, Orange Vale," ca. 1892, Center for Sacramento History, no. 2002/092/001; OVCC, *A Souvenir of Orange Vale*, 6; "Orange Vale: Making Rapid Progress," *Folsom Telegraph*, February 18, 1893, 2; G. Walter Reed, ed., *History of Sacramento County, California* (Los Angeles: Historic Record Co., 1923), 599; Sacramento Chamber of Commerce, *Sacramento, California*, 5–7; Sacramento County Board of Supervisors and Sacramento Chamber of Commerce, *Resources of Sacramento County, California, compiled from reports of the State Board of Agriculture, and other reliable sources* (Sacramento: [Sacramento County Board of Supervisors and Sacramento County Chamber of Commerce, 1899]), 7; *Sacramento County: In Heart of California* ([Sacramento]: Sacramento County Board of Supervisors and Exposition Commissioners, [1915]), 21, 39; Sacramento Valley Development Association, *Sacramento Valley, California*, 43; West, "Northern California's First Successful Colony," 28; White and Lawson, "Northern California," *Harper's*, 2100; and Wilson, "Among the Cowboys," *Farm, Field and Fireside*, 756.

29 OVCC, *A Souvenir of Orange Vale*, 6; and Sacramento County Chamber of Commerce, *Fruit Growing is California's Greatest Industry*, 7.

30 *Greater Sacramento*, no page number; and Sacramento Chamber of Commerce, *Fruit Growing is California's Greatest Industry*, 6.

31 See, "Orange Vale: Making Rapid Progress," 2; McClatchy & Company, *Sacramento County and its Resources*, 24; and West, "Northern California's First Successful Colony," 28.

32 SCPD, *Fair Oaks Community Plan*, 2.

33 Avella, *Sacramento*, 59, 67–68, 81, 119 for both Orangevale and Fair Oaks, and 122 for Fair Oaks, and 124 for Orangevale. See also, for example, John Cook, "Orangevale Named for Citrus Trees," *Sacramento Union*, May 31, 1959, 1; Laucher, *History of Orangevale*, [3]; SCPD, *Fair Oaks Community Plan*, 2; Julie Mims and Kevin Mims, *Sacramento: A Pictorial History of California's Capital* (Virginia Beach: Danning, 1981), 80–81; *Fair Oaks Guide* ([Fair Oaks]: Fair Oaks Chamber of Commerce, 1988), 6.

34 Cook, "Orangevale Named for Citrus Trees," 1; and Laucher, *History of Orangevale*, [3].

35 Fair Oaks Historical Society, *Newsletter*, volume 73 (July 2005), available online at www.fairoakshistory.org; and Fair Oaks Historical Society, *Newsletter*, volume 78 (October 2006), available online at www.fairoakshistory.org.

36 John Mellencamp, quoted in "About Us," Farm Aid website, updated 2007, available online at www.farmaid.org.

37 Kathleen Underwood, *Town Building on the Colorado Frontier* (Albuquerque: University of New Mexico Press, 1987), xv–xvii. The Canby quote, found on page xv, originally appears in Henry S. Canby, *The Age of Confidence* (1934), 1. The *Time* article comes from the May 24, 1976, issue, page 16, according to Underwood. Lastly, Underwood provides a great bibliography on small towns and historiography on page 133, endnote 3.

38 Dumke, *Boom of the Eighties*, 107. See also, Gentilcore, "Ontario, California," 87. For more recent accounts, see, among others, Garcia, *A World of Its Own*; Sackman, *Orange Empire*; and Vaught, *Cultivating California*.

39 F. W. Hart, *Ontario Colony* (Ontario, CA), quoted in Gentilcore, "Ontario, California," 87.

40 *The Ontario Record Twenty-Fifth Anniversary Edition*, November 1907, 3.

41 For rail lines, see Austen, *Ontario*, 41; Conley, *Dreamers and Dwellers*, 3–5; and Rounds, *Ontario*, 62. For cooperatives and packing houses, see Austen, *Ontario*, 60–70; Conley, *Dreamers and Dwellers*, 72–101; and Rounds, *Ontario*, 84–86. For Holt and agricultural fairs, see Conley, *Dreamers and Dwellers*, 95. For Hotpoint, see, among others, Max van Balgooy, "A Factory Midst the Orange Grove: Hotpoint and Ontario, California in the Early Twentieth Century," a senior thesis presented to the faculty of the department of history, Pomona College, Claremont, December 9, 1983, Model Colony History Room; Austen, *Ontario*, 49–50; and Conley, *Dreamers and Dwellers*, 11. Grape information came from footnote, marked with †, in Alexander, *Life of George Chaffey*, 58.

42 For 1910 and 1920 US Census data, see Historical Census Browser, from the University of Virginia, Geospatial and Statistical Data Center, http://fisher.lib.virginia.edu/collections/stats/hist census/index.html. For conversion of relative value for dollars, see Lawrence Officer and Samuel Williamson, "Purchasing Power of Money in the United States from 1774 to 2007," Measuring Worth, 2008, available online at www.measuringworth.com/ppowerus.

43 For references to Orangevale and Fair Oaks as "fruit colonies," "choice subdivisions," "colonization enterprises," see, among many others, Avella, *Sacramento*, 67; Bryan, *Souvenir of the Capital*, 5, 7–8; John Burns, ed., *Sacramento: Gold Rush Legacy, Metropolitan Destiny* (Carlsbad, CA: Heritage Media, 1999), 93; Hayes, *Lower American River*, 98–99; McGowan, *History of the Sacramento Valley*, vol. 1, 410; "Orange Vale: A Sacramento Fruit Colony Enterprise," 3; Sacramento County Board of Supervisors and Sacramento Chamber of Commerce, *Resources of Sacramento County, California*, 6; *Sacramento County: In Heart of California*; and West, "Northern California's First Successful Colony."

44 Burns, *Sacramento*, 93; and McGowan, *The Sacramento Valley*, 34.

45 See, for example, Davis, *Sacramento County, California*, 13; FODC, *Fair Oaks*, 12; Fair Oaks Historical Society, *Fair Oaks*, 8; Howard & Wilson, advertisement for "San Juan Colony," 5; Howard & Wilson, *Heart of California*; "Orange Vale: An Excursion to the Sacramento Colony Near Folsom," 1; "Orange Vale: Making Rapid Progress," 2; Sacramento County Board of Supervisors and Sacramento Chamber of Commerce, *Resources of Sacramento County, California*, 6, 9; Sacramento Chamber of Commerce, *Fruit Growing is California's Greatest Industry*, 3 (picture of "Young Orchard at Fair Oaks"); Sacramento Chamber of Commerce, *Sacramento, California*, 5, 8; Sacramento Valley Development Association, *Sacramento Valley California*, 43; Wilson, "Among the Cowboys," *Farm, Field and Fireside*, 756; and Wilson, "Among the Fair Oaks of Sunset Colony," *Farm, Field and Fireside*, 788–89.

46 Sacramento County Board of Supervisors and Sacramento Chamber of Commerce, *Resources of Sacramento County*, 6.

47 Wilson, "Among the Cowboys," *Farm, Field and Fireside*, 756.

48 Lord, *Sacramento Saga*, 287.

49 OVCC, *A Souvenir of Orange Vale*, 6.

50 *Fair Oaks Guide*, 32.

51 For example, see Fair Oaks Historical Society, *Fair Oaks*, 40; Hayes, *Lower American River*, 98, 101; McGowan, *History of the Sacramento Valley*, vol. 1, 411–12; Orangevale Chamber of Commerce, "History," Orangevale Chamber of Commerce website, www. orangevalechamber.com; "History of Fair Oaks," www.fairoakshistory.org; and SCPD, *Fair Oaks Community Plan*, 2.

52 Starr, *Material Dreams*, 16.

53 National Park Service, United States Department of the Interior, National Register of Historic Places website, www.cr.nps.gov/nr, weekly list, September 2, 2005, www.cr.nps.gov/nr/listings/20050902.htm; and Historic American Buildings Survey/Historic American Engineering Record (HABS/HAER), Euclid Avenue, 1997, Library of Congress website, http://hdl.loc.gov/loc.pnp/hhh.ca2323. Euclid Avenue was determined eligible in 1979.

54 HABS/HAER, Euclid Avenue, 1.

55 *Ontario, Located in San Bernardino County*, 30; Widney, *Ontario*, 7; Ontario Land and Improvement Company, *Ontario*, 4; *An Illustrated History of Southern California*, 473; "Ontario," *Land of Sunshine*, 247; *Ontario Record Industrial Review Edition*, 1903, front page [1]; and Smith, "A City of Ten-Acre Lots," 66.

56 Alexander, *Life of George Chaffey*, 49–50.

57 Upland Elementary School, *Historical Essays*; Ontario Diamond Jubilee Committee, *Ontario Diamond Jubilee*; Ontario Bicentennial Commission, *A Bicentennial Salute*; and Rounds, *Ontario*.

58 For "urban planning," see Starr, *Material Dreams*, 16.

59 "Fair Oaks Colony: Sacramento's Suburban Site for Little Farms," ca. 1900, ad, reprinted in Fair Oaks Historical Society, *Fair Oaks*, 2 (see also p. 7).

60 Bryan, *Souvenir of the Capital*, 7–8; Davis, *Sacramento County California*, 239; "Fair Oaks Colony," 2; FODC, *Fair Oaks*, title page; *Fair Oaks Guide*, 4; Laucher, *History of Orangevale*, [6]; McClatchy & Company, *Sacramento County and its Resources*, 60; McGowan, *History of the Sacramento Valley*, vol. 1, 410–11; "Orange Vale: An Excursion to the Sacramento Colony Near Folsom," 1; OVCC, *A Souvenir of Orange Vale*, 16; Sacramento Chamber of Commerce, *Fruit Growing is California's Greatest Industry*, 3; and Sacramento County Board of Supervisors and Sacramento Chamber of Commerce, *Resources of Sacramento County*, 6.

61 FODC, *Fair Oaks*, 3.

62 Bryan, *Souvenir of the Capital*, 5, 8; Davis, *Sacramento County, California*, 238–39; FODC, *Fair Oaks*, 3; *Greater Sacramento*, no page number (picture of "Typical California Bungalow . . ."); Laucher, *History of Orangevale*, [10]; McClatchy & Company, *Sacramento County and its Resources*, 60; McGowan, *History of the Sacramento Valley*, vol. 1, 411–12; "Orange Vale: A Sacramento Fruit Colony Enterprise" (1888), 3; "Orange Vale: Making Rapid Progress," 2; Sacramento Chamber of Commerce, *Fruit Growing is California's Greatest Industry*, 7; *Sacramento County: In Heart of California*; and "History of Fair Oaks," www.fairoakshistory.org.

63 OVCC, *A Souvenir of Orange Vale*, 20; *Greater Sacramento*, no page number (picture of "Typical California Bungalow . . ."); "A Suburban Railroad to Fair Oaks," 4; Hayes, *Lower American River*, 101; and "Orange Vale: Making Rapid Progress," 2.

64 Greenback Lane is the present-day name of the road the promoters named Orange Vale Avenue, which is not to be confused with the contemporary road named Orangevale Avenue. For more, see Sandul and Swim, *Orangevale*, 69–72. Likewise, the present-day Fair Oaks Boulevard section that runs through the commercial district of Fair Oaks originally had the name Howard Avenue—though a contemporary Howard Avenue exists as well in Fair Oaks and was likely a part of the original road, to add confusion. Specifically, the contemporary Fair Oaks Boulevard is a series of streets and roads that are noncontiguous. Therefore, one of the older sections of Howard Avenue retained its original name despite other sections becoming a part of Fair Oaks Boulevard.

65 "Orange Vale: A Sacramento Fruit Colony Enterprise," 3; and Hack, *History of Orangevale*, 5.

66 *Sacramento County: In Heart of California*, 21.

67 Bodnar, *Remaking America*, 120–21; and Glassberg, *Sense of History*, 62. See also, Diane Barthel, *Historic Preservation: Collective Memory and Historical Identity* (New Brunswick: Rutgers University Press, 1996), 31.

68 Beatrice Paxson Lee, "The History and Development of the Ontario Colony," Master's thesis, University of Southern California, 1929, Model Colony History Room; Upland Elementary School, *Historical Essays*; and Lois Griffin, *Ontario*, with students from Lois Griffin's Social Living Class, Chaffey High School, Ontario, 1937, Model Colony History Room.

69 "George Chaffey Buried After Simple Services," *Los Angeles Times*, March 5, 1932, A8; "A Real Empire Builder," *Los Angeles Times*, March 10, 1932, A4; "Chaffey [High School] Planning

Memorial Library," *Los Angeles Times*, November 7, 1933, 10; "The Giants of the West," *Los Angeles Times*, November 18, 1934, A7; "Chaffey Library Will Be Opened Today," *Los Angeles Times*, September 19, 1935, 8; and "Memorial Library Dedicated," *Los Angeles Times*, September 20, 1935, 8; "What He Gave; His Monument," in the following issues of the *Los Angeles Times*: January 28, 1936, 5; January 28, 1938, 9; January 28, 1940, A2; and January 28, 1941, 6; "Chaffey Historical Room to Be Dedicated Today," *Los Angeles Times*, March 16, 1951, 29; and "Chaffey Day at Ontario Pays Tribute to Founder," *Los Angeles Times*, January 29, 1952, 17. For more on "living memorials," see Glassberg, *Sense of History*, particularly 62.

70 Ontario Bicentennial Commission, *A Bicentennial Salute*, 2–3.

71 This is similar to Bernard Finn's take on technology in museum exhibits. Bernard Finn, "Exhibit Reviews—Twenty Years After," *Technology and Culture* 30, no. 4 (October 1989): 993–1001.

72 Appleby, *Inheriting the Revolution*; and Kimmel, *Manhood in America*. See also Rotundo, *American Manhood*.

73 For more on pioneers and patriots in American public memory and vectors of memory, see Bodnar, *Remaking America*, particularly 115–37. See also Barthel, *Historic Preservation*, 69–72.

74 Wilson, "Among the Cowboys," *Farm, Field and Fireside*, 789; FODC, *Fair Oaks*, 5; Sacramento County Board of Supervisors and Sacramento Chamber of Commerce, *Resources of Sacramento County, California*, 6; "Orange Vale: An Excursion to the Sacramento Colony Near Folsom," 1; "A New Deal At Fair Oaks," 4; Sacramento Chamber of Commerce, *Fruit Growing is California's Greatest Industry*, 7; Sacramento Valley Development Association, *Sacramento Valley California*, 43; McClatchy & Company, *Sacramento County and its Resources*, 59; and FODC, *Fair Oaks*, 17.

75 FODC, *Fair Oaks*, 6; McClatchy & Company, *Sacramento County and its Resources*, 62; and West, "Northern California's First Successful Colony," 27.

76 "Orange Vale: Making Rapid Progress," 2; and Sacramento Chamber of Commerce, *Hub of Western Industry*, 4.

77 Reed, *History of Sacramento County*, 599.

78 Indeed, geographer James Vance in "California and the Search for the Ideal," concluded that California's residential and suburban expansion "showed more force if less pattern." Vance, "California and the Search for the Ideal," 186.

CHAPTER 7
_____

1 *Fair Oaks Guide*, 13.

2 Kammen, *Mystic Chords of Memory*, 3.

3 Richard Wohl and A. Theodore Brown, "The Useable Past: A Study of Historical Traditions in Kansas City," *The Huntington Quarterly* 23 (May 1960): 237–59; and Hobsbawm and Ranger, *Invention of Tradition*, 4. See also, Blake McKelvey, "A History of Historical Writing in the Rochester Area," *Rochester History* 6, no. 2 (April 1944): 1.

4 Friedrich Nietzsche, *Untimely Meditations: On the Uses and Disadvantages of History for Life* (1874; repr., New York: Cambridge University Press, 1997), 67–77. Monumental history is history, which is celebratory, romantic, congratulatory, and exceptional in a positive context. Monumental history serves life, since in its proper amount it inspires or encourages the striving of individuals to better themselves because it celebrates, "through which alone greatness goes on living" (68). See also, Stanton, *Lowell Experiment*, 37, 57, 67, and, especially, 171.

5 Paul Connerton, "Seven Types of Forgetting," *Memory Studies* 1, no. 1 (January 2008): 64. For similar arguments and conceptions of something like structural amnesia, though with different terminology, see also Barthel, *Historic Preservation*, 9; Glassberg, *Sense of History*, 26–27; Carol Kammen, "Local History—In Search of Common Threads," in *The Pursuit of Local History: Readings on Theory and Practice*, ed. Carol Kammen (Walnut Creek, CA: AltaMira, 1996), 12–13; Marianne Hirsch, *Family Frames: Photography, Narrative, and Postmemory* (Cambridge: Harvard University Press, 1997), 22; Hobsbawm and Ranger, *Invention of Tradition*, 4; Wertsch, *Voices of Collective Remembering*, 50, 119; and James Young, *The Texture of Memory: Holocaust Memorials and Meaning* (New Haven: Yale University Press, 1993), xi. Also informative is a growing literature on forgetting, of which Connerton is just one. See also, Barbara Mills, "Remembering While Forgetting: Depositional Practices and Social Memory at Chaco," in *Memory Work: Archaeologies of Material Practices*, ed. Barbara Mills and William Walker (Santa Fe: School for Advanced Research Press, 2008), 81–108. In fact, Mills opens her study with an overview of the process of forgetting and, in turn, provides a useful bibliography as well. Finally, see also Paul Ricoeur, *Memory, History, Forgetting* (Chicago: University of Chicago Press, 2004), especially ch. 3, "Forgetting," of Part III, "The Historical Condition," 412–56.

6 Benedict Anderson, *Imagined Communities: Reflections on the Origin and Spread of Nationalism* (New York: Verso, 1983). For devices of cohesion, see Émile Durkheim, *The Division of Labor in Society* (1893; repr., New York: Free Press, 1997), 73–130.

7 Hobsbawm and Ranger, *Invention of Tradition*, 1.

8 McKelvey, "A History of Historical Writing," 1.

9 David Russo, "Some Impressions of the Nonacademic Local Historians and Their Writings," in Kammen, *Pursuit of Local History*, 39. In fact, the celebration of local pioneers has been a salient feature of local history and memory works for a rather long time as the great amateur historian Salma Hale called attention to local "actors" in contrast to a "national" focus on "men of power" in 1832. Nevertheless, Hale's call was not one for including "average" people, especially ethnoracial minorities, but rather a call for highlighting the local powers that be. See Selma Hale, "An Address Delivered Before the New-Hampshire Historical Society," *Collections of the New Hampshire Historical Society* 3 (1832), in Kammen, *Pursuit of Local History*, 61–65; and James Dave Butler Jr., *Deficiencies in Our History: An Address Delivered Before the Vermont Historical and Antiquarian Society, October 16, 1846*, in Kammen, *Pursuit of Local History*, 66–75.

10 Conley, *Dreamers and Dwellers*, 102–81.

11 Susan Powell quoted in Monica Rodriquez, "Paying Homage to History," *Inland Valley Daily Bulletin* (Ontario), October 15, 2005, accessed via LexisNexis, http://web.lexis-nexis.com/universe.

12 "Statue of Ontario pioneer monumentally a good idea," *Inland Valley Daily Bulletin*, November 18, 1993, B6.

13 See "George Chaffey: The Final Dream," collection of materials concerning the creation of a George Chaffey statue, Model Colony History Room; and Robert E. Ellingwood Collection, Box 2, folder 6, collection of materials concerning the creation of the Chaffey statue, Model Colony History Room.

14 Contrary evidence shows that recreational vehicles date further back, even before the automobile. See Carlton M. Edwards, *Homes for Travel and Living: The History and Development of the Recreation Vehicle and Mobile Home Industries* (East Lansing: Carol Edwards and Associates, 1977).

15 "Chaffey statue set for reveal," San Bernardino Sun, October 15, 2005, accessed via LexisNexis, http://web.lexis-nexis.com/universe.

16 See Barthel, *Historic Preservation*; Bodnar, *Remaking America*; Glassberg, *Sense of History*; Hayden, *Power of Place*; James Oliver Horton and Lois Horton, eds., *Slavery and Public History: The Tough Stuff of American Memory* (New York: New Press, 2006); Hamer, *History in Urban Places*; William Murtagh, *Keeping Time: The History and Theory of Preservation in America* (Pittstown, NJ: Main Street Press, 1988); Norkunas, *Politics of Public Memory*; and Russo, "Some Impressions of the Nonacademic Local Historians."

17 For 2000 data, see Table DP-1, Profile of General Demographic Characteristics: 2000, Geographic Area: Ontario, city, California, p. 1, 2000 Census, United States Census Bureau, accessible online at the US Census Bureau website: http://censtats.census.gov/cgi–bin/pct/pctProfile.pl. For 2010 data, see US Census Bureau, "State and County Quick Facts," Ontario City, California, Census 2010, US Census Bureau website, www.census.gov.

18 United States, Department of the Interior, National Park Service, National Register of Historic Places Inventory—Nomination Form for the Frankish Building, 200 S. Euclid Avenue, Ontario, CA, prepared by Vicki Alexander, President, Ontario Historic Landmark Society, Montclair, CA, entered into the National Register of Historic Places by the Keeper, National Park Service, United States, Department of the Interior on August 1, 1980, NRHP-L-80-839 (report on file at the Archaeological Information Center, San Bernardino County Museum, Redlands).

19 United States, Department of the Interior, National Park Service, National Register of Historic Places Inventory—Nomination Form for the Hofer Ranch (Ballou Ranch, Ben Haven), 11248 South Turner Avenue, Ontario, prepared by Philip Hardison, Ramussen & Associates, Ventura, March 26, 1993, entered into the National Register of Historic Places by the Keeper, National Park Service, United States, Department of the Interior in 1993, NRHP-L-93-596 (report on file at the Archaeological Information Center, San Bernardino County Museum, Redlands).

20 City of Ontario, Planning Department, Historic Preservation Program, "Designated Historic Districts," City of Ontario website, www.ci.ontario.ca.us.

21 Interview with the City of Ontario Planning Department staff by Paul J. P. Sandul, January 30, 2007, City Hall, 303 East B Street, Ontario 91764.

22 Austen, *Ontario*; and Rounds, *Ontario*.

23 This is precisely what Dolores Hayden attempted to do with her Power of Place Project in Los Angeles. See Hayden, *Power of Place*, 168–87. For other examples, see Horton and Horton, *Slavery and Public History*; Stanton, *Lowell Experiment*; and Karen E. Till, "Artistic and Activist Memory-Work: Approaching Place-Based Practice," *Memory Studies* 1, no. 1 (January 2008): 99–113.

24 The contention that the commission is seeking political support for preservation efforts came from the interview with the City of Ontario Planning Department staff by Sandul, January 30, 2007.

25 See Hayden, *Building Suburbia*; Lewis, *Manufacturing Suburbs*; and Nicolaides and Wiese, *Suburb Reader*.

26 City of Ontario, Planning Department, City of Ontario website, www.ci.ontario.ca.us.

27 Preservation and public recollections reveal much about Ontario's relationship to its past because commemoration mediates between many things: individual testimony and collective remembrance, remembered experience and written works, and remembering and forgetting.

28 For population and other figures concerning Orangevale, see Sacramento County Planning Department (SCPD), *Orangevale Community Plan: Technical Report* (Sacramento: SCPD, 1976), 9–10; California Department of Finance, "Population Totals by Township and Place for California Counties: 1860 to 1950"; US Census Bureau, Census 2000 Summary File 4, Orangevale, California CDP, available online at www.census.gov; and US Census Bureau, Census 2010 Summary File, Orangevale, California CDP, available online at www.census.gov. For population and other figures on Sacramento County, see US Bureau of the Census, 1990 Census of Population and Housing, Summary Tape File 1, Sacramento County, California, available online at www.census.gov; US Census Bureau, Census 2000 Summary File 4, Sacramento County, California, available online at www.census.gov; and US Census Bureau, Census 2010 Summary File, Sacramento County, California, available online at www.census.gov.

29 For example, since 1978, Orangevale, along with other communities in California's 5th Assembly District, such as Fair Oaks, has elected 6 straight Republicans to represent them in California's State Assembly, and, since 1966, for California's 1st Senate District, has elected 5 straight Republicans to represent them in the State Senate.

30 Sigmund Freud, *Civilization and Its Discontents*, in *The Freud Reader*, ed. Peter Gay (New York: W. W. Norton, 1999), 751.

31 Philip Deloria, *Playing Indian* (New Haven: Yale University Press, 1998), 7.

32 Spickard, *Almost All Aliens*, 7.

33 SCPD, *Orangevale Community Plan*, 8.

34 For more on the Orangevale Pow Wow Days, see Orangevale Chamber of Commerce, "Pow Wow Days History," Orangevale Chamber of Commerce website, www.orangevalechamber.com; and Sandul and Swim, *Orangevale*, 124–26.

35 "Orangevale," *Sacramento Union*, April 29, 1972.

36 US Census Bureau, Population Division, Table 1A. Population in Metropolitan and Micropolitan Statistical Areas in Alphabetical Order and Numerical and Percent Change for the United States and Puerto Rico: 1990 and 2000, in Ranking Tables for Population of Metropolitan Statistical Areas, Micropolitan Statistical Areas, Combined Statistical Areas, New England City and Town Areas, and Combined New England City and Town Areas: 1990 and 2000, available online at www.census.gov; and US Census Bureau, Population Division, "Annual Estimates of the Population of Metropolitan and Micropolitan Statistical Areas: April 1, 2010 to July 1, 2011," available online at www.census.gov.

37 US Census Bureau, Population Division, "Annual Estimates of the Population of Combined Statistical Areas: April 1, 2010 to July 1, 2011," 2011 Population Estimates, available online at www. census.gov. A Combined Statistical Area includes adjacent metropolitan (areas of at least 50,000 people) and micropolitan statistical areas (areas of 10,000 to 49,999 people). The Combined Statistical Area is listed as the "Sacramento—Arden–Arcade—Yuba City, CA–NV Combined Statistical Area," and includes the Gardnerville Ranchos, NV Micropolitan Statistical Area, Sacramento—Arden–Arcade—Roseville, CA Metropolitan Statistical Area, Truckee–Grass Valley, CA Micropolitan Statistical Area, and the Yuba City, CA Metropolitan Statistical Area.

38 SCPD, *Orangevale Community Plan*, 5.

39 Historic Environment Consultants, Historic Resources Survey: Report for Harvard Place Subdivision, Orangevale, California; Warhaftig Property, Prepared for the Department of Environmental Review and Assessment, Sacramento County Environmental Impact Section (Sacramento: Historic Environment Consultants, 1990), 6; 10; and 11, California History Room.

40 Historic Environment Consultants, Historic Resources Survey: Report for Harvard Place Subdivision, Orangevale, California; Warhaftig Property, 9–10. For more on the Stick Style, see Scully, *The Shingle Style*.

41 Historic Environment Consultants, Historic Resources Survey: Serve Our Seniors Project, Orangevale, California, prepared for the Department of Environmental Review and Assessment, Sacramento County Environmental Impact Section (Sacramento: Historic Environment Consultants, 1990), 13, California History Room.

42 For Fair Oaks population figures, see California Department of Finance, "Population Totals by Township and Place for California Counties: 1860 to 1950"; US Bureau of the Census, 1990 Census of Population and Housing, Summary Tape File 1, Fair Oaks, California, CDP, available online at www.census.gov; US Census Bureau, Census 2010 Summary File, Fair Oaks, California, CDP, available online at www.census.gov. For population and other figures on Sacramento County, see US Bureau of the Census, 1990 Census of Population and Housing, Summary Tape File 1, Sacramento County, California, available online at www.census.gov; US Census Bureau, Census 2000 Summary File 4, Sacramento County, California, available online at www.census.gov; and US Census Bureau, 2005–2007 American Community Survey, Sacramento County, California, available online at www.census.gov.

43 Bodnar, *Remaking America*.

44 "History of Fair Oaks," www.fairoakshistory.org.

45 Amy Whitlatch, "Fair Oaks Historical Society: Building a History Center," MA Thesis, Public History, Department of History, California State University, Sacramento, 2003, 19.

46 See Simpson and Sandul, *Fair Oaks*, 22, 26, 30, 59, 127.

47 "Walking Tour," Fair Oaks Historical Society website, www.fairoakshistory.org.

48 I visited the Hermitage and encountered postings firsthand concerning the ongoing process of uncovering the slave past in the summer of 2007. See also the Hermitage website, http://www.thehermitage.com, as well as Kevin Bartoy (Director of Archaeology at The Hermitage), "The Other Hermitage: The Enslaved at the Andrew Jackson Plantation," BlackPast.Org, An Online Reference Guide to African American History, www.blackpast.org; Aaron Russell, "Material Culture and African-American Spirituality at the Hermitage," *Historical Archaeology* 31, no. 2 (1997): 63–80; Samuel Smith, "Plantation Archaeology at the Hermitage: Some Suggested Patterns," *Tennessee Anthropologist* 2, no. 2 (1977):152–63; and Brian William Thomas, "Power and Community: The Archaeology of Slavery at the Hermitage Plantation," *American Antiquity* 63, no. 4 (1998): 531–52.

49 All newsletters can be found online under the "Newsletter" heading and "Archives" heading at the Fair Oaks Historical Society website, www.fairoakshistory.org.

CONCLUSION

1 "The Big Idea," found at the Agriburbia website, last updated in 2010, at www.agriburbia.com.

2 Matthew Redmond, quoted in "Agriburbia Takes Hold in Colorado," Spatial Sustain: Promoting Spatial Design for a Sustainable Tomorrow, blog site, by Matt Ball, October 24, 2009, accessed online at http://www.sensysmag.com/spatialsustain/agriburbia–takes–hold–in–colorado.html.

3 "About Agriburbia," found at the Agriburbia website, last updated in 2010, at www.agriburbia.com.

4 "Key Personnel," found at the Agriburbia website, last updated 2010, at www.agriburbia.com.

5 "TSR Agristruction," found at the Agriburbia website, last updated in 2010, at www.agriburbia.com.

6 See "Public Lands" and "Private Land," under "Land Use" section, found at the Agriburbia website, last updated in 2010, at www.agriburbia.com.

7 For Farmstead, see "New Developments" under the "Land Use" section, found at the Agriburbia website, last updated in 2010, at www.agriburbia.com; and for Milliken, see "Markets" under "The Big Idea" section, found at the Agriburbia website, last updated in 2010, at www.agriburbia.com.

8 See the homepage for the Agriburbia website, last updated in 2010, at www.agriburbia.com.

9 See "Land Use" section the Agriburbia website, last updated in 2010, at www.agriburbia.com.

10 Margret Aldrich, "At Home in Agriburbia," September 22, 2011, "The Sweet Pursuit Blog" of Former Associate editor Margret Aldrich, found online at http://www.utne.com/The-Sweet-Pursuit/At-Home-in-Agriburbia-New-Ruralism.aspx#ixzz2HDxEssHL.

11 See homepage, "Big Idea" section and "Land Use" section, found at the Agriburbia website, last updated in 2010, at www.agriburbia.com.

12 Homepage, found at the Agriburbia website, last updated in 2010, at www.agriburbia.com.

13 See the sidebar under the "Land Use" section, found at the Agriburbia website, last updated in 2010, at www.agriburbia.com.

14 See "Land Use" section, found at the Agriburbia website, last updated in 2010, at www.agriburbia.com.

15 For more on New Urbanism, see Congress for the New Urbanism, "Who We Are," found online at the Congress for the New Urbanism website at http://www.cnu.org/who_we_are; Duany, Plater–Zyberk, and Speck, Suburban Nation; Peter Katz, ed., The New Urbanism: Toward an Architecture of Community (New York: McGraw–Hill, 1994); and Kunstler, Geography Of Nowhere. For New Ruralism, see Sibella Kraus, "A Call For New Ruralism," Frameworks (Spring 2006) available online at http://www.farmlandinfo.org/documents/37270/new-ruralism.pdf; and David Moffat, "New Ruralism: Agriculture at the Metropolitan Edge," Places (December 2006) available at http://escholarship.org/uc/item/43b9c9xw. For Agricultural Urbanism, see Janine de la Salle and Mark Holland, eds., Agricultural Urbanism: Handbook for Building Sustainable Food Systems in 21st Century Cities (Sheffield, VT: Green Frigate Books, 2010).

16 See the Hampstead website at http://www.hampsteadliving.com/hampstead_farms.php.

17 Harvey, Condition of Postmodernity, 295.

18 Jackson, *Crabgrass Frontier*, 296; Lefebvre, *Production of Space*, 89, 335, 349; Logan and Molotch, *Urban Fortunes*, 236; Marc Weiss, *The Rise of the Community Builders: The American Real Estate Industry and Urban Land Planning* (New York: Columbia University Press, 1987); and Gyan Prakash, "Introduction," in Prakash and Kruse, *Spaces of the Modern City*, 7. See also, Cronon, "A Place for Stories"; Cronon, *Nature's Metropolis*, 5–19; Davis, *City of Quartz*, especially chapter 1, "Sunshine or Noir," 17–97; Bella Dicks, *Culture on Display: The Production of Contemporary Visitability* (Maidenhead, U.K.: Open University Press, 2003); Feld and Basso, *Senses of Place*; Stanton, *Lowell Experiment*, 65–67; Harvey, *Condition of Postmodernity*, 295; Hayden, *Power of Place*; Prakash and Kruse, *Spaces of the Modern City*; Soja, *Thirdspace*; Ward, *Selling Places*; and Yi-Fu Tuan, *Space and Place*.

19 For some examples, see Fishman, *Bourgeois Utopias*, especially chapter 7, "Beyond Suburbia: The Rise of the Technoburb," 182–207; Anthony Flint, *This Land: The Battle Over Sprawl and the Future of America* (Baltimore: Johns Hopkins University Press, 2006); "The Future of Suburbia," chapter 16 of *Suburb Reader*, edited by Nicolaides and Wiese, 469–97; Garreau, *Edge City*; Hayden, *Building Suburbia*, especially chapter 9, "Rural Fringes," 181–97; Robert Hugh Kargon and Arthur Molella, *Invented Edens: Techno-Cities of the Twentieth Century* (Cambridge: MIT Press, 2008); Katz, *New Urbanism*, especially the essay "The Neighborhood and the District," by Andres Duany and Elizabeth Plater-Zyberk; and James Russell, "When Suburbs Become Mega-Suburbs," *Architectural Record* 191, no. 8 (August 2003): 76–81.

20 Historian Carl Abbott provides a good overview of many of these communities in California in his "Garden Cities" chapter of *How Cities Won the West*, 88–99. See also, for Fresno, Pisani, *From the Family Farm to Agribusiness*; Vaught, *Cultivating California*; for Runnymede and Little Landers Colonies, Michelson and Solomonson, "Remnants of a Failed Utopia"; Hine, *California's Utopian Colonies*, 145–49; and Lee, "The Little Landers Colony," 26–48.

21 Abbott, *How Cities Won the West*; Garcia, *A World of Its Own*; Orsi, *Sunset Limited*; Sackman, *Orange Empire*; Starr, *Americans and the California Dream*; Starr, *Inventing the Dream*; Starr, *Material Dreams*; Stoll, *Fruits of Natural Advantage*; Tyrrell, *True Garden of the Gods*; David Vaught, *After the Gold Rush: Tarnished Dreams in the Sacramento Valley* (Baltimore: Johns Hopkins University Press, 2007); and Vaught, *Cultivating California*.

22 See Kruse and Sugrue, *New Suburban History*, 1–10; Lassiter, "The New Suburban History II," 75–88; O'Mara, "Suburbia Reconsidered," 229–44; Nicolaides and Wiese, *Suburb Reader*, 5–11; Seligman, "New Suburban History," 312–33; and Sies, "North American Urban History," 28–42.

23 Patillo-McCoy, *Black Pickett Fences*; Herbert J. Gans, *Levittowners: Ways of Life and Politics in a New Suburban Community* (New York: Pantheon Books, 1967); and William Whyte, *The Organization Man* (New York: Simon and Schuster, 1956). Also of note are works citing a strong sense of community, such as John Seeley, R. Alexander Sim, and Elizabeth Loosley, *Crestwood Heights* (New York: Basic Books, 1956); Sylvia Fleis Fava, "Contrasts in Neighboring," in *The Suburban Community*, ed. William Dobriner (New York: G. P. Putnam's Sons, 1958); S. F. Fava, "Suburbanism as a Way of Life," *American Sociological Review* 21 (February 1956), 34–38; Claude Fischer and Robert Max Jackson, "Suburbanism and Localism," in *Networks and Places*, Claude Fischer et al. (New York: Free Press, 1977).

24 Archer, "The Places We Love to Hate."

25 Berglund, *Making San Francisco American*; Bodnar, *Remaking America*; Deverell, *Whitewashed Adobe*; Glassberg, *Sense of History*; Graff, *Dallas Myth*; Hayden, *Power of Place*; Kropp, *California*

Vieja; Lindgren, *Preserving Historic New England*; Norkunas, *Politics of Public Memory*; Otero, *La Calle*; Stanton, *Lowell Experiment*; West, *Domesticating History*; and Wilson, *Myth of Santa Fe*.

26 Review of *California Vieja: Culture and Memory in a Modern American Place* by Phoebe Kropp, reviewed by Anne Petersen, *The Public Historian* 30, no. 1 (February 2008): 130.

27 Review of *La Calle: Spatial Conflicts and Urban Renewal in a Southwest City* by Lydia Otero, reviewed by Paul J. P. Sandul, *The Public Historian* 34, no. 1 (Winter 2012): 136.

28 Richard Handler and Eric Gable, *The New History in an Old Museum: Creating the Past at Colonial Williamsburg* (Durham, NC: Duke University Press, 1997); and Stanton, *Lowell Experiment*.

29 Michael Frisch, *A Shared Authority: Essays on the Craft and Meaning of Oral and Public History* (Albany: SUNY Press, 1990), xx.

30 For critiques, and praise, of shared authority, see "Special Feature: Shared Authority," in *The Oral History Review* 30, no. 1 (Winter/Spring 2003): 23–113.

31 Nietzsche, *Untimely Meditations*, 67–77.

32 Antonio Gramsci, in *Culture, Ideology and Social Process: A Reader*, ed. Tony Bennett, et al. (London: The Open University Press, 1989), 210–14.

33 Certeau, *Practice of Everyday Life*, xix; and Soja, *Thirdspace*.

34 Michael Frisch, "Oral History and *Hard Times*: A Review Essay," *Red Buffalo* 1, nos. 2–3 (1972): 217–31; Ronald Grele, *Envelopes of Sound: The Art of Oral History* (Chicago: Precedent Publishing, 1985), 127–54; Luisa Passerini, "Work Ideology and Consensus Under Italian Fascism," *History Workshop* 8 (1979): 84–92; Alessandro Portelli, "The Peculiarities of Oral History," *History Workshop* 12 (1981): 96–107; and Paul Thompson, *The Voice of the Past: Oral History, Third Edition* (New York: Oxford University Press, 2000), 173–89.

SELECTED BIBLIOGRAPHY

THE SOURCES LISTED BELOW include most of the books, articles, and archival material referred to throughout the book, but first cited in the endnotes, of course. To be clear, all sources cited and/or referenced to or used in some capacity appear in the endnotes. Nevertheless, this selected bibliography excludes materials used only once or just a handful of times, but, again, appear in the endnotes. In addition, the criteria for the selected bibliography further narrowed on sharing primary sources, especially as they concern the case study sites, but also relevant secondary sources related to suburbs, California, and critical theory, especially concerning memory. Moreover, the intention is to provide a list that is relatively easy to navigate and, it is hoped, that much more helpful and useful to others seeking to locate the more pertinent sources behind this book and its principal content and ideas. Finally, to aid the reader further, the bibliography subdivides. Following identification of the archives and repositories used, a selection of general primary sources appears, typically those that deal with California broadly and suburban image-makers, such as Olmstead, Beecher, and Downing, as well as census material. Second, I also packaged together sources about just Ontario, Orangevale, and Fair Oaks, under a subheading of "Collected Memory Sources (Memory Works)," which includes both primary and secondary source material about each site and its respective metropolitan regions. While I explain this more just before that section, I did this to not only make finding such material easier, but also to serve as corroborating evidence of the existence of a robust collected memory about these sites. Also, it makes distinguishing between primary and secondary source material here somewhat moot when placed under the microscope of memory—as all become primary source material in that regard. Lastly, secondary sources wrap up the selected bibliography, focused primarily on works about suburbs, California, and memory.

ARCHIVES AND REPOSITORIES

- California History Room, California State Library, Sacramento, CA. Hereafter referred to as California History Room.
- California State Archives, Sacramento, CA. Hereafter referred to as Cal State Archives.
- Center for Sacramento History, Sacramento, CA. Hereafter referred to as Center for Sacramento History.
- Fair Oaks History Center, Fair Oaks Historical Society, Fair Oaks, CA. Hereafter referred to as History Center, Fair Oaks.

- Fair Oaks Library, Fair Oaks, CA. Hereafter referred to as Fair Oaks Library.
- Ontario Museum of History and Art, Ontario, CA. Hereafter referred to as Ontario Museum.
- Orangevale Public Library, Orangevale, CA. Hereafter referred to as Orangevale Library.
- Robert E. Ellingwood Model Colony History Room, City Library, Ontario, CA. Hereafter referred to as Model Colony History Room.
- Sacramento Room, Sacramento Central Library, Sacramento, CA. Hereafter referred to as Sacramento Room.

PRIMARY SOURCES

"Annual Review, 1888–1889." *California Fruit Grower,* August 17, 1889, 5–28.

Beecher, Catharine. "American People Starved." *Harper's New Monthly Magazine* 32, no. 192 (May 1866): 762–72.

———. "A Christian Neighborhood." *Harper's New Monthly Magazine* 34, no. 203 (April 1867): 573–84.

———. *The Duty of American Women to Their Country.* New York: Harper & Brothers, 1845.

———. "How to Redeem Woman's Profession." *Harper's New Monthly Magazine* 31, no. 186 (November 1865): 710–16.

———. *Letters to Persons who are Engaged in Domestic Service.* New York: Leavitt & Trow, 1842.

———. *Letters to the People on Health and Happiness.* New York: Harper & Brothers, 1855.

———. *A Treatise on Domestic Economy, for the use of Young Ladies at Home, and at School.* 1841. Reprint, New York: Source Book Press, 1970.

Beecher, Catharine and Harriet Beecher Stowe. *American Woman's Home: or, Principles of Domestic Science; Being a Guide to the Formation and Maintenance of Economical, Healthful, Beautiful, and Christian Homes.* 1869. Reprint, New York: Arno, 1971.

———. *Principles of Domestic Science; as Applied to the Duties and Pleasures of Home; A Text–book for the Use of Young Ladies in Schools, Seminaries, and Colleges.* New York: J. B. Ford, 1870.

Bell, Horace. *Reminiscences of a Ranger; or, Early Times in Southern California.* Los Angeles: Yarnell, Caystile & Mathes, 1881.

Bishop, William. *Old Mexico and Her Lost Provinces.* New York: Harper & Brothers, 1883.

Bowen, Daniel. *A History of Philadelphia, with a Notice of Villages in the Vicinity.* Philadelphia: D. Bowen, 1839.

Brook, Harry Ellington. *Los Angeles: The City and County.* Rev. ed. Los Angeles Chamber of Commerce: Home Printing Company, 1911.

California Department of Finance. "Population Totals by Township and Place for California Counties: 1860 to 1950," compiled by Campbell Gibson, 2005. Available online at the California Department of Finance webpage: www.dof.ca.gov.

California Immigrant Union. *Memorial and Report of the California Immigrant Union to the Legislature of the State of California.* Sacramento: T. A. Springer, 1872.

"California—Its Character and Climate." *The United States Democratic Review* 20, no. 108 (June 1847): 556–61.

California Legislature. *Appendix to the Journals of the Senate and Assembly of the 21st Session of the Legislature of the State of California.* Vol. 1. Sacramento: State Printing, 1876.

California Office of State Engineer. *Irrigation Development: History, Customs, Laws, and Administrative Systems Relating to Irrigations, Water-Courses, and Waters in France, Italy, and Spain; the Introductory Part of the Report of the State Engineer of California, on Irrigation and the Irrigation Question.* By William Hammond Hall. Sacramento: James A. Ayers, 1886.

California State Agricultural Society. *Transactions, 1868–1869.* Sacramento: [s.n.], [1870].

———. *Transactions, 1882.* Sacramento: [s.n.], [1883].

———. *Transactions, 1888.* Sacramento: [s.n.], [1889].

Cleveland, H. W. and W. S. Backus. *Village and Farm Cottages.* New York: Appleton, 1856.

Clifford, Josephine. "Tropical California." *Overland Monthly* 7, no. 4 (October 1871): 297–312.

Davis, Alexander Jackson. *Rural Residences: Consisting of Designs, Original and Selected, for Cottages, Farm-Houses, Villas, and Village Churches.* 1838. Reprint, New York: Da Capo, 1980.

Downing, Andrew Jackson. *Architecture of Country Houses: Including Designs for Cottages, Farm Houses, and Villas, with Remarks on Interiors, Furniture, and the Best Modes of Warming and Ventilating.* Introduction by George B. Tatum. New York: D. Appleton and Company, 1850. Reprint, New York: De Capo, 1968.

———. *Rural Essays.* New York: Leavitt and Allen, 1857 Reprint, New York: Da Capo, 1974.

———. *A Treatise on the Theory and Practice of Landscape Gardening.* New York: George P. Putnam, 1850.

Fish, A. C. *The Profits of Orange Culture.* 2nd ed. Los Angeles: Semi Tropic Land and Water Company, 1890.

Historical Census Browser. University of Virginia, Geospatial and Statistical Data Center, http://fisher.lib.virginia.edu/collections/stats/histcensus.

Hudson, Henry Holly. *Modern Dwellings in Town and Country.* New York: Harper and Brothers, 1878.

James, George Wharton. *B. R. Baumgardt and Co.'s Tourists' Guide Book to South California: For the Traveler, Invalid, Pleasurist and Home Seeker.* Los Angeles: B. R. Baumgardt, [1895].

"Landscape-Gardening: Llewellyn Park." *Crayon* 4 (August 1857). In *Building the Nation: Americans Write About Their Architecture, Their Cities, and Their Landscape,* edited by Steven Conn and Max Page, 263–64. Philadelphia: University of Pennsylvania Press, 2003.

Lindley, Walter and Joseph Widney. *California of the South: Its Physical Geography, Climate, Resources, Routes of Travel and Health-Resorts, Being a Complete Guide–Book to Southern California.* New York: D. Appleton, 1888.

"Llewellyn Park." *Every Saturday* 11 (September 2, 1871): 227. In *Building the Nation: Americans Write About Their Architecture, Their Cities, and Their Landscape,* edited by Steven Conn and Max Page, 264. Philadelphia: University of Pennsylvania Press, 2003.

Madden, Jerome. *Southern Pacific Company, California: Its Attractions for the Invalid, Tourist, Capitalist, and Homeseeker, with General Information on the Lands of the S.P.R.R. Co.* San Francisco: Crocker, 1890.

Marks, Bernard. *Small-Scale Farming in Central California*. San Francisco: Crocker, 1882.

Nordhoff, Charles. *California For Health, Pleasure and Residence*. New York: Harper & Brothers, 1882.

Olmsted, Frederick Law. *Civilizing American Cities: A Selection of Frederick Law Olmsted's Writings on City Landscapes*. Edited by S. B. Sutton. Cambridge: MIT Press, 1971.

———. *The Papers of Frederick Law Olmsted*. Edited by Charles E. Beveridge and David Schuyler. 3 vols. Baltimore: Johns Hopkins University Press, 1983.

Olmsted, Frederick Law and Staten Island Improvement Commission. *Report of a Preliminary Scheme of Improvements, submitted to the Staten Island Improvement Commission*. New York: James Sutton, 1871.

Olmsted, Vaux, and Company. "Letter to the Riverside Improvement Company." September 1, 1868. In *Building the Nation: Americans Write About Their Architecture, Their Cities, and Their Landscape*, edited by Steven Conn and Max Page, 265–68. Philadelphia: University of Pennsylvania Press, 2003.

———. *Preliminary Report upon the Proposed Suburban Village at Riverside, near Chicago*. New York: Sutton, Browne and Co., 1868.

Phillips, David L. *Letters from California: Its Mountains, Valleys, Plains, Lakes, Rivers, Climate and Productions*. Springfield: Illinois State Journal Co., 1877.

San Diego "Our Italy": Illustrative and Descriptive of the Natural Resources, Developments and Prospects of San Diego County; Containing Information for the Capitalist, Home Seeker, Tourist and Invalid. Compiled under direction of the San Diego Chamber of Commerce by the Literature Committee. [San Diego: San Diego Chamber of Commerce], 1895.

Shinn, Charles Howard. "Our Duty and Destiny." In *California Anthology; or, Striking Thoughts on Many Themes; Carefully Selected from California Writers and Speakers*, edited by Oscar T. Shuck. San Francisco: Barry & Baird, 1880.

———. "Social Changes in California." *The Popular Science Monthly* 38, no. 6 (April 1891): 794–803.

———. "Southern California." *The Californian* 3, no. 17 (May 1881): 446–49.

Sloan, Samuel. *City Homes, Country Houses, and Church Architecture*. Philadelphia: Claxton, Remsen, and Haffelfinger, 1871.

Southern California Bureau of Information. *Southern California: An Authentic Description of Its Natural Features, Resources, and Prospects; Containing Reliable Information for the Homeseeker, Tourist, and Invalid*. Los Angeles: Bureau of Information Print, 1892.

Southern Pacific Company. *California Industries: Personal Testimonies of Experienced Cultivators*. San Francisco: Southern Pacific Company, 1902.

Southern Pacific Company. *Catalogue of the Products of California*. New Orleans: Press of W. B. Stansbury, 1886.

Spalding, William Andrew. *The Orange: Its Culture in California*. Riverside: Press and Horticulturist Steam Print, 1885.

Suburban Homes on the West Jersey Railroad. Philadelphia: Allen, Lane, and Scott Printers, 1881. In *Building the Nation: Americans Write About Their Architecture, Their Cities, and Their Landscape*, edited by Steven Conn and Max Page, 268–70. Philadelphia: University of Pennsylvania Press, 2003.

Truman, Benjamin C. *Homes and Happiness in the Golden State of California: Being a Description of the Empire State of the Pacific Coast, Its Inducements to Native and Foreign-born Emigrants, Its Productiveness of Soil and its Productions, Its Vast Agricultural Resources, Its Healthfulness of Climate and Equability of Temperature, and Many Other Facts for the Information of the Homeseeker and Tourist.* San Francisco: Passenger Department of the Central Pacific Railroad Company, 1883.

_____. *Semi-Tropical California: Its Climate, Healthfulness, Productiveness, and Scenery.* San Francisco: A. L. Bancroft, 1874.

Van Dyke, Theodore S. *Southern California: Its Valleys, Hills and Streams; Its Animals, Birds, and Fishes; Its Gardens, Farms and Climate.* New York: Fords, Howard & Hulbert, 1886.

Vaux, Calvert. *Villas and Cottages.* 1857. Reprint, New York: Da Capo Press, 1968.

Warner, Charles D. "The Golden Hesperides," *Atlantic Monthly* 61, no. 363 (January 1888): 48–57.

The Weekly Call. California as It Is. San Francisco: The San Francisco Call Company, 1881.

Wheeler, Gervase. *Homes for the People, in Suburb and Country.* New York: Scribner, 1855.

Whittier, J. G. "Eldorado: Adventures in the Path of Empire." *The International Magazine of Literature, Art, and Science* 1, no. 3 (July 15, 1850): 74–77.

Wickson, Edward. *California Fruits and How to Grow Them.* 7th ed. San Francisco: Pacific Rural Press, 1914.

_____. *California Garden-Flowers, Shrubs, Trees and Vines.* San Francisco: Pacific Rural Press, 1915.

Collected Memory Sources (Memory Works)

Often a secondary source can be a primary source when concerning a history that pays particular attention to a variety of memory works composed as collected memory, regardless of their creator or publication date. Instead of forcing primary or secondary source classifications or categories, these sources are considered useful as primary sources and as memory works. They are what constitute the collected memory of Ontario, Orangevale, and Fair Oaks (though, of course, the list cannot be considered all-inclusive). Nevertheless, the focus here is on works that discuss the early developmental years of Ontario, Orangevale, and Fair Oaks because they correlate to the years that growth machines promoted these areas as agriburbs. A focus on these years is also what serves as the basis for the determination of a dominant cultural memory and narrative.

The material type is difficult to characterize. Sources that addressed Ontario, Orangevale, or Fair Oaks, as well as principal players such as George Chaffey or Harris Weinstock, were what ultimately determined their inclusion. Much of the material observably concerns larger themes beside Ontario, Orangevale, and Fair Oaks, such as California or county histories. The agriburb sites, however, are still included, typically, though not always, in five to ten pages. Combining a variety of dates, types, lengths, formats, creators, and topics is what gives a history concerning the memory of the agriburbs particular legitimacy. For example, histories that devote a paragraph to the history of Ontario, Orangevale, or Fair Oaks compare with 200–page *magnum opuses*, student papers compare to academic publications, government reports compare to privately published material, and city histories compare to regional histories and state histories. In addition, material comes from every decade from the 1870s to the 2000s and includes physical sites of memory such as statues, plaques, and public spectacles.

COLLECTED MEMORY OF ONTARIO

Please note that sources relating to Upland or Etiwanda are relevant because Upland was formerly a part of Ontario and Etiwanda was a previous project of the Ontario founders George and William Chaffey.

1998 George Chaffey Jr.'s 150th Anniversary Calendar. [Rancho Cucamonga]: The Etiwanda Historical Society, 1997. Model Colony History Room.

Alexander, Joseph. *Life of George Chaffey: A Story of Irrigation Beginnings in California and Australia.* Melbourne, Australia: Macmillan, 1928.

Alford, Grace and Lillian Halfpenny. "Survey of Ontario." Written for Sociology 121: Community Organization, Second Semester, 1928, Term Paper and Project. [Department of Sociology, University of Southern California, Los Angeles, or Pomona College, Pomona], 1928. Model Colony History Room.

Allen, David. "Upland reveals plans for centennial fetes." *Inland Valley Daily Bulletin*, August 11, 2005, LexisNexis, http://web.lexis–nexis.com/universe.

———. "With his RV, Chaffey jumped on the bandwagon." *Inland Valley Daily Bulletin*, December 17, 2005, LexisNexis, http://web.lexis-nexis.com/ universe.

"An Account of the Life of Capt. Joseph S. Garcia." In *Autobiographies and Reminiscences of California Pioneers.* Vol. 7. Vault–6E, the Society of California Pioneers Collection of Autobiographies and Reminiscences of Early Pioneers, Institutional Records Digitization Project: Reminiscences of Early Pioneers: 1900–1904, Society of California Pioneers, San Francisco. Collection and text available at the Online Archives of California website: www.oac.cdlib.org.

Andre, Rich. *The Comprehensive General Plan Report Ontario, California.* [Ontario: s.n., 1966]. Model Colony History Room.

Austen, Ruth. *Ontario: The Model Colony; An Illustrated History.* Produced in cooperation with the Ontario Chamber of Commerce. Chatsworth, CA: Windsor Publications, 1990.

Balgooy, Max van. "A Factory Midst the Orange Grove: Hotpoint and Ontario, California in the Early Twentieth Century." Senior thesis presented to the faculty of the Department of History, Pomona College, Claremont, California, 1983. Model Colony History Room.

Bancroft, Hubert. *History of California, Volume 7: 1860–1890.* Vol. 24 of *The Works of Hubert Howe Bancroft.* San Francisco: The History Company, 1890.

Banham, Reyner. *Los Angeles: The Architecture of Four Ecologies.* Berkeley: University of California Press, 2000.

Bank of America, Economics Department. *Economic Growth and Development in the San Bernardino–Riverside–Ontario Area.* N.p.: [Bank of America], 1961.

Beland/Associates, Inc. *Draft Master Environmental Assessment (MEA): Environmental Impact Report (EIR).* Part 2 of *Proposed General Plan, City of Ontario, California.* In association with Ontario City Planning Department, the Natelson Company, Inc., Kunzman Associates, and Aron W. Clemens. Los Angeles: Beland/Associates, Inc., [1981]. Model Colony History Room.

———. *Proposed General Plan, City of Ontario, California.* In association with Ontario City Planning Department, the Natelson Company, Inc., Kunzman Associates, Aron W. Clemens. Los Angeles: Beland/Associates, Inc., 1981. Model Colony History Room.

Black, Esther Boulton. *Tunneling For Water Begun in 1883.* [Upland]: Friends of the Upland Library, 1977. Model Colony History Room.

Blitstein, J. Frederic. "Ontario." In "Blitstein, America's Turmoil: A View from the Suburbs," by Frederic J. Blitstein, 170–85. A dissertation submitted to the faculty of Claremont Graduate School, Department of Government, Claremont College, 1971. Model Colony History Room.

Bolton, Mabel Moore. "The Chaffey Experiment: The History of a Unique Community Project in Ontario California." Master's thesis, University of Southern California, Department of Education, 1929. Model Colony History Room.

Brief History: Ontario, Model Colony. Collection of essays, articles, and ephemera compiled by the Ontario City Public Library, [1960s]. Model Colony History Room.

Brown, Jr., John and James Boyd, editors. "Ontario." In *History of San Bernardino and Riverside Counties,* 229–37. Vol. 1. Chicago: The Lewis Publishing Company, 1922.

California, California Department of Finance, Budget Division. *Report to the City of Ontario on its Population Growth, 1950–1959.* [Sacramento: s.n., 1960].

California, Department of Parks and Recreation. Historic Resources Inventory of the Frankish Building, 200 S. Euclid Avenue, Ontario. Prepared by Cathy Warren and G. Worthington, Ontario Planning Department, Ontario, June 1984. Report on file at the Archaeological Information Center, Redlands.

———. *Points of Historical Interest: The Bank Block, 300 S. Euclid Avenue, Ontario, CA.* Recommended by the Chairman of San Bernardino County Board of Supervisors on December 2, 1974, and approved by Chairman of Historical Landmark Advisory Committee, January 9, 1975. Registration no. SBr-043, January 17, 1975. Archaeological Information Center, Redlands.

California, Employment Data and Research Division. *Report of Major Employment Opportunities, Riverside–San Bernardino–Ontario LMA.* [Sacramento: s.n., 1959].

Chaffey Community Art Association Museum of Art. San Bernardino County Point of Historical Interest. North Wing of the J. Filippi Winery, 12467 Base Line Road, Rancho Cucamonga, California. Although primarily a venue for art, the museum, like numerous other institutions, organizations, and businesses (not all of which are mentioned here), is a living memorial to George Chaffey because residents and visitors are provided a culturally valued institution for their daily use.

"Chaffey Day at Ontario Pays Tribute to Founder." *Los Angeles Times,* January 29, 1952, 17.

"Chaffey Historical Room to Be Dedicated Today." *Los Angeles Times*, March 16, 1951, 29.

Chaffey Letters. Transcriptions of original letters complied by Ron Baker and transcribed by M. Tikfesi. Book 1: January 23, 1882 to March 10, 1885, letters 1–265. Book 2: March 15, 1883 to November 14, 1883, letters 1–175. Model Colony History Room.

"Chaffey Library Will Be Opened Today." *Los Angeles Times*, September 19, 1935, 8.

"Chaffey Planning Memorial Library." *Los Angeles Times*, November 7, 1933, 10.

"Chaffey sculpture due in early summer." *Inland Valley Daily Bulletin*, May 10, 2005, LexisNexis, http://web.lexis-nexis.com/universe.

"Chaffey statue set for reveal." *San Bernardino Sun*, October 15, 2005, LexisNexis, http://web.lexis–nexis.com/universe.

"Chaffey unveiling set for September." *San Bernardino Sun*, July 29, 2005, LexisNexis, http://web.lexis-nexis.com/universe.

Chapman, Charles. *History of the Ontario National Guard Unit.* Prepared by the National Guard Unit of Ontario, Ontario, 1994. Model Colony History Room.

Clucas, Donald Laine. *Light over the Mountain: A History of the Rancho Cucamonga Area.* Upland, CA: [n.p.], 1979. Model Colony History Room.

The Colony Tour: An Experience of Ontario's Heritage. Prepared by Ontario Historic Landmarks Society in cooperation with the Ontario Centennial Committee, 1991. Model Colony History Room.

Color Ontario, 1881–1991. A Centennial Project of the Ontario City Library. Printing of booklet funded by Friends of Ontario City Library. Ontario: Ontario City Library, 1991. Model Colony History Room.

Conley, Bernice Bedford. *Dreamers and Dwellers: Ontario and Neighbors; An Offering of the Years of Research into the Beginnings of the Model Colony and its Neighbors in the Boom Years of Southern California.* [Ontario]: Privately published, 1982. Model Colony History Room.

———. *Pages from the Past.* [Ontario: Privately published, 1982]. Model Colony History Room.

The Daily Report. Fiftieth Anniversary of the Founding of the Model Colony. Ontario: The Daily Report, 1932. Model Colony History Room.

David Evans and Associates. Draft Environmental Impact Report for the Proposed Amendment No. 1 to the Redevelopment Plan for the Ontario Redevelopment Project No. 2. Prepared for the Ontario Redevelopment Agency. Ontario: [Ontario Redevelopment Agency], 1994.

———. Initial Study for the Proposed Amendment No. 1 to the Redevelopment Plan for the Ontario Redevelopment Project No. 2. Prepared for the Ontario Redevelopment Agency. Ontario: [Ontario Redevelopment Agency], 1994.

Drury, Aubrey. "Heart of the Southland." In *California: An Intimate Guide*, by Aubrey Drury, 113–16. New York: Harper & Row, 1935.

Dumke, Glenn. *Boom of the Eighties in Southern California.* San Marino: Huntington Library, 1944.

Etiwanda: Young and Old. Compiled and edited by Mrs. White's 1977–78 Sixth Grade Class, Etiwanda Intermediate School. Etiwanda: Etiwanda Intermediate School, 1978. Model Colony History Room.

Euclid Avenue. Runs north to South from Upland to Ontario. Listed on the National Register of Historic Places. Euclid Avenue was listed for its historical association with the development of Upland and Ontario, as well as its architectural significance as a doublewide avenue.

Euclid Avenue Fountain. San Bernardino County Point of Historical Interest. Front of the Ontario Museum, 225 South Euclid Avenue, Ontario. The fountain was placed near the Southern Pacific Railroad Depot, where, according to a few sources, such as Rounds (Ontario), Chaffey sprayed water on passing train passengers to show off the Model Colony's irrigation technology and plethora of water.

Frankish, Jack. "Some Early History of Ontario." *Pomona Valley Historian* 4, no. 4 (October 1968): 176–80.

Frankish Building. Listed on the National Register of Historic Places. 200 S. Euclid Avenue, Ontario. Site was listed for its association with the commercial growth of the community and Frankish as a pioneering "step–founder."

Freeman, Eleanor. "Ontario." In *Ingersoll's Century Annals of San Bernardino County, 1769–1904, edited by Luther A. Ingersoll*, 565–81. Los Angeles: Ingersoll, 1904.

Galvin & Associates. The City of Ontario's Historic Context for the New Model Colony Area. Prepared for City of Ontario Planning Department. Sacramento: Galvin & Associates, 2004. Model Colony History Room.

Galvin Preservation Associates. Historic Context for the City of Ontario's Citrus Industry. Prepared for City of Ontario Planning Department. Redondo Beach, CA: Galvin Preservation Associates, 2007. Model Colony History Room.

Garcia, Matt. *A World of Its Own: Race, Labor, and Citrus in the Making of Greater Los Angeles, 1900–1970*. Chapel Hill: University of North Carolina Press, 2001.

Gentilcore, R. Louis. "Ontario, California and the Agricultural Boom of the 1880s." *Agricultural History* 34, no. 2 (April 1960): 77–88.

"George Chaffey Buried After Simple Services." *Los Angeles Times*, March 5, 1932, A8.

"George Chaffey—The Final Dream." Collection of material concerning the failed erection of the George Chaffey Statue and Plaque in Ontario, 1993. Model Colony History Room.

George Chaffey: His Life in Newspaper Account at the Time of His Death. Compilation of unidentified newspaper articles. [Compiled between 1932 and 1933]. Model Colony History Room.

George Chaffey Jr. Plaque and Statue. Located in front of Upland City Hall, 460 Euclid Avenue, Upland.

"The Giants of the West." *Los Angeles Times*, November 18, 1934, A7.

"The Greater Chaffey." *FASTI*, Ontario High School Yearbook, 1912. On file at the Chaffey High School, Ontario.

Griffin, Lois, ed. *Ontario*. With students from Lois Griffin's Social Living Class, Chaffey High School, Ontario, CA, 1937. Model Colony History Room.

Guinn, J. M. "Ontario and Upland." In *History of California and an Extended History of Its Southern Coast Counties, also Containing Biographies of Well-known Citizens of the Past and Present*, 413–15. Vol. 1. Los Angeles: Historical Record Company, 1907.

Hickcox, Robert L. *A History of Etiwanda*. 2nd ed. Etiwanda: Etiwanda Historical Society, 1995. Model Colony History Room.

Hinrichsen, Kenneth Connard. "Pioneers in the Beginnings of Hydroelectric Power in Southern California: Chaffey and Baldwin." Master's thesis, University of California, Berkeley, 1949. Model Colony History Room.

Historic American Buildings Survey/Historic American Engineering Record (HABS/HAER). Euclid Avenue, 1997. Available at the Library of Congress website, http://hdl.loc.gov/loc.pnp/ hhh.ca2323.

Historical Essays by the Students of the Upland Elementary School. Upland: privately printed, 1931. Model Colony History Room.

"History of Ontario." City of Ontario website, www.ci.ontario.ca.us, 2006. Available online, www. ci.ontario.us/index.cfm/21956/17099.

Hofer Ranch (Ballou Ranch, Ben Haven). Listed on the National Register of Historic Places. 11248 South Turner Avenue, Ontario. Was listed for its associational history with the agriculture vitality and importance in Ontario, as well as architectural significance for one of the few, if not only, remaining agricultural homesteads in Ontario.

Holmes, Elmer Wallace. *History of Riverside County, California: With Biographical Sketches of the Leading Men and Women of the County Who Have Been Identified with its Growth and Development from the Early Days to the Present.* Los Angeles: Historic Record Company, 1912.

Holt, Raymond. "L. M. Holt: The Man Behind the Avenue." *Pomona Valley Historian* 9 (Winter 1973): 81–85.

Hundley Jr., Norris. "Localism and the Search for Alternatives." In Hundley, *The Great Thirst: Californians and Water, A History, Revised Edition*, 104–07. Berkeley: University of California Press, 2001.

Hunt, Rockwell, ed. *California and Californians.* Vol. 4. Chicago: Lewis Publishing, 1932.

_____. *California in the Making: Essays and Papers in California History.* Caldwell, ID: The Caxton Printers, 1953.

Hunt, Rockwell and Nellie van de Grift Sánchez. *A Short History of California.* New York: Thomas Y. Crowell, 1929.

Hutchison, W. H. *California: Two Centuries of Man, Land, and Growth in the Golden State.* Palo Alto: American West, 1969. 218–20.

An Illustrated History of Southern California: Embracing the Counties of San Diego, San Bernardino, Los Angeles and Orange, and the Peninsula of Lower California, from the Earliest Period of Occupancy to the Present Time; together with Glimpses of their prospects; also, Full-Page Portraits of some of their Eminent Man, and Biographical Mention of Many of their Pioneers and of Prominent Citizens of to-day. Chicago: Lewis Publishing, 1890.

The Image of Ontario: Completed Interviews. Compiled by Beth McClain, Landscape Architecture, College of Environmental Design, California State Polytechnic University, Pomona, March 8, 1991. Model Colony History Room.

"Irrigation of the Delta of the Colorado." *Scientific American* 85, no. 23 (December 7, 1901): 358.

Jolliffe, Emma. "Ontario." *Rural Californian* 7 (November 1884): 214–16.

Kershner, Jr., Frederick. "George Chaffey and the Irrigation Frontier." *Agricultural History* 27 (October 1953): 115–22.

Landman, Ruth Hallo. "Some Aspects of the Acculturation of Mexican Immigrants and their Descendents to American Culture." PhD Dissertation, Department of Anthropology, Yale University. New Haven: Yale University, 1954. Ontario is the site of Landman's investigation.

Lee, Beatrice Paxson. "The History and Development of the Ontario Colony." Master's thesis, University of Southern California, 1929. Model Colony History Room.

"Long Beach." Los Angeles Times, July 10, 1893, 3.

McWilliams, Carey. Southern California: An Island on the Land. New York: Duell, Sloan & Pearce, 1946.

"Memorial Library Dedicated." Los Angeles Times, September 20, 1935, 8.

The Model Colony: A Time Machine; A Walking Tour of Old Ontario. Prepared for the Centennial Celebration, March 1982, by the Tour Committee of the Ontario Historic Landmarks Society. Ontario: Ontario Historical Landmarks Society, 1982. Model Colony History Room.

Mule Car Marker and Mule Car. San Bernardino County Point of Historical Interest. Marker and restored mule car are at the intersection of Euclid Avenue (State Route 83) and B Street, in the median on Euclid Avenue, Ontario. The mule car, also known as the gravity car, was a streetcar that required two mules to pull passengers north toward San Antonio Canyon (in Upland), which took approximately 90 minutes. Then, the mules were placed on a cart in the rear, as the tram relied on gravity to take it downward south to Ontario. The tram is recognized as a technological novelty, as well as a vital transportation mechanism needed in the young colony (operating from 1895 to 1902).

Museum of History and Art, Ontario. 225 South Euclid Avenue, Ontario. Museum provides as stunning variety of exhibits devoted to the history of Ontario, as well as galleries devoted to local artists. Larger exhibits include "Road Maps," which highlight important transportation corridors in Ontario, such as Euclid Avenue, agriculture, particularly citrus and viniculture, and, of course, Chaffey. The museum also frequently gives tours to local schools, providing them with a history of the founding of Ontario, and provides lecture nights, such as one given by a descendent of the Hofer family commenting on the growth of Agriculture in Ontario's past (the Hofer Ranch is a National Register site).

_____. Road Ways, Road Maps, "Pride of Place Tour," Euclid Avenue. Pamphlet accompanying exhibit (as of March 2007). Ontario: Museum of History and Art, [2006].

_____. Road Ways, Road Maps, "Street Smarts Tour," Holt Blvd. and Three Highways. Pamphlet accompanying exhibit (as of March 2007). Ontario: Museum of History and Art, [2006].

_____. Teachers Resource Packet from the exhibit "From the Ground Up: Architecture and Community Building," May 12, 1993, through April 10, 1994. Ontario: Museum of History and Art, 1993.

Nadeu, Remi. City-Makers: The Men Who Transformed Los Angeles from Village to Metropolis During the First Great Boom, 1868–76. Garden City: Doubleday, 1948.

Neales, Isabel. "Social Life in Early Ontario." Pomona Valley Historian 4, no. 4 (October 1968): 181–84.

"Ontario." Classified ad, Los Angeles Times, December 7, 1884, o_3.

"Ontario." Display ad, Harper's Weekly 27, no. 1379 (May 26, 1883): 336.

"Ontario." Land of Sunshine 3, no. 6 (October 1895): 247–50.

"Ontario." In San Bernardino City and County Directory, 1891, 256–73. Riverside: George Bagot, 1891.

Ontario: A Compilation of Historical Articles and Booklets. Compiled in 1964. Model Colony History Room.

Ontario: From A to Z. Scrapbook collection of essays, articles, and ephemera. [Compiled by Ontario City Library, 1960s]. Model Colony History Room.

Ontario: George Chaffey's Model Colony. Articles from *Ontario Herald* in 1937–38, compiled by James Neill Northe [1938]. Model Colony History Room.

Ontario Bicentennial Commission. *A Bicentennial Salute: An Historical Review of Ontario, California and our Nation, 1776–1976.* Ontario: Ontario Bicentennial Commission, 1976. Model Colony History Room.

Ontario, California. [Ontario: Ontario Chamber of Commerce, 1949]. Model Colony History Room.

Ontario City Library. *Ontario City Library: Commemorative History; Century of Books and Services, 1885–1985.* Upland: Helen's Place Printing, 1985. Model Colony History Room.

Ontario Diamond Jubilee Committee. *Ontario Diamond Jubilee: Historical Review: Pictures and Events of Ontario and Surrounding Communities.* Ontario: Ontario Diamond Jubilee Committee, 1957. Model Colony History Room.

Ontario Fruit Grower, March 22, 1883.

Ontario Land and Improvement Company. *Ontario, California: The City that Charms.* Ontario: Ontario Publishing Company, 1908.

———. *Ontario, Gem of the Foothills of Southern California.* [Ontario: Ontario Land and Improvement Company, 1897].

Ontario, Located in San Bernardino County, California on the Southern Pacific Railroad. Riverside: Press and Horticulturist Press, 1883.

"Ontario—The Model Settlement." Classified ad, *Los Angeles Times,* August 10, 1883; August 11, 1883; September 6, 1883; September 7, 1883; October 23, 1883; October 26, 1883; and October 30, 1883. Ad is on p. o_1 for all articles.

The Ontario Record 18, no. 12 (1903). *The Ontario Record Industrial Review Edition.*

The Ontario Record 20, no. 31 (August 5, 1905). *The Ontario Record Industrial Souvenir Edition.*

The Ontario Record 22, no. 47 (November 1907). *Twenty-Fifth Anniversary Edition.* Copied by Bernice Bedford Conley. Model Colony History Room.

"Ontario Survey." Pomona, CA: California State Polytechnic University, Dept. of Urban Planning, 1973. Model Colony History Room.

Osborne, Sherrill. *Ontario Colony, California.* [Ontario: Ontario Chamber of Commerce, 190–?]. Model Colony History Room.

Our Local History. Reprints of articles published in the *Upland News,* 1946. Compiled by Una R. Winter. Model Colony History Room.

Palasek, Dwayne. "A History of the Ontario–Montclair School District, 1883–1973." Master's thesis, Department of Education, California State University, Fullerton, 1974. Model Colony History Room.

Pictorial Memories of the Inland Valley. Produced by the *Inland Valley Daily Bulletin.* Ontario: Heritage House Publishing, 1995. Model Colony History Room.

Pioneer Title Insurance Company. *The Story of San Bernardino County.* San Bernardino County: Pioneer Title Insurance Company, 1958.

"A Real Empire Builder." *Los Angeles Times,* March 10, 1932, A4.

Redlands Board of Supervisors. *San Bernardino County, California: Historical, Descriptive, Prophetic.* Redlands: Redlands Board of Supervisors, 1903.

Richards, Betty. "The Chaffeys: Saga of a Southern California Family." *Pomona Valley Historian* 7 (April and July 1971): 56–69.

Robert E. Ellingwood Model Colony History Room City Library. 215 East C Street, Ontario. The history room is simply an amazing local archive, which houses thousands of photos, original manuscripts, including Chaffey's personal diaries and correspondences, and hundreds of materials related to the history of the community. The history room obviously proved invaluable to this project, with the vast majority of the work used concerning Ontario coming from there. Still, the Model Colony room further memorializes Ontario as the "Model Colony" and prominently displays a picture of George Chaffey—and William.

"Robert M. Widney." *Los Angeles Times,* November 16, 1929, A4.

Rodriquez, Monica. "Paying Homage to History." *Inland Valley Daily Bulletin* (Ontario), October 15, 2005, LexisNexis, http://web.lexis–nexis.com/universe.

Rolle, Andrew. *California: A History.* Based in part upon *A Short History of California,* 1929 by Rockwell Hunt and Nellie Van de Grift Sánchez. New York: Thomas Y. Cromwell, 1963.

Rounds, Michael. *Ontario: The Gem of the Foothills.* Carlsbad, CA: Heritage Media Corp., 1999.

"*San Antonio Community Hospital, 1907–1969.*" Hospital Historical Bulletin. N.p.: s.n., [1969]. Model Colony History Room.

San Bernardino Board of Trade. *San Bernardino, California and its Environments.* [San Bernardino: San Bernardino Board of Trade, 1910].

San Bernardino County Museum Association. *Historical Landmarks of San Bernardino County.* Special Issues of *San Bernardino County Museum Association Quarterly* 28, nos. 1–2 (Fall and Winter, 1980).

"San Fernando Water Deal." *Los Angeles Times,* May 29, 1901.

Schuiling, Walter. *San Bernardino County: Land of Contrast. Produced in association with the San Bernardino County Museum Association.* Woodland, CA: Windsor Publications, 1984.

"Sensational Litigation Promised in South: Management of Big Corporation Said to Have Looted It." *San Francisco Call,* December 20, 1905, 1.

"Sleuths Watch Robber at Work: Entrap Son of a Prominent Los Angeles Capitalist." *San Francisco Call,* March 12, 1902, 3.

Smith, Bertha H. "A City of Ten-Acre Lots: Something About the Orange Grove Prosperity of Ontario, California." *Sunset* 19, no. 1 (May 1907): 65–69.

Southern California Panama Expositions Commission. "Ontario." In *Southern California: Comprising the Counties of Imperial, Los Angeles, Orange, Riverside, San Bernardino, San Diego, Ventura,* 178–81. San Diego: Southern California Panama Expositions Commission, 1914.

Starr, Kevin. *Material Dreams: Southern California Through the 1920s.* New York: Oxford University Press, 1990.

"Statue of Ontario pioneer monumentally a good idea." *Inland Valley Daily Bulletin,* November 18, 1993, B6.

Stumpf, Marcia. *Grapevines and Peppertrees: Family Stories from Guasti.* Phoenix: Marcia Stumpf, 2002.

Swett, Ira L. "The Ontario & San Antonio Heights Railroad Company: Pacific Electric in Ontario & Claremont." *Interurbans Magazine* 26, no. 2 (Summer 1969): 1–117.

"To Honor Memory of Town Builder." *Los Angeles Times,* August 16, 1920, II3.

Tyrrell, Ian. *True Garden of the Gods: Californian–Australian Environmental Reform, 1860–1930.* Berkeley: University of California Press, 1999.

United States Department of the Interior, National Park Service. National Register of Historic Places Inventory—Nomination Form for the Frankish Building, 200 S. Euclid Avenue, Ontario. Prepared by Vicki K. Alexander, President, Ontario Historic Landmark Society, Inc., Montclair, CA. Entered into the National Register of Historic Places by the Keeper, National Park Service, United States, Department of the Interior on August 1, 1980, NRHP–L–80–839. Report on file at the Archaeological Information Center, Redlands.

———. National Register of Historic Places Inventory—Nomination Form for the Hofer Ranch (Ballou Ranch, Ben Haven), 11248 South Turner Avenue, Ontario. Prepared by Philip Hardison, Ramussen & Associates, Ventura, March 26, 1993. Entered into the National Register of Historic Places by the Keeper, National Park Service, United States, Department of the Interior in 1993, NRHP–L–93–596. Report on file at the Archaeological Information Center, Redlands.

———. National Register of Historic Places Inventory—Nomination Form for the Old San Antonio Hospital, 792 West Arrow Highway, Upland. Prepared by Sita E. Chaney, Editorial Manager, Astara, Inc., Upland, July 5, 1979. Entered into the National Register of Historic Places by the Keeper, National Park Service, United States, Department of the Interior in 1980, NRHP–L–80–840. Report on file at the Archaeological Information Center, Redlands.

———. National Register of Historic Places Inventory—Nomination Form for the Ontario State Bank Block (The Grand Palace Pavilion of Antiques), 300 S. Euclid Avenue, Ontario. Prepared by Vicki K. Alexander, President, Ontario Historic Landmark Society, Inc., Ontario, February 12, 1979. Entered into the National Register of Historic Places by the Keeper, National Park Service, United States, Department of the Interior on January 8, 1982, NRHP–L–82–2242. Report on file at the Archaeological Information Center, Redlands.

Upland: Yesterday. Pomona: Pomona First Federal Savings and Loan Association, 1975. Model Colony History Room.

Wescott, Peter. "Chaffey, George, and Chaffey, William Benjamin." In *Australian Dictionary of Biography, Volume 7: 1891–1939, A–Ch.,* edited by Bede Nairn and Geoffrey Serle, 599–602. Carlton, Victoria, Australia: Melbourne University Press, 1979.

"What He Gave; His Monument." *Los Angeles Times,* January 28, 1936, 5; January 28, 1938, 9; January 28, 1940, A2; and January 28, 1941, 6.

White, Edward. "The Drift Wealth to Los Angeles." *Banke* 72, no. 6 (June 1906): 872.

Widney, Robert M. *Ontario: Its History, Description, and Resources; Valuable Information For Those Seeking Homes in Southern California.* Riverside: Press and Horticulturist Steam Printing House, 1884.

COLLECTED MEMORY OF ORANGEVALE AND FAIR OAKS

Adams, Edward and C. E. Grunsky. *Memorial to Harris Weinstock: First President of the Commonwealth Club of California, 1903–1907, Born, September 18, 1854, Died, August 22, 1922*. Issued by the Commonwealth Club of California. [San Francisco]: The Club, 1922.

Avella, Steven. *Sacramento: Indomitable City*. Charleston: Arcadia Publishing, 2003.

Bates, J. C., ed. *History of the Bench and Bar of California*. San Francisco: Bench and Bar, 1912.

Bryan, William. *Souvenir of the Capital of California: Sacramento City and Country as seen through the Camera*. Issued by the *Sacramento Union*. San Francisco: Stanley–Taylor, 1901. California History Room.

Buckley and Taylor (Sacramento). *Abstract of Title to the San Juan Tract, Sacramento County, California: On Which is Located the Farm, Field and Fireside's Sunset Colonies, Fair Oaks and Olive Park*. [Sacramento: Buckley and Taylor, 1895]. California History Room.

Burns, John, ed. *Sacramento, Gold Rush Legacy, Metropolitan Destiny*. Carlsbad, CA: Heritage Media Corp., 1999.

The Calder Guest House. Built in the 1890s, the Calder House is probably the most recognized building in Orangevale today. Beginning in the 1970s, the house has been the site of a restaurant. William Calder, a famous Shakespearean actor who entertained the likes of John Barrymore while at Orangevale, is one of the more prominent names in Orangevale.

California Department of Transportation. *Historic Bridges of California*. Sacramento: California Department of Transportation, 1990. Caltrans Library, Sacramento.

_____. *Request for Determination of Eligibility for Inclusion in the National Register*. Report submitted to the California SHPO. Sacramento: California Department of Transportation, 1985. Report on file with the California SHPO.

Citizens to Save the Bluffs. "History." SaveTheBluffs.org, Citizens to Save the Bluffs, Fair Oaks, CA, December 31, 2005. Available online at www.savethebluffs.org/pages/321131/index.htm.

"Clarke, Crawford W." Bio Info File, 1–2, California History Room.

Colwell, Neal. "The Cultural Landscape of Fair Oaks." BA in Environmental Studies, University of California, Santa Cruz, 1993. Fair Oaks Public Library; and the California History Room.

Comstock, Timothy. *The Sutter Club: One Hundred Years*. Sacramento: The Sutter Club, 1989.

Cook, John. "Orangevale Named For Citrus Trees." *Sacramento Union*, May 31, 1959, 1, continued on p. 3.

Davis, Winfield. *An Illustrated History of Sacramento County, California: Containing a History of Sacramento County from the Earliest Period of its Occupancy to the Present Time*. Chicago: Lewis Publishing, 1890.

_____. *Sacramento County, California: Its Resources and Advantages*. Sacramento: Board of Supervisors of Sacramento County, 1905.

Fair Oaks Bluff overlooking the American River. A favorite site of locals for over 100 years and a favorite of promoters in advertising images. Recently, the Citizens to Save the Bluffs has worked to purchase the property to conserve the area. The price of the property was $1.2 million. On August 3, 2001, Citizens to Save the Bluffs purchased half the land for $735,000, and Sacramento County became the owner of that half plus the recreation easement. On January 31, 2002, Citizens to Save the Bluffs purchased the remaining land for $465,000 with the help of a loan from

American River Bank for $326,000. The Fair Oaks Recreation and Park District was the signatory on the loan. On December 29, 2005, the outstanding loan balance of $124,705 was paid off with the help of funds from the Park District, Sacramento County, and community donors. Their remaining obligation is to raise funds for the Donor Recognition Plaza. See http://www.savethebluffs.org.

Fair Oaks Chicken Festival. Beginning in 2006 locals and neighbors are invited out to dance, dine, and drink yet again in the center of town. Essentially a replica of Fair Oaks Fiesta, the Festival pays tribute to Fair Oaks's legendary roosters and chickens that frolic freely throughout the downtown district despite the hustle and bustle of human and automobile traffic.

Fair Oaks Development Company. *Fair Oaks, California: The Paradise of the Fruit Grower, Health Seeker and Tourist. In the Valley of the Celebrated Gold-Bearing American River, Fourteen Miles from Sacramento.* Sacramento: The Fair Oaks Development Company, 1900. California History Room.

Fair Oaks Fiesta. Annually held in May, the Fiesta, or at least some type of local parade and gathering, has been going on since the 1950s. Recently changing the name to "Fair Oaks Spring Fest," one can go and enjoy frog jumps, the sun run, a car show, parade, food and craft vendors, special entertainment, and children's games.

Fair Oaks Fruit Company. 1901–1902. A Record Book of Director's Meetings for the Fair Oaks Fruit Company. Sacramento Collection, Sacramento Room.

———. 1902–1908. A Record Book of Director's Meetings for the Fair Oaks Fruit Company. Sacramento Collection, Sacramento Room.

Fair Oaks Guide. Contributing writers Judy Kemper, Hugh Gorman, Maggie Upton. Fair Oaks: P. D. Willey, 1984. California History Room.

Fair Oaks Guide. [Fair Oaks]: Fair Oaks Chamber of Commerce, 1988. California History Room.

Fair Oaks Historical Society. *Fair Oaks: The Early Years.* Fair Oaks: Fair Oaks Historical Society, Centennial History Book Committee, 1995.

———. *Newsletters.* All issues published in the first decade of the twenty-first century are available online at the Fair Oaks Historical Society Webpage, www.fairoakshistory.org.

Fair Oaks Historical Society and History Center. A Museum is operated out of the Old Fair Oaks Library Building, erected in 1912. According to the Society, "The Fair Oaks Historical Society and History Center is dedicated to collecting, preserving, and presenting the historical record of Fair Oaks and its inhabitants." See www.fairoakshistory.org.

Fair Oaks Plaza Muriel by Hugh Gorman. Local resident and artist's public art of the history of Fair Oaks, located of Fair Oaks Blvd. in the Fair Oaks Park in the "Village" area.

Fair Oaks Presbyterian Church. *Fair Oaks Presbyterian Church: Celebrating 50 Years, 1952–2002.* Fair Oaks: The Church, 2002. Fair Oaks Library; and Fair Oaks Presbyterian Church.

Fair Oaks Woman's Thursday Club. *Fair Oaks: The Way it Was, 1895–1976.* [Fair Oaks: Woman's Thursday Club of Fair Oaks, 1976]. Reprint, Fair Oaks: Fair Oaks Historical Society, 2007, available online on the Fair Oaks Historical Society Webpage at http://www.fairoakshistory. org. All citations are to the Fair Oaks Historical Society edition.

Fairoaks [sic] Library Association. Miscellaneous Documents. Fair Oaks: The Association, 1908–1921. Sacramento Collection, Sacramento Room.

Final Environmental Impact Report for Fair Oaks Bluff Overlook. Prepared by the County of Sacramento Department of Environmental Review and Assessment. Sacramento: The Department, 1991. Sacramento Collection, Sacramento Room.

Friends of the Sacramento City and County Museum. *Historic Landmarks of the City & County of Sacramento.* Published by Friends of the City and County Museum and Pipper Parrish Printery. Sacramento: Pipper Parrish Printery, 1975. California History Room.

Greater Sacramento: Her Achievements, Resources and Possibilities. Sacramento: Kelman, 1912. Sacramento Room.

Greenback Lane, Orangevale, and Citrus Heights. One of the first roads built in Orangevale is also one of the largest today and has possibly one of the most fascinating stories associated with it: Greenback Lane. The legend maintains, according to residents and local historians, that Chinese laborers (presumably from Folsom) built Greenback Lane sometime in the 1860s and 1870s and received payment in America's first wide-circulating paper money, demand notes, or greenbacks. Greenback Lane, paved in 1916 and for a time a part of the famous US 40 route, remained the only major road in Orangevale until Madison and Hazel avenues became major roads in the 1960s following the large population growth in the region and the construction of Hazel Avenue Bridge.

Hack, Catherine. *A History of the Orangevale Community.* N.p., 1990. California History Room.

"Hall, Thomas." Bio Info File, California History Room.

Hayes, Peter, ed. *The Lower American River: Prehistory to Parkway.* Carmichael, CA: American River Natural History Association, 2005.

Historic Environment Consultants. Historic Resources Survey: Report for Harvard Place Subdivision, Orangevale, California; Warhaftig Property. Prepared for the Department of Environmental Review and Assessment, Sacramento County Environmental Impact Section by Historic Environment Consultants. Sacramento, CA: Historic Environment Consultants, [1990s?]. California History Room.

_____ . Historic Resources Survey: Serve Our Seniors Project, Orangevale, California. Prepared for the Department of Environmental Review and Assessment, Sacramento County Environmental Impact Section by Historic Environment Consultants. Sacramento: Historic Environment Consultants, [1990s?]. California History Room.

"A History of Fair Oaks." Fair Oaks: Fair Oaks Historical Society, 2005. Accessible at the Fair Oaks Historical Society's website, http://www.fairoakshistory.org.

History of Sacramento County, California. Oakland: Thompson & West, 1880.

History of Sacramento County, California. With Illustrations and with introduction by Allan R. Ottley. Berkeley: Howell-North, 1960. Sacramento Room.

The History of St. Mel's Catholic Church, Fair Oaks, California, 1921–1985. Tappan: Custombook, 1985. On file at the Fair Oaks Library; and St. Mel's Catholic Church, Fair Oaks.

Houghton, A. N. *Map of Fair Oaks City in Sacramento County California.* Boston: A.N. Houghton, 1900. Available at California History Room.

Howard, Charles, ed. *The Advance.* Chicago: *The Advance* Co., 1867–1917. LC Control Number: sn 82007018, call number: Newspaper 7574–X, Library of Congress, Washington, DC.

_____. *The National Monthly Farm Press, Devoted to the Welfare of the Farmer and his Family; An Illustrated Agricultural Journal.* Chicago: Howard & Wilson Publishing Co., [1895]. LC Control Number: ca 09000973, call number: S1 .N4, Library of Congress, Washington, DC.

Howard, Otis McGaw. *General Charles H. Howard: A Short Outline of a Useful Life.* Chicago: Privately Printed, 1925.

Howard & Wilson Publishing Company. *Farm, Field and Fireside, 1892–1906.* 15 Volumes. LC Control Number: 09009915, call number: S1 .N4. Library of Congress, Washington, D.C. Pieces of this collection can also be found at the Wisconsin Historical Society in Madison, as well as the New York Public Library and the Library of the New York Botanical Garden in New York City.

_____. *Farm, Field and Stockman.* LC Control Number: ca 09000972, call number: S1 .N4. Library of Congress, Washington, D.C. This collection is the predecessor of the *Farm, Field and Fireside* published by the Howard & Wilson Publishing Company.

_____. *Heart of California.* Chicago: Howard & Wilson, 1897. Sacramento Collection, Sacramento Room.

_____. *Sunset Colonies: Fair Oaks and Olive Park, In Heart of California / Farm, Field and Fireside and Western Rural, Colony Department.* Chicago: Farm, Field and Fireside and Western Rural, Colony Dept., 1896. Sacramento Collection, Sacramento Room.

Irvine, Leigh Hadley. *A History of the New California: Its Resources and People.* New York: Lewis Publishing, 1905.

LaDuke, Sheila. *The History of Orangevale.* [Shelia LaDuke]: Vintage Typographics, 1980. Orangevale Library.

Larsen, Grace. "A Progressive in Agriculture: Harris Weinstock." *Agricultural History* 32, no. 3 (July 1958): 187–93.

Laucher, Mary. *History of Orangevale.* N.p., 1962. California History Room.

Lord, Myrtle Shaw. *A Sacramento Saga: Fifty Years of Achievement—Chamber of Commerce Leadership.* Sacramento: Sacramento Chamber of Commerce, News Publishing Company, 1946.

Map of Orangevale, Proposed Town Center. Cal. Label & Maccabe Lith Co. [Sacramento, CA, s.n., 1892]. California History Room.

Marty, Jason, "Old Fair Oaks Bridge." Memorial plaque located on the north side of the Fair Oaks Bridge on Bridge Street in Fair Oaks. Sponsored by American River Bank, Fair Oaks, February 20, 1989.

McClatchy, James & Company. *Sacramento County and its Resources: A Souvenir of the Bee.* Sacramento: H. S. Crocker, 1894.

McClatchy, Valentine S. *McClatchy Letter Books*, September 8, 1898, to April 24, 1900, Eleanor McClatchy Collection, Center for Sacramento History.

_____. *McClatchy Letter Books*, April 28, 1900, to January 21, 1902, Eleanor McClatchy Collection, Center for Sacramento History.

McGowan, Joseph. *History of the Sacramento Valley.* 3 vols. New York: Lewis Publishing, 1961.

Menefee, Selden, Patricia Fitzgerald, and Geraldine Fitzgerald, eds. *Fair Oaks and San Juan Area Memories.* Fair Oaks: *San Juan Record* Press, 1960.

Millard, Frank. *History of the San Francisco Bay Region.* Vol. 2. Chicago: American Historical Society, 1924.

Mims, Julie and Kevin Mims. *Sacramento: A Pictorial History of California's Capital.* Virginia Beach: Danning, 1981. California History Room.

"A New Deal at Fair Oaks: The Old Land Company is Now Out of it; Prominent Eastern People Are Negotiating for Homes in Sacramento County." *Sacramento Union,* May 31, 1900, 4.

The Old Fair Oaks Bridge, Bridge Street, Fair Oaks. Crosses over the American River. Listed on the National Register of Historic Places. Built in 1907, the bridge replaced the original 1901 structure and served as the only major crossing over the American River in Eastern Sacramento County for nearly 50 years.

Old Fair Oaks Downtown Area, a.k.a. Fair Oaks Village. Fair Oaks Village is the old central business district of Fair Oaks and has served as the main business thoroughfare in the community for over 100 years. In addition to the Fair Oaks Plaza, Slocum House, and the Old Library Building (which are mentioned elsewhere), they are also the site of several older buildings, built in the early to mid-twentieth century, such as the Bank Building (c. 1910), Community Center (site of the first school house), and Tudor-Style business offices (though they were built in the 1980s). Currently, the Fair Oaks Historical Society offers a walking tour that privileges this area, and the Society hopes to nominate the areas as a Historic District.

Orange Vale Colonization Company. "A Map of Sacramento County, Orange Vale." 1892. Center for Sacramento History, no. 2002/092/001.

———. *Map of Sacramento County Showing Location of Orange Vale: Property of The Orange Vale Colonization Company, Sacramento County, Cal., comprising 3,200 acres cultivated land.* [Sacramento: The Company, 1892]. California History Room.

———. *A Souvenir of Orange Vale.* Sacramento: Orange Vale Colonization Co., 1894, distributed by H. S. Crocker Co. California History Room.

"Orange Vale: An Excursion to the Sacramento Colony Near Folsom." *Sacramento Union,* June 16, 1890, 1.

"Orange Vale: Making Rapid Progress." *Folsom Telegraph,* February 18, 1893, 2.

"Orange Vale's Water System." *Sacramento Union,* July 27, 1889, 5.

Orange Vale Water Company. *Information Bulletin.* Orangevale: Orange Vale Water Company, 1958.

———. *One Hundred Years of Service.* Orangevale: Orange Vale Water Company, 1996.

Orange Vale Water Company Papers. Orangevale: The Company, [1896]. Sacramento Room.

"Orangevale." *Sacramento Union,* April 29, 1972.

"Orangevale: A Sacramento Fruit Colony Enterprise." *Sacramento Union,* May 8, 1888, 3.

Orangevale Chamber of Commerce. "Pow Wow Days History." Ca. 2000s. Orangevale Chamber of Commerce website, www.orangevalechamber.com.

Orangevale's "Pow Wow Days." Beginning in 1963 as a "neighborhood" parade, residents of Orangevale have also enjoyed an annual parade and fair each spring, Pow Wow Days. The parade features floats from local businesses, organizations, and clubs, as well as pancake breakfasts, barbeques, horse shows, dancing, music, crowning of a queen, and a carnival complete with rides.

Pitzer, Gary. *150 Years of Water: The History of the San Juan Water District*. Prepared by the Water Education Foundation. Sacramento: The Foundation, distributed by San Juan Water District, Granite Bay, 2004.

Reed, Walter, ed. *History of Sacramento County, California: With Biographical Sketches of the Leading Men and Women of the County Who Have Been Identified with its Growth and Development from the Early Days to the Present*. Los Angeles: Historic Record Company, 1923.

Sacramento Board of Supervisors and Sacramento Chamber of Commerce. *Resources of Sacramento County, California*. Sacramento: Sacramento Board of Supervisors and Sacramento Chamber of Commerce, [1899]. California History Room.

Sacramento Chamber of Commerce. *Fruit Growing is California's Greatest Industry: Sacramento County is the Very Heart of its Greatest Production; Possesses a Climate Unsurpassed for its Equilibrity*. Sacramento: Sacramento Chamber of Commerce, [1904]. California History Room.

_____. *Hub of Western Industry: Sacramento, California*. Sacramento: Sacramento Chamber of Commerce, 1944. Sacramento Room.

_____. *Industrial Survey of Sacramento, 1925*. [Sacramento, CA]: Sacramento Chamber of Commerce, 1925. California History Room.

_____. *Resources of Sacramento County, California*. Sacramento: Press of the H. S. Crocker Co., [1903]. California History Room.

_____. *Sacramento, California: The World's Garden Valley*. Sacramento: Anderson Printing Co., [1926]. California History Room.

_____. *Sacramento and its Tributary County*. Sacramento: Sacramento Chamber of Commerce, [1904]. Sacramento Room.

Sacramento City and County Directory, 1893. Dallas: R. L. Polk, 1893.

Sacramento City and County Directory, 1901. Dallas: R. L. Polk, 1901.

Sacramento: The Commercial Metropolis of Northern and Central California. Sacramento: A. J. Johnston & Company, 1888. California History Room.

Sacramento County Board of Supervisors. *Sacramento County in Heart of California*. Issued under direction of the Board of Supervisors and Exposition Commissioners of Sacramento County. Sacramento: Alvord & Young, [1915]. Sacramento Room.

Sacramento County Planning Department. *The Fair Oaks Community Plan*. Adopted by the Sacramento County Board of Supervisors, Resolution no. 75–12, January 8, 1975.

_____. *Orangevale Community Plan: Technical Report*. Sacramento: Sacramento County Planning Department, 1976.

Sacramento County Recorder Collection. Articles of Incorporation of the California Olive and Fruit Growers Association of Fair Oaks, October 27, 1896, case file no. 716, Center for Sacramento History.

_____. Articles of Incorporation of the Fair Oaks Development Company, September 8, 1900, case file no. 828, Center for Sacramento History.

_____. Articles of Incorporation of the Fair Oaks Fruit Association, May 28, 1901, case file no. 872, Center for Sacramento History.

_____. Articles of Incorporation of the Fair Oaks Fruit Company, October 30, 1902, case file no. 963, Center for Sacramento History.

_____. Articles of Incorporation of the Fair Oaks Water Company, September 8, 1900, case file no. 829, Center for Sacramento History.

_____. Articles of Incorporation of the Orange Vale Colonization Company, September 2, 1887, case file no. 505, Center for Sacramento History.

_____. Articles of Incorporation of the Orange Vale Orchard and Vineyard Company, January 16, 1907, case file no. 48853, Cal State Archives.

_____. Articles of Incorporation of the Orange Vale Water Company, May 29, 1896, case file no. 25503, Cal State Archives.

_____. Articles of Incorporation of the Orangevale Townsite Company, October 17, 1908, case file no. 55191, Cal State Archives.

_____. Articles of Incorporation of the Sacramento, Fair Oaks and Orange Vale Railway Company, July 12, 1895, case file no. 690, Center for Sacramento History.

Sacramento Valley and Foothill Counties of California. Compiled and edited by Emmett Phillips and John H. Miller, under the direction of the Sacramento Valley Exposition. Sacramento: Sacramento Valley Exposition, 1915.

Sacramento Valley Development Association. *Sacramento Valley, California.* San Francisco: Sunset Magazine Homeseekers' Bureau, [1911]. California History Room.

Sacramento Valley Sunbeam: Devoted to the Interests of Ideal County Homes. Sacramento: B. F. Hulings, March 1909.

"The San Juan Colony: Its Advantages Explained to Eastern People." *Sacramento Union*, April 23, 1895, 5.

Sandul, Paul J. P. and Tory D. Swim. *Orangevale.* Images of America Series. Charleston: Arcadia Publishing, 2006.

"Shasta Retreat & Shasta Mineral Springs, Siskiyou, California." In "Summer Holidays Among The Hills," *Sunset Magazine* 1, no. 2 (June 1898): 21–24.

Simpson, Lee M. A. and Paul J. P. Sandul. *Fair Oaks.* Charleston: Arcadia Publishing, 2006.

Slocum House & Restaurant, 7992 California Avenue, Fair Oaks, CA, 95628. Listed as a California Historical Landmark. The former home of Charles Slocum, a prominent businessmen and civic leader in the late nineteenth and early twentieth century. Today the house is a five-star restaurant.

Stoll, Steven. *Fruits of Natural Advantage: Making the Industrial Countryside in California.* Berkeley: University of California Press, 1998.

"A Suburban Railroad to Fair Oaks: It is Expected that the Line Will be in Operation by the First of April—It Will be a Great Thing for the County, As it Will Likely Promote a Goodly Suburban Population." *Sacramento Bee*, March 1, 1901, 1.

"Sunset Colonies." Display ad in *Sacramento Union*, September 10, 1895, 12.

A Volume Of Memoirs And Genealogy of Representative Citizens Of Northern California, Including Biographies of Many of Those who have Passed Away. Chicago: Standard Genealogical Publishing Co., 1901.

"Wake Up Sleepy Folsom." *Sacramento Union,* May 28, 1889, 3.

Weinstock, Harris. California Commissioner to investigate disturbances in San Diego. *Report of Harris Weinstock, commissioner to investigate the recent disturbances in the city of San Diego and the County of San Diego, California.* Sacramento: Superintendent of State Printing, 1912.

_____ . California, Special Labor Commissioner. *Report on the labor laws and labor conditions of foreign countries in relation to strikes and lockouts.* Prepared for the information of His Excellency Governor James N. Gillett. Sacramento: W. W. Shannon, Superintendent State Printing, 1910.

_____. California, State Market Commission. *The Burden for Better Marketing Rests with the Farmer and Not with the State.* [Sacramento: State Market Commission, 1918].

_____. *Harris Weinstock Papers, 1878–1922.* Judah L. Magnes Jewish Museum, Berkeley, CA (WJHC 1969.035).

_____. *Jesus the Jew: And Other Addresses.* New York: Funk & Wagnalls, 1902.

_____. *The Nation's Chief Need of the Hour.* [San Francisco: Harris Weinstock], 1907.

_____. "Observation as a Commercial Asset." A lecture to the students of the College of Commerce, February 20, 1905. Reprint from the *University Chronicle* 8, no. 3. California History Room.

_____. *Scrapbooks: A Collection of Newspaper Clippings.* S.l.: s.n., 1893–1922. Available at the Bancroft Library, Berkeley, CA.

_____. *Statement of Harris Weinstock, State Market Director, in answer to the criticisms of Senator Wm. E. Brown of Los Angeles relative to the administration of the California state market law.* San Francisco: [Harris Weinstock], 1917.

West, Carol Anne. "Northern California's First Successful Colony: The Orange Vale Legacy." [Orangevale, CA]: Carol Anne West, 2001. California History Room.

Whitlatch, Amy. "Fair Oaks Historical Society: Building a History Center." MA Thesis, Public History, Department of History, California State University, Sacramento, 2003.

Who's Who in the Pacific Southwest: A Compilation of Authentic Biographical Sketches of Citizens of Southern California and Arizona. Los Angeles: Times-Mirror Print & Binding House, 1913.

Willis, William Ladd. *History of Sacramento County, California: With Biographical Sketches of the Leading Men and Women of the County who have been Identified with its Growth and Development from the Early Days to the Present.* Los Angeles: Historic Record Company, 1913.

Wilson, James. *Farm, Field, and Fireside's Financial Catechism.* Chicago: Howard-Wilson Publishing Co., [1896]). LC Control: ca 07006659, call number HG562 .W77 1896, Library of Congress, Washington, D.C.

_____. *Wilson's Financial Catechism.* Chicago: Howard-Wilson Publishing Co., 1898. On microfiche, microfc E178.P24 1978, Regenstein, Microforms, Floor 3, University of Chicago Library.

Wooldridge, Jesse Walton. *History of the Sacramento Valley, California.* Chicago: Pioneer Historical Publishing Company, 1931. Sacramento Room.

Wright, George, ed. *History of Sacramento County*. Berkeley: Howell-North, 1960.

SECONDARY SOURCES

Abbott, Carl. *How Cities Won the West: Four Centuries of Urban Change in Western North America*. Albuquerque: University of New Mexico Press, 2008.

Alamillo, José. *Making Lemonade: Mexican American Labor and Leisure in a California Town, 1880–1960*. Urbana: University of Illinois Press, 2006.

Anderson, Benedict. *Imagined Communities: Reflections on the Origin and Spread of Nationalism*. New York: Verso, 1983.

Archer, John. *Architecture and Suburbia: From English Villa to American Dream House, 1690–2000*. Minneapolis: University of Minnesota Press, 2005.

_____. "Country and City in the American Romantic Suburb." *Journal of the Society of Architectural Historians* 42, no. 2 (May 1983): 139–56.

_____. "The Place We Love to Hate: The Critics Confront Suburbia, 1920–1960." In *Constructions of Home: Interdisciplinary Studies in Architecture, Law, and Literature*, edited by Klaus Stierstorfer. New York: AMS Press, 2010, 45–82.

Avila, Eric. *Popular Culture in the Age of White Flight: Fear and Fantasy in Suburban Los Angeles*. Berkeley: University of California Press, 2006.

Barraclough, Laura. *Making the San Fernando Valley: Rural Landscapes, Urban Development, and White Privilege*. Athens: University of Georgia Press, 2011.

Barthel, Diane. *Historic Preservation: Collective Memory and Historical Identity*. New Brunswick, NJ: Rutgers University Press, 1996.

Berglund, Barbara. *Making San Francisco American: Cultural Frontiers in the Urban West, 1846–1906*. Lawrence: University Press of Kansas, 2010.

Binford, Henry. *First Suburbs: Residential Communities on the Boston Periphery, 1815–1860*. Chicago: University of Chicago Press, 1985.

Blumin, Stuart. *Emergence of the Middle Class: Social Experience in the American City, 1760–1900*. New York: Cambridge University Press, 1989.

Bodnar, John. *Remaking America: Public Memory, Commemoration, and Patriotism in the Twentieth Century*. Princeton, NJ: Princeton University Press, 1992.

"Citriculture and Southern California." Special issue of *California History* 74, no. 1 (Spring 1995).

Clark Jr., Clifford Edward. *American Family Home, 1800–1960*. Chapel Hill: University of North Carolina Press, 1986.

Connerton, Paul. *How Societies Remember*. New York: Cambridge University Press, 1989.

_____. "Seven Types of Forgetting." *Memory Studies* 1, no. 1 (January 2008): 59–71.

Cronon, William. "A Place for Stories: Nature, History, and Narrative." *Journal of American History* 78, no. 4 (March 1992): 1347–76.

Danbom, David. *Born in the Country: A History of Rural America.* 2nd ed. Baltimore: Johns Hopkins University Press, 2006.

Danhof, Clarence. *Change in Agriculture: The Northern United States, 1820–1870.* Cambridge, MA: Harvard University Press, 1969.

Daniel, Cletus. *Bitter Harvest: History of California Farmworkers, 1870–1941.* Berkeley: University of California Press, 1981.

Deverell, William. *Whitewashed Adobe: The Rise of Los Angeles and the Remaking of its Mexican Past.* Berkeley: University of California Press, 2004.

Dumke, Glenn. *Boom of the Eighties in Southern California.* San Marino, CA: Huntington Library, 1944.

Erll, Astrid and Ansgar Nunning, eds. *A Companion to Cultural Memory Studies.* New York: De Gruyter, 2010.

Fishman, Robert. *Bourgeois Utopias: The Rise and Fall of Suburbia.* New York: Basic Books, 1987.

Garcia, Matt. *A World of Its Own: Race, Labor, and Citrus in the Making of Greater Los Angeles, 1900–1970.* Chapel Hill, NC: University of North Carolina Press, 2001.

Glassberg, David. *Sense of History: The Places of the Past in American Life.* Amherst, MA: University of Massachusetts Press, 2001.

Gonzalez, Gilbert. *Labor and Community: Mexican Citrus Worker Villages in a Southern California County, 1900–1950.* Urbana: University of Illinois Press, 1994.

Halbwachs, Maurice. *The Collective Memory.* Translated by Francis J. Ditter Jr. and Vida Yazdi Ditter. New York: Harper & Row, 1980.

———. *On Collective Memory.* Edited by Lewis A. Coser. Chicago: University of Chicago Press, 1992.

Harris, Richard and Robert Lewis. "Constructing a Fault(y) Zone: Misrepresentations of American Cities and Suburbs, 1900–1950." *Annals of the Association of American Geographers* 88, no. 4 (1998): 622–41.

———. "The Geography of North American Cities and Suburbs, 1900–1950: A New Synthesis." *Journal of Urban History* 27, no. 3 (March 2001): 262–92.

Hayden, Dolores. *Building Suburbia: Green Fields and Urban Growth, 1820–2000.* New York: Vintage Books, 2003.

———. *Power of Place: Urban Landscapes as Public History.* Cambridge: MIT Press, 1996.

Henderson, George. *California and the Fictions of Capital.* New York: Oxford University Press, 1999.

Hobsbawm, Eric and Terence Ranger, eds. *The Invention of Tradition.* New York: Cambridge University Press, 1983.

Hurt, R. Douglas. *American Agriculture: A Brief History.* Rev. ed. West Lafayette, IN: Purdue University Press, 2002.

Irwin–Zarecka, Iwona. *Frames of Remembrance: The Dynamics of Collective Memory.* New Brunswick, NJ: Transaction, 1994.

Jackson, Kenneth T. *Crabgrass Frontier: The Suburbanization of the United States.* New York: Oxford University Press, 1985.

Jonas, Andrew E. G. and David Wilson, eds. *The Urban Growth Machine: Critical Perspectives Two Decades Later.* Albany: State University of New York Press, 1999.

Kammen, Michel. *Mystic Chords of Memory: The Transformation of Tradition in American Culture.* New York: Knopf, 1991.

Kimmel, Michael. *Manhood in America: A Cultural History.* New York: Free Press, 1996.

Kropp, Phoebe. *California Vieja: Culture and Memory in a Modern American Place.* Berkeley: University of California Press, 2007.

Lefebvre, Henri. *The Production of Space.* 1974. Reprint, Oxford, UK: Blackwell, 1991.

Lewis, Robert, ed. *Manufacturing Suburbs: Building Work and Home on the Metropolitan Fringe.* Philadelphia: Temple University Press, 2004.

Logan, John and Harvey Molotch. *Urban Fortunes: The Political Economy of Place.* Berkeley: University of California Press, 1987.

Marsh, Margaret. *Suburban Lives.* New Brunswick: Rutgers University Press, 1990.

Marx, Leo. *Machine in the Garden: Technology and the Pastoral Ideal in America.* New York: Oxford University Press, 1964.

McClelland, Peter. *Sowing Modernity: America's First Agricultural Revolution.* Ithaca: Cornell University Press, 1997.

McWilliams, Carey. *California: The Great Exception.* 1949. Reprint, Berkeley: University of California Press, 1999.

————. *Factories in the Field: The Story of Migratory Labor in California.* 1935. Reprint, Berkeley: University of California Press, 1999.

————. *Southern California: An Island on the Land.* New York: Duell, Sloan & Pearce, 1946.

Molotch, Harvey. "The City as a Growth Machine: Toward a Political Economy of Place." *American Journal of Sociology* 82, no. 2 (September 1976): 309–22.

Mumford, Lewis. *City in History: Its Origins, Its Transformations, and Its Prospects.* New York: Harcourt, Brace & World, 1961.

Nicolaides, Becky M. and Andrew Wiese, eds. *Suburb Reader.* New York: Routledge, 2006.

Norkunas, Martha. *The Politics of Public Memory: Tourism, History, and Ethnicity in Monterey, California.* Albany: State University of New York Press, 1993.

Olick, Jeffrey, Vered Vinitzky-Seroussi, and Daniel Levy, eds. *The Collective Memory Reader.* New York: Oxford University Press, 2011.

Orsi, Richard J. "Selling the Golden State: A Study of Boosterism in Nineteenth-Century California." Dissertation, University of Wisconsin, 1973.

————. *Sunset Limited: The Southern Pacific Railroad and the Development of the American West, 1850–1930.* Berkeley: University of California Press, 2005.

Otero, Lydia. *La Calle: Spatial Conflict and Urban Renewal in a Southwest City.* Tucson: University of Arizona Press, 2010.

Pisani, Donald. *From the Family Farm to Agribusiness: The Irrigation Crusade in California and the West, 1850–1931.* Berkeley: University of California Press, 1984.

Sackman, Douglas. *Orange Empire: California and the Fruits of Eden.* Berkeley: University of California Press, 2005.

Scully Jr., Vincent. *Shingle Style and the Stick Style: Architectural Theory and Design from Richardson to the Origins of Wright.* New Haven: Yale University Press, 1971.

Self, Robert. *American Babylon: Race and the Struggle for Postwar Oakland.* Princeton: Princeton University Press, 2003.

Soja, Edward. *Thirdspace: Journeys to Los Angeles and Other Real-and-Imagined Places.* Cambridge: Blackwell, 1996.

Stanton, Cathy. *Lowell Experiment: Public History in a Postindustrial City.* Amherst: University of Massachusetts Press, 2006.

Starr, Kevin. *Americans and the California Dream, 1850–1915.* New York: Oxford University Press, 1973.

———. *California: A History.* New York: Modern Library, 2005.

———. *Inventing the Dream: California Through the Progressive Era.* New York: Oxford University Press, 1985.

———. *Material Dreams: Southern California through the 1920s.* New York: Oxford University Press, 1990.

Stoll, Steven. *Fruits of Natural Advantage: Making the Industrial Countryside in California.* Berkeley: University of California Press, 1998.

Underwood, Kathleen. *Town Building on the Colorado Frontier.* Albuquerque: University of New Mexico Press, 1987.

Urry, John. *Consuming Places.* New York: Routledge, 1995.

Vaught, David. *Cultivating California: Growers, Specialty Crops, and Labor, 1875–1920.* Baltimore, MD: Johns Hopkins University Press, 1999.

Walker, Richard. *The Conquest of Bread: 150 Years of Agribusinesss in California.* New York: New Press, 2004.

Walker, Richard and Robert Lewis. "Beyond the Crabgrass Frontier: Industry and the Spread of North American Cities, 1850–1950." *Journal of Historical Geography* 27, no. 1 (January 2001): 3–19.

Walkowitz, Daniel and Lisa Maya Knauer, eds. *Memory and the Impact of Political Transformation in Public Space.* Durham, NC: Duke University Press, 2004.

Ward, Stephen. *Selling Places: The Marketing and Promotion of Towns and Cities, 1850–2000.* New York: Routledge, 1998.

Warner Jr., Sam Bass. *Streetcar Suburbs: The Process of Growth in Boston, 1870–1900.* 1962. Reprint, New York: Athenaeum, 1976.

Wertsch, James. *Voices of Collective Remembering.* New York: Cambridge University Press, 2002.

Williams, Raymond. *Country and the City.* New York, Oxford University Press, 1973.

INDEX

ABOUT THE AUTHOR

Paul J. P. Sandul is an Assistant Professor of History at Stephen F. Austin State University, where he teaches courses in American history, urban and suburban history, public history, oral history, and cultural memory. In addition to *California Dreaming*, he is a coeditor (with John Archer and Katherine Solomonson) and a contributor to a new anthology called *Making Suburbia: New Histories of Everyday America*, forthcoming from the University of Minnesota Press (Spring 2015). Past publications include a chapter concerning suburban development and the environment in Sacramento for *River City and Valley Life: An Environmental History of the Sacramento Region* (University of Pittsburgh Press, 2013), articles for the *Sound Historian, Agricultural History*, and *East Texas Historical Journal*, and two books about California suburbs for Arcadia Press. Sandul is also heavily involved in public history projects and oral history (directing the Charlie Wilson Oral History Project about the famed congressperson), and he serves on advisory committees and boards for both professional and local historical societies and journals.